Assessment in Music Education

G-7170

Assessment in Music Education: Integrating Curriculum, Theory, and Practice

Proceedings of the 2007 Florida Symposium
on Assessment in Music Education

University of Florida

Timothy S. Brophy, PhD, Editor

Kristen Albert

Janet R. Barrett

William I. Bauer

Mary Birkner

Timothy S. Brophy

Rebekah Burcham

Ming-Jen Chuang

Richard Colwell

Colleen Conway

David Edmund

Helen Farrell

Dee Hansen

Aurelia W. Hartenberger

Sarah Hearn

Christopher Heffner

Maud Hickey

Al D. Holcomb

Charles R. Hoffer

Paul R. Lehman

Jay McPherson

James D. Merrill

Glenn E. Nierman

Denese Odegaard

Douglas C. Orzole

Mary Palmer

Kelly A. Parkes

Tara Pearsall

Patricia Riley

Philip Shepherd

Scott C. Shuler

Bret P. Smith

Robyn Swanson

Sandra K. (Tena) Whiston

Melanie Wood

Ching Ching Yap

GIA Publications, Inc.
Chicago

G-7170

GIA Publications, Inc.
7404 South Mason Avenue
Chicago, IL 60638
www.giamusic.com

ISBN: 978-1-57999-714-4

Contents

Part 3   Large-Scale Music Assessment

Part 4   Facilitating Music Assessment Practice

Facilitating Practice in K-12 Music Classrooms

Facilitating Practice in Music Teacher Education

Acknowledgements

This symposium was possible only with the assistance of many people. First, I want to thank Dr. Russell L. Robinson, my colleague in music education at the University of Florida, for finding financial support for this meeting when he was serving as Interim Association Dean of Academic Affairs in the University of Florida College of Fine Arts. I also acknowledge my other colleague, Dr. Charles R. Hoffer, for his support and help with the symposium. Dr. John Duff, Director of the University of Florida School of Music, also provided important financial support for this meeting. I especially appreciate his welcoming remarks at the symposium, as well as those by Dr. Lucinda Lavelli, Dean of the College of Fine Arts. I am also deeply grateful to the reviewing committee for this symposium. They spent many hours reviewing papers, many more than any of us expected.

In addition to the financial support provided by the University of Florida School of Music and the College of Fine Arts, I want to acknowledge the University of Florida Office of Research and Graduate Programs for their support. We also received grants from the Florida Division of Cultural Affairs and the Alachua County Tourism Bureau.

Thirty-four undergraduate and graduate students participated in the symposium as CMENC hospitality desk workers, session hosts, work session scribes, and room assistants. These bright young people worked many hours to ensure that the symposium ran smoothly. I am very grateful to the following students for their assistance:

Graduate Students
- Merissa Beth Amkraut
- Mary Elizabeth Birkner
- Nate Bisco
- Rebekah Watson Burcham
- Jian-Jun Chen
- David Edmund
- Julie Ann Franklin
- Dilek Gokturk
- Christopher James Heffner
- Alena V. Holmes
- Ineta I. Jonusas
- Timothy M. Mutschlechner
- Moises Abraham Paiewonsky
- Joshua E. Pitts
- Ilkay E. Tuncer

Undergraduate Students
- Ross P. Amkraut
- Philip G. Barton
- Anthony Robert Bolton
- Stefy Britton
- Carolyn De Simone
- Danielle Drapiza
- Michelle Marie Gossard
- Dakeyan C. Graham
- Melanie Anne Hilden
- Derrick Michael Johnson
- Lauren E. Kingry
- Thomas Jefferson LeMaster
- Charlotte Sarah Manes
- Carrie Hand Olson
- Lalaine Arroyo Papel
- Harry Waldo Pardee
- Adlai Salvant
- Brenda Rose Zell

Finally I acknowledge the support of my wife, Frances, to whom this book is dedicated. She worked tirelessly behind the scenes to ensure the symposium guests were greeted with Southern hospitality and was responsible for organizing the special gifts that each presenter received.

Timothy S. Brophy, PhD
Organizing Chair

Introduction

The music education faculty of the University of Florida School of Music hosted *Integrating Curriculum, Theory, and Practice: A Symposium on Assessment in Music Education*, from March 29–31, 2007, at the University of Florida Hilton Hotel and Conference Center in Gainesville, Florida. This symposium brought together assessment scholars, researchers, music administrators, and practicing K–12 and higher education music educators to share current thought, research, and practices of music assessment.

Four keynote speakers accepted my invitation to share their expertise with symposium attendees: Dr. Edward Asmus, Dr. Richard Colwell, Dr. Paul Lehman, and Dr. Cornelia Orr joined me to address the participants each morning and afternoon of the symposium. Four special guest presenters also accepted my invitation to share their experience and knowledge with our participants: Dr. Lynn Brinckmeyer, Dr. Maud Hickey, Dr. Scott Shuler, and Dr. Sandra K. "Tena" Whiston presented their ideas and work each of the first two mornings of the symposium. Of the forty presenters we accepted for the symposium, and we were very fortunate to have thirty-eight of them travel to Gainesville to deliver their presentations. I am deeply grateful for all of the presenters' contributions.

The symposium was focused on the following key questions:

1. What is the purpose and role of assessment in music education in an increasingly politicized, data-driven, accountability-focused educational environment?
2. In what ways can effective assessment practice in K–12 music education be facilitated?
3. In what ways can assessment data be most effectively used to improve music teaching and learning?
4. What are the current research priorities for assessment in music education?

To address these questions, symposium attendees met each afternoon in focus groups that were facilitated by pairs of keynote speakers and special guest presenters. Through their discussions, shared experiences, and collective thought, the participants in these work sessions yielded valuable ideas and suggestions for facilitating assessment practice and future directions in music assessment in the United States. David Edmund, Mary Birkner, Rebekah Burcham, and Christopher Heffner served as scribes for these sessions, and they have summarized these sessions in their paper, *Identifying Key Issues in Assessment in Music Education*.

A total of twenty-seven papers are presented in these Proceedings. The papers fall into four general categories.

Part 1 of this collection presents papers related to exploring the purpose and role of assessment in music education by Richard Colwell, Paul Lehman, Charles Hoffer, Douglas Orzolek, and David Edmund, et al.

Part 2 presents papers contributed by Dee Hansen, Aurelia Hartenberger, Janet Barrett, and Jay McPherson that examine music assessment and curriculum, and present ways to connect the two effectively. We welcomed representatives from three states—Bret Smith (Washington), Robyn Swanson and Melanie Wood (Kentucky), and Ching Ching Yap and Tara Pearsall (South Carolina)—who shared their work on state-level, large-scale assessments in music.

Part 3 of this book presents their papers, along with my keynote address on the association-driven model of test development we have created in Florida, and Scott Shuler's suggestions for developing large-scale assessments of music performance.

Part 4 presents papers focused on facilitating assessment practice, and are divided into two sub-categories. Papers that share research and explore facilitating assessment practice in K–12 music classrooms by Maud Hickey, Ming-Jen Chuang, Helen Farrell, and Glenn Nierman are presented here. We were also very pleased to have several practicing K–12 teachers present their classroom assessment work. Sandra K. "Tena" Whiston, James Merrill, Sarah Hearn, and Denese Odegaard provide important insights into how they deal with assessment in their music classrooms. Papers that explore facilitating assessment practice with pre- and in-service teachers and in higher education by Al Holcomb, Colleen Conway, and Mary Palmer, Kelly Parkes, Patricia Riley, Kristen Albert, and William Bauer round out this collection.

The papers presented here provide a representation of where we are in music assessment at this time in the history of our profession. We still have much to do, but readers will likely agree that we are moving in the right direction.

Timothy S. Brophy, PhD
Organizing Chair

PART 1

The Role and Purpose of
Assessment in Music Education

Music Assessment in an Increasingly Politicized, Accountability-driven Educational Environment

Keynote Address

Richard Colwell
Professor Emeritus, University of Illinois
New England Conservatory of Music

Preface

The editor of this volume deserves a spirited panegyric for this remarkable work, for he has assembled an excellent and representative number of research studies that describe the present status of assessment in music education. The political situations described in the following chapter did not draw directly on any of the music education research cited in this book. It is likely, however, that the politics of today's milieu in an accountability-driven culture affected the studies in some way.

The American Federation of Teachers (AFT), in its effort to establish music as an essential liberal art, selected Wynton Marsalis to provide an answer believable and supportable by its membership. His response:

> Over the past twenty-something years, I've seen a generation of Americans who are culturally ignorant, who lack a basic connection to, and an understanding of, the arts—of music, of theatre, of dance, and of the visual arts. I also see a government that is just unwilling to invest in turning this situation around. And in a nation that's as rich in culture and dollars as ours, that's truly unacceptable. It's not the kids; they act on what we give them. Many times, what's offered in the schools is a watered-down version of the latest pop song and as a result, our kids don't even know what a classic is. School bands should play a Sousa march, a Scott Joplin rag, a symphonic dance by Bernstein, or a Duke Ellington swing... (Marsalis, 2006, 15)

The interviewer, apparently surprised at this answer, responded by asking, "But don't the young people in the band want to play their favorite music?" (2006, 15). Marsalis replied:

> If so, it's because they've never heard the music that so many of the world's great musicians learned from, or even the great music from our country. The job of the music teacher is to broaden students' musical taste. The foundation of any music

education cannot be found in the Top 40 this week. That's not how you train the ears of a musician or even a non-musician. That's not how you lead kids into a deeper understanding of who they are or who they will be which is even more important. We're sending our kids into the world with their skills and talents untapped and underdeveloped. Our nation is really much poorer for it" (Marsalis, 2006, 15).

Is Marsalis making a statement about an increasingly politicized accountability-driven educational environment? Is the American Federation of Teachers taking a stand on curricular issues in music? I think so. Marsalis' concern is about federal arts policy and he selected the AFT, with its strength in urban schools, to disseminate his admonition. He has connected policy, objectives, and assessment.

The political side of today's education reform movement is enormous and is affected by national and international events. Ronald Dworkin opens his 2006 book on democracy with these words: "American politics are in an appalling state" (2006, 1). The British *Financial Times* (Editorial, 2007, A6) summed it up in an editorial—the cure-all super policy applied to intractable problems of every sort: put it in the school curriculum and leave the kids to worry about it. In the United States, education is widely believed to be the solution to major social challenges, including those of workplace productivity, economic competition, social equity, civic behavior, technology, cultural knowledge and effective democracy (Levin 2006, 166). Politics, however, may not materially affect music teaching and learning. All of the pother I shall discuss excites bureaucrats, and they pass on their concerns to the profession's leaders, who race to podiums to inform us what we should be doing to respond to these politically motivated and ill-formed, top-down ideas. My topic, suggested by Dr. Brophy, required that I think deeply about relationships among politics, education and music education in the past few decades. Most of what I say will not be original, and will necessarily be gleaned from the media, which is not unbiased. Education topics that have a controversial hue have likely been spotlighted. There are opposing sides and often a hidden agenda. I will not suggest that today's considerable political influence on education is negative or positive; it exists on a powerful scale and, depending upon the authority and influence of the players, can have considerable influence on teaching and learning. As Neal McCluskey says:

> Throughout American history, public schooling has produced political disputes, animosity, and sometimes, even bloodshed between diverse people. Such clashes are inevitable in government-run schooling because all Americans are required to support the public schools, but only those with the most political power control them. (2007, 1)

Political—and sometimes even physical—conflict has thus been an inescapable public schooling reality; McCluskey continues with examples of conflict over dress codes, intelligent design, freedom of expression, book banning, multiculturalism, and more. The need is for us to be more curious about policies affecting music education than we have been. The theoretical thrust of my presentation is based on Karl Popper's (2002) understanding of knowledge when he argues that knowledge is used to justify belief and to justify the authority of leaders and that we can never know the truth. We can, however, be thoughtful and critical and aspire to know what is most true about issues affecting music education. That aspiration is based on being as objective as possible and learning from criticism.

4

The brevity of my remarks on important issues borders on parody. For example, I will only mention the Getty Center for Education in the Arts, whose political muscle was important in establishing the standards, acceptance of the arts as a core subject, and promoting their assessment. Issues in teacher assessment are certainly political, and Samuel Hope has spoken to policy issues for decades.

All politics may be local, but education issues have advanced up the taxonomy to state and federal levels (McDermott 2007, 77). Today's political environment is not limited to education. Think foreign policy, minimum wage, global warming, immigration, social security, education, and support for the arts. Assessment and its use are driven by policies, and music educators have historically been uninterested in studying and researching policy formation and implementation. Policy can hurt as much as it can help. If we behave like lemmings and follow the loudest voices, the practical and technical aspects of our assessment procedures can be misused. It is not only numbers that determine policy. Cooperation, coordination, and consultation are key elements to good governance. I'll return to the critical national issues, but first a remark about the status of music education assessment.

Music educators have two ideas about assessment: (1) we assess continually or (2) our goals cannot be assessed. Murphy (2007, 361) phrases this dichotomy as either "ardent passion or blithe disregard." Other than our fascination with aptitude tests, individual assessment has been informal, and used in private instruction. Group assessment has been conducted in classes, contests, festivals, and concerts. The professional literature in assessment is focused on program assessment. However, music education, K–12, has no identifiable programs.

Perhaps the first person to question assessment procedures in the arts was Frank Hodsoll in *Toward Civilization* with his statement that "the arts are in triple jeopardy: they are not viewed as serious; knowledge itself is not viewed as a prime educational objective; and those who determine school curricula do not agree on what arts education is" (1988, 19). He asked,

> What should teachers teach in the arts...what should be required, what should be taught separately, what should be integrated into the teaching of other subjects? Nor is there any consensus in arts education about the relative emphasis that should be placed on teaching history, skills, and critical judgment (Hodsoll, 1988, 25).

In assessment, he stated,

> Schools have little or no idea what their students are learning about the arts. Nowhere in the country is there any systematic, comprehensive, and formal assessment of student achievement in the arts; nor is the effectiveness of specific arts programs in local school districts generally measured (Hodsoll, 1988, 26).

Hodsoll intended his remarks to be constructive and to aid in the acceptance of the arts as an important subject in the curriculum. There is, however, little evidence of change during the past two decades in the profession or in the priorities of his organization, the National Endowment for the Arts.

The federal government's Performance and Results Act of 1993 (U. S. Government Printing Office, 1993) intended to improve the confidence of the American public in the capability of the federal government by systematically holding federal agencies accountable for achieving program results. State bureaucracies have followed suit with similar acts to improve program effectiveness by promoting a new focus on results, service quality, and customer satisfaction. The impetus for assessment, however, remains with the federal government as state evaluators are bureaucratic by definition, are in a political environment, report to a variety of audiences, operate under severe constraints of time and human and financial resources, and tend to be reactive in mode (Smith 1981, 82; Sunderman and Orfield, 2006, 545; McDermott, 2007, 102).

The extent to which these federal and state acts have affected election results cannot be determined with any precision, but most individuals aspiring for public office actively champion better accountability in government. Priorities change. In 1958 with the passage of the NDEA, the interest was in high-achieving students. Lyndon Johnson's social/educational programs (ESEA) dissipated this interest. After the publication of *A Nation at Risk* in 1983 (which Rod Paige [2006, 41] terms blatantly political), attention returned to the strengthening of values and excellence in education, and the standards movement was born. In the background there was always Edward Kennedy, prompted by concerns of brother Robert, reminding congress that the federal government should not support the school's "tired old practices" (Weiss, 1998, 9; Kanto and Lowe 2006, 480). The dual interest in equity and achievement did not last long, as accomplishing both was obviously difficult if not impossible.

Economists think that educators are using resources inefficiently, as the pattern of payments of resources does not reflect the relative values of the regression coefficients in their input-output studies (Murname, 1982, 7). Politics has moved from policy to management and from government to governance. The problem of school efficiency has taken precedence over the political debate about educational values and goals (Rochex, 2006, 165). In the past, political leaders acted upon their own political beliefs and opinions; today the trend is to rely upon facts—those that reveal school efficiency (actual return on public educational expenditure) and those used to promote educational reforms (comparable outcome indicators). This has led from evaluating student knowledge and ability for a successful life to an evaluation of the different school systems, different teachers, schools, and practices (Rochex, 165). Policymakers' reports of findings overestimate school solutions and the importance of teachers' and school staff personnel's room to maneuver. Such reporting is a real misuse of school effectiveness research.

To a large extent, assessment policies represent a political solution to an educational problem (McDonnell, 2005, 35). The definition of those problems to which standards and assessments are the solution has a decidedly political cast. The assumption is that politicians, educators, parents, and the public will act on the information made available by testing, and their actions will improve educational quality and student achievement (McDonnell, 2005, 37). The theory behind democratic accountability assumes that citizens can and should hold their elected officials accountable. State standards reflect value choices about what is most important for students to learn and what constitutes mastery of that knowledge. But different constituencies have different ideas about success.

There are several parts to my discussion, although they often overlap. First, I began by mentioning a few policies and assessment in and about education as the general concerns of schooling affect music education. I do want to be on record, however, that a major problem in music education is our following the lead of professional educators at the expense of concern for the outcomes of music. I wrote at length on this issue, with respect to teacher education, in the last two issues of *Arts Education Policy Review* (Colwell, 2006a, 2006b).

Second, I'll remark briefly about standards, then NCLB, Advocacy, and NAEP, make a few statements about what we might be doing to improve assessment in today's climate, and end with an assessment policy statement of one Sam Hope.

Standards

The adoption of national content standards, which, with state involvement is seldom voluntary, carried with it the assumption that there would be accompanying assessment measures, as the premise of establishing a standard is to determine an individual or a group's relationship to that standard. The focus on content standards has been an egregious error on the part of the music education profession. The idea that music teachers were deficient in knowing the content of music was misplaced. However, performance standards—which describe how well students should perform at various age levels—are more important; most important is the *opportunity to learn standards*. There is no point in getting excited about assessment if the student has not had an opportunity to learn the material. The music content (Consortium of National Arts Education Associations, 1994) and performance standards (MENC, 1996) were based on the premise of a qualified teacher with a minimum of nintey minutes of instructional time per week in the elementary gradesand at least forty-five minutes every other day at both the middle and high school. Other resources requisite to the standards besides time are listed in the relatively unknown *Opportunity-to-learn Standards for Arts Education* (Consortium of National Arts Education Associations, 1995). What the public needs to understand and support is the necessity for resources to attain the performance standards that accompany content standards.

The acceptance of the standards in music was most certainly the result of considerable political maneuvering. One political decision was to declare that the arts, not music, were core subjects. The successes and failures of the visual arts with Discipline Based Arts Education were a major factor and an "academic" hue was given to the standards by including history, criticism, and aesthetics as outcomes of a valid instructional program.

The idea of any standards cannot be accepted as noncontroversial. The recent report on *Tough Choices for Tough Times*, authored by the National Center on Education and the Economy (NCEE) (2007), states that the standards in the United States are anything but coherent. They are the result of a brokering process among teachers and others who have no incentive to create coherent standards. There are no examples of clear thinking, good analysis, fine writing, or skillful problem solving (NCEE, 2007, 83). The authors of *Tough Choices* would support arts education primarily for the value of the arts to the entertainment industry, an important U. S. export and not for our curricular goals as suggested by the MENC press release on *Tough Choices*.

David Elliott (2006) views the standards in music negatively; he argues that MENC reduced the nature and values of music to a list of simply stated behaviors and then outlined how teachers should measure these behaviors via simplistic summative assessment statements (p. 47). He suggests that "political" is the standards and "practical" is the everyday world (p. 53).

I'm aware that the national standards in music have had minimal impact upon the classroom although they have been politically powerful. I would guess that music does not differ substantially from the finding of Kendra Arnold (2006, 23), who reports that less than half of the art educators she contacted knew that art had been defined as a core subject. The arts standards provide an extremely flimsy platform from which to launch any effort to improve teaching and learning in music. They are so broad that almost any musical activity at any grade level can be justified by reference to one or more of the standards and when the states have adopted their standards they have usually added to the breadth rather than tightened the focus. Wyoming determined that standards for music were not necessary and that arts standards would provide sufficient guidance. As one who has worked in assessment with all four arts, I find that visual arts instruction differs considerably from that in music education. This course lends support to the critics who suggest that educators have talked for decades about learning to learn but that we know very little about how to build a curriculum that helps students do that. In that music educators have not been able to agree on any sequence that leads to *progressive* outcome standards, the standards could eventually be a serious encumbrance to improvement in the profession. The arts standards of 1994, most certainly out-dated by now, resulted from a strategic move by arts leaders responding to the 1989 conference of governors and Goals 2000, a movement that Congress allowed to die because these goals were not even close to attainment in 2000. The idea was that the arts should be combined for their political influence and power and that all subjects should have standards similar to the 1989 math standards. We might profit from the experience with the math and language arts standards, as they have been revised at least three times, with math subjected to careful study, especially in the state of Michigan (Spillane, 2005). Spillane concluded that math standards were not a great success, but neither a total failure (p. 9); what was important was that everyone involved—teachers and students—understood the principles of the standards. We also need to consider Brent Wilson's (1996, 3) suggestion that individual standards do not form a coherent vision of the purposes of arts education. Sam Hope (2006b, 4) argues that music as a core subject is distant from reality.

Even in accepted core subjects, the standards are continuing to be a tough sell. With few exceptions, there is no groundswell for national standards. The business community would like national standards, and Dannenberg (2006) suggests that the country is on an inexorable march toward national education standards. If so, it might be time for music to bail out of the standards movement.

States

In implementing the standards at the state level, most states' education officials have made a mess of their test-based accountability programs (Stufflebeam, 2001). They simply have too many content standards that are poorly conceptualized for teaching or testing (Popham, 2006, 87). In some states, the content standards are little more than category labels describing collections of curricular aims in particular content areas, a valid description of the music standards. In other states, like Illinois, assessors of the state standards refused to allow art educators to use the term creativity because creativity cannot be measured with multiple-choice tests (Freedman, 2007, 206).

Some states have flirted with the idea of using a smaller number of broader "power standards." State bureaucrats have resisted this, as the curriculum specialists in state departments are reluctant to abandon cherished skills or knowledge that they would like students to possess.

States have become powerful authorizing environments that create policies focused on the evaluation of social welfare programs. States have generally been unsuccessful in carrying through any local evaluation because of the variety of stakeholders. At least forty-four state legislatures have program evaluation offices, but these are under-resourced and cannot provide the needed assessment expertise. Assessment professionals are commanding higher salaries than states can afford; thus, outsourcing has become the norm. State departments of education simply do not have the financial or personnel resources to construct valid and reliable tests. It is understandable that a gap exists between state assessments and the federal NAEP. Basically there is a lack of understanding about what content standards mean in terms of enacted curriculum, in terms of instructional materials requirements, and often in terms of test content. No goal can be both challenging to and achievable by all students across the achievement distribution. Standards can be either minimal and present little challenge to typical students or challenging and unattainable by below average students. No standards can simultaneously do both—hence proficiency for all children is, by definition, an oxymoron. Accountability must begin with realistic goals that recognize human variability (Rothstein, Jacobsen, and Wilder, 2006). An interesting philosophical question is: If those at the bottom will attain proficiency by 2014, what achievement level do we expect of others by that date?

No Child Left Behind

The present policy elephant in the room is, of course, No Child Left Behind (NCLB), a product of frustration and promoted by Bush's comment of soft bigotry of low expectations. Zhao terms it "simply fool's gold" (2007, 3). Kanto and Lowe (2006, 485) argue that the greatest shortcoming is the lack of vision relating education and the political economy. Many individuals mistakenly believe this act to be a continuation of the standards movement that began with a Nation at Risk. NCLB is the result of a political compromise; to get it passed the conservatives were tossed a bone—with money would come accountability. Students would have to take tests from time to time (Bethell, 2006–2007, 66). In Washington, almost all the forces are arrayed on one side. The teacher unions and the education industry press for more money, and the public mostly believes that more money will translate into better education (think of all of the states faced with lawsuits because of unequal per-student funding despite the data that amount of support per student has little relationship to student outcomes (West and Peterson, 2007—there are other, more powerful influences.) Legislators who vote for spending increases have reason to expect they will be rewarded by re-election. No educator believes that the goals can be accomplished within the time frame, and probably not ever without adjusting the curriculum and standards. NCLB is certainly not a continuation of the original standards movement, nor is the Thompson-Barnes revision (Thompson and Barnes, 2007), as there is almost no concern for gifted or average students; it is a failure-prevention measure. The political fires are stoked as much by "administrivia" as by substantive content. Reading First is part of NCLB and is a billion-dollar-a-year investment to improve reading (Stern, 2007, 100; Glenn, 2007). Thus, we have a lawsuit in Georgia on whether all programs were fairly considered in issuing contracts related to Reading First; and Chris Doherty is accused of a "lack of integrity and ethical values" for strong-arming education officials in some states to adopt a phonics-based reading program based on Direct Instruction, and blocking Reading Recovery (Glenn, 2007). With 5600 schools in 1700 school districts participating, more than a few individuals have an opinion on how reading should be taught.

Laura Chapman (2004, 10), a visual arts educator, has analyzed NCLB on behalf of the arts and concluded that it is the result of a political doctrine with an agenda shaped in large measure by conservative think tanks, corporate leaders, and nonprofits set up to represent their interests in education. Starnes (2007, 474) suggests that NCLB is not an educational plan, it is a political knee-jerk that has created a huge market for textbook and testing companies, the workshop and consultant industry, and the production of narrow, meaningless research. It is a soapbox from which a constant war is raged against public education (Starnes, 474). We are told NCLB is a cause of problems ranging from obesity to head lice.

A National Curriculum

And then Linda Darling-Hammond (2005) speaks out: "It is hard to imagine why the teaching knowledge needed to instruct first graders to read, write, and compute should vary from state to state but vary it does" (p. 61). NCLB and state assessments are leading many to think about a national curriculum. The idea makes sense as the "voluntary" part of the standards is not voluntary on the part of students, teachers, schools, or state school boards. Education policy and expectations about alignment are muddled and contradictory because core issues of meaning, values, and outlook have not been addressed completely. Does standards alignment automatically equal support for a national curriculum for K–12 schools or for teacher preparation programs? Related to this, does standards alignment imply a national examination for elementary and secondary school children or for individuals seeking a state teaching certificate or license?

The educational director of *The Journal* (Fletcher, 2007) changed his mind about a national curriculum when one parent in the Federal Way School District was able to get the school board to place a moratorium on the showing of Al Gore's documentary on global warming. Thus, a parent can dictate what teachers can use to teach about a subject, in this case global warming. Music educators know that a parent can influence a school board to prevent a teacher from using simple hymns in teaching form, phrasing, and four-part harmony. Hence, there is increasing support for the Chris Dodd-Vernon Ehler bill, "Standards to Provide Educational Achievement for Kids," that will create, adopt, and implement voluntary core American education content standards in math and science while providing states incentives to adopt them. The incentives include federal funds to bolster NCLB, additional time to meet NCLB requirements, and funds to implement the merging of state standards with the national. The rationale for the legislation rests on the assessment data comparing the U. S. with other countries. In a similar mode, Edward Kennedy and Christopher Dodd have promised incentives (like 4 million competitive dollars) if states align their state tests with NAEP, thus allowing for state by state comparisons. In addition they propose 200 million for state grants to establish PreK–16 preparedness councils that would engage education, business, and military communities in aligning state standards with the skills needed for college and the workplace. An additional 75 million is to be allocated for state consortia and more rigorous tests. The National Education Association and the Great City Schools Council, as well as conservative think tanks, have endorsed this national approach (Olson, 2007). New bills would prod states toward a national view on standards. Relying on business is a slippery slope, as their issues can more easily be resolved by immigration rather than educational reform.

Advocacy

Advocates believe in using the political process to attain their goals. Angelo Codevilla (2007, 9) says there is nothing worse for a good cause than bad advocacy. Advocates and lobbyists share a specific approach, which is to make the public aware of a need so political pressure can be brought to bear on policy makers. Advocacy is a strength of MENC and it works with a host of organizations, including Americans for the Arts and Richard Deasy's arts partnership organization. As desperate-sounding as are some of the arguments for arts education, one would think there is little or no support for arts education in the public schools. In their glee at finding a reported benefit of some arts participation, advocates could be changing the public's perception of what music education is all about, as Constance Gee (2006) recently pointed out in a talk to the National Association of Schools of Music. She argues that what is said about why music is important is far removed from what students actually want to learn about music. This "marketing of music" resonates with Julia Koza's (2002) concerns about MENC's cooperation with Jeep, ASCAP, the Girl Scouts, Walt Disney, and Pepsi Cola. Marketing benefits that Gee identified positively with MENC included patriotism, national identity, cohesiveness, self-esteem, good citizenship, and wholesome attitudes. Gee continues listing claims that the study of music improves not only reading, writing, and math skills, but also spiritual and moral development. Further, students better know themselves and better relate to and communicate with those around them; participation in music fosters tolerance and appreciation for cultural and ethnic diversity; improves attitude toward school; teaches discipline; promotes a host of brain and skill development such as stimulating creativity, critical thinking, and higher order thinking skills; offers a competitive edge for getting a job in the future; and in health, music increases serum melatonin levels. The American Music Conferences argues that a recreational music program shows potential to combat the nursing shortage (Gee, 2006). Gee faults publications such as *Gaining the Arts Advantage* and *Critical Links* for obscuring the true reality, the intrinsic qualities of music itself. Her hope is that achievement excellence in music will replace marketing, in that performance excellence has long been all that was necessary for a program that reached most students deeply. She failed to include James Catterall's (Catterall, 1998) advocacy statements that music students watch fewer hours of television, are less bored in school, are less likely to drop out, and perform more community service.

Professional musicians are also skeptical about the need for this political approach. Eric Booth (2006) reported that his impressions of UNESCO's first worldwide arts education conference were actually painful, as by the end of the first day speakers had named fourteen different purposes of arts education—every social crisis from a global explosion of mental health problems in youth, to poverty, to AIDS, to ecological abuse, worldwide economic disparity and human rights were given to arts educators to resolve. This performing artist suggested that advocacy should be about changing beliefs, and that good research data can help. As a non-certified teacher, he recognizes that an objective such as creativity is not automatic; a student can spend a year with a clarinet and not become more creative (Booth, 222). Lynch (2006), president of Americans for the Arts, most recently has suggested that involvement in the arts increases a student's ability to express anger appropriately.

National Assessment of Educational Progress (NAEP)

NAEP is still incredibly contentious, initially opposed by the National Education Association and school administrators. Cut scores, even in math and language arts, remain fundamentally flawed and achievement levels do not appear to be reasonable (Jones and Olkin, 2004, 32). Bob Stake (2007, 17) concludes that NAEP has been a bad influence on pedagogy and curriculum, and what could be worse is that others model items based on this test. Evaluation and advocacy are a bad fit (Stake, 15). Yet NAEP is considered as the basis for the standards movement in many subjects—though fortunately it is not yet the standard in the arts. NAEP is the nation's report card and the backdoor to national exams. I would be alarmed if states construct tests in music based upon the 1997 NAEP. It was a political, not an evaluation instrument. Wondrously, ETS accepted new assessment strategies for the arts, group assessment, videotapes, and more, but did not attempt to solve the substantive assessment issues in the arts. The faults are as much ours as ETS'. The purpose of NAEP has changed at least three times since the 1960s, and there are now three NAEP tests, yet we have not adjusted our thinking to the most recent purposes. Professional item writers were not adequate as NAEP found; Cronbach suggested that music's requirements were too technical; the 1997 arts test was the only subject where achievement levels could not be established; Item response theory (IRT) is based on a hypothetical 500-item test, and also depends on a twofold hypothesis. Whatever items a person passes, he or she should obtain the same level of performance on the global scale, and the processes and ways of answering a question should be similar and could be organized on a continuum; NAEP's incomplete block design does not work in music nor does item anchoring (Jones and Olkin, 2004). There is no accepted hierarchy of difficulty in our standards and objectives, and the aggregation of items is invalid.

Teacher Education

I wish to make a quick comment that supplements my comments in *Arts Education Policy Review* (Colwell, 2006a, 2006b). A shift is occurring at the policy level that places the responsibility for closing the achievement gap on the teacher and not the student. Two assessment issues are involved. First, it would be an immoderate mistake to use any present music assessment measures as an indicator or student achievement. And, second who among us believes that either a PRAXIS test or NBPTS is an adequate measure of music teaching competence or even potential for teaching? In addition, state bureaucrats who exercise policy power believe teaching competence can be regulated. Thomas Brewer (2006), a visual arts educator and the 2007 arts educator of the year, suggested that with the plethora of teacher education requirements, students now need an attorney to make certain that all state-mandated requirements are being met (p. 269). He argues that methods courses are short-changed in favor of less important requirements and that teacher education in Florida has gone from raising teaching standards to an ultra-functionalist, vocation education concern for staffing, the aim being more about job training than the pursuit of learning (Brewer, 282).

Assessment in Music

Although not necessarily related to the politics of policymaking, let me comment on the profession's general assessment competence. Formative assessment is friendly and widely accepted. Music teachers, however, believe that formative assessment refers to any assessment conducted by teachers who then tell students the results. Formative assessment does not occur unless some learning action follows from the testing, otherwise it is merely frequent summative assessment. Assessments are formative only if something is contingent on their outcomes and the information is used to alter what would have happened in the absence of the information (Black and Wiliam, 2004, 30).

Again, I refer to Karl Popper (2002). We can strive to know the truth, but to do so requires a deep curiosity about what we are doing and why. Debbie Meier's questions (Meier, 1995, 41) adapted from Popper (2002) pertain: How do you know that? Who said it and why? What led to it and what else happened? What if? And who cares? As a profession, we must be more self-critical.

Sam Hope (2006a) began his report to the NASM membership this past November with this policy-influencing story. "I was speaking with a wise friend the other day and he suggested that we both ponder a possibility. Manic focus on assessment, accountability, and status usually appears when vision is lacking or faltering in terms of content, intellect, individual mind, and spirit. When the vision turns to power and control of the achievement of empty things, assessment, accountability, and status become masters and not servants. If vision is centered in the humanistic and spiritual, in the essence, the world of evaluation and assessment are servants and assistants in achieving the vision."

The good and the bad influences of past and present policy and politics on education will remain long after the current federal administration is history. The issues are sufficiently complex that the entire music education profession cannot be expected to master them all. Within the profession, however, there must be a group of music educators who continually exercise informed criticism, are expert in evaluation and are sufficiently knowledgeable about policy and politics that we can answer the Meier-Popper queries in all four areas at the basic, if not the proficient, level.

References

Arnold, K. 2006. New Mexico arts educators and educational policy. *Arts Education Policy Review, 107* (5):23–29.

Bethell, T. 2006–2007. Reform movement and NCLB: Spending more, learning less. *American Spectator, 39* (10):66–69.

Black, P., and William, D. 2004. The formative purpose: assessment must first promote learning. In Wilson, Mark, ed. *Towards coherence between classroom assessment and accountability.* 103rd yearbook of the NSSE, Part II:20–50. Chicago: University of Chicago Press.

Booth, E. 2006. Global impressions: Inside UNESCO's first worldwide arts education conference. *Teaching Artist Journal, 4* (4):220–229.

Brewer, T. 2006. Teacher preparation solutions: Rumbling for quality just won't do. *Studies in Art Education, 47* (3):269–285.

Catterall, J. S. 1998. Does experience in the arts boost academic achievement? A response to Eisner. *Art Education, 51* (4):6–8.

Chapman, L. 2004. No child left behind in art? *Arts Education Policy Review, 106* (2):3–17.

Codevilla, A. 2007. Words and deeds: A response to Norman Podhoretz. *American Spectator, 40* (1):9.

Colwell, R. 2006a. Music teacher education in his century: Part I. *Arts Education Policy Review 108* (1):15–27.

Colwell, R. 2006b. Music teacher education in this century: Part II. *Arts Education Policy Review, 108* (2):17–32.

Consortium of National Arts Education Associations. 1994. *National standards for arts education: What every young American should know and be able to do in the arts.* Reston, VA: MENC, The National Association for Music Education.

Consortium of National Arts Education Associations. 1995. *Opportunity-to-learn standards for arts education: dance, music, theatre, visual arts.* Reston, VA: Music Educators National Conference.

Dannenberg, M. 2006, March 10. *National Education Standards.* Live discussion sponsored by *Education Sector.*

Darling-Hammond, L. 2005. Licensure reform. In L. Darling-Hammond and L. Baratz Snowden (Eds.), *A good teacher in every classroom: Preparing the highly qualified teachers our children deserve,* 60–61. San Francisco: Jossey Bass.

Dworkin, R. 2006. *Is democracy possible here? Principles for a new political debate.* Princeton, NJ: Princeton University Press.

Editorial. 2007, February 10. *Financial Times:* A6.

Elliott, D. 2006. Music education and assessment: Issues and suggestions. In P. Taylor, ed. *Assessment in arts education,* 41–56. Portsmouth: Heinemann.

Fletcher, G. 2007. Rethinking a national curriculum. *The Journal, 34* (2):8.

Freedman, K. 2007. Artmaking/troublemaking: Creativity, policy, and leadership in art education. *Studies in Art Education 48* (2):204–217.

Gee, C. B. 2006. *Future of art music: Advocacy that works.* Paper presented to the 2006 annual Meeting of the National Association of Schools of Music, Chicago, Illinois.

Glenn, D. 2007 Reading for Profit. *Chronicle of Higher Education, LIII* (22):A8.

Hodsoll, F. 1988. *Toward civilization: A report on arts education.* Washington, D. C.: National Endowment for the Arts.

Hope, S. 2006a, November. *Oral report of the executive director: 2.* Presented at the meeting of the National Association of Schools of Music, Chicago, Illinois.

Hope, S. 2006b. Characteristics of a "basic" discipline in elementary and secondary education. *Arts Education Policy Review, 108* (2):3–5.

Jones, L., and Olkin, I., eds. 2004. *The nation's report card: Evaluation and perspectives.* Bloomington: Phi Delta Kappa and Washington: American Educational Research Association.

Kanto, R., Lowe, R. 2006. From new deal to no deal: No child left behind and the devolution of responsibility for equal opportunity. *Harvard Educational Review 76* (4):474–502.

Koza, J. E. 2002. A realm without angels: MENC's partnerships with Disney and other major corporations. *Philosophy of Music Education Review, 10* (2):72–79.

Levin, H. 2006. Why is this so difficult? In F. M. Hess, ed. *Educational entrepreneurship: Realities, challenges, possibilities,* 165–182. Cambridge: Harvard University Press.

Lynch, B. (2006, Fall). Youth ARTS development project, *ArtsLink,* 1–2.

Marsalis, W. 2006. On America's musical classics. Interview. In The neglected muse: Why music is an essential liberal art. *American Educator, 30* (3):14–15.

McCluskey, N. 2007. Why we fight: How public schools cause social conflict. *Policy Analysis, 587:*1–59.

McDermott, K. 2007. "Expanding the moral community" or "Blaming the victim"? The politics of state education accountability policy, *American Educational Research Journal. 44* (1):77–111.

McDonnell, L. 2005. Assessment and accountability from the policymaker's perspective. In J. Herman and E. Haertel, eds. Uses and misuses of data for educational accountability and improvement, 35–54. *104th Yearbook of The NSSE Part II.*

Meier, D. 1995. *The Power of their ideas: Lessons for America from a small school in Harlem.* Boston: Beacon Press.

Murname, R. 1982. Input-output research in education: Accomplishments, limitations, and lessons. *New Directions for Testing and Measurement, 15:*5–16.

Murphy, R. 2007. Harmonizing assessment and music in the classroom. In L. Bressler, ed. *International handbook of research in arts education, Part I:*361–380. Dordrecht, The Netherlands: Springer.

MENC: The National Association for Music Education. 1996. *Performance standards for music: Strategies and benchmarks for assessing progress toward the national standards, grades pre-K–12.* Reston, VA: Author.

National Center on Education and the Economy (NCEE). 2007. *Tough choices or tough times.* Hoboken, NJ: John Wiley and Sons.

Olson, L. 2007, January. New bills would prod states to take national view on standards. Electronic version. *Education Week, 26* (18):1, 19.

Paige, R. 2006. *The war against hope: How teachers' unions hurt children, hinder teachers, and endanger public education.* Nashville, TN: Thomas Nelson, Inc.

Popham, W. J. 2006. Content standards: The unindicted co-conspirator. *Educational Leadership, 64* (1):87–88.

Popper, K. 2002. *The logic of scientific discovery.* London: Routledge.

Rochex, J. 2006. Social, methodological, and theoretical issues regarding assessment: Lessons from a secondary analysis of PISA 2000 literacy tests. In J. Green and A. Luke, eds. Rethinking learning: What counts as learning and what learning counts. Special issue. *Review of Research in Education, 30:*163–212.

Rothstein, R., Jacobsen, R., and Wilder, T. 2006, November. Proficiency for all is an oxymoron: Accountability should begin with realistic goals that recognize human variability. Electronic version. *Education Week, 26* (13):32, 44,

Smith, N. 1981. Creating alternate methods for educational evaluation. *New Directions,* 12:77–94.

Spillane, J. 2005. Standards deviation: How schools misunderstand education policy. *Policy Briefs, 43*:1–9.

Stake, Robert. 2007. NAEP, Report cards and education: A review essay. *Education Review 10* (1):1–22.

Starnes, B. 2007. Thoughts on teaching. *Phi Delta Kappan, 88* (6):473–474.

Stern, S. 2007. The Bush education reform really works. *City Journal, 17* (1):100–107.

Stufflebeam, D. 2001. Evaluation models. In *New Directions for Evaluation*, vol. 89, entire issue. San Francisco: Jossey Bass.

Sunderman, G., and Orfield, G. 2006. Domesticating a revolution: No child left behind reforms and state administrative response. *Harvard Educational Review, 76* (4):526–556.

Thompson, T. G., and Barnes, R. E. 2007. *Beyond NCLB: Fulfilling the promise to our nation's children.* Washington, D. C.: The Aspen Institute.

U. S. Government Printing Office. 1993. Section 2. *Government Performance and Results Act.* 1993 Congress. Washington, D. C.: Author.

Weiss, C. 1989. *Evaluation*, 2nd ed. Upper Saddle River: Prentice-Hall.

West, M. and Peterson, P., eds. 2007. *School money trials: The legal pursuit of educational adequacy.* Washington: Brookings Institution Press.

Wilson, B. 1992. A primer on arts assessment and a plethora of problems. *Design for Arts in Education, 93* (3):34–44.

Zhao, Y. 2007. Education in the flat world: Implications of globalization on education. *EDge, 2* (4):3–19.

Getting Down to Basics

Keynote Address

Paul R. Lehman
Professor Emeritus, University of Michigan

I want to thank Tim Brophy and the University of Florida for sponsoring this Symposium, and I want to congratulate every one of you for having the good judgment to be here. I've thought for several years, and especially since the national standards were published, that finding ways to improve our assessment practices is one of the most urgent needs facing education today. That's true in all of education, not just music. And one way to begin is to get together and discuss the issues in settings like this.

My remarks today will fall under three headings: First, I'll suggest some principles that can serve as a basis for improving our efforts in assessment; second, I'll outline some beliefs and assumptions that should underlie our efforts; and third, I'll describe some obstacles to effective assessment and explore what can be done to minimize their impact.

Four Principles for Improving Our Efforts

Principle no. 1: Improving instruction

To begin with, I propose that we focus first on improving instruction. At first glance it may be unclear how this relates to improving assessment. But I think it becomes clear if we look at the larger picture and consider not merely how to improve our assessment techniques, but more importantly how to improve the overall educational process. When we focus on assessment but ignore instruction we distort the process and we place a burden on assessment that it cannot be expected to carry.

To see how this can work, consider the No Child Left Behind (NCLB) Law. Despite its good intentions, NCLB suffers from serious shortcomings. One shortcoming is that it places too much emphasis on testing and not enough on improving instruction. Oh, it says all the right things about good teaching, but its most conspicuous features are the penalties it imposes on schools for failure to perform. It contains bigger sticks than carrots, and lots more of them. NCLB is clearly based on the assumption that teachers and schools could do a better job if only they would try harder.

But trying harder by itself is not enough. And high-stakes testing by itself is not enough. It has to be accompanied by efforts to help teachers and schools to improve. And here's where NCLB fails. The reason it fails is that improving teaching is tough. It takes effort. And it costs money. It's easier to mandate tests and let someone else figure out how to prepare the kids to pass them. Trying to improve education by legislating tests is like trying to eliminate crime by making it illegal.

In my view, the most urgent need in education today is for a massive, systematic, all-out effort to improve the quality of teaching. There's nothing that would do more to improve America's schools. If we emphasize better teaching, then we'll lessen the very real danger of assessment driving the curriculum. Assessment can resume its proper function of documenting student achievement, and the focus of education can return once again to teaching and learning.

Principle no. 2: Integrating assessment and instruction effectively

The second principle I propose is that we integrate assessment with instruction more effectively. Too often assessment is thought of as a separate process that's added on at the end of instruction. It's an afterthought. And it simply can't be done properly that way. Assessment has to be planned along with instruction from the very beginning because the relationship between the two is intimate and inherent. If you plan the assessment along with the instruction, not only will you have better assessment but also the instruction itself will be better because the very act of planning the assessment will force you to think about how you want the student to behave differently after the instruction than before.

Assessment occurs not only at the end of a grading period, but it occurs every time a student answers a question in class or plays a passage in rehearsal. It occurs continuously, minute after minute, day after day, often in an informal, unstructured format. We need to merge our formative assessment with our summative assessment. When we improve our instruction we'll improve our assessment, and vice versa.

In teaching we typically begin with a desired goal and we assign students certain learning tasks that will lead sequentially to that goal. Often there are many tasks that can lead to a given goal, and there are many tasks that can demonstrate that the goal has been achieved.

Consider for a moment the universe of tasks that can demonstrate that a goal has been achieved. We can think of assessment as sampling randomly from that universe of tasks. And it's essentially the same as the universe of tasks that we drew from in selecting the learning experiences. We select one sampling for learning and a different sampling for assessment. If it's a routine, low-level goal, maybe a single task will do for assessment. If it's a high-stakes assessment, we need a larger sampling to achieve higher reliability.

Now I turn my focus to the curriculum. We speak of the school curriculum as though it were a single entity, but in most schools there is not one curriculum but as many as four curricula. First there is the official curriculum. That's the curriculum that exists in the curriculum guides. That's the face the school presents to the outside world. It's based on the standards adopted by the state or the district. But it's not the whole story.

In fact there is a second curriculum, and the second curriculum is the curriculum that the teachers teach. Now, of course, these two ought to be the same, but everyone knows they're not always, and sometimes the discrepancies can be significant.

Then, in addition to the official curriculum, and the curriculum that the teachers teach, there's a third curriculum—the curriculum that the students learn. Again, that curriculum ought to coincide with the other two, but sometimes what students learn is very different from what their teachers intended to teach.

Then, in addition to the official curriculum, and the curriculum that the teachers teach, and the curriculum that the students learn, there is a fourth curriculum—the curriculum that's tested. And the gap between this curriculum and the first three can be vast as well.

I remember once reading the results of the state assessment in the Ann Arbor newspaper. The story reported that the local kids had done badly on one section of the exam, and a school official was explaining why this had happened. The problem wasn't that the teachers didn't teach that material, he said; they taught it. The problem was that the students didn't learn it.

Hey, hold on a minute. That's like saying the automobile salesman sold the car, but the customer didn't buy it. That official seemed to define teaching as merely telling. I don't believe one can say there has been teaching unless there has been learning.

These four curricula need to be reconciled and unified. That's a prerequisite to valid assessment, and it's a prerequisite to improving our nation's schools.

We sometimes hear complaints about teachers "teaching to the test." This is spoken of as something that teachers are forced to do because of overemphasis on test results, and it's done to the detriment of teaching what students ought to know. Is that criticism justified? Well, if the test is valid, the answer is no. In other words, if the fourth curriculum matches the first, it's not justified.

Why not? Because the curriculum is based on the standards and expectations of the school district, and the test also is based on the standards and expectations of the school district. If that's the case, then there can be no inconsistency between the two. We know from algebra that quantities equal to the same quantity are equal to each other.

However, we also know that in practice some schools, especially urban schools, have to spend much of their time on repetitive drills geared to teaching their students strategies and formulas for answering narrowly focused, small-minded questions. They have no time for reading novels or listening to music or creating art, or any of the other higher-level learning activities that wealthier suburban schools have the luxury of engaging in.

But the fault lies with poor tests—tests that measure only the superficial, and fail to capture the breadth and depth of what we really want for our students as reflected in the first curriculum. We know that the pressures of NCLB have forced some states to abandon their more sophisticated test-development efforts, which have included, for example, open-ended questions, and analytic essays, and problems requiring complex solutions. Instead, they've had to adopt cheap, unimaginative, off-the-shelf, multiple-choice tests. Not only are we guilty of trying to use assessment to solve problems that are essentially instructional in nature, but we're also guilty of failing to provide the resources necessary to do good assessment.

I served for a while in the late 1960s as Music Specialist in the Department of Education in Washington. By the way, do you know what a specialist is? A specialist is someone who knows a great deal about very little and keeps learning more and more about less and less until he knows virtually everything about practically nothing.

Anyway, the 1960s was a time of great interest in assessment also, and I can remember receiving phone calls from music supervisors around the country asking me to recommend a standardized music test they could use. It usually became clear quickly that they didn't really care whether the test fit their curriculum or whether it was technically adequate. They were under pressure to test and they simply needed something they could use right away. Unfortunately, I sense a touch of that same hysteria in the air today. We always need to insist that assessment be valid.

Principle no. 3: Seeking maximum transparency in assessment

The third principle I propose is that we seek maximum transparency in assessment. One reason that students may not learn what their teachers want them to learn is that they don't know exactly what it is that their teachers want them to learn. And the best way to let students know what they're supposed to learn is to show them how they'll be assessed. Sometimes we'll be surprised to find how little else we have to do. Students should be able to see on a daily basis how well they're doing. There should be no mystery about the process, and no big surprises at the end of the grading period. Mystery is the enemy of assessment.

The entire process of assessment ought to be open to review by all interested parties. That includes not only students but also parents, and school officials, and the public, all of whom should be given enough information that they too can make judgments about what their kids are learning and how their schools are performing. Otherwise their views of the music program may be shaped solely by watching the marching band at football games or by reading in the newspapers the ratings the kids received in competitions.

Principle no. 4: Interpret results cautiously

Fourth, we need to be cautious in interpreting the results of assessment. Any assessment is only an approximation of the truth, and we have to recognize that limitation, especially when the stakes are high. There's an error component in every obtained score. An obtained score is the sum of a true score and an error score. In the case of the true score, we can never know for certain what it is. If we take a number of obtained scores, they'll tend to cluster around the true score, but the true score remains a hypothetical construct. In the case of the error score, we not only don't know how great it is, we don't know its direction, either. So we don't know whether the obtained score is above or below the true score. We can sympathize with the student whose obtained score falls just below an arbitrary cut-off point, because we know that his true score may lie above that point. At the same time we should recognize that, thanks to the error of measurement, for every student in that situation there is another student whose obtained score falls just above the cut-off point but whose true score may lie below it.

Beliefs and Assumptions

Next I'd like to list some beliefs and assumptions that should underlie our assessment efforts.

1. Every child can learn music.

Every child has the potential to sing, and play instruments, and learn about music. If we don't believe that, we shouldn't be in this business. Kids may be seriously disadvantaged when we don't give them enough opportunities early enough, but every child has the potential to learn music. I suspect there's no controversy here.

2. Assessment in music is both possible and necessary.

We have a long history of assessing music performance, although we've sometimes had difficulty with certain other types of music learning. However, once we develop standards stated in terms of what students should know and be able to do, then assessment becomes possible. But standards do more than make assessment possible. They make it necessary. We cannot have standards without assessment. The two go hand-in-hand. Standards are useless if we don't know whether or not they're being met, and the only way we can know that is through assessment. One of the most important results of the standards movement is that it has made assessment both possible and necessary.

3. The purpose of assessment is to improve learning and teaching.

It does this in many ways: It can provide information concerning progress toward meeting the standards of the school. It can clarify the types of learning and the levels of achievement sought. It can motivate student learning. It can furnish teachers with information on the effectiveness of instruction and thereby provide a basis for improvement. And it can provide information to policy-makers to aid in decision-making.

There are many things that assessment can do, but there are some things that it should not do. It should not be used to punish teachers, or to weed out students, or to penalize schools. The purpose of assessment is to improve learning and teaching, and any other use is a misuse.

4. Assessment requires various techniques in various settings.

This is a cliché, of course, but it's true. The sheer variety of cognitive, affective, and psychomotor learning we seek in music requires diverse assessment techniques. And our student populations are enormously diverse. We always need to ensure that we have an appropriate match between the assessment instrument and the population or the skill being assessed. And we need to remember that no single measure can provide a comprehensive picture of music learning.

5. Reports to parents should be standards-based.

Grading has always been a challenge for music teachers because the problems are so complex. I believe we need to accept as a basic principle that grades should be standards-based. And I'll say more about this later.

Obstacles to Assessment and What We Can Do About Them

Now I'd like to point out some obstacles to effective assessment and explore what might be done to minimize their impact.

1. Music assessment is difficult, time-consuming, and costly.

As a profession we've made much progress in recent years in solving some of the problems we face in music assessment. And I'm grateful to several of you, including Sandra Whiston and Janice Smith, for showing us yesterday some creative ways in which assessment can be done with large numbers of students, as in the elementary classroom and the large ensemble.

Is music assessment worth the effort? I think the answer is *yes*. I've known teachers who reject the whole idea of assessment in music because they claim that much music learning is too highly subjective. No test, they say, can measure a student's creative ability, or her perceptual skills, or her love of music. No test can measure the chill that goes up the spine when we hear an emotionally moving performance.

Well, perhaps not, but we can assess the skills and knowledge associated with those phenomena. It may be difficult or even impossible to assess the most intangible and exalted qualities of musicianship at the highest levels, but we can assess the skills and knowledge called for in a set of standards. Those skills and knowledge don't represent the highest levels of music achievement, but they are prerequisites for achieving at the highest levels. We cannot refuse to do what is possible on the grounds that some things are not possible. If our instruction is effective, then the student will behave differently in some way as a result. And if the student behaves differently as a result of instruction, then there is a basis for assessment.

At the same time, most people, even teachers, underestimate the difficulty of competent assessment. Anyone can write a test, we think; after all, we've taken lots of tests and we know what tests are like. But the fact is that it's very difficult to write good tests. Test-writing is not a skill we simply absorb. As a profession, we're far too unmindful to the technical flaws in our classroom assessments. Assessment skills should be taught in our teacher education programs, beginning at the undergraduate level.

2. Many music teachers have too many students and too little time with them.

This is especially a problem at the elementary level. We all know that. The first step toward a solution is to do what we can to ensure that every school district meets the standards for instructional time and staff outlined in the *Opportunity-To-Learn Standards for Music Instruction* published by MENC. In many schools this will require more music teachers.

In addition, let's ask the classroom teacher to play a greater role in the process. She sees the students more than the music teacher does, she knows them better, and we hope she carries on music instruction when the music teacher's not there. Let's ask for her help.

Technology can play an important role in assessment just as it does in instruction. This is especially true in music because much of what musicians do is media-based. Student performances, compositions, and improvisations can be recorded, evaluated, and revised using technology. Every day creative music teachers are developing computer-based procedures for these purposes, and hand-held hardware is making the task easier. Students themselves can play a role in the process, and they're usually not only willing but often eager to contribute self-assessments and help in other ways.

Many music teachers are finding portfolios to be useful in assessment. Portfolios can provide a more comprehensive basis for assessment by giving teachers a wider array of raw materials on which to assess. But portfolios can't solve the most basic problems. We still need teachers to determine which materials to look at, what the scoring rubrics will be, and whether each given piece of work meets the criteria.

Also, we need to be more aggressive and systematic in learning how other schools are solving some of the common problems we face in assessment. We need to create a "best practices" culture in education, which means finding ways to share what we do that works, so we can all benefit from the experiences of our colleagues. We do astonishingly little of that today, and what we do is largely on an individual, ad hoc basis. We need to build a culture in which sharing our best practices is not an exception or an aberration but a commonplace and expected part of our everyday work.

3. There is widespread confusion and disagreement concerning the criteria on which to grade students.

I'm speaking now about reporting to parents. This is often the crux of the issue when it comes to assessment. This is where our idealistic tendencies can collide head-on with the practical requirements of our school district.

Historically as a profession we haven't done a very good job of this. Sometimes we've based our grades entirely or largely on attendance. This borders on fraud. It's certainly not the way kids are graded in other basic disciplines, and it's often seen by other educators as evidence that music lacks substance. One result of this practice is that music grades are often disregarded by college admissions officers.

Some teachers claim to emphasize effort as distinguished from achievement. They ask why a student should be "penalized" for lack of talent or lack of good previous instruction. But how do we judge effort? Where are the reliable and valid instruments for assessing effort? I have yet to see any.

Some teachers claim to grade on progress rather than achievement. Progress is a legitimate concern, but this emphasis too distorts the process. It's much easier for a student to make progress if he begins at a low achievement level. This is unfair to the student who begins at a high level.

The problem with these criteria is that they have nothing to do with music itself. Anyone reading a transcript has a right to assume that a good grade indicates knowledge and skill in the subject matter. A grade is not just misleading, it's dishonest if it means merely that the student has come to class, or tried hard—or, more accurately, given the appearance of trying hard. No student who does poorly in algebra or biology can expect a good grade solely because she tried hard or came to class. Why should music be different?

On the other hand, the mere fact that grades tend to be high in music courses is not in itself evidence of a lack of serious assessment. Students in bands and orchestras, for example, tend to be highly selected, highly motivated, and often they've studied their instruments for years. The grade distribution in an elective course in music cannot be expected to resemble the distribution in a required course in English or history.

Still, we need a reporting system that provides meaningful information to parents. Traditional grades are not very helpful, and neither are prose reports if they're filled with educational jargon and platitudes. In my view, the most useful way to report student progress is to present a profile for each student that indicates progress toward each separate goal or standard adopted by the district. That requires a more complex reporting format than either parents or teachers are accustomed to. But standards-based reporting can be reconciled with traditional letter grades if necessary by equating A, B, C, and D with advanced level, proficient level, basic level, and "needs improvement."

4. It's difficult to determine how good is good enough.

Norm-based assessment, in which students are assessed relative to the rest of their group, has been generally abandoned in favor of criterion-based or standards-based assessment. Today we typically set up assessment tasks based on our standards and we establish scoring rubrics and criteria for passing. We usually have several levels, often a basic level, a proficient level, and an advanced level.

But there are problems immediately apparent. First, what adjectives can we use that are precise enough to be helpful in judging student responses? The standard may say, "Play with a good tone." But "good" is a slippery and imprecise descriptor, and judges may not agree on whether a given student's tone is, in fact, good. Most other descriptors we can think of are equally vague and fuzzy. We can help considerably if we provide an audio example of a good tone. But that requires good audio equipment at every site, and it probably requires separate examples for every instrument.

And there are more questions: How high should our expectations be? And by what process do we decide this? One way to begin is to ask, item-by-item, "What level of proficiency do our kids really need in this specific task?" And, if we want support from the community, at some point parents and the public should be allowed to participate in this process.

Then as we begin getting results from our assessment we should check to confirm that our standards are realistic and achievable. All standards should be subject to a reality check. But no standards can be realistic and achievable unless we have the proper conditions for learning in terms of time and staff and materials and equipment. No district can expect to achieve any reasonable standards if its elementary music teachers see their students for, say, fifteen minutes every two weeks. But if we can get agreement within a community on what students should know and be able to do in music, then there is ownership of those expectations by the community, and that ownership can serve as a lever to get the time and materials and so forth we need to meet the standards.

The question "How good is good enough?" burst into the public consciousness a few years ago when states began mandating tests that kids had to pass to graduate from high school or to be promoted—typically to fourth grade or eighth grade. These are high-stakes exams, and states found that large numbers of kids were failing. I remember reading that when Florida began to require third graders to pass a reading exam for promotion to fourth grade several years ago, 23% failed the first year. And in California just last year 41,700 high school seniors failed the test required to receive diplomas.

Popular reaction in state after state has taught us that widespread failure is politically unacceptable. It alienates the public. And it discourages kids and causes them to drop out of school. How have states responded to these challenges? They have done one of two things: Either they have lowered the passing score or they have made the tests easier.

Does that make sense to you? Both of these responses underscore the stunningly arbitrary nature of the criterion-setting process.

Of course, there is another option, and that is actually to improve learning. That was always the purpose of the test in the first place, but a mandate without a plan for implementation and without adequate funding has no more chance of success at the state level than it does at the national level. Again, that's trying to eliminate crime by making it illegal.

And here, too, NCLB, however well intentioned, demonstrates a monumental naiveté. It requires that students make so-called "adequate yearly progress," but leaves it up to the states to define "adequate yearly progress." What kind of requirement is that? It requires that all teachers be "highly qualified," but it lets the states define what that means. The fox is guarding the chickens here.

Other provisions are even more mind-boggling in their lack of contact with reality. All students—*all* students—must be proficient in reading and math by 2014. Congress is good at lofty rhetoric but sometimes hasn't a clue about how things work in the real world. The only way that goal could be met is by setting the proficient level so low as to be laughable. Provisions like these constitute a clear and open invitation to states for manipulation, and gimmickry, and gamesmanship with the assessment results. NCLB not only allows the states to mislead the public, but some would say that it requires them to do so.

5. *Overemphasis on testing has caused some schools to cut back on music and the other arts.*

In the annual Phi Delta Kappa Gallup Poll last year, 68% of the public said that NCLB was hurting the performance of the public schools in their communities, or that it was making no difference, and only 29% said it was helping. And those who were actually familiar with the law had a more negative opinion of it than the general public.

A survey of school principals by the Council for Basic Education shows that the amount of instructional time devoted to reading, math, and science has been increasing, but the liberal arts are being squeezed and the curriculum is being forcibly narrowed. Of the principals surveyed, 25% reported a decrease in instructional time for the arts in their schools. And these trends are most pronounced in schools with large minority populations.

Causation is often difficult to prove, but surely it's more than coincidence that these shifts in the allocation of instructional time are occurring just as the NCLB mandates for tests in reading, math, and science are taking effect. Let's not forget that the definition of the core academic disciplines in NCLB includes the arts. And let's not allow education decision-makers to forget that either. The arts are core academic disciplines under NCLB. Of course we want no child left behind. We also want no discipline left behind, especially a discipline that directly affects the quality of life for every American.

In contrast to the rigid but manipulatable requirements we now have, a more sensible system might look something like this:

> *First.* National voluntary standards and model assessment instruments in each
> core discipline are developed through the National Assessment program.

Second. If desired, state or local standards and assessment instruments are developed in the same format as the national models so that differences between the two levels are readily apparent.

Third. The state or district reports to the public at set intervals on the percentage of kids who meet the standards-based assessment by the state or district.

Fourth. The district reports regularly to parents whether their kids are meeting the standards.

Fifth. Decisions regarding promotion continue to be made on an individual basis.

Sixth. Serious remedial efforts are undertaken for the kids who fall short.

There's a danger lurking beneath the surface in the present system. In some quarters of the public there's a strong presumption that in education what's tested is what's important. One corollary is that what's important is what's tested. Another corollary is that what's not tested is not important. Of course, none of this is true, but truth doesn't matter here. All that matters is perception.

I recently ran across a song that relates to this issue. The title is "It's Not on the Test." I don't have the music, so I can't sing it, which is probably just as well, but let me share with you the first and last verses:

"Go to sleep now, third grader of mine,
The test is tomorrow, but you'll do just fine.
It's reading and math. Forget all the rest.
You don't need to know what is not on the test.

"The School Board is faced with No Child Left Behind.
With rules but no funding, they're caught in a bind.
So music and art and the things you love best
Are not in your school 'cause they're not on the test.

Assessment can be a powerful tool to improve education. But it can become detrimental and counterproductive if it's misused. It's up to us as teachers to insist that assessment be done competently, with an emphasis on quality not quantity. And it's up to us to not allow misguided efforts in assessment to shift the emphasis in American schools away from the broad humanistic goals they've traditionally pursued.

Conclusion

It is not the purpose of education to teach kids how to take tests. The purpose of education, in my view, is the pursuit of truth and beauty, and the development of human capacities, and the improvement of the quality of life. If we can maintain our perspective and guarantee that the assessment we do is done well, and if we can ensure that assessment is used to document student learning and not allowed to drive the curriculum, and if we can distinguish between useful innovations and passing fads, then maybe we can manage to run our schools in a rational manner, and maybe we can achieve the musical vision we all hold for the young people of America.

Issues in the Assessment of K–12 Music Instruction

Charles R. Hoffer
University of Florida

Abstract

This paper presents four significant considerations in assessing learning in K–12 music classes. One is the need for teachers to be very clear about what they want students to learn. The second emphasizes the value of assessment for both teachers and students. The third points out the need to assess individual as well as group learning. The fourth is the importance of assessing learning in the cognitive, affective, and psychomotor domains.

Five recommendations are offered. The first is to assess individual students in addition to evaluating groups. Second, to achieve useful assessments, teachers must have clearly stated curricular objectives. The third recommendation is to develop curriculum guides that provide a bedrock course of study for elementary and middle schools. Fourth, directors of secondary school performing ensembles should plan for more than performances. The fifth recommendation is that college music methods classes devote more attention to practical ways of assessing students' learning.

Assessing learning in real world situations involves many issues and considerations. Five are especially important for music teachers in the schools, and these issues promote several recommendations for improving the assessment of learning in music.

Content and Curriculum

The first consideration for assessment is actually a curricular question: What, if anything, should students be learning in music classes and rehearsals? If teachers have little idea of what they want their students to learn, there can be little to assess. Objectives and the assessment of those objectives are actually two sides of the same coin. Without a clear idea of what students are to learn, assessment is no more possible than "pigs can fly," to quote an old phrase.

For a number of reasons, the content of music classes is largely the responsibility of each music teacher. They can generally teach what they want to teach, which is good or bad, depending on the teacher. If one observes many teachers in the schools, one realizes that many of them exhibit limited interest in teaching content, and consequently, in assessment.

For some music teachers, the goal (expressly stated in some instances) is that the students "have fun."[1] What their students learn—or don't learn—seems unimportant to them.

Large school districts often have curriculum guides for music at the elementary and middle school levels, which often make use of one of the basal music series books. Music courses in the secondary schools consist almost entirely of elective performing ensembles and vary enormously from one to another in type and quality. Curriculum guides and textbooks at this level are rare. One has the impression that in school districts where they do exist, curriculum guides usually have a limited effect on what most teachers actually attempt to teach. Some of the time this is so because the guides are not of useful quality, whereas at other times it's because teachers prefer to teach something else.

The Importance of Assessing Learning

There is a compelling reason why music teachers should assess how well their students are learning: *They need indicators of how well their students have learned so that they can then make adjustments in what they teach in subsequent classes and how they teach it, which will then contribute to greater student learning.* Assessment is a part of a cycle consisting of *what* (content), *how* (method), *to whom* (students), and *assessment* (indications of results), with assessment leading back to the beginning of the cycle. Self-evaluation in terms of what students have learned is also the chief means by which teachers can improve their teaching.

The reason for the recent interest in assessment is not, however, that many teachers have suddenly become interested in doing a better job of teaching—unfortunately. Instead, it is largely the result of the No Child Left Behind (NCLB) Act and its progeny in the various states. The basic purpose of NCLB is to make sure that all students meet certain minimum standards, a lofty and commendable goal. That's the good news.

But there is also bad news. Instead of a comprehensive curriculum, the NCLB has focused almost all the attention on reading and math. A couple of other areas may soon be included in some states, which would be good. In Florida some elementary school music teachers have had portions of their assignments changed from music to reading. The American Federation of Teachers reports that 87% of its members—across all grade levels—responded that "increases in testing have pushed important subjects and activities out of the curriculum" ("Teachers Question Testing," 2006, p. B2). NCLB has had the effect of promoting a major curricular distortion—the educational equivalent of the arms of the comic strip character Popeye.

The situation in Florida has been exacerbated by the fact that schools are graded based on these assessments, and the grades have been made public and given much attention in the media. One can easily imagine the pressure that school principals and teachers must feel to have their school receive a good grade! The unfortunate fact is that in the eyes of the media and the public, the purpose of assessment is to make schools shape up with regard to the limited subject matter areas being assessed.[2]

---

1 The only known measure of fun is, "More fun than a barrel of monkeys," which is hardly practical for assessment purposes!

2 In Florida, Dr. Timothy S. Brophy is leading an effort to assess music instruction on a statewide basis. At this

Traditionally, assessment has been closely associated with giving students grades. Music teachers have been doing so for generations now, but usually not in a very valid way. It's difficult for elementary music specialists to give a valid grade to each of the hundreds of students they teach in group situations for only forty minutes a week. (In fact, it takes many weeks just to learn their names!) Grading doesn't get much better at the middle and high school levels, where students expect high grades, or else they may choose another elective. Admission interviews here at the University of Florida reveal the fact that most high schools now weight grades, so that a grade in a music course counts for less than grades in traditional academic subjects in computing students' grade point averages. Grading practices are no better in some areas at the college level, where all students who show up faithfully for rehearsals of performing groups are awarded an A. Professors who teach in the academic areas do only a little better. They face a phenomenon called grade inflation, which has caused some law and medical schools to set percentage allocations for the grades professors can award.

Levels of Sophistication

Whether they realize it or not, almost all music teachers make rudimentary judgments about their students' learning in groups, especially their performance of music. Elementary school classes sing songs or move to music and secondary school ensembles play or sing works. Based on what they see or hear, music teachers usually make decisions about how well a class or ensemble did on the particular activity and decide what further actions need to be taken. Usually these judgments are not systematic, and their effects are not carefully analyzed. But they can be a foothold leading to systematic assessment of learning in music classes and rehearsals.

The word *assessment* often conjures up thoughts of a sophisticated activity that is limited to researchers who have a special interest and expertise in the topic. In real world school situations, however, it can't be that way. There simply isn't time in music classes for intensive assessment procedures. Nor do most teachers have the time in their crowded teaching schedules to do it. But they can systematically sample their students' achievements by asking individual students to play or sing a short passage in rapid succession or ask several students short questions. By taking such actions, teachers will have a far better idea of what the students have learned than would otherwise be true.

If one is referring to doctoral dissertations and/or articles for the *Journal of Research in Music* Education, this is a quite different matter. Assessment at that level is complex and time consuming. It also involves several thorny issues regarding validity and reliability. One such issue is the use of statistics to report and analyze phenomena. Statistical analysis requires converting an aspect of human behavior into numbers, a process that rests on a host of assumptions such as: The units are of equal size, they can be analyzed mathematically, and they truly represent units of the particular phenomenon. Usually the phenomena being assessed are mental constructs that can only be inferred from examining indicators of them.

---

point, the effort is not part of the Florida Comprehensive Assessment Test (FCAT). One wishes him and his colleagues well, because it could have a major positive impact on how school boards and administrators view music.

The limitations involved with converting phenomena into numerical values for statistical analysis have encouraged some researchers to reject their use. Instead, they have turned to descriptive data consisting of qualitative, subjective impressions. Usually their subjective conclusions cannot be generalized to other situations, and both the reliability and validity of such research are questionable. For these reasons, in spite of the limitations and problems with quantitative analysis, it represents the best and most useful means available for analyzing most phenomena at the level expected for professional publications.

Individual and Group Assessment

Music teachers often make decisions based on how well a group has performed. At the elementary school level, music teachers hear a class sing or observe as it engages in an activity. Secondary schools also have a long tradition of contest/festivals in which once or twice a year ensembles perform for adjudicators and are given ratings. Usually these group assessments are rendered on three works the ensemble has prepared; sometimes one additional work is read at sight. The results are reported by categories such as Excellent or Good. The ensembles are also provided general comments about aspects such as technique, intonation, interpretation, and so on.

A modest number of individual secondary school students voluntarily prepare solos that are evaluated at contest/festivals. They receive the same limited type of comments and ratings that ensembles are given. Students are given grades individually in music in both elementary and secondary schools, but the questionable validity of these grades was cited earlier in this paper. The assessment of individual learning in music classes and rehearsals is rare.

Comprehensiveness of Assessment

Music is a multifaceted art that involves information, attitudes, and performing skills. Assessments of learning in music, therefore, need to include each of its aspects. Although first published fifty years ago, the concept of the three domains of learning and their taxonomies developed by Bloom, Krathwohl, and others still remains useful today.

Cognitive Domain. Assessment in the cognitive domain of information and understanding is rather easily accomplished, at least at its lower levels, which consist largely of rudimentary knowledge (Bloom, Krathwohl, and Masia, 1956). Questions about notation and musical terms, for instance, are not difficult to write and score, but they are of limited significance.

The higher levels of the taxonomy (analysis and synthesis) represent a greater challenge, because answers are not as clear-cut as they are at the lower levels. For this reason, scoring the responses is more complicated and usually involves judgments, which make the process more time-consuming and less precise. Nevertheless, these higher-order cognitive levels are important, and they certainly should be a part of efforts at assessment.

Listening questions can be considered both cognitive in the sense that they involve knowledge and psychomotor because they require perceptive hearing. However one classifies them, they are important, because listening is such an integral part of music. Several computer programs that help students improve their ability to hear and recognize features in music have been developed in the past fifteen years (Hoffer, 2007). Often these programs include quizzes that can be used for assessment purposes.

Affective Domain. Assessment in the affective domain of attitudes, beliefs, and commitments presents a different challenge (Krathwohl, Bloom, and Masia, 1964). The two assessments conducted by the National Assessment of Educational Progress included a sizable number of items dealing with students' attitudes toward music, but the 1997 assessment conducted under auspices of the U. S. Department of Education did not (National Assessment of Educational Progress, 1981). The committee that worked on the music portion of the *National Standards for Arts Education* discussed including standards in the affective domain, but decided against doing so (personal participation). Yet, how music instruction affects students' attitudes toward music is an important matter.

It seems entirely possible to gather data about changes in students' attitudes for a class or group, *if* the students respond anonymously. If asked individually, they may be tempted to answer the way they think the teacher wants them to. They may also think their answer might affect their grade. It is fair to ask students if they know or can perform something, but they should not be required to like what they perform or learn. There is a difference between education and indoctrination!

Psychomotor Domain. Performing ensembles have a tradition of giving concerts at various times throughout the school year. At the secondary school level they also participate in contest/festivals in which their performance skill as a group is evaluated, as was mentioned earlier. What is played or sung varies from year to year and occasion to occasion. The music in the students' folders at a particular time is tantamount to the curriculum. The performance skill of the group is what matters most; what is learned in conjunction with performing the music seems secondary.

The writers of the *National Standards for Arts Education* attempted to strike a balance between the doing and knowing aspects of music with four standards dealing with the making and creating music and four involving knowledge and understanding. The fifth standard, which deals with reading music, includes both skill and knowledge (Music Educators National Conference, 1994). This proportion represents a desirable goal for the total music program, but it will of course vary depending on the type of class. It does suggest to all music teachers, however, that both aspects of music education are necessary.

Recommendations

1. Individual students must be assessed.

The assessment of individual students is required for meaningful assessment. The assessment of group performance involves only a group, and it's usually confined to the performance of music. It is useful for groups, but it says little about how much, for example, each of the thirteen sopranos in a choir is learning in terms of singing skill, information about music, and attitude toward what is being taught.

Due to the severe limitations on time, music teachers need to be extremely efficient in assessing individual students. Skill development can, for example, be assessed by asking individual students to play or sing a short phrase in rapid succession as the teacher rates the performance. These ratings can be as robust as a two-point scale or rubric in elementary schools to more refined ratings at the secondary school level.

Technology can make listening to individual students much more convenient. The SmartMusic programs, for example, allow students to perform exercises or melodies, which are then presented on the computer monitor in original notation with any incorrect rhythms or notes shown in a different color (MakeMusic, Inc., 2006). The program also allows students to email their performances to their teacher for grading and assessment purposes.

In the case of obtaining information, teachers can have students take short quizzes consisting of as few as one or two questions. Or teachers can ask several students short questions verbally to sample how well they have understood a point. Attitudes can be assessed by observing student behavior and anonymous questionnaires.

The fundamental suggestion here is that music teachers consciously make systematic efforts to find out how well their students individually have learned. These efforts do not need to be carefully controlled research studies. They can, however, provide teachers with the feedback necessary to complete the teaching process described earlier.

2. *Devote more time to music content.*

As was mentioned early in this paper, objectives and the assessment of the learning of those objectives are two sides of the same coin. For this reason, music teachers generally need to devote more attention (*much* more in some cases) to the content they teach. Just entertaining the public and keeping students happy simply isn't enough.

3. *Develop and use an effective curriculum guide.*

An effective curriculum guide can help teachers in planning and assessing. There is not space here to describe many of the features of such a guide, but a few can be mentioned. One is that it be specific about what is to be learned; just providing a list of activities is not enough. Another is that the guide be planned so that the specified activities require roughly 50 percent of the time for an average class or group. The remaining 50 percent allows for differences among schools and the varied interests and abilities of teachers. A third condition is that a beta version of a guide be developed by a small committee. Then it should be field tested and critiqued by *all* music teachers appropriate for the guide. Every teacher needs to feel a sense of ownership in the guide, or else it will probably be largely ignored. Finally, the guide should never be considered final and finished; improving it should be a continuing process.

4. *Plan and implement curricula for secondary performance ensembles.*

Most curriculum planning has been for general music classes in elementary and middle schools. Secondary school performing ensembles should also have planned curricula. Just preparing for one performance after another usually results in haphazard learning. In addition, students in high school ensembles receive grades and credits, which imply courses with planned content.

5. University teachers should devote more time to teaching assessment methods.

Music education methods classes and textbooks need to devote more attention to the reasons for and efficient ways of assessing learning in K–12 music instruction. Future music teachers are often urged to assess student learning, but in many cases they need specific, practical ideas for doing so, as well as systematic follow-up in their field experiences and student teaching.

Music teachers who fail to assess their students' learning systematically are operating on faith, not facts. Objective assessment of what students have learned is an essential aspect of effective teaching.

References

Bloom, B., Krathwohl, D., and B. Masia, B. 1956. *Taxonomy of educational objectives: Book I, Cognitive domain.* New York: David McKay.

Hoffer, C. 2007. Active listening guides. *Music listening today*, 3rd ed. (ancillary materials). Belmont, CA: Thomson-Schirmer.

Krathwohl, D., Bloom, B., and B. Masia. 1964. *Taxonomy of educational objectives: Book II, Affective domain.* New York: David McKay.

MakeMusic, Inc. 2006. SmartMusic version 10.0. (computer software). Eden Prairie, MN: Author.

Consortium of National Arts Education Associations. 1994. *National standards for arts education: What every young American should know and be able to do in the arts.* Reston, VA: MENC—The National Association for Music Education.

National Assessment of Educational Progress (NAEP). 1981. *Results from the second national assessment* (Report 10-MU-01). Denver: Educational Commission of the States.

Teachers Question Testing. 2006, August 4. *The Gainesville Sun*: B2.

Navigating the Paradox of Assessment in Music Education

Douglas C. Orzolek
University of St. Thomas

Abstract

Assessment has become inseparable from formal education—and it is here to stay. The problem for many educators is that the term *"assessment"* is full of paradox, and has taken on different meanings for different people. At the same time, there has been a philosophical shift as education has moved its emphasis to learning and away from teaching. Assessment practice should reflect that shift but still have meaning to all of education's stakeholders. Can assessment of that kind be done? This paper suggests that the answer may lie in considering the paradox of assessment *and* assessment as paradox as an approach to meet that end.

Like many in the field of education, I follow the path of the assessment paradigm with great interest. Through the efforts of "No Child Left Behind" and the many accountability systems put into place in our states and districts, assessment of student learning is on the minds of many. One would only review a listing of presentations at professional development workshops, any educational journal, or the editorial pages of your local paper for support of the notion that assessment has become a part of our country's educational landscape.

Assessment has become inseparable from formal education—and it is here to stay. The problem for many educators is that the term *"assessment"* is full of paradox, and it has taken on different meanings for different people. Assessment has become a driving force and factor in the funding of schools, teacher evaluation, curriculum development, the adaptation of curriculum and testing for special needs learners, determining mission and vision for schools, the retention of administrators and even the re-election of politicians. Assessment can also help to explain, determine, monitor, and promote student learning.

The editors of *Educational Leadership*, the periodical of the Association for Supervision and Curriculum Development, in an effort to meet the needs of their wide spectrum of readers, fell prey to this paradox as well. The frames for the November 2005 issue were "assessment that promotes learning" and "an examination of the role of all kinds of assessment." Yet, in further describing the aims of this issue, contributors were asked to consider how data can monitor progress, inform instruction, meet diversity requirements, determine how homework fits in, and decide whether or not assessment is valid and appropriate. Sure, all of this fits together in some respects, but this seems to be asking a lot of one test.

The Paradox in Assessment

It's not anyone's fault. Paradox is found throughout current thinking in educational assessment, so in honing my thoughts, I began where I usually do, and found help in the "good book"—the dictionary. However, the definition of the word *"assessment"* is really where the paradox begins! Assessment can mean many things: performance evaluation (as in learning), value (as in property), or simply a judgment about something. But, as any good etymologist knows, by looking at the origin and root of a word, we can learn something more. According to my American Heritage Dictionary of the English Language, *assessment*, which is derived from *"assess,"* actually comes from the Latin word *"assidere,"* meaning "to sit beside as an assistant judge." I suppose that you could derive a lot of different meanings from that, but I use the following: It means that the educator (assistant judge) would merely sit next to the learner and offer advice or ideas as they assess themselves!

Our particular content area, music, is rich with examples of paradox. Richard Colwell (2003), a noted music education scholar, smartly summarizes this situation by citing several paradoxes he has experienced. The heart of the matter, in his opinion, is that the profession has spent more time "attacking the problem rather than solving the problem" (11). He's right. The amount of time and money that has gone into debating the merits of assessment could have been spent building many new schools. We've got to accept our responsibility to be accountable to all of the stakeholders in the educational community (students, teachers, parents, administrators, boards, communities, politicians) and work to an end. We must solve the assessment problem.

Colwell (2003) also cites that assessment will *not* provide more respect for the profession of music education—another paradox. Many in my area believe that a standardized test might put music on par with English and Math. In a recent discussion with a state politician, I asked whether testing in the arts would make a difference in funding. His reply was quick and simple, "Nah, what do you need a test for? We know why the arts are important." (12). Colwell was right.

Colwell was right about something else related to assessment and respect. He also suggested that few stakeholders could accurately describe an outstanding arts program. During a visit to a state conference of school board members, I asked a group of volunteers how they assessed their high school music programs. The answers were not that surprising: no complaints or letters from parents or students, "good" concerts, "good" trips, a strong pep band for games, trophies and awards, and good numbers. And then, the fatal blow—"What else is there?" It was clear that their form of assessment was working for them. As I share this with music education colleagues, they cringe. We truly do much more for kids than helping them to attain awards. We don't need assessments for this purpose; we simply need to better explain ourselves and what we do in our classes.

Colwell (2003) also suggests that teachers have not been granted enough training in assessment to truly grasp what it might accomplish. He offers: "If we can't help teachers with assessment, we should just hang up the fiddle" (17). As a result, we have workshops and lots of them. I've attended many workshops about assessment with hopes to find the key

that will unlock my understanding of assessment. But it never fails that a gifted presenter ends a brilliant demonstration of the assessment tools used in his/her setting by saying, "Now, this probably won't work for you, but you'll probably need to adapt it for your use." Not what I was hoping to hear. Or, when providing a session on the process I've gone through to determine an appropriate assessment for my students, it never fails that someone asks me to just get to the point and explain how to use the rubric on the last page. Or, how about this "one? "There is more than one way to assess." While this is true, this creates more ambiguity in an already ambiguous area.

There's more. Since we haven't figured out ways to integrate assessment well, now we have mandated assessment in the form of high-stakes testing from both the federal and state levels. The paradox here is that assessment used as an accountability tool. Think about this for a second: 'We're testing students on content to determine whether schools and educators are doing their job. I've heard many stories of students who have simply taken the day off to avoid the long hours of filling in bubbles—they've got it figured out, too! Sometimes the tests have high stakes—a student may not advance to the next grade. But, most often, the results are used to determine funding or remove administrators from schools where improvement is not seen as sufficient.

I ask: Is high-stakes testing the way to go? Assessment to improve learning is best formulated in the classroom (Colwell, 2003, 12); it shouldn't come in the form of a test written by people who aren't familiar with the needs of individual students. Furthermore, education should focus on individuals and their specific learning needs. Colwell writes, "...assessment must be credible and illuminating, inform decisions, and motivate learning" (2003, 17). Other than a number, students rarely receive any feedback about their results. Teachers rarely see the results, either. There is no way these assessments can be used to inform instruction and the resultant learning if more details aren't made available.

Tests are something tangible. The results of tests can be considered a product of what students know and are able to do. But, are they? Learning theory speaks to the importance of "process over product." How do the students work their way through a problem and ultimately solve it? Many suggest that the effort and experience attained in that process is far more important and valuable than any grade could ever explain. Paradox? In other words, not everything that is important is tested, and not everything that is tested is important!

School *without* assessments might be a good thing. In many states, music education (or arts education) is required by law. All but one state has specific academic standards in place for these areas. Yet, only a few states have any sort of assessment to measure whether this requirement is being met. Many states have declared that it is the districts' responsibility to determine whether or not students are fulfilling state standards. That is a good thing, except for the fact that the state does not require districts to report on any of it! There is no reporting mechanism in place. Under the strain of budget cuts, many administrators have decided to forego or reduce arts education for that reason and to spend more time in areas that are reported, creating more paradox.

What about the students? Assessment should provide students with feedback on progress and their learning. It should offer suggestions of what needs to be reviewed. It should offer the teacher a "teachable moment""": "'Here's what you should do next time." It should motivate students to learn more or dig deeper into a new, more complex problem. (I'll share more on this point later.) With all the wonderful things assessment can and should do for them, it does one important thing in the eyes of students—it gives them a grade. How important are grades? Students reminding us how they need to get an A in our course to get into a good college have approached us all. The paradox is found within them as well.

With all of this in mind, it is not difficult to understand why assessment has become so ubiquitous in today's educational climate.

Solving the Problems of Assessment in Music Education

How do we solve these problems? To what extent is it possible to improve assessment in music education to void the many paradoxes that exist in today's thinking?

The simple truth may be that we do nothing. We should come to accept that assessment has become paradoxical and look at it and use it with that knowledge in hand. Assessment can be used in a number of ways and mean many different things to many different stakeholders. We should consider it from every angle and create numerous and varied tools to assist in the learning of our students. Education in this vein is here to stay. It is important that we begin to view the learning of music in this light if we are to get over this latest hurdle and advance music education.

If we embrace the shift in education that has moved the emphasis to student learning and away from teaching, we will need to extend our thinking about assessment. My experiences have taught me that music education, however, has yet to embrace those changes. Our model of teaching students is very teacher-driven: fix this rhythm; sing it this way; use this fingering; shape the phrase this way. In essence, when we assess a student's learning in much of today's music education, we are truly assessing the teaching. There are many who are adapting more "learner-oriented" approaches to music education. These approaches (inquiry-based, problem-based, constructivist, and many others) are based on the learning theories extensively studied by other educators while music teachers are focusing so deeply on content and performance. In other words, the profession may need to re-think how music education is being delivered.

While that may be a highly desirable end for music education as a whole, let's take a step back and consider how assessment might be improved upon in the more teacher-oriented setting. We might get started by asking ourselves a few questions when considering assessment in our teaching. What is the purpose of the assessment? Who is it for and why do they want it? How are the data/results to be used? What will be gained from this assessment? Or, to make it even simpler, just start with these two: What are you trying to accomplish? And, how will you know when it's been done? And, I've found that many of my best teaching moments have come as the result of considering the assessment of a lesson before I actually determine the lesson procedures. Having a clear eye on where I'd like to go generally leads to a better overall experience for everyone. I've also used my final assessment as a pre-test to determine what my students may already know—yes, assessment as a starting point.

I've often found that those two questions are enough to foster a great deal of thought about what assessments I will use. In the area of music, we have traditionally used a wide range of assessment tools. In these cases, we are assessing a product (not the process) through tools like: written tests on musical concepts; performance auditions; listening tests; analysis of musical works in written papers; written reviews of musical performances attended; proper use of musical elements in composition projects; and, even multiple-choice, standardized tests. All of these have their value and place and can offer the teacher and a student a certain type of feedback. All of these tools are readily at hand and have been used by educators for many years.

As inquiry-based and constructivist approaches work their way into music education, new possibilities aimed at assessing a student's process are also arising. Teachers are asking their students to solve musical problems much like those that real composers, performers or listeners might be required to solve. Let's consider a lesson where students are asked to compose a variation on their school song. Students can build upon the knowledge and insights they have gathered from their experiences as musicians. Teachers can monitor their progress by assessing the procedure students used to solve the problem as well as the final outcome—a piece of music. Here, the same project—writing a composition—can be used to assess both product and process. Students will learn from both assessments! Again, music educators must be trained and encouraged to teach this way.

If we believe that assessment should motivate students to learn more or dig deeper into a new, more complex problems, then we need to rethink our assessment tools even further. Lately, music educators are considering more assessments that allow students to learn more from the experience—like rubrics designed to assess performance progress on an instrument. These rubrics can include terminology and information that can suggest where a student might work to improve before the next performance. I would propose this area as a means for further exploration for the profession. In my setting, students are recording their practice once a week and electronically submitting their sessions for assessment by professors, fellow students, and outside evaluators from all over the country. After reviewing several weeks of recordings, it is easy to determine the progress that has been made and the measures that can be taken to improve further.

Now that we have a variety of assessment tools at hand and now that we have compiled a variety of data and information about our learners, music educators need to find effective ways to share them with the stakeholders in their schools. But, we must first understand what each of the stakeholders wants to know about student learning. It seems that this may be the greatest paradox of all. My perception is that they are all interested in something different. Parents and students are interested in progress, principals are often interested in the individual cognitive development of students (McCoy, 1991), school boards and community members are often concerned with how each student is meeting curricular goals, the state is interested in each student meeting state standards, and the federal leadership seems interested in test scores of schools. This may seem overwhelming, but if we take the broad and student-centered approach in our teaching and assessing previously described, we merely need to find a way to report the results to *all* of the people involved.

One reporting mechanism might be the individualized student portfolio. It can include all and any kinds of work—written tests, standardized tests, recordings of performances, compositions, papers, anything! Many music educators are keeping this information in electronic formats ("e-folios") on websites that anyone can access. The variety of information here can provide a strong view of how a student has done on tests and how they have made their way through the process of learning music. There seems to be something here that all of the stakeholders can use to make their own assessment of student learning.

I also believe that it is important for music educators to summarize and report all of their assessment data and information to the stakeholders in a one page, holistic accountability report (see Appendix 1: Sample Accountability Report for an example of what this may look like for an entire music department). We must learn to accept the serious responsibility of accountability to all of the stakeholders as a part of the terms of our employment. We should be able to describe what our students have learned in music to each of the groups listed above.

Finally, I firmly believe that any dialogue about assessment in education is only going to produce positive results for students. What I am most excited about, however, is that the education has moved its emphasis to learning and away from teaching. And, for me, there is the most important paradox of them all—assessment should be about what students have learned and not what has been taught to them. It is not about us as teachers, it is about our students. That means that assessment practice should reflect that shift. Can assessment of that kind be done? Considering the assessment from every possible angle may be the best answer. I challenge all of you to do just that.

References

Colwell, R. 2003. The status of arts assessment: Examples from music. *Arts Education Policy Review, 105* (2):10-17.

McCoy, C. 1991. Grading students in performing groups: A comparison of principals' recommendations with directors' practices. *Journal of Research in Music Education, 39* (3):181-190.

Scherer, M., ed. 2005. Assessment (Special issue). *Educational Leadership, 63* (3).

Accountability Report

Instrumental Music Education Department

Mission Statement : High Quality, Comprehensive Music Education

Goals/*Results* for 2003-2004

- Increase number of national standards completed / *Implemented composition unit this year*
- Improve student rankings in state portfolio assessments / *See below*
- Enhance music theory understanding by adapting new software / *New software purchased and implemented*
- Provide outstanding performance opportunities for students / *Performances were well received - CD attached!*
- Exemplary School Award 2004-5

National Standards

This year we added a composition (Standard 4) unit to our instruction. Several guests spoke of their experiences as composers, we took a field trip to the American Composer's Forum and wrote our own pieces that were performed during our recital at the end of the year.

State/District Standards

11th grade portfolios were sent to our neighboring schools for evaluation and assessment by music educators in those districts. The following are the results based upon established rubrics:

- 4 (Exemplary) - 15% (10% in 2002)
- 3 (Proficient) - 45% (40% in 2002)
- 2 (Developing) - 35% (45% in 2002)
- 1 (Poor/Incomplete) - 5% (5% in 2002)

The results suggest that our students are performing well in these assessments of their work. This year's scores show an improvement from the previous year.

Comments from Professional Reviews

"Strongest performing group I have heard in years" - Leonard Bernstein

Student/Peer Comments

- "I feel like I have a better understanding of my instrument after I've studied a composer and her intentions"
- "Billy's perceptions of the performance were much different than mine. But, I appreciated his points - they reminded me that music can be something different for everyone.
- "Opera - I still don't like it."

Testing Results for 2003-2004

- 9th Graders completed the NAEP music skills written portion and scored in the 72 percentile nationally.
- Music reading skills measured by the Watkins-Farnum performance scale continue to improve. The mean etude completed by students in grades 9-12 was #6 in 2004 and rose to #8 in 2005.
- Average SAT score of a student in band was 1425 (out of 1600).

Other Highlights

- 97% of our students participated in the MN solo/ensemble festival this year. 35% received Superior and 40% received Excellent ratings.
- Our Concert Band earned the top ranking of Superior at the large group festival.
- Our Marching Band was selected to perform in the Rose Parade.
- We commissioned a new work from composer Libby Larsen.
- 6 band members were selected to perform with the All-State band.
- Our students gave 60 public performances during this past year.
- 80% of senior band members are planning to attend a 4 year college.

Identifying Key Issues in Assessment in Music Education

David Edmund
University of Florida

Mary Birkner
University of Florida

Rebekah Burcham
University of Florida

Christopher Heffner
Lebanon Valley College

The papers, posters, Keynote Addresses, and Special Guest Presentations delivered during *Integrating Curriculum, Theory, and Practice: A Symposium on Assessment in Music Education* were organized around four key questions. These questions were:

1. What is the purpose and role of assessment in music education in an increasingly politicized, data-driven, accountability-focused educational environment?
2. In what ways can effective assessment practice in K–12 music education be facilitated?
3. In what ways can assessment data be most effectively used to improve music teaching and learning?
4. What are the current research priorities for assessment in music education?

Participants were divided into four groups, and at the end of each of the first two days these groups each considered and discussed one of these questions. Each group was assigned a different question each day, so that each question was considered by two different groups of participants. Discussions were facilitated by pairs of keynote speakers and special guest presenters who led and guided the discussions. The facilitators utilized a think tank format, and session notes were scribed by University of Florida music education doctoral students. This paper is a summary of the results of these sessions.

The following summaries are organized by key questions. The facilitators' names are included. The responses to the key questions are treated as identifying key issues regarding assessment in music education. Though the questions for each session differ, many of the answers and resulting key issues are related.

Key Question 1: What is the purpose and role of assessment in music education in an increasingly politicized, data-driven, accountability-focused educational environment?

Facilitators: Scott Shuler and Richard Colwell

The question for this breakout session required participants to consider assessment critically. Determining purposes and roles of assessment established this session as a form of assessment in itself. Music educators identified key issues, including teacher/student growth, advocacy, communication, and most prominently, political gamesmanship. Objectives were laid forth for the effective use of assessment, as well as challenges associated with assessment in music education.

Like the other breakout sessions, purposes and roles of assessment were addressed by two separate groups of symposium participants. Between the two separate sessions, a few common themes evolved. While the participants in the first session initiated discussions noting the importance of politics, one participant ended the second session with the statement "The answer to the question is political!" Other common themes emerged. In both sessions, participants mentioned the importance of making things happen at the state level. Likewise, discussions during each session focused on advocacy.

Participants from the second session suggested that advocacy entities such as Minnesota's Citizen for the Arts program and Florida's Arts Work in Education (AWE) play a role in improving instruction and accountability. This session opened with a discussion on advocacy, and the majority of the discussion during the second session pertained to advocacy. A noted problem with advocacy groups is that they sometimes fail to draw a connection to participation in the arts and future impact/involvement in society. A list of purposes for music education emerged from this advocacy discussion:

1. Preparation of students for the workplace.
2. Preparation of students for citizenship.
3. Guidance of students toward having fulfilling lives.
4. Preparation of students for college.

It was determined that music advocates should place focus on intrinsic musical values rather than extrinsic ones. This is paradoxical, however, as evidenced by the suggestion that visibility is an important purpose of assessment. It was noted that visibility might be obtained through informing the public of music benchmarks (which should emphasize more intrinsic values).

Statewide Assessment

Some teachers are reluctant to assess students' musical achievement based upon performance. If we are to assess more than student participation, it was suggested that some type of assessment be implemented at the state level. The issue of statewide assessment led participants to consider if large-scale assessment might be a way to improve politicians' views of school music programs. Communicating the value of music education with politicians who lack knowledge about the arts is tricky. Yet, politicians are largely concerned with facts and figures, meaning that assessment may provide a way to "speak their language." Participants noted that conceptually, individual musicianship is different from institutional musicianship, which bears implications for large-scale testing. Another challenge stems from the "scientific, grid-like structure" of standardized tests. Balancing rigid testing structures and assessing musical performance is an issue of concern. One particularly thought-provoking question was: "If your state organized a meeting to discuss a music achievement test, what topics should be brought up for discussion?" Answers included the following:

1. Teacher fear of documentation (as opposed to fear of assessment).
2. Accuracy of multiple-choice testing in music assessment.
3. Not all students participate in music.
4. Teachers must avoid "teaching to the test."
5. Testing methods must vary, taking the standards into consideration.
6. Factual knowledge versus musical ability.
7. For action to take place, acceptance and excitement need to be instilled in today's music educators.

Challenges Associated with Assessing Music Performance

Discussions ensued regarding problematic issues regarding assessment in music. The subjective nature of quality in musical performance makes accurate assessment difficult. One educator commented that "music cannot be accurately assessed in a multiple-choice test." Some worry that assessment "separates music from its communication aspect." Perhaps what is meant by this statement is that the expressive component of musical performance is not assessment-friendly. It is felt that music is more profound than statistics can reveal. Others expressed concern that performance-based assessments are not practical because of time and cost constraints. Another cautious observation is that the necessity for assessments to be specific should not result in a narrowing of the curriculum.

Many agree that the goal of teaching standards should not supersede the joy of music making. Each positive aspect of assessment seems to correspond with a negative or challenge. While statewide testing is not ideal for music performance, it could help identify programs lacking in certain areas. This could lead to improvement, but some argued that it would lead to singling out schools and/or educators, which may or may not be beneficial. The competitive aspect of assessment is a concern for some. Implementing assessment in music education reminded one participant of Kurt Lewin's change theory: For every driving force associated with assessment, there seems to be one or more resisting forces.

The Future of Assessment in Music Education

As assessment plays an increasingly crucial role in education, it is up to music educators to use it most effectively. Session participants felt that music should establish itself as a subject worthy of concentrated assessment. To do this, music educators need to define the music's importance as an academic subject. An important first step would involve designing a list of benchmarks with the purpose of increasing public understanding of what students should know musically at certain ages. Though many state Department of

Education and music education leaders have established benchmarks for music, they are often not actively communicated to the public. Another important step would be to increase emphasis on music literacy. Schools are placing increased emphasis on reading fluency and comprehension. Musical literacy is likewise important for our students. Fostering creativity is another important goal of music education. Assessment may help to improve our understanding of creativity as well as our methods of teaching musical creativity.

Standards and benchmarks serve as a curriculum framework for music programs, and their content identifies essential knowledge and skill components for music educators. Session participants suggested that music standards be accompanied by specific models. Scott Shuler noted that music educators do a lot of assessing; and instead of creating more assessments, perhaps our focus should be on improving effectiveness of assessment. Paul Lehman remarked in his keynote address that the purpose of assessment is simply to improve learning and teaching. Session participants note that assessment needs to result in change. Whether we aim for advocacy, accountability, or improvement of teaching and learning, it appears clear that assessment will play a prominent role.

Key Question 2: In what ways can effective assessment practice in K–12 music education be facilitated?

Facilitators: Paul Lehman and Sandra K. "Tena" Whiston

Participating music educators were asked to formulate ideas that would help to facilitate effective assessment practices in music programs. The thoughts and ideas of the participating music educators fell into three broad categories:

1. Education and professional development.
2. Frameworks and models.
3. Dissemination of resources and materials.

Education and Professional Development

The first area of concern for participants was the need for continued education and professional development in the matter of assessment for teachers. The following concerns and suggestions were raised:

1. The teacher certification process should include evidence that music teachers can implement appropriate assessment practices.
2. University undergraduate music teacher education programs should include an assessment course and/or embed assessment knowledge and skills across the program.
3. In addition to pre-service inclusion of assessment practices, there is a need for in-service teacher training in assessment. Music educators need continued training and models of assessment throughout their teaching careers.

48

4. Additional symposia that address assessment in schools are needed. These symposia can play an important role in networking with music educators in other states and would be pivotal for professional growth.

Frameworks and Models

The second area of concern related to the need for frameworks and models for teachers to facilitate assessment practices in music classrooms. A related concern emerged regarding the frequency of music assessments in school music programs.

Participants agreed that music educators need benchmark assessment examples and models. These benchmarks and models would be invaluable for teachers, and could be revisited throughout the school year. For performance ensembles, one benchmark example might be a series of well-made recordings that present high-quality performances that model components such as tone, articulation, releases, diction, etc. The recordings could be used at home as well as in the classroom, extending learning beyond the school day.

Assessment for many performance ensembles happens only once per year as a seating audition. Participating educators asked: "Is it fair to assess students on a performance task once? Students have bad days and should have opportunities for second chances." Participants agreed that music educators generally need to incorporate more music assessment opportunities. Increasing the frequency of assessment in music ensembles for students would help educators to be more accurate in determining the students' achievement. Increasing the frequency of music assessment could also help to lower anxiety for students. Routines in student assessment should be established. When goals and objectives are clarified and a schedule for assessment is provided, students are able to prepare for assessment activities without anxiety or surprise. One participant commented: "Scope and sequence are critical." For music educators who are reluctant to lose rehearsal time for assessment, participants suggested the use of taped performance excerpts. One strategy was that "students should have to tape themselves and submit the recording at the end of the week." By using taped examples, teachers could listen to performances at their leisure. The routines and standards are still intact without the loss of rehearsal time.

Dissemination of Resources and Materials

Technology is a useful tool in assessment. Participating educators stated that a safe and secure environment should be established so that students feel confident to sing or play in front of their classmates. Participants acknowledged that there are different cultures that exist from choir to band to orchestra. Teachers felt that instrumental students are more comfortable playing by themselves than choir students. In an attempt to eliminate anxiety, educators suggested the use of directional microphones to record students during rehearsal. This would allow students to perform in an ensemble setting and be assessed simultaneously. Music educators could use directional microphones to record students onto audiotapes or computer files. Having the ability to incorporate computer software allows individual recordings to be saved indefinitely so the teacher could listen to each individual quickly and conveniently.

Participants discussed the value of web sites and the Internet as a tool for information dissemination. The Internet is a powerful tool to use as a follow-up to symposia. Web sites could be used to share information and materials with others. Web site topics included:

1. Teacher sharing of quality assessment tools divided into levels and curricular area or standard.
2. Use of chat rooms to discuss successes and failures.
3. The web may be a place to share rubrics/templates.
4. Streaming video from assessment symposium sessions for educators unable to attend.
5. Websites may be used to post models of quality performance standards.

Overall, the session discussions yielded several useful tools that music educators can use in the classroom to lower student anxiety levels while increasing ease and accessibility for teachers. It was agreed that events like this symposium are key opportunities for teachers to expand their knowledge of assessment strategies as well as broaden their view of the larger issues of assessment beyond their own classrooms.

Question 3: In what ways can assessment data be most effectively used to improve music teaching and learning?

Facilitators: Bill Bauer and Lynn Brinckmeyer

During these work sessions many factors were identified that strengthen and weaken the assessment process in music education. The discussions focused on how to effectively use assessment data in the music classroom. The discussion topics fell into three broad categories:

1. How to use and interpret data from the school to the national level.
2. Teaching teachers how to use data properly and effectively through foundations classes and professional development.
3. How standards and benchmarks have effected this issue.

There were two common themes that emerged from both sessions. The first theme revolved around the identification of ways that assessment data can effect change in teaching and learning. Discussions within this theme yielded four primary ways for using assessment data to:

1. Identify needs for professional development purposes.
2. Help establish age- and developmentally appropriate goals and standards.
3. Help teachers identify what their students know and what needs to be taught.
4. Provide academic credibility.

The second theme concerned ways to use assessment data to effect change in curriculum and standards. These discussions also yielded four primary issues for using assessment data to:

50

1. Develop effective standards.
2. Help determine the effectiveness of current standards.
3. Determine the extent to which students understand the standards put before them.
4. Provide evidence of whether or not group success equals individual student learning.

How Can Using Assessment Data Effect Change in Teaching and Learning?

Participants agreed that assessment data helps to determine professional development needs. This is an issue not only for seasoned teachers, but new and pre-service teachers as well. Teachers must have knowledge in this area to be able to use assessment effectively. It was agreed that pre-service teachers should be introduced to the issue of assessment before entering the workforce, and that they should possess knowledge of different types of assessment in music, scoring procedures, how to collect data, how to write rubrics, and what to do with the data collected before becoming certified. It was suggested that an assessment course be required for undergraduate music education majors or that assessment topics be included in all methods courses. Throughout the discussions it was clear that participants believed that consistent, periodic training was imperative. Assessment is quickly becoming a top professional development need for in-service teachers.

Participants expressed concerns over the incorrect use of data, as well as the incorrect use of assessment. Assessment in music might facilitate interdisciplinary opportunities, possibly a collaboration among classroom teachers in the elementary schools or among secondary music teachers and other secondary teachers who teach in outside fields.

Another key point in the discussion centered on the use of assessment data to help determine age and developmentally appropriate outcomes. To accomplish this, the music teachers in a school district need to engage in a collaborative effort to obtain such data. This may prove helpful in restructuring curriculum. The following questions emerged from this discussion:

1. How do we know students are learning?
2. Is learning always visible?
3. Is learning always tangible?
4. How can we show that students are learning?

Assessment data collected in the music classroom could be used in many different ways to help teachers determine if students are learning. Participants suggested some guiding questions for teachers when they review the data they collect, such as: Are the students getting from point A to point B and understanding how to do so? Are they using critical thinking skills? Examining and analyzing assessment information is the primary way for a music teacher to determine if the student is retaining what is being taught.

Immediate feedback based on assessment data is crucial for teachers and learners alike. Because of their scope, large-scale assessments do not provide immediate feedback. Participants believe that it is important that data from large-scale statewide assessments be distributed as soon as possible so that teachers may improve teaching and learning immediately.

Data from music assessments could also be useful when new students enter the music program. If a student enters a school in the middle of the year, previous assessment data

51

could help the new teacher determine where the student is academically and developmentally, and prepare a learning plan using the information. This data also helps teachers avoid teaching students material with which they may already be familiar. Participants viewed this data as evidence of what has been accomplished in music.

Academic credibility is very important today. Teachers are being held responsible for students' academic successes or failures. Using data from assessment in music can help provide evidence to administration, other faculty, and those in the community of the importance of music in schools. Well-organized and presented assessment data could help demonstrate to those outside the music classroom that, if given the proper financial support and less time constraints, students can accomplish much in the music classroom.

Another main point discussed during the session was that assessment data could be used to ensure the quality of music education at city, district, and county levels. Data could also be used to compare school programs and unify a grading system among them. Assessment data in music can also determine if rubrics and tests administered are reliable and valid.

How Can Using Assessment Data Effect Change in Curriculum and Standards?

When discussing the use of assessment data in changing curriculum and standards, the majority agreed that the standards came first and assessment of these came later. Some participants considered this a major shortcoming of the original National Standards for Music, because music teachers need to know how to assess the standards. The key to solving this issue is the revision of the standards and addition of assessments to correspond with the revised standards.

Data from assessments completed in the music classroom may produce results that provide information on how realistic the standards are. This information would provide evidence of the consistency of music education across the nation. With data from state and national assessments, standardized documents could be created.

Participants also discussed the need for students to understand benchmarks and standards set before them. If the student does not understand what is expected of him or her then assessment data might not precisely gauge what he or she is learning. It is the responsibility of both the student and teacher to understand the objectives found within standards and benchmarks.

Another area of concern pertained to the use of assessment data to provide evidence of whether or not group success is equal to individual student learning. The concerns regarding this issue were:
1. How does one assess many students in a short time, especially in a performance-based curriculum?
2. Can the student answer the question, "What did you learn?"
3. How do teachers collect data quickly, and then effectively distribute it to their administration?
5. How can teachers be most time efficient when assessing their students?
6. Are data being used to determine individual progress or group progress?
7. Are changes to curriculum affecting exams and program and student data?

The results of this discussion reveal that music educators have much to consider. At the end of the teaching day we must relinquish ourselves to the fact that we cannot solve every problem and concern stated above. Nevertheless, participants agreed that music educators must do everything possible to use assessment data most effectively.

Question 4: What are the current research priorities for assessment in music education?

Facilitators: Ed Asmus and Maud Hickey

This session provided the opportunity to identify that which is currently important for researchers to examine in music assessment. Participants recognized the need to better prepare music educators in assessment techniques and how best to implement valid assessment practices. Discussions also focused on the effects of assessment on music teaching and learning as well as student and teacher attitudes toward music assessment. Specific areas of research were identified based on these categories.

Better preparation of music educators in assessment techniques was a main focus of the breakout session. Concern over a current a lack of schema regarding assessment for collegiate music education students was voiced. Participants expressed concern that university method courses do not necessarily cover assessment techniques and collegiate students are unfamiliar with assessment because the students themselves were not assessed. While some collegiate students are provided the opportunity to take classes in assessment, these students may not be charged with the task of thoroughly developing ideas or practice tactics pertaining to assessment. As a result, university students are left with few tools to draw upon during their own teaching experiences and, as future teachers, may not understand the importance of assessment.

Undergraduate courses must present skills and knowledge for implementing effective and developmentally appropriate assessments. One proposed solution to the problem involves music education professors teaching undergraduate music education students how to create well-written rubrics. Rubrics should contain well-defined criteria to be assessed. The use of such rubrics should be incorporated as a frequent classroom activity during which college students practice writing rubrics and use them to evaluate classmates. It was further suggested that a national data bank be developed to which students can contribute well-developed rubrics. Research priorities related to the issue of teacher preparation in assessment include the following:

1. There is a need for case studies dealing with university music programs and the necessity (or lack thereof) for assessment instruction in undergraduate coursework.
2. There is a need to determine what helps teachers to be better assessors.
3. There is a need for a clearinghouse of measurement tools accessible to collegiate music education students and current music educators.

The implementation of valid assessment practices was also deemed a significant issue by breakout session participants. The use of quality assessment tools has become a concern at all levels of education. For example, one participant observed that college studios and juries often lack quality assessment. Many university professors do not want the burden of justifying their students' grades. Many professors have resisted change and the use of assessment tools such as rubrics. At the primary and secondary levels, valid assessment is often overlooked in music, as music teachers are not held widely accountable for student learning. School principals are not usually aware of how to measure student success in music, and thus, may not effectively evaluate a music teacher. Likewise, there is no standardized testing in place to measure student learning in music, which requires music teachers to be held accountable for student learning. As a result, assessment in music education is inconsistent from teacher to teacher and may not be based on valid practices.

Research priorities related to the issue of validity include the following areas:

1. There is a need to determine the best (most valid) assessment practices.
2. There is a need to determine when, developmentally speaking, we assess specific skills.
3. What are the essential musical behaviors warranting assessment?
4. Are rubrics useful for studio instructors at the collegiate level? Are rubrics valid at other levels of instruction?
5. There is a need to find and develop the best rubrics.
6. There is a need to study whether *SmartMusic* and the use of other technological tools are valid in assessment.
7. There is a need to determine the effectiveness and validity of portfolios in assessment.
8. The validity and reliability of state contest ratings needs to be explored.
9. Examining assessment tools currently available may be a helpful place to start. Can we alter strategies already being used in assessment?

The effects of assessment on music teaching and learning were also discussed. For example, how are student and teacher attitudes toward music assessment influenced? How do communities perceive music as an environment for learning as opposed to a mere activity? The study of music currently involves a standards-based system that focuses on the individual student. Assessment, then, is often individually based. One session participant voiced concern regarding whether individual assessment is compatible with traditional music education at the secondary level where large ensembles exist. The effects of assessment on music teaching and learning will undoubtedly influence the ways in which music is taught. Research priorities related to this issue include the following areas:

1. There is a need for qualitative versus quantitative research of what assessment tactics are working.
2. There is a need to determine the impact of instructional time on student achievement.
3. We must determine which resources have the greatest impact on student success.
4. We must investigate how to most efficiently provide assessment feedback.
5. There is a need to determine how to best keep data and records on large numbers of students.
6. There is a need to examine which assessment techniques are the most efficient.

Many research priorities were identified for assessment in music education. This breakout session provided participants the opportunity to identify that which is currently important for researchers to examine in music assessment. Overall, there is a great need for case studies regarding assessment use. It was determined that case studies should include regional trends and differences in assessment. Assessment in music education must be examined at all levels and from a variety of angles including the implementation of assessment, the outcomes of assessment, and teacher preparedness in assessment tactics. Further research will help music educators to better develop assessment tactics that are effective, efficient, and valid.

PART 2

Music Assessment and Curriculum

The Alignment Loop: A Curriculum Planning Sequence and Critical Inquiry as Catalysts for Sound Assessments

Dee Hansen
The Hartt School of Music
University of Hartford

Abstract

Effective assessment in music education is ideally informed by a myriad of systemically linked elements. This paper offers a curriculum design sequence, *The Alignment Loop,* which describes these interacting components of the overall curriculum design process. Each component in the loop is intrinsically influential to the other components, resulting in valuable assessments and useful resulting data. In order to accomplish *The Alignment Loop,* the paper cites a curricular design model, *Understanding by Design* (UBD) (Wiggins and McTighe, 1998), which proposes a sequence of steps necessary for creating curriculum, lesson units, and assessments, Finally, the paper reviews research by Marzano (2003) which validates effective instructional strategies, generally obtained through district-level professional development opportunities. Critical inquiry is offered as an example of an instructional strategy that can be utilized as a way of promoting sound instruction as well as assessments—thus contributing to the alignment loop.

In observing teachers' attempts to create assessments for their curriculum, whether district or personal, I find that gaps appear in the process of identifying what is taught and what is actually assessed. The procedures for this process require a thoughtful, reflective, and purposeful sequence of planning steps. One purpose of this paper is to define and clarify those steps so that valid and effective assessment can occur. *The Alignment Loop,* as described in the paper, reviews the many considerations with which school districts must grapple in order to help teachers effectively instruct, assess, and collect data on their students' progress. Instructional strategies reside at the heart of the loop. *Understanding by Design* (UBD) (Wiggins and McTighe, 1998) is cited as a method for further refining this planning process in curricular design and assessment. Because the third step in UBD is instructional planning, critical inquiry will be additionally examined in some depth as an instructional strategy significant for the music classroom. Skillful questioning and guiding statements encourage problem-solving, open-ended responses, and student demonstration of learning through performance, all necessary for assessment, effective instruction, and student learning—each a critical component of *The Alignment Loop.*

The Alignment Loop

School districts must consider a broad and comprehensive array of interacting forces as they build and implement curriculum. The following chart, *The Alignment Loop* (Hansen, 2001), categorizes and sequences these forces. Further explanations are found following the chart.

Figure 1: The Alignment Loop (Hansen, 2001)

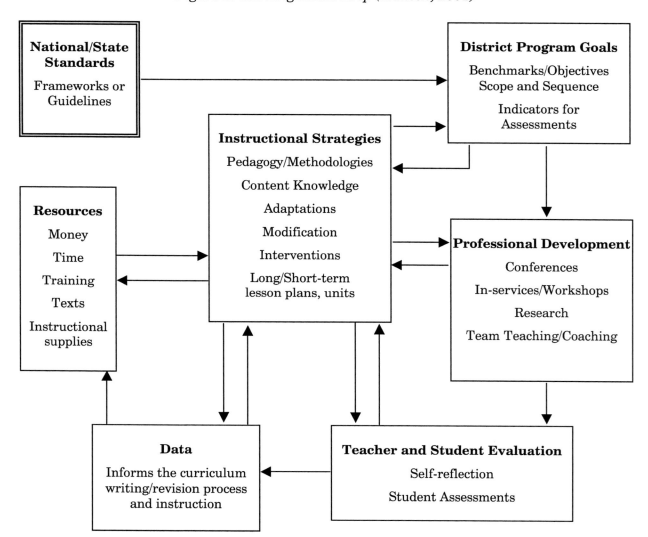

National/State Standards

Nearly all school districts involve classroom teachers in the curriculum writing process. For music educators, the National Standards for Music Education (1994) have provided a framework and high-level goals for what students should be able to know and do in music. Many states have adopted or adapted the National Standards. States title their standards differently; some are called Standards, others Frameworks or Guidelines. Regardless of the title, these are generally broad and written in order to provide a structure for school district curriculum development. The work at the state level, the school district, and for the classroom teacher is to narrow and refine the National Content and Achievement Standards so that they are achievable in each respective learning environment.

District Program Goals

The alignment process, then, begins with the National and/or State Standards. Many district curricula have also adopted what are called Educational Goals or Exit Outcomes. Often these will include Program Goals, Objectives, Benchmarks, and/or Indicators—specific statements of learning content. The Scope and Sequence is also written as a means of assuring that the agreed-upon content is taught at certain grade levels. Certainly within any given town, the amount of instruction, the demographic characteristics of a community, its cultural aspects, and the socio-economic levels of individual schools significantly impact the effectiveness with which a teacher addresses the standards. In "best practice" situations, school districts require an ongoing rotation of curriculum revisions for every subject area. The resulting curriculum advises the choice of textbook, instructional resources, and the nature and depth of assessments.

Professional Development

The teacher in the classroom is ultimately where the responsibility rests for providing a rich and standards-based curriculum for his or her students. But teachers don't magically master effective instruction. Ongoing professional development, whether at local or national levels, is imperative to strengthen teachers' tool chests of instructional approaches. School curriculum alignment and assessment must guide the teacher to facilitate student learning, given their particular environment.

Instructional Strategies

While professional development is offered in most school districts, many music educators lament the lack of direct training in music skills. Often, teacher in-services revolve around strategies to enhance reading and mathematics instruction, those areas tested through the No Child Left Behind Act. While the strategies may seem distant and unrelated to music instruction, many can be artfully crafted to succeed in the music classroom. This paper will review the research on successful teaching strategies and suggest some specific applications for music teachers.

Teacher/Program Evaluation and Data

Evaluation and assessment occur at many levels and in a wide berth of complexities. Assessment can be a valuable tool for teachers and students alike, providing information (data) that leads to improved instruction and stronger performance by both parties. Or it can be an exercise in futility. If a mismatch exists between what is taught and what is assessed, then the resulting data information is not a meaningful reflection of the impact of the instruction. At this point, we must look back and review *The Alignment Loop* in order to emphasize the significance of these steps. When the National and State standards are reflected in the District Program Goals, appropriate professional development can be implemented to assist teachers in meeting the goals. Presumably, more skillful and informed instruction will result in stronger student achievement. But professional development is no silver bullet by any means. Teachers must have deep content knowledge and continually work to refine their pedagogical skills, as in any profession. Explaining *The Alignment Loop* is relatively simple; successfully implementing it is not.

Resources

State and district resources are often based on the results of student data. To reiterate: the resources needed to assure student achievement must be the result of carefully conceived alignment process as described above. It is no secret that state and district funds can be misdirected if based on incorrect conclusions from poorly conceived assessments. How can this gap be avoided?

A Planning Process for *The Alignment Loop*

The critical components of the *Alignment Loop* that are directly applicable in the classroom are the use of state and national standards or goals, teacher and program evaluations and assessments, and instructional strategies. *Understanding by Design* (UBD) (Wiggins and McTighe, 1998) presents further clarification to these portions of the loop by describing a comprehensive planning process. Wiggins and McTighe describe a "Planning Backwards" process by which the teacher literally begins at the end—by identifying the desired results of the instruction. For the "end," the teacher first considers the national and state standards, the district curriculum, scope and sequence, and finally building and classroom goals. This of course represents the beginning of *The Alignment Loop*. This sweep of curricular guidelines is often overwhelming for music teachers, given their limited amount of planning time. It is, however, critical. For each music program or grade level, teachers must take the time to consider this first step in lesson planning. Once in place, the daily, weekly and yearly plans fall together with more coherence and connectivity. Let us examine how this works using a 6th-grade general music classroom as the model.

UBD Step One: Identify the Desired Results

Alignment Loop Components:
  • Aligning National/State Standards
  • Aligning District Benchmarks and goals
  • Professional Development

Composition is a skill that has been highlighted for this grade level in Ms. G's school district. By 6th grade, students should be able to "compose short pieces within specified guidelines, demonstrating how the elements of music are used to achieve unity and variety, tension and release, and balance (National Content Standard 4, Composing and Arranging music, MENC, 1994). Ms. G's district curriculum aligns with the national standards, and she emphasizes composition, using computer software as well as traditional notation. She believes that her students need to have conceptual understanding of how music elements interplay in musical composition. For her, this most important understanding, or "Enduring Understanding," as described by Wiggins and McTighe (1998), will be assessed when her students are asked to effectively utilize music elements in their compositions. The desired result—the Enduring Understanding, aligns with the national, state, and district standards and program goals. Ms. G then seeks professional development either through in-services, workshops, or peer mentoring in order to successfully craft her composition unit.

UBD Step Two: Determine Acceptable Evidence

Alignment Loop Components:
  • Teacher and Program Evaluation
  • Data Collection

What will be assessed and how the assessment will be structured is the next step in designing this instructional unit. Because this unit is intentionally placed at the beginning of the school year, it serves as a review of past instruction as well as an introduction to new learning. The students will be assessed through a multi-achievement level, multi-criterion rubric below. The criteria will include use of dynamic symbols, use of articulation symbols (e.g. staccato, marcato, and accents), manipulation of pitch to heighten text meaning, and performance of their compositions. The criteria will be rated on a point scale of 0–5 (Figure 2: Text-Painting Rubric)[1].

Ms. G considers this task and assessment to be formative in nature. Her plans are to continue to reinforce learning the Enduring Understanding through increasingly complex and challenging tasks. The engaging learning experience, however, is motivating and fun. It lays the foundation for future composition tasks. As she leads her students through this process of learning to compose, she will glean data from each formative assessment, thereby informing the nature of the summative assessment and her success at teaching the composition unit.

---

[1] I wish to thank Kennedy Center Master Artist, Marcia Daft, for her music text painting exercise with Shel Silverstein's poem, *Medusa*.

Music Elements	5	3	0
Dynamic Symbols	Use of dynamics effectively enhances the text.	Dynamic markings are used, but the text is not always enhanced as a result.	Dynamic markings are not used.
Articulation Symbols	Articulation symbols effectively enhance the text.	Articulation symbols are used with some success, but the text is not always enhanced as a result.	Articulation symbols are not used.
Pitch Manipulation	Symbols are used to indicate use of vocal pitch manipulation so that the meaning of the text is effectively heightened.	Some pitch manipulation is used, but the text is not always enhanced as a result.	No pitch manipulation is used.
Performance	The student performance of the poem reflects their application of the required musical elements.	The student performance of the poem at times reflects their application of musical elements.	The student performance of the poem does not reflect their application of musical elements.

UBD Step Three: Plan Learning Experiences and Instruction

Alignment Loop Component:
* Instructional Strategies

As her assessment task, Ms. G has chosen to have her students "paint" the text of the Shel Silverstein poem, *Medusa* (1996). The students with whom she has worked in her elementary school have previously studied dynamic and articulation markings. They have had limited work in applying them to composition, however. Several new students have little or no background in these elements. In step three, Ms. G must determine what facts, concepts, principles and/or skills (procedures) are needed to accomplish the text-painting task. She plans her learning experiences and instruction based on the students' needs. Prior to initiating the assessment task, she plans several learning experiences that either review or teach the needed concepts and vocabulary.

This sequence of planning steps seems straightforward enough. The teacher has identified the most important understandings that will be taught and assessed.

The assessment tool reflects program goals and objectives. The gaps between instruction and assessment are eliminated as a result. However, further refinement of this process is needed; the actual prompts (questions or statements) that engage the students in the learning experiences can help the students achieve the desired results.

The Heart of *The Alignment Loop*: Effective Instructional Strategies

Step three of the UBD planning sequence is to plan the learning experiences and instruction. But writing the lesson plan and delivering the lesson are two different skill sets. Now we will pinpoint the actual language used by a teacher to initiate a learning experience.

In his publication *What Works in Schools: Translating Research into Action* (ASCD, 2003), Robert Marzano synthesizes the results of several studies that ranked instructional strategies. Marzano reports the average effect size, percentile gain, number of effect sizes and standard deviation for each category (2003, 80). The instructional strategies include:

- Identifying similarities and differences
- Summarizing and note-taking
- Reinforcing and providing recognition
- Homework and practice
- Nonlinguistic representations
- Cooperative learning
- Setting objectives and providing feedback
- Generating and testing hypotheses
- Questions, cues, and advance organizers

This portion of the paper will highlight questions and cues. Familiarity with questioning strategies and thoughtful preparation of cues or prompts are proven instructional strategies (Marzano, 1998). Many school districts or state and teachers' organizations provide in-services for learning questioning strategies. Inquiry is a skill that can become second nature with practice. As the facilitator of learning, rather than the provider of information, a teacher can guide students to greater and deeper understanding of concepts and skills. While music is a performing art, the learning process takes many forms. Conceptual learning is acquired not only through doing but also through metacognitive reflection. Effective questioning strategies afford us the opportunity to instruct and assess. Let us consider an example.

A recognized researcher and author in language arts, Taffy Rafael (1986) has written extensively about questioning. Her model, Question-Answer-Responses (QARs) refers to four types of questions: Q1: Right There, Q2: Think and Search, Q3: The Author in Me, and Q4: In My Head or On My Own. Raphael created QARs as a procedure for enhancing students' ability to answer comprehension questions of varying degrees of difficulty. QARs are easily transferable to music and the arts. A teacher guides the questions with respect to the degree of prior knowledge their students possess. Integral to QARs is having students identify the response demands of various questions and create their own questions.

Figure 3: Question-Answer Relationships (QARs) (Raphael, 1986)

Q1: Right There

Text: Literal questions easily found in the text. The words used to make up the question and words used to answer the question are "right there" in the same sentence.

In music   These questions relate directly to the fundamental, easy-to-identify elements of music, e.g., starting pitch, line, tempo and dynamic markings, key signature.

Q2: Think and Search

Text: The answer is in the story, but you need to put together different story parts to find it. Words for the question and words for the answer are not found in the same sentence. They come from different parts of the text.

In music   These questions require students to look around and through the score or song to find the answer. With text, the questions are similar to what a reading teacher would ask. When the music lacks text, questions revolve around the manipulation of the music elements, such as including melody, harmony, tonal center, or form. Teachers can ask both text and non-text Think and Search questions.

Q3: Author and Me

Text: The answer is not in the story. The reader needs to think about what they already know and what they read in the text and fit the two together. Questions require students to use critical thinking skills.

In music: These questions require some prerequisite knowledge on the part of the student. The student must think about what he/she already knows and respond based on his/her own experiences. These questions deal with perceived emotional responses, comparisons to other works of art, interpretation of the meaning or theme, etc. Often these questions involve higher-order thinking and several national standards areas.

Q4: On my Own (In My Head)

Text: The answer to the question is not in the text. A reader could answer the question without having read the targeted text. The reader's own experiences are the basis for the answer.

In music At this level of questioning the responses to the questions require thinking "outside of the box." Students may not have heard or played the music before. Responses to the questions might prompt students to create a product, predict an ending, solve a creative problem, or evaluate a performance containing a theme or structure related to the music or art studied. Responses are open-ended and with no correct answer. On My Own may serve as a summative task or assessment or may initiate a new unit of instruction as an "anticipatory set."

Question Answer Response Examples in the Music Classroom

Q1: Right There

These questions are typical in music classrooms. In this instance, Ms. G is familiarizing her students with expression markings in a score in preparation for their *Medusa* project.

Ms. G: Class, on the screen you see a musical score. Let's make a list of the dynamic markings you see. What other expression markings do you find?

Q2: Think and Search

Ms. G's goal is to help her students understand the relationship between the meaning of the text and how music elements are used to enhance the text.

Ms. G Find a place in the score where the dynamic markings seem to enhance the words or lyrics. Are there other places in the music where this happens?

Q3: Author and Me

In this instruction, Ms. G is helping her students make the transition between text-painting examples of experienced composers to doing their own text painting.

Ms. G: Work with a partner and decide how you could change the meaning of the text by changing the dynamic marking or expression marking in the music.

Q4: On my Own (In my Head)

Q4-prompting statements or questions can be used to begin a unit or create a summative lesson. In this case, Ms. G will prepare the students for her first formative task and assessment. These types of statements or question prompts require the teacher to allow for responses that she/he may not expect. While the responses should be within acceptable parameters, the student may think of answers that the teacher has not considered. The arts are rich fodder for such lines of questioning, often missing in other curriculum area studies.

Q4 questions might take this form in Ms. G's class:

Ms. G: Class, which do you prefer—if I say the word "snake" with a long hissing sound at the beginning or I add a staccato above the word "snake" and say it quickly?

Student: It sounds better to say snake with a hiss, since that's the sound they make.

Ms. G: What type of symbol could we make up to indicate that we want that type of sound?

Student: We could draw an arrow above the "s" so we know to say it longer.

Ms. G   Great idea. Now, write down this passage. "It was a dark and scary night." Using the dynamic markings on the board and symbols that you make up, paint the words."

Student: I used the pianissimo symbol (pp) over the sentence and put an arrow over the *s* in scary.

Ms. G   Okay, read your interpretation. The student reads his sentence and others are asked to read as well. More examples are presented in order to practice and reinforce the concept.

Ms. G   Let's listen to a piece of music. Write in your journals how the composer has used musical elements we've studied to heighten the musical expression. Be specific with your musical language. We have studied many different types of dynamic and articulation symbols. You have made up some of your own. Be sure to use your musical vocabulary in your journal reflections.

This process continues as the students refine and reinforce their ability to use the elements of music in composition. They are now ready to text paint Shel Silverstein's *Medusa* poem as the first formative task and assessment of their composition unit.

Final Thoughts

Curriculum alignment is a systemic process in which each component is critical to the success of the next. Because music educators are interested in learning about what works in instruction, we assess, research, and analyze data in an attempt to impact instructional and student work. A significant consideration is this, however: We can use our assessments and data to inform a discreet instructional practice, to effectively teach a certain skill or impart certain concepts. But, when we place these findings in context with the entire curriculum design process, teachers and students alike will benefit from the broader perspective of coherent and comprehensive curriculum and instruction. Assessment cannot be an end unto itself. As part of an overall systemic process, the entire alignment loop must be considered in order for the assessments and the resulting data provide informative feedback.

References

Bloom, B. S., ed. 1984. *Taxonomy of educational objectives*: *Book 1, Cognitive domain*, rev. ed. New York: Longman.

Consortium of National Arts Education Associations. 1994. *National standards for arts education*. Reston, VA: MENC—The National Association for Music Education.

Hansen, D. 2001. *Handbook of music supervision*. Reston, VA: MENC—The National Association for Music Education.

Lowery, L. F. 1998. *Asking effective questions*. Workshop handout. Lawrence Hall of Science, Graduate School of Education, University of California: Berkeley.

Marzano, R. J. 1998. *A theory-based meta-analysis of research on instruction*. Aurora, CO: Mid-Continent Research for Education and Learning. ERIC Document Reproduction Service No. ED 427 087.

Marzano, R. J. 2000. *A new era of school reform: Going where the research takes us*. Aurora, CO: Mid-continent Research for Education and Learning. ERIC Document Reproduction Service No. ED 454 255.

Marzano, R. J. 2003. *What works in schools: Translating research into action*. Alexandria, VA: Association for Supervision and Curriculum Development.

Raphael, T. E. 1986. Teaching question answer relationships, rev. *The Reading Teacher* *39*:516-522.

Silverstein, S. 1996. *Falling up: Poems and drawings by Shel Silverstein*. New York: Harper Collins Children's Books.

Wiggins, G. and J. McTighe. 1998. *Understanding by design*. Alexandria, VA: Association for Supervision and Curriculum Development.

Connecting Assessment to Standards through Core Conceptual Competencies

Aurelia W. Hartenberger
University of Missouri—St. Louis

Abstract

A key concern among writers of standards-based curricula is the appropriate alignment of the curriculum with the standards, and the effective implementation and assessment of the standards-based curriculum. The purpose of this paper is to address this concern through the Core Conceptual Competencies Model. More specifically, it addresses the question: "How do I better align, implement, and connect the standards to assessment?" The Core Conceptual Competencies Model has three major components: (a) Alignment, (b) Expectations, and (c) Cognitive Understanding. These standards-based competencies are the conceptual extensions of behavioral objectives that provide a snapshot of the desired achievement/results at pre-determined levels of achievement. The Core Conceptual Competencies Model is a simple yet powerful strategy that supports appropriate alignment and implementation of the standards for assessment, and provides teachers with a practical strategy to help quantify and qualify the characteristics that inform teaching and assessment.

The purpose of this paper is to introduce a model to facilitate alignment and implementation of music education standards in instructional practices and assessments. The backward design model of Wiggins and McTighe (1999) requires that teachers design unit tasks first, and then design the learning experiences leading up to the assessment of performance. The idea is to facilitate student success by teaching with the end, or outcomes, in mind. At first sight, some might call this model an "assessment-driven" design approach. While this is an important strategy, it is only one aspect of this model.

Many current educational assessments consist of content and process objectives. While critical content and individual skill-building is essential in curriculum development, the basis for comprehension comes from the development of conceptual understanding through the executive function processes, i.e., the mental operations applied to knowledge such as planning, problem-solving, and analyzing, rather than the mastery of facts.

Designing assessments that are standards-based requires the development of what I call Core Conceptual Competencies (CCCs). The CCCs define the *big ideas* that are important to understanding and transfer of knowledge, once basic skills and knowledge are mastered. They must be stated so that the teacher can easily connect standards to assessment practices that support all three dimensions identified in the National Standards—what students should know, be able to do, and understand—at the various levels of achievement

(Consortium of National Arts Education Associations, 1994). The process of aligning assessments to standards should engage analytical, interpretative, critical and creative thinking skills.

Core Conceptual Competencies are the conceptual extension of behavioral objectives. They serve as anchors for curriculum and assessment development that define both the expectation of knowledge and/or performance by the students, and identify the cognitive demands of understanding, as implied by the performance objectives.

The Core Conceptual Competencies Model for assessment has three major components:

1. Alignment
2. Expectations
3. Conceptual Understanding

Alignment

National and state standards serve schools by providing a framework for the school curriculum. Standards serve teachers by providing the learning goals that their students should achieve. The National Standards for Arts Education (Consortium of National Arts Education Associations, 1994) are written in two levels: (a) Content Standards, which specify broadly what students should know and be able to do, and (b) Achievement Standards, which specify the understanding and levels of achievement that students are expected to attain in the content standards.

National and state standards provide strong and comprehensive statements of expectations that serve to ensure quality and accountability in the school music programs. They serve as the learning targets for building the Core Conceptual Competencies.

When writing and aligning the CCCs, teachers should keep in mind that the standards are interdependent and spiraled in levels of achievement. While this encourages breadth and depth for writing the competencies, care should be taken to make sure the focus does not become too broad and unattainable. Once the K–4 Achievement Standards are accomplished by all children, the 5–8 and 9–12 Achievement Standards require the teacher to guide students toward achievements that focus more specifically on the needs of their specific levels of students. One example where this focus is articulated can be found in National Achievement Standard 1a for Grades 9–12: "Students sing with expression and technical accuracy a large and varied repertoire of vocal literature with a level of difficulty of 4, on a scale of 1 to 6, including some songs performed from memory" (Consortium of National Arts Education Associations, 1994, 59).

Expectations

Educational expectations identify specifically the components of learning, including knowledge and skills, which can be demonstrated (behavioral results) in the standards. For example, in the National Achievement Standard 1b for Grades 5–8: "Students sing expressively, with appropriate dynamics, phrasing, and interpretation" (Consortium of

National Arts Education Associations, 1994, 26). In this standard, the general components of learning can be assessed by having the children demonstrate dynamics, phrasing, and interpretation while singing. This Achievement Standard identifies the musical concepts—dynamics, phrasing, and interpretation—which the teacher will further support with declarative knowledge (loud, soft, etc) and procedural knowledge (the individual skill-building task of singing).

Conceptual Understanding

Once students practice and memorize the declarative and procedural knowledge contained in a standard, *thinking* often stops. If we want students to be able to develop transferable ideas that support a depth of understanding beyond facts and skills, we must add the third element—conceptual understanding.

Conceptual understanding comes from the act of forming a concept (an idea) so that meaning and prior knowledge can be transferred to new learning experiences. We simply cannot assume students understand something just because they have memorized it. To connect declarative and procedural knowledge to ideas of conceptual significance (meaning), we must stimulate complex thinking skills by consciously asking students to demonstrate conceptual understanding.

Concepts support understanding that involves the holistic performance of a meaningful, complex task. In teaching, multiple interrelated activities that focus on a common concept, and the flexible organization of concepts/ideas into generalizations and principles, will support the construction of new meaning and learning, promoting cognitive flexibility and knowledge interconnectedness.

In the National Standards for Arts Education (Consortium of National Arts Education Associations, 1994), the Content Standards are performance-based and represent a macro-concept, while the Achievement Standards, also performance-based, provide the supporting micro-concepts. To find the micro-concepts in performance-based standards, one merely needs to remove the action verb. For example, National Standard 4.1a for Grades K–4 states: "Students sing independently, on pitch and in rhythm, with appropriate timbre, diction, and posture, and maintain a steady tempo" (Consortium of National Arts Education Associations 1994, p.26). The micro-concepts for musical elements are pitch, rhythm, timbre, diction, posture, and steady tempo.

Nevertheless, the goal of the CCCs is not only to have students define musical concepts, but more importantly, to have them understand their relationships. To accomplish this, the teacher must develop a conceptual framework of cognitive processes to help structure their assessments of conceptual learning.

While the sequential framework of Bloom's Taxonomy has served teachers for many years in the tasks of formulating objectives and test questions, the primary focus of this taxonomy appears to be the testing of memory. Cognitive psychologists Anderson and Krathwohl (2001) have incorporated new thoughts into the framework of Bloom's Taxonomy by changing the one-dimensional taxonomy framework to a two-dimensional classification, which they have labeled: 1) the Cognitive Process Dimension—"How to do something, methods of inquiry, and criteria for using skills, algorithms, techniques, and methods" (29), and 2) the Dimension of Knowledge—Factual, Conceptual, Procedural, and Metacognitive.

The first three processes of the Anderson and Krathwohl framework correlate to a dimension of knowledge. However, at level 4, Anderson and Krathwohl group the processes of Analyze, Create, and Evaluate into one dimension of knowledge: Metacognitive. To better correlate the six dimensions of process to the knowledge dimensions, I have modified Krathwohl's Taxonomy Table to include six dimensions, rather than the four, as each of the processes will result in different ways of knowing. These additional classifications of knowledge types better align to the Cognitive Process Dimension and I believe merit recognition as distinctive types of knowledge (see Figure 1). This taxonomy will also provide the framework for designing assessment.

Figure 1. Core Conceptual Competencies Taxonomy Table

Knowledge Dimensions		Cognitive Process Dimension					
		1. Capture	2. Connect	3. Utilize	4. Analyze	5. Create	6. Evaluate
Level 1	Factual/Specified	(to Name)					
Level 2	Conceptual/Comprehension		(to Understand)				
Level 3	Procedural/Application			(to Do)			
Level 4	Contextual/Analysis				(to Examine)		
Level 5	Synthesis/Inventive					(to Reflect/Construct)	
Level 6	Metacognitive/Evaluative						(to Assess)

Note. Modified from Anderson and Krathwohl, Revised Bloom's Taxonomy of Education Objectives (2001)

Beginning with the Knowledge Dimensions, I offer a conceptual framework for organizing musical content understanding, using the music concepts that spiral through the critical thinking process of Bloom's Taxonomy of the Cognitive Domain: Factual/specified knowledge, conceptual/comprehension, procedural/application, contextual/analysis, synthesis/inventive, and metacognitive/evaluative (Hansen, Bernstorf, Stuber, 2004, 85), (see Figure 2).

Figure 2. Levels of Conceptual Understanding in Music (Hansen, Bernstorf, and Stuber, 2004, 85)

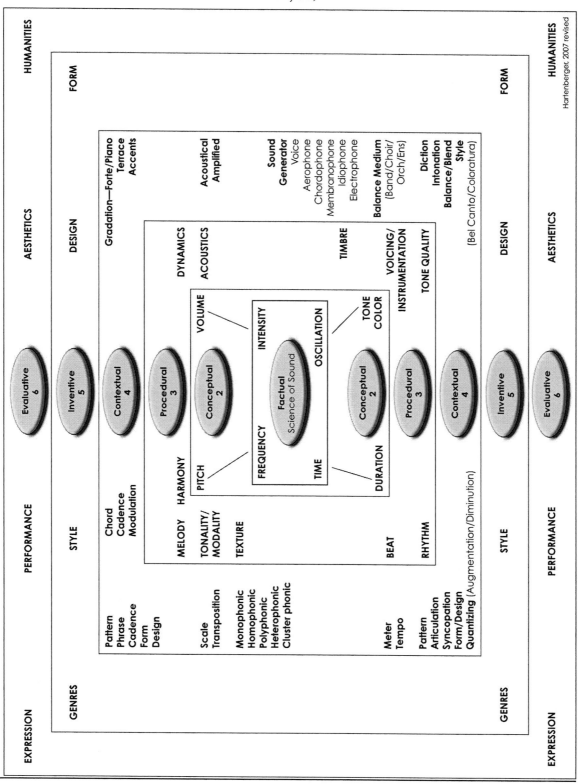

An important factor in the evaluation of these Knowledge Dimensions is their varying degrees of complexity. For example, in Procedural/Application—Level 3, the utilization of processes and skills vary in degree of complexity of the procedural knowledge when playing a recorder versus playing a clarinet. Even the terms *process* and *skill* show degrees of complexity, as process is often considered steps of conscious manipulation, whereas skill is the acquired automatic unconscious execution of an act. Also to be considered in the degrees of complexity is the number of steps required to complete a task.

In assessment, these varying degrees of complexity are spiraled as in a sequential process and can serve as benchmarks for teachers. For example, in Contextual/Analysis—Level 4, the degree of complexity is determined by the descriptive attributes. As an example, assessment of the concept *dynamics* for a first grader would be to have the student differentiate between the terms *loud* and *soft*, while for the high school student, differentiation would be between the terms *piano, mezzo piano, forte,* and so forth. Pre-assessment of the students' Knowledge Domain for degrees of complexity is an essential strategy. Figure 3 shows qualifying degrees of complexity for each of the Knowledge Dimensions of the CCCs model. A matrix based upon the degrees of complexity can serve as a scope and sequence tool to support the assessment of the Knowledge Domain.

Figure 3. Knowledge Domain Degrees of Complexity

LEVEL	KNOWLEDGE Dimensions	RANGE OF COMPLEXITY Simple to Complex
1	Factual/Specified	Concrete to Abstract
2	Conceptual/Comprehension	Acknowledge to Meaning
3	Procedural/Application	Process to Skill
4	Contextual/ Analysis	Descriptive Attributes
5	Synthesis/Inventive	Convergent to Divergent
6	Metacognitive/Evaluative	Reflective to Habits of Mind

The components of the Cognitive Process Dimensions are expressed as verbs because thinking is an action verb. With the use of verbs, assessment possibilities become embedded in the CCCs statement. These processes also provide teachers with an organizational pattern that leads to the performance expectations, which describe the desired achievement/result.

In music, intrinsic learner motivation and attention that allows personal connection to music are essential for developing aesthetic sensitivity, and are particularly reflected as behavior becomes consistent and characterizing. This positive attitude toward learning is a vital element in the success of all learning and is an enabling skill that supports all the processes. With this in mind, critical for arts learning is the opportunity for children to construct a foundation of new knowledge through enabling artistic processes that are not necessarily learned sequentially, but through the interplay of the various cognitive levels, while performing, responding to, and creating music. These processing foundations are built formally and informally, through guided practice, and guided inquiry. I provided a sequential framework of the levels of artistic processes (in Hansen, Bernstorf, and Stuber, 2003, 224;

see Figure 4). It is important to note that these processes do not represent levels of complexity, which is in contrast to Bloom's Taxonomy (Anderson and Krathwohl, 2001).

Nevertheless, there is a hierarchy of the level of conscious processes that is required, as these Artistic Processes are the mental operations applied to knowledge. Furthermore, Figure 5 illustrates how sequential levels of Artistic Processes relate to Krathwohl's Taxonomy of the Affective Domain and Simpson's Psychomotor Domains (Abeles, Hoffer, and Klotmann, 1994). With careful consideration of the students' physical maturity, intellectual ability, and previous experiences, the Artistic Processes can easily align with the corresponding cognitive domains. Thus, when developing assessments, the Artistic Processes become the performance content for conceptual understanding.

Using the structure of Artistic Processes, a prescribed list of verbs is provided to assist teachers in writing their CCCs for assessments (Figure 7). These processing verbs equate to the transferable skills that support conceptual development. The teacher should be careful not to confuse them   with activities or content objectives. For example, "Students play an instrument expressively using dynamics" is a transferable skill, but "Students play an instrument expressively using dynamics in Robert W. Smith's *Liturgical Fanfare*" is a specific activity to help develop the skill. The CCCs isolate and name the transferable skills identified in the standards so that in the assessment planning they are certain to be tested.

Figure 4. Artistic Processing (from Hansen, Bernstorf, and Stuber, 2004, p 224).

ARTISTIC PROCESSING
Aurelia Hartenberger

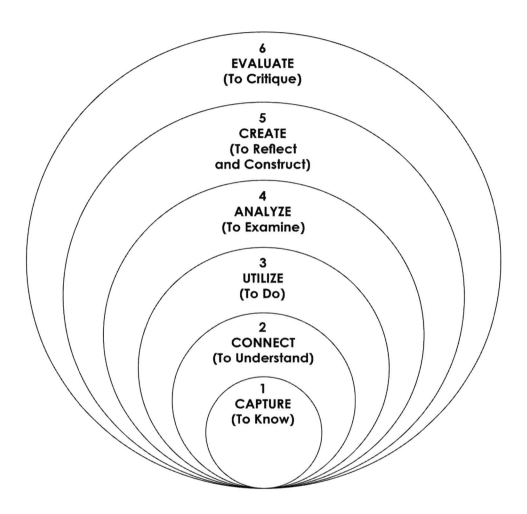

Figure 5. Sequential Relationship of the Core Conceptual Competencies Model of Artistic Processes to Krathwohl's Affective Domains and Simpson's Psychomotor Domains

Level	Artistic Processes		Level	Krathwohl's Affective Domains		Level	Impson's Psychomotor Domains	
1	CAPTURING	Conscious Selection of Activities	1	RECEIVING	Giving attention to	1	PERCEPTION	Awareness
2	CONNECTING	Listening, Reading, Writing	2	RESPONDING	Interacting, Interested	2	SET	Mental, Physical, Emotional preparatory adjustments
3	PERFORMING [UTILIZING]	Singing, Moving, Playing an Instrument, Audiating	3	VALUING	Expressing attitude	3	GUIDED RESPONSE	Imitation followed by trial and error
4	RESPONDING [ANALYZING]	Describing, Analyzing, Critiquing, Comparing	4	ORGANIZATION	Considering interrelated values, Developing a value system	4	MECHANISM	Habit-forming skill
5	CREATING	Improvising, Arranging, Transposing, Composing	5	CHARACTERIZATION BY A VALUE OR VALUE COMPLEX	Observable lifestyle of consistent characteristic behaviors	5	COMPLEX OVERT RESPONSE	Resolution of uncertainty leading to automatic performance skills
	VALUING [EVALUATING]	Creating meaning from Selecting, Developing personal response				6	ADAPTATION	Change by altering performance to make more suitable
6	CHARACTERIZING	Actively supporting by presenting performances, Pursuing as an avocation or vocation				7	ORIGINATION	Ability to develop new skills

Implementing the Core Conceptual Competencies for Assessment

Goals for Assessment

Using the CCCs model, teachers begin with the identification of Educational Goals. These Goals are the broad or general instructional objective statements that a school district or music department has aligned and/or integrated with the National and/or State Standards. Usually, they are written to ensure a scope and sequence based on Strands, such as Performance Product, Elements of Music, Artistic Perception, Interdisciplinary Connections, and Historical and Cultural Contexts. For the strand Performance Product, the goal may be, for example, "Students will be able to develop and apply skills to perform and communicate through the arts."

The learning objectives are derived from the Educational Goals and reflect achievement standards. The CCCs taxonomy serves to support and clarify the learning and assessment of performances that reveal the student's depth of understanding. Its emphasis is not only on the end, but also the means. For example, what a student does while performing in the recital may be the end objective, but how the student prepared the music, acquired their performance technique, and developed conceptual understanding of musical style are just as important. Using the convention of Anderson and Krathwohl in terms of how objectives should be stated, each sentence begins a phrase that describes the performances that support the Educational Goals. For example, the stem, "Students will be able to" is followed by a (Artistic Processing) verb that acts upon the (Knowledge Domain) object.

Prior Enabling Expectations

The ability to think and use information begins with self-knowledge. By conducting a pre-assessment, teachers will be informed of their students' present achievement levels and will be able to discern if any remedial work is needed. This pre-assessment will also help the teacher identify prior enabling expectations that will support the acquisition of new information. It may also provide for students a review of their prior knowledge, skills, and understanding, and serve as preview or warm up for what is to come. Objectives that identify prior knowledge may include:

Grade 1
Students will have:
- Respect for the rights, responsibilities and contributions of self and others
- Practiced speaking out loud and whispering
- Known the meaning of *same* and *different*
- Skills in quite listening

Declarative and Procedural Knowledge

Once the Educational Goal and learning objective is determined and student prior knowledge identified, teachers clarify the supporting information in terms of declarative and procedural knowledge. Declarative Knowledge, or information knowledge, includes vocabulary terms, phrases, and facts. These facts present information about specific people, places, things, and events. In Procedural Knowledge, both mental and psychomotor procedures are included. As Marzano and Kendall (2007) differentiate, "procedural knowledge is executed, whereas informational is recognized and recalled." (30) For assessment, it identifies what you want the student to know and to do. Objectives identifying knowledge content may include:

Grade 1
Students know:

- Dynamics are the loud and soft of sound   (Declarative Knowledge)
- Whispering demonstrates soft   (Procedural Knowledge)
- Movement is a form of interpretation   (Declarative Knowledge)
- Large movements demonstrate loud   (Procedural Knowledge)

Generalization

To comprehend and understand, students must connect prior knowledge, skills, and understanding with the new information. This process involves identifying concepts that are articulated in the Educational Goals and Standards and integrating prior understandings with new information, creating generalizations, and principles for comprehension. These generalizations are broad statements of conceptual relationships that are generally timeless, universal, and can transfer across cultures. According to Marzano and Kendall (2007), generalizations are identified as categories and classifications of information; while principles deal with relations in knowledge, such as cause-effect principles and correlational principles. He stated that "the process of generalizing is neither purely inductive nor purely deductive," and that the concept of *retroduction*, the act of generating and shaping an idea based upon prior and new experiences, is a concept advanced by many philosophers (49). As both inductive and deductive reasoning are involved in different aspects of the process for creating CCCs, retroduction best serves as the process for creating the generalizations. For example, the standard, "Students sing expressively, with appropriate dynamics, phrasing, and interpretation" (Consortium of National Arts Education Associations, 1994, 26) may be generalized in the following manner (see Figure 6):

Figure 6. Writing a Generalization

Learning Objective [Achievement standard]:		"Students will be able to sing expressively with appropriate dynamics, phrasing, and interpretation."		
Grade Level:		First Grade		
STEPS	GUIDELINES	EXAMPLE		
1	*Focus on specific information without making assumptions*	Expressive singing includes the use of appropriate dynamics, phrasing, and interpretation.		
2	*Classify information*	**CONCEPT A:**	Expressive elements in music may include dynamics and tempo. The loudness of sound is called dynamics and may be identified as loud and soft. Tempo is the speed of the beat and may be identified as fast and slow.	
		CONCEPT B:	Musical interpretation may include the use of expressive elements in music.	
3	*Connect information and patterns, using active, present-tense verbs to support the generally timeless and universal conceptual relationships*	**GENERALIZATION:**		
		The elements of dynamics and tempo create musical expression.	or	The singer's interpretation of the dynamics and tempo can affects the mood of the music.

Essential Question

The generalizations above move the behavioral learning objective of the Educational Goal, "Students will be able to sing expressively with appropriate dynamics, phrasing, and interpretation," to a statement of conceptual understanding. To further engage and direct thinking towards conceptual understanding, the essential questions of "why" and "how" will extend and bridge the processes with the generalizations.

- Essential Question:

  Grade 1: How are the expressive musical elements of dynamics and tempo used in a lullaby? in a march?

  Grade 1: How can the singer show expression in music? create an expressive musical performance?

Enabling Processes

The enabling processes of the Artistic Processes can serve to answer the essential questions of "how" and "why" and can move understanding to varying levels of conceptual sophistication. These processing verbs are the tools that support teachers in creating assessments that frame the enabling process levels of capturing, connecting, utilizing, analyzing, creating, and evaluating information. Objectives identifying Artistic Processes may include:

Grade 1
Students will be able to:

- Listen and identify the dynamic levels of loud and soft in a song (Connecting)
- Demonstrate loud and soft by whispering and speaking out (Utilizing)
- Demonstrate loud and soft through movement (Utilizing)

Using these enabling processes, students are asked to demonstrate depth of understanding by "connecting" and "utilizing" their knowledge, which results in varying levels of conceptual sophistication. Figure 8 shows the processes and possible levels of operations for sequencing the assessment tool.

Core Conceptual Competencies

These levels of conceptual sophistication are then represented in the Core Conceptual Competency: "Students listen and demonstrate musical expression by moving to and singing with dynamics to show the mood in music." The CCCs are the conceptual extension of behavioral objectives that explicitly identifies the target of what students are expected to come to understand for assessment. They identify and represent the ideas, processes, relationships, and questions of understanding in performing, responding, and creating music. (For additional samples of CCCs see Figure 9.)

Specification of these Core Conceptual Competencies as educational objectives has implications for assessment in that it makes clear what should be assessed (see Figure 10 for the assessment format). Using the CCCs, the focus of assessment is no longer on memorization of facts and simply recall and recognition of items. The CCCs support assessments that ask students to apply their skills and knowledge in meaningful ways to demonstrate understanding. Figure 11 depicts the framework for developing the CCCs Model for assessment.

Figure 7. Artistic Processing Verbs for Music

LEVELS	ARTISTIC PROCESSES	ACTION VERBS	
1	CAPTURING	Recall Remember Recognize Name Recite	Define Identify Retrieve List Memorize
2	CONNECTING	Interpret Match Translate Summarize Describe Discuss Explain Read musical notation/icons	Compare Infer Classify Sort Categorize Listen
3	UTILIZING	Execute Carry out Implement Bow Move Notate Sing Sight-read	Solve Use Perform Clap Journal Play an Instrument Auriate Demonstrate
4	ANALYZING	Discriminate Take apart Distinguish Analyze Research	Differentiate Organize Attribute Reflect Compare
5	CREATING	Arrange Plan Design Transpose Improvise Formulate	Produce Compose Invent Construct Orchestrate Theorize
6	EVALUATING	Critique Judge Appraise Evaluate Assess	Rate Score Justify Defend Validate

Figure 8. Strategies for Assessment

Level	Processes	Mode	Processing Operations		
			Level 1	**Level 2**	**Level 3**
1	Capturing	Responding	*The student...* recognizes	*The student...* names identifies	*The student...* recalls defines
2	Connecting	Responding	*The student...* matches sorts describes classifies	*The student...* discusses explains	*The student...* reads musical notation/ icons infers translates
3	Utilizing	Responding/ Performing	*The student...* uses claps executes	*The student...* performs sings moves sight-reads	*The student...* plays an instrument journals
4	Analyzing	Responding	*The student...* compares distinguishes between	*The student...* attributes reflects	*The student...* analyzes researches
5	Creating	Creating	*The student...* arranges transposes	*The student...* formulates improvises designs	*The student...* composes invents produces
6	Evaluating	Responding/ Creating	*The student...* rates scores assesses	*The student...* critiques evaluates appraises judges	*The student...* defends validates

Figure 9. Sample of Core Conceptual Competencies

National Standards Code	Achievement Standard*	Grade Level	Core Conceptual Competencies
NA.K–4.4a	Students create and arrange short songs and instrumental pieces within specified guidelines.	1	Students *create* echo-clapping patterns and *rate* their level of difficulty.
NA.5–8.1b	Students perform expressively using dynamics, phrasing, and interpretation.	1	Students *listen* and *perform* expressively using dynamics and interpretation to show the mood of the music.
		3	Students *perform* expressively using dynamics and interpretation, so as to *distinguish* when to use the appropriate volume to support balance within musical parts.
NA.5–8.8b	Students describe ways in which the principles and subject matter of other disciplines taught in the school are interrelated with those of music.	8	Students *identify* patterns of repetition in music and art forms and *attribute* to how patterns give balance to unity and variety across disciplines.
NA.5–8.7a	Students develop criteria for evaluating the quality and effectiveness of music performances and compositions and apply the criteria in their personal listening and performing.	8	Students *listen,* and *analyze* the quality and effectiveness of music to *create* a standard for music performance and composition, and to *critique* the quality of their own music listening and/or performance.
NA.9–12.2a	Students perform with expression and technical accuracy a large and varied repertoire of instrumental literature with a level of difficulty of 4, on a scale of 1 to 6.	10	Students *perform* with expression and technical accuracy a large and varied repertoire of instrumental literature with a level of difficulty of 4, on a scale of 1 to 6, and *produce* consistency in stylistic treatment of the elements of music that they *assess* as appropriate for the literature.

*Consortium of National Arts Education Associations, 1994.

Figure 10. Assessment Format for Core Conceptual Competencies

Assessment Planning	Tools for On-going Assessment
Prior Knowledge	
Students will have...	
Declarative and Procedural Knowledge	Anecdotal Record
Students knows...	Checklist—Student
	Checklist—Teacher
	Constructed Response—Close
	Constructed Response—Extended
	Constructed Response—Open
	Direct Observation
Generalization	Multiple Choice (Selected Response)
Students will understand...	Oral examination/Interview
	Reading Responses
	Scoring Guide—Analytic
	Scoring Guide—Holistic
Essential Question	Student—Peer Evaluation
Students answer why and how...	Student—Self Evaluation
	Student Oral Responses
	Student—Teacher Conferencing
	Writing and Project Journals
	Portfolio
Enabling Processes	
Students will be able to... Capture... Connect... Utilize... Analyze... Create... Evaluate...	
Core Conceptual Competencies	Performance task using scoring guide
	Portfolio—scoring guide

Figure 11. Core Conceptual Competencies Framework

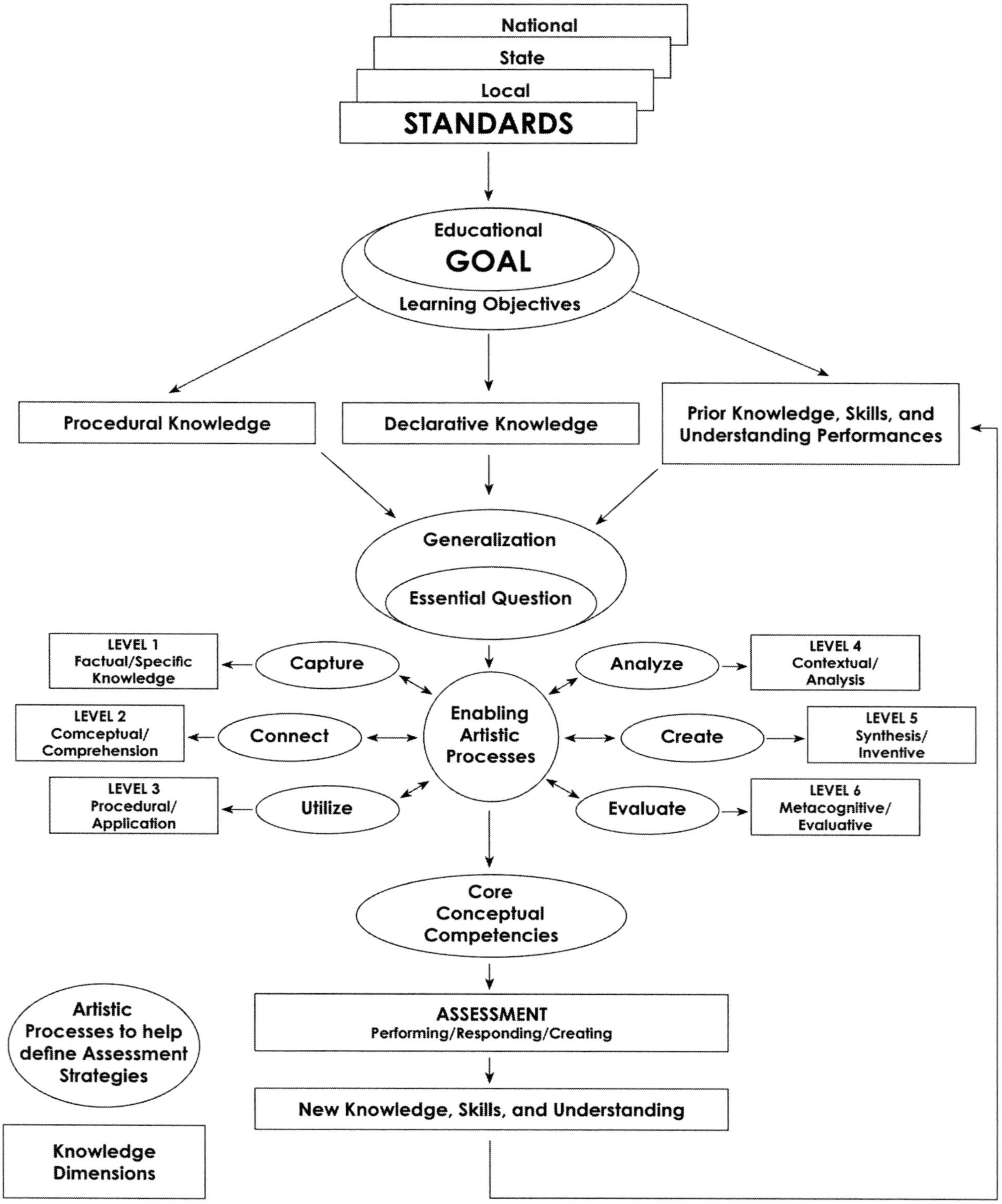

References

Abeles, H. F., C. R. Hoffer, and R. H. Klotman. 1994. *Foundations of music education*, 2nd ed. Belmont, CA: Thomson Higher Education.

Anderson, L. W., and D. R. Krathwohl, eds. 2001. A *taxonomy for learning, teaching, and assessing: A revision of Bloom's taxonomy of educational objectives*. New York: Addison-Wesley Longman.

Hansen, D., E. Bernstorf, and G. M. Stuber. 2004. *The music and literacy connection*. Reston, Virginia: MENC: The National Association for Music Education.

Marzano, R. J. and J. S. Kendall. 2007. *The new taxonomy of educational objectives*, 2nd ed. Thousand Oaks, CA: Corwin Press.

Consortium of National Arts Education Associations. 1994. *National standards for arts education*. Reston, VA: MENC—The National Association for Music Education.

Wiggins, G., and J. McTighe. 2005. *Understanding by design*. Alexandria, VA: Association for Supervision and Curriculum Development.

Integrating Music Curriculum and Assessment in a Standards-Referenced Environment: A Perspective from New South Wales (Australia)

Jay McPherson
Board of Studies, New South Wales, Australia

Abstract

The Board of Studies (New South Wales, Australia) has introduced educational reforms across the curriculum in the form of standards-referenced assessment and reporting. Central to this is the development of curriculum that clearly defines the learning expectations through explicit outcomes and content in syllabus documents, support for teachers in making consistent judgments and a clear method of reporting standards to students, parents, and the wider community. Concurrently, the philosophy of assessment for learning was introduced into curriculum documents to emphasise the importance of integrating quality curriculum with quality assessment practices. This paper explores the New South Wales Music curriculum, the philosophy of assessment for learning that is embedded in this curriculum and describes the methods used to determine and communicate standards.

New South Wales has a centralized curriculum authority with all curriculum and public examinations being developed and conducted by the Board of Studies and the Office of the Board of Studies. Of the 20.6 million people in Australia, 1.2 million attend New South Wales schools and the Board of Studies is responsible for all curricula for these students. The *Education Act 1990* (NSW) sets out minimum curriculum requirements for primary (elementary) schools. It requires that courses of study must be provided in each of the six key learning areas for primary education for each child during each year. In particular, the Act states that "courses of study in both art and music are to be included in the key learning area of Creative and Practical Arts." At secondary level, NSW is the only state in Australia to have mandated music studies where students must undertake a music subject with a minimum of 100 indicative hours, usually studied in Years 7 and 8 as part of the requirements for the New South Wales School Certificate (Stevens, 2003, 11). Beyond this mandatory requirement students may also elect to study more music for either 100 or 200 hours, which is also credentialed for the School Certificate. The end of secondary schooling credential, the Higher School Certificate, provides students the opportunity to study music at a much higher level. The NSW Higher School Certificate allows students access to three different courses of study—Music 1, Music 2 and Music Extension. Both Music 1 and Music 2 are comparable and the Music Extension course is designed for the most capable students. The K–12 continuum is constructed with links to both years of schooling and stages of development (see Figure 1). Outcomes and content for each stage are based on student achievement expected to be gained by most students as a result of effective teaching and learning at the end of each stage.

Central to the curriculum at each stage is that students engage with the concepts of music (see Figure 2) and are actively engaged in an integrated way in musical learning experiences (see Figure 3) though repertoire from a range of musical styles, periods, and genres.

Figure 1: Table showing the links between
years of schooling and stages of development

Early Stage	Kindergarten
Stage 1	Years 1 and 2
Stage 2	Years 3 and 4
Stage 3	Years 5 and 6
Stage 4	Years 7 and 8
Stage 5	Years 9 and 10
Stage 6	Years 11 and 12

Figure 2: Musical concepts studied through each stage[1]

Stage/s	Musical Concepts	Examples from "Duration" from simple to complex
Early Stage 1 to Stage 3	Duration Pitch Dynamics Tone Color Structure	Singing, playing and moving to music with a regular beat Recognizing patterns of sounds and silences Performing in a range of tempi Recognizing strong, weak and accented beats
Stages 4 and 5	Duration Pitch Dynamics and Expressive Techniques Tone Color Texture Structure	Performing with changing beat at various tempi Rhythmic devices such as syncopation Mixed meter Complex rhythmic patterns including devices such as triplets and duplets
Stage 6	Duration Pitch Dynamics and Expressive Techniques Tone Color Texture Structure	Polymetres Rhythmic devices such as diminution, augmentation, and polyrhythms

McPherson and Jeanneret (2005) propose that that the New South Wales curriculum has been heavily influenced by milestone programs developed in the USA throughout the 1960s, most significantly the Contemporary Music Project for Creativity in Music Education (CMP), the Manhattanville Music Curriculum Program (MMCP) and the Hawaii Music Curriculum Program (HMCP). They further speculate that the building of this K–12 continuum in music education is an example of a sustained commitment to important aspects of the CMP, MMCP and the HMCP, highlighting their strengths and the possibilities for music curriculum development and implementation that were intended by each of these programs (McPherson and Jeanneret, 2005, 196; Jeanneret, McPherson, Dunbar-Hall and Forrest, 2003, p.137).

---

[1] Examples taken from Board of Studies, NSW Syllabuses—Creative Arts K–6 (2000), Music Years 7–10 (2003) and Music 2 and Music Extension (1999).

Figure 3: Learning experiences studied through each stage[2]

Stage/s	Learning Experiences	Examples from "Composing" from Simple to Complex
Early Stage 1 to Stage 3	performing organizing sound listening	creates own rhymes, games, songs and simple musical compositions explores, creates, selects and organizes sound in simple structures uses symbol systems to represent sounds improvises musical phrases, organizes sounds and explains reasons for choices
Stages 4 and 5	performing composing listening	demonstrates an understanding of musical concepts through exploring, experimenting, improvising, organizing, arranging and composing notates own compositions, applying forms of notation appropriate to the music selected for study uses different forms of technology in the composition process
Stage 6	performance composition musicology aural skills	composes, improvises and analyses melodies and accompaniments for familiar sound sources in solo and/or small ensembles stylistically creates, improvises, arranges and notates music which is representative of the mandatory and additional topics and demonstrates different social, cultural and historical contexts composes with highly developed technical skill and stylistic refinement demonstrating the emergence of a personal style demonstrates a sophisticated understanding of the concepts of music and their relationship to each other with reference to works composed.

Integrating Curriculum and Assessment: Assessment *for* Learning

To many music educators, assessment is so much part of instruction (Colwell, 2002, 1130). Music teachers must spend time on thinking about what the most important outcomes of music instruction are and plan their instruction and assessment strategies accordingly (Abeles, et al., 1995, 304).

In 2003 the Board of Studies published revised syllabuses in all subjects for the Years 7–10 of schooling. An integral part of this revision was the inclusion of references to, and the advocacy of assessment *for* learning. Assessment for learning is designed to enhance teaching and improve learning. It gives students opportunities to produce the work that leads to development of their knowledge, understanding, and skills. Assessment for learning involves teachers in deciding how and when to assess student achievement, as they plan the work students will do, using a range of appropriate assessment strategies, including self-assessment and peer assessment (Board of Studies, 2003a, 56).

---

[2]   Examples taken from Board of Studies, NSW Syllabuses—Creative Arts K–6 (2000), Music Years 7–10 (2003) and Music 2 and Music Extension (1999).

Black and Wiliam (2004) describe assessment for learning in the following way:

Assessment for learning is any assessment for which the first priority in its design and practice is to serve the purpose of promoting students' learning. It thus differs from assessment designed primarily to serve the purposes of accountability, or of ranking, or of certifying competence. An assessment activity can help learning if it provides information that teachers and their students can use as feedback in assessing themselves and one another and in modifying the teaching and learning activities in which they are engaged. Such assessment becomes "formative assessment" when the evidence is actually used to adapt the teaching work to meet learning needs (10).

The underpinning philosophy of this approach is predicated on the notion that assessment should occur as an integral part of the teaching and learning process and the information gained from this assessment assists teachers in formulating further work that extends student learning or, in fact, remedies learning that has not taken place as anticipated. In using this approach it is hoped that students will be able to monitor and evaluate their own learning through actively encouraging both peer and self-assessment.

Central to this philosophy is that the syllabus outcomes are integral to the decisions teachers make about the learning to be undertaken and the evidence of learning that needs to be collected with the view to determining how well students are achieving in relation to the outcomes and to provide students with feedback on their learning (Board of Studies, 2004, 7–8). This model is summarised in Figure 4.

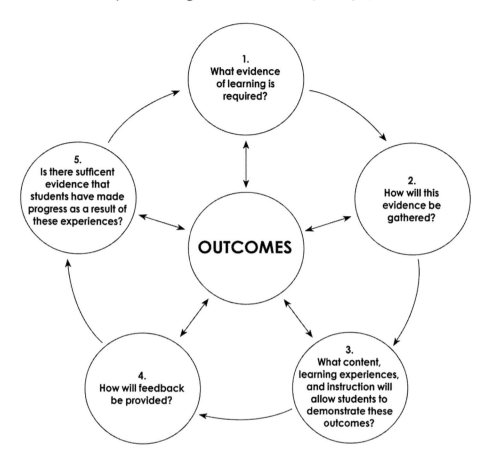

Figure 4: Model demonstrating philosophy of assessment for learning (Board of Studies, 1994, 8)

This model highlights the need for teachers to be explicit about the outcomes and content they are addressing and the corresponding evidence required to demonstrate student learning. It reinforces the need to give explicit feedback to students and that teaching and learning methods may need to be adapted to meet the particular learning needs of the students.

Bransford et al. (2000) argue that ongoing formative assessments that are designed to make students' thinking visible to both teacher and student are essential. Formative assessment, involves the use of assessments (usually administered in the context of the classroom) as sources of feedback to improve teaching and learning. These assessments permit the teacher to understand student preconceptions, progress and allow them to design instruction accordingly. In the assessment-centered learning environment, formative assessments should be learner-friendly and assist both teachers and students to monitor progress. Opportunities for formative assessment increase students' learning and transfer and they learn to value opportunities to revise (Bransford, et al., 2000; Black and Wiliam, 1998).

Another key aspect of the assessment for learning philosophy is the use of self-assessment and peer assessment techniques. Black and Wiliam (1998a) argue that the link between formative assessment and self-assessment is not an accident, it is merely inevitable and that it is, in fact, an essential component of formative assessment. They explain that students are usually particularly honest and reliable in assessing themselves and others (if not too hard on themselves), but these assessments can only take place when they have a clear understanding of the criteria or targets that their learning is meant to attain. When these targets are understood students become effective and more committed learners (6). This is also supported by Bransford et al. (2000) when they argue that self-assessment is an important part of the metacognitive approach to instruction.

Black and Wiliam (2004) also make some interesting observations on the importance of peer assessment. They remark that "peer assessment is uniquely valuable because students may accept criticisms of their work from one another that they would not take seriously if the remarks were offered by a teacher." They further state that peer work is also valuable because "the interchange will be in language that students themselves naturally use and because students learn by taking on the roles of teachers and examiners of others" (2004, p.14).

Representation of Standards in Curriculum and Assessment in Public Examinations

In contemporary society there is strong support for the view that money spent on education should lead to improvements in student learning, or at least to no declines. Thus, a public examination system that does not enable explicit judgments to be made as to whether students are achieving required standards is of limited value (McPherson and Bennett, 2004, 127).

To enable such judgments to be made, and thus to exact full value from a curriculum-based examination, student performance needs to be related to some form of pre-defined standards. When these standards are expressed in terms of course outcomes, professional judgment can be used to reference student performance to these standards. That is, student performance will be related to the things students know and can do. In addition, the use of standards will enable the equating of different examinations. This will allow a direct comparison of the performances of different cohorts across time within the same course, even though they have attempted entirely different examinations. Refer to Figure 5: The Relationship between Syllabus and Performance Standards.

The context for this work is the New South Wales Higher School Certificate (HSC) examinations. The NSW Higher School Certificate is a high-stakes credential awarded to students at the end of secondary education. Each year approximately 65,000 students complete the requirements for the Higher School Certificate in 83 subjects and 146 courses. The courses students take relate to the traditional subject disciplines, such as English, Mathematics, History, French, and Music, as well as subjects ranging from Aboriginal Studies to Visual Arts. In 2006 approximately 5,500 students sat for Music examinations. During the final year of school, students typically study five or six courses with their achievement in these courses since 2001 being reported using a standards-based approach. An external examination conducted by the NSW Board of Studies and an assessment program conducted by their school is used to measure a student's final achievement. The examinations are closely based on course curricula, and employ a variety of different item types, as appropriate.

Figure 5: The Relationship between Syllabus and Performance Standards.

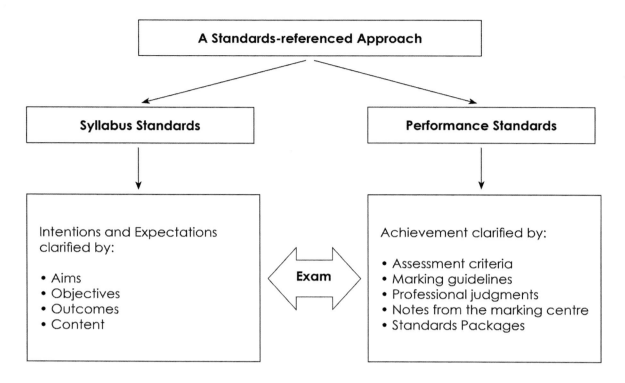

Most examinations consist of written response-type items that are scored polytomously. Some examinations also include multiple-choice and short-answer items. Written components generally consist of short or extended responses or the solution to a mathematics problem. However, in some courses there are other, more substantive, manifestations of student work. For example, in Visual Arts, students submit for assessment a piece of artwork they have created. In the examinations for foreign languages, items that assess listening and speaking skills are employed. In Music and Drama, students are assessed on components such as the quality of their performance of pieces of music or short plays they have prepared.

In each course a new examination is prepared each year. While the general structure of an examination paper, including the number and type of the items and the maximum possible score for each item, remains similar from year to year, new items are included in the examinations every year, and once an examination is sat it is publicly available.

In 2004, McPherson and Bennett described the process for determining and setting standards in the New South Wales Higher School Certificate. This process was based on the work of Bennett (1998), in which he developed and tested a multi-staged Angoff-based standards-setting procedure that could be applied in the context of the NSW Higher School Certificate examinations. It is a procedure that uses teams of highly experienced teachers employing professional judgment informed by certain appropriate statistical data and student examination responses to determine what examination marks correspond to the borderlines between the different performance bands established for that course (McPherson and Bennett, 2004, 128). Prior to this process, teams of experienced teachers using data and student responses to past examinations met to prepare statements describing five different levels of achievement in their course. These statements were the first component of the standards that were to be set for each course. The levels were designated as Band 2 to Band 6 with Band 6 being the highest level. A sixth level of achievement, Band 1, was considered to be below the minimum standard expected and did not have a description (refer to Appendix 1 for a sample of the Draft Performance Bands). During the marking of examinations benchmarks are developed. These benchmarks show, using student work, the typical responses and descriptions of the qualities of responses expected of student in different mark ranges. The benchmarks are developed by a Supervisor of Marking and Senior Markers who undertake this leadership role as well as the monitoring of the marking process to ensure consistency in judgement from the markers. In the case of performance and *viva voce* examinations, the benchmarks consist of video footage and markers undergo an extensive briefing prior to the commencement of the examination period.

An essential part of any standards-based approach to examination and reporting is to be able to effectively communicate the expectations of standards to key stakeholders in the education world—most particularly teachers, students and parents. For standards to be consistent, valid and reliable from year to year, shared understanding of standards must be developed and made available.

In New South Wales, this involved the development of a Standards Package for each course. The packages produced on CD-ROM contained the syllabuses, band descriptions, the examination paper, marking guidelines and samples of responses of students at each borderline, and other statistical information were collected and incorporated into what is referred to as a Standards Package. The material was presented in such a way that teachers, students, and others can most effectively develop a clear understanding of the standards that have been developed for each course.

Representation of Standards in Curriculum and Assessment in Music from Kindergarten to Year 10

In New South Wales there are no Board of Studies public examinations for Music from Kindergarten to Year 10. Therefore it is essential that when curriculum is developed, a clear sense of standards be represented within syllabus and curriculum documentation and support materials. In syllabus design, therefore, content standards must be made explicit (refer to Figure 6).

Figure 6: The Relationship between Syllabus and Performance Standards.

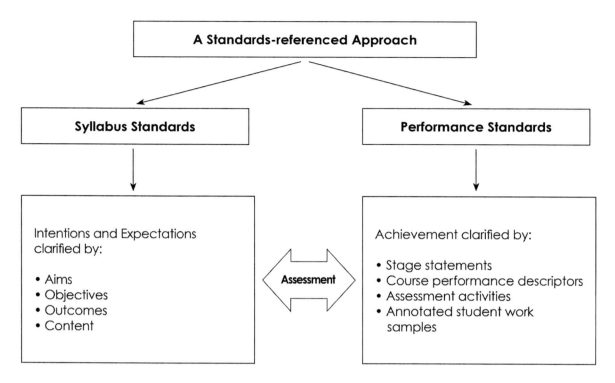

This occurs through the provision of course objectives, learning outcomes, and content that states what students must learn to do and what they must learn about. In the primary (elementary) years of schooling this also includes a set of indicators for each learning outcome. Indicators provide examples of the typical sorts of behaviors a student would be exhibiting if they were working toward the achievement of that particular outcome.

At the end of Year 10, if a student has undertaken an elective course of either 100 or 200 hours of Music, they will receive a grade on the credential of the New South Wales School Certificate. Schools are responsible for awarding each student a grade from A to E from the Course Performance Descriptors (CPDs) that summarizes the student's achievement in the course. To attempt parity across subjects, all CPDs are based on a set of generic descriptors that summarizes the standard (or quality) of achievement associated with each grade. The scale describes the depth of knowledge and understanding and the range of skills that students working at that standard typically show (see Figure 7).

Figure 7: Generic Course Performance Descriptors.
Board of Studies ARC Website, Retrieved 21 September 2006.

A	The student has an extensive knowledge and understanding of the content and can readily apply this knowledge. In addition, the student has achieved a very high level of competence in the processes and skills and can apply these skills to new situations.
B	The student has a thorough knowledge and understanding of the content and a high level of competence in the processes and skills. In addition, the student is able to apply this knowledge and these skills to most situations.
C	The student has a sound knowledge and understanding of the main areas of content and has achieved an adequate level of competence in the processes and skills.
D	The student has a basic knowledge and understanding of the content and has achieved a limited level of competence in the processes and skills.
E	The student has an elementary knowledge and understanding in few areas of the content and has achieved very limited competence in some of the processes and skills.

In applying the subject specific CPDs, teachers are required to make professional and on-balance judgments. The CPDs are not intended to represent a checklist or comprehensive description of student performance, but rather the best overall description of the student's achievement. This judgment is made through a series of school-determined formal assessment tasks as well as information gathered through less formal assessment of student work on an ongoing basis through the philosophy of "assessment for learning" which underpins this syllabus (for a copy of the Stage 5 Course Performance Descriptors, refer to Appendix 2).

Each time a syllabus is developed it is accompanied by a set of support materials designed to assist teachers in understanding the syllabus, provide key messages, and assist in the implementation of this document. In 2003, the Music Years 7–10 Syllabus was revised and accompanied by two support documents: *Advice on Programming and Assessment* (2003b) and the CD-ROM *Music Years 7–10 Assessment for Learning in a Standards-Referenced Framework* (2004). This CD-ROM also provided teachers with a significant number of student work samples, with accompanying commentary to assist in clarifying student achievement of the learning outcomes of the course.

The Creative Arts K–6 Syllabus was published in 2000. It provides teachers with clear expectations of student learning and teaching strategies. This syllabus contains a number of art forms, but each art form is presented as a discrete body of knowledge, skills, and understanding. Accompanying this syllabus was the *Creative Arts K–6 Units of Work Support Document*. This document was designed more specifically to show the generalist primary teacher a series of strategies, both in classroom management and pedagogy, that would assist them in implementing the syllabus.

The Assessment Resource Centre (ARC)

In September 2006, the Board of Studies launched the Assessment Resource Centre (ARC). The aim of this website is to support and enhance professional practice in the assessment and reporting of student achievement across Years K–12. While it has been developed primarily for teachers, parents and students may also find it useful (see arc.boardofstudies.nsw.edu.au).

The website provides teachers with advice on awarding grades using the A to E system, recognizing standards within their classrooms, and methods of reporting student achievement. Importantly, it promotes the understanding of standards through becoming familiar with the standards by reading the descriptions for each grade, viewing student work samples, and comparing the grade commentaries.

The provision of student work samples that come from real classrooms and were administered by practicing teachers is a commitment to assisting teachers to understand standards and ultimately be able to make consistent judgments. The samples come from a range of schools. Many samples have already been graded, and the grades agreed by a number of experienced practicing teachers based on the characteristics of work typically produced by students performing at that grade. Explanations called grade commentaries are provided to illustrate the reasons for each grading. The grade commentaries are an important role linking the work samples and the grades. They are designed so that when teachers read them they can think of their own experiences with other students who have produced similar work. Consistency of judgments within and between schools will therefore eventually come through following common syllabuses, using a common grading scale, and understanding standards through shared student work samples.

To facilitate this, a grade-alignment process is undertaken. This process aims to show, through work samples, standards that are typically produced by students whose overall performance, on balance, best matches that grade description. Practicing teachers are employed to make a professional judgment about each work sample, based on their knowledge and experience of teaching students in that subject area at that stage. In making these judgments, teachers are asked to consider the grade descriptions from a common grade scale, and pictured the types of knowledge, skills, and understandings in the subject area that students at each of the grade levels typically demonstrate. In doing this, they looked closely at the syllabus outcomes and content for the stage. This website is designed as an ongoing and dynamic project where additional tasks can be trialed and student work samples and grade commentaries can be continually updated. Of particular importance will be the advice provided to the general primary school teacher.

Conclusion

The Board of Studies (New South Wales) has made a commitment to standards-referenced assessment and reporting over several phases of curriculum development. Key to the success of this reform is clearly articulating standards. This has occurred through clearly defining learning expectations through outcomes and content in syllabus documents, introducing philosophies that inextricably link curriculum planning and assessment and the introduction of standards-based assessment and reporting. Throughout this process, teachers, parents, and students have had access to materials that assist them to understand each of these standards though careful descriptions of student achievements, which are supported by samples of student work. In a subject area such as Music, there are inherent obstacles that need to be addressed. These include issues of web-based copyright, the need to be able to represent standards across a large range of musical styles, periods and genres, and the problem with providing lower end samples of video footage that clearly identify students. Despite these obstacles and the relative infancy of these reforms, the framework is in place to ensure that the integration of curriculum and assessment in New South Wales provides students with a high-quality education and that their relative standards can be clearly reported in a consistent manner to students, parents, and the wider community.

References

Abeles, H. F., C. R. Hoffer, and R. H. Klotman. 1995. *Foundations of music education*, 2nd ed. New York: Schirmer.

Bennett, J. 1998. *A process for equating curriculum-based public examinations using professional judgment informed by the psychometric analysis of response data and student scripts*. Unpublished doctoral thesis. University of New South Wales, Sydney, Australia.

Black, P. and D. Wiliam. 1998. *Assessment and classroom learning: Principles, policy and practice*. Special issue. *Assessment in Education*, 5 (1):7–75.

Black, P. and D. Wiliam. 1998a. *Inside the black box: Raising standards through classroom assessment*. London: School of Education, King's College.

Board of Studies, NSW. 1999. *Stage 6 syllabus—Music 2 and music extension*. Sydney: Author.

Board of Studies, NSW. 2000. *Creative arts K–6 syllabus*. Sydney: Author.

Board of Studies, NSW. 2003a. *Music years 7–10 syllabus*. Sydney: Author.

Board of Studies, NSW. 2003b. *Stages 4 and 5—music years 7–10 syllabus*. Sydney: Author.

Board of Studies, NSW. 2004. *Music years 7–10 syllabus advice on programming and assessment*. Sydney: Author.

Board of Studies, NSW. 2006. Assessment Resource Centre website. Retrieved 21 September 21, 2006, from http://www.arc.boardofstudies.nsw.edu.au

Bransford, J., A. Brown, and R. Cocking, eds. 2000. *How people learn. Brain, mind, experience and school*. National Research Council. Washington, DC: National Academy Press.

Colwell, R. 2002. Assessment's potential in music education. In R. Colwell and C. Richardson, eds., *The new handbook of research on music teaching and learning—A project of the Music Educators National Conference*: 1128–1175. New York: Oxford University Press.

Jeanneret, N., J. McPherson, P. Dunbar-Hall, and D. Forrest. 2003. Beyond Manhattanville, Paynter, and cultural identity: The evolution of the NSW music curriculum. In L. C. R. Yip, C. C. Leung, and W. T. Lau, eds., *Curriculum innovation in music—Asia-Pacific symposium of music education research (APSMER)*:137–141. Hong Kong: Hong Kong Institute of Education.

McPherson, J. and J. Bennett. 2004. Representing syllabus and performance standards in external music examinations within a standards-referenced framework: the New South Wales experience. In D. Forrest, ed., *The Puerto papers: Conference proceedings of the 12th biennial international seminar of the ISME commission on Music in Cultural, Educational and Mass Media Policies in Music Education*: 125–140. Puerto de la Cruz, Tenerife, Canary Islands.

McPherson, J. and N. Jeanneret. 2005. *Connections and curriculum development: Foundations of the New South Wales K–12 music curriculum*. In D. Forrest, ed., *A celebration of voices: ASME XV national conference*: 190–196. Melbourne, New South Wales, Australia: The University of Melbourne.

Stevens, R. 2003. *National report on trends in school music education provision in Australia*. Sydney: Music Council of Australia. Retrieved September 16, 2006 from http://www.mca.org.au/StevensReport.htm

Appendix 1: Draft Performance Bands—Music 2

MUSIC 2

The typical performance in this band:

Band 6	Displays extensive knowledge, skills, and understanding of music in social, cultural and historical contexts and of music as an art form.
	Makes high-level musical observations reflecting comprehensive musical experiences.
	Demonstrates excellent development of ideas, musical discrimination, and stylistic understanding in composition.
	Performs with expertise displaying stylistic interpretation and a high level of technical skill.
	Demonstrates comprehensive analytical skills supported by an excellent understanding of the musical concepts.
Band 5	Displays detailed knowledge, skills, and understanding of music in social, cultural, and historical contexts and of music as an art form.
	Makes detailed musical observations reflecting diverse musical experiences.
	Demonstrates successful development of ideas, stylistic and technical competence in composition.
	Performs stylistically with musical sensitivity and technical accomplishment. by a thorough understanding of the musical concepts.
Band 4	Displays sound knowledge, skills, and understanding of music in social, cultural, and historical contexts and of music as an art form.
	Makes sound musical observations based on broad musical experiences.
	Demonstrates musical merit and stylistic awareness in composition.
	Performs with musical style and proficiency.
	Demonstrates broad analytical skills based on a good understanding of the musical concepts with
Band 3	Displays basic knowledge, skills, and understanding of music in social, cultural, and historical contexts and of music as an art form.
	Makes musical observations based on their musical experiences.
	Demonstrates inconsistent musical merit and stylistic awareness in composition.
	Performs competently but inconsistently.
	Demonstrates basic analytical skills and understanding of the musical concepts.
Band 2	Displays limited knowledge, skills, and understanding of music in social, cultural, and historical contexts and of music as an art form.
	Makes simple musical observations.
	Demonstrates limited musical merit in composition.
	Performs with limited interpretive and technical skills.
	Demonstrates limited analytical skills and simple understanding of the musical concepts.
Band 1	Below the minimum standard expected.

Appendix 2: Stage 5 Music Course Performance Descriptors

Grade E	A student performing at this grade typically:	Demonstrates elementary understanding of music as an art form in a limited range of styles, periods and genres.
		With support, engages in some musical experiences demonstrating an elementary understanding of the concepts of music.
		With assistance, is able to perform a limited range of repertoire and engage in group music-making.
		With support, constructs limited musical compositions.
		With support, explores the capabilities of some instruments.
		With support, uses limited notational forms in their own work.
		Describes aspects of style, demonstrating a limited awareness of the social, cultural and historical contexts of the music studied.
Grade D	A student performing at this grade typically:	Demonstrates a basic understanding of music as an art form in a range of styles, periods and genres and with guidance, makes some connections across a range of music.
		Engages in a range of musical experiences demonstrating a basic understanding of the concepts of music.
		Engages in group music-making and may perform some solo repertoire.
		With support, explores, improvises, and constructs basic musical compositions.
		With guidance, explores the capabilities of some instruments to create effects.
		With support, notates their own work demonstrating some understanding of notational conventions.
		Describes aspects of style, demonstrating some awareness of the social, cultural and historical contexts of the music studied.
Grade C	A student performing at this grade typically:	Communicates an understanding of music as an art form in a range of styles, periods and genres and makes connections across a range of music.
		Engages in a range of musical experiences demonstrating a sound understanding of the concepts of music.
		Performs a range of repertoire in solo and group situations.
		Explores, improvises, and constructs musical compositions.
		Explores the capabilities of some instruments and how musical concepts can be manipulated for various effects.
		Notates their own work, demonstrating understanding of notational conventions.
		Discusses style and interpretation, demonstrating some awareness of the social, cultural and historical contexts of the music studied.
Grade B	A student performing at this grade typically:	Clearly communicates an understanding of music as an art form in a range of styles, periods and genres and makes connections across a

		range of repertoire.
		Confidently engages in a range of musical experiences, demonstrating understanding of the concepts of music within a range of repertoire.
		Performs a range of repertoire as a solo performer, and/or takes prominent roles within group performances.
		Explores, improvises, and constructs coherent musical works.
		Explores the capabilities of a range of instruments and how musical concepts can be manipulated for a range of effects.
		Notates their own work, choosing notational forms and conventions appropriate to the style, period or genre being explored.
		Critically discusses style and interpretation, demonstrating an awareness of the social, cultural and historical contexts of the music studied.
Grade A	*A student performing at this grade typically:*	Clearly and perceptively communicates an understanding of music as an art form in a comprehensive range of styles, periods and genres and is able to make connections across a range of repertoire.
		Confidently engages in a range of sophisticated musical experiences demonstrating a perceptive understanding of the concepts of music within a broad range of repertoire.
		Confidently performs a range of repertoire as a solo performer, and/or takes prominent roles within group performances.
		Explores, improvises, and constructs coherent and stylistic musical works.
		Explores the capabilities of a range of instruments and understands how musical concepts can be manipulated for a range of effects.
		Confidently notates their own work, choosing notational forms and conventions appropriate to the style, period or genre being explored.
		Analyses and critically discusses style and interpretation, demonstrating a clear awareness of the social, cultural and historical contexts of the music studied.

Assessing the Strength of Interdisciplinary Connections in the Music Curriculum

Janet R. Barrett
Northwestern University

Abstract

Interdisciplinary approaches to education promote the worthy goal of enhancing students' abilities to draw meaningful connections across school subjects or domains of knowledge. In this paper, I argue that interdisciplinary approaches in music education are complicated and compromised by several misconceptions about the definition, extent, and instructional expectations for interdisciplinary work. Musical understanding depends upon constructing relationships of meaning between and among musical works as well as relationships with works, subjects, and domains outside of music. In order to strengthen interdisciplinary approaches within music education, the strength and scope of these connections needs to be clarified. A conceptual model is presented that includes dimensions for assessing students' knowledge of the relationships among works or disciplines, as well as criteria that can be used to examine the extent and degree of students' relational thinking.

Music teachers often witness the serendipitous and spontaneous connections students make as they relate what they are learning in music classrooms to other subjects or to their lives outside of school. Explicitly *teaching* for connections conveys to students that music is a pervasive and integral dimension of everyday experience, and that music influences other aspects of our lives, just as other aspects of our lives influence music. When music is taught comprehensively, teachers strive for this kind of rich and meaningful interconnectedness in music classrooms. When this work is labeled *interdisciplinary*, though, some music teachers become wary, concerned that such curricular initiatives represent a threat by replacing serious music study with superficial exposure to music, or by relegating music to a secondary role by supporting student achievement in core subjects. Their hesitation is understandable in the current climate of accountability, and given the range of interdisciplinary projects and proposals and considerable conceptual confusion about the purposes and permutations of connecting school subjects. Although comprehensive views of the music curriculum provide strong support for an interdisciplinary emphasis (Barrett, McCoy, and Veblen, 1997; Detels, 1999), the extent to which interdisciplinarity contributes to students' musical understanding has not been widely explored. Clarifying how we assess connected thinking will help us clarify the importance of relating music to other disciplines within a comprehensive music classroom.

Before discussing how music educators might assess the strength of connections that students construct, I describe some common assumptions about interdisciplinary approaches that complicate our path in moving toward comprehensive curricular goals and assessing students' work. Next, I will address how musical understanding and the development of students' relational thinking can be integrated. Principles to guide the alignment of curriculum, instruction, and assessment in interdisciplinary work prefaces the presentation of a conceptual model that can be used to examine the types of *relationships among works and disciplines,* and qualities of *relational thinking,* or processes, used to form these connections.

Interdisciplinary Entanglements

Music educators have been fascinated by the relationship of music to the other arts, culture, history, and disciplines and fields outside the arts for over a century (Barrett, 2006). Yet at the moment, interdisciplinary curricula, projects, and research are entangled in a twisted skein of claims, configurations, and contexts. The term is used so broadly that it prompts a flood of questions and concerns. What are the benefits of implementing an interdisciplinary approach? To what extent and in what circumstances is the study of related disciplines appropriate within a comprehensive music curriculum? What principles foster the development of meaningful connections? Who is responsible for planning these interdisciplinary experiences and for what settings? How do we know that the time spent thinking about subjects outside of music enhances students' understanding of music? The answers to these questions require thoughtful and ambitious responses, but a start can be made by clearing up some areas of confusion that stand in the way of progress. The three that I address here include entanglements related to assumptions that the benefits of interdisciplinary curricula only accrue in one direction—from music to other subjects; from muddled terminology used to describe curricular patterns of organization; and from the common misconception that interdisciplinary work is dependent upon collaboration across classrooms and among teachers.

Accountability in American education is predominantly focused on improving student achievement, defined most narrowly as raising test scores in reading and math. Correspondingly, many interdisciplinary initiatives that involve music in some way are targeted toward establishing the effect of music study on achievement in subjects outside of music. Burton, Horowitz, and Abeles (2000) call this an unfortunate "leitmotif of arts education" (228), particularly since the putative influence of music on extra-musical subjects is rarely explored in the reverse. Secondarily, interdisciplinary initiatives may be targeted toward music's role in the transfer of general cognitive capacities and dispositions such as creativity, self-discipline, or motivation that enhance learning in any subject. The arts may indeed contribute to academic achievement or foster general cognitive dispositions, but the overwhelming impression of many music educators is that interdisciplinary initiatives are too often one-sided and aimed at using music for the benefit of other subjects. The question—What are the benefits of studying other subjects to the study of music?—is rarely asked. This complementary and balanced position is critical in order to change the perception that interdisciplinary work only serves extra-musical aims.

Discussing complex ideas in interdisciplinary curriculum is particularly difficult, since there are few terms that have widespread common meanings (Russell and Zembylas, 2007). Categories to represent various curricular schemes and relationships, such as interdisciplinary, multidisciplinary, crossdisciplinary, transdisciplinary, parallel instruction, integrated instruction, and others, are intended to provide useful distinctions and to portray a continuum in the degrees of coordination between subjects (even to point of dissolving disciplinary distinctions in some infused models). Comparing the way that these terms are used in literature for practitioners and researchers reveals that little agreement exists in labeling interdisciplinary efforts by type or degree. Although delineating terms can tease out useful conceptual distinctions, the spirit of interdisciplinarity is aptly and succinctly described as that which "enables students to identify and apply authentic connections between two or more disciplines and/or to understand essential concepts that transcend individual disciplines" (Consortium of National Arts Education Associations, 2002, 3).

Interdisciplinary work is often assumed to involve, and even require, collaboration among teachers of diverse subjects. Music teachers may respond cautiously to interdisciplinary proposals because meaningful collaboration is increasingly difficult and rare in the current climate of intensified expectations for teachers and their work (Hargreaves, Earl, Moore, and Manning, 2001). Seldom is interdisciplinary work characterized as that which transpires *within* the music classroom, as music teachers and students work together to seek meaningful connections between music and other subject areas. Although collaboration benefits from shared expertise among teachers and across classrooms, it is not an essential requirement for interdisciplinary work. Music teachers can act on their own as interdisciplinarians, and can encourage similar tendencies in students.

Fortunately, assessment can serve as the great clarifier. Through assessment, teachers come to terms with what is essential, aligning curricular content and instructional strategies with forms of evidence that substantiate learning. As the music curriculum becomes more comprehensive in scope, it necessarily becomes more interdisciplinary in nature. Seeking clarity about the kinds of connections students make, and testing the strength of those connections will help to untangle the skein of competing claims and assumptions. Within the context of the classroom, assessment brings purposes, plans, and progress into sharp relief.

Musical Understanding and Interdisciplinarity

The nature of understanding in music relies upon students' conceptions of music, and the ways that those conceptions are organized and interrelated. Although not specifically focused on interdisciplinary connections *per se*, descriptions of musical understanding are grounded in connected knowing. Reimer (2003), for example, relates knowledge, the "mental material one has available to draw on to make connections," to understanding, "the ability to make relevant, genuine connections among discriminations" and the process of "configuring . . . connections to make meaning" (212). Zenker (2002) describes how this understanding is dynamic, fluid, and individualized as "we react to and interact with music based on patterns we recognize in the music, and the social/cultural context of the music mingled with our personal musical history, experiences, and theoretical knowledge" (47).

Experience bears this out. Many of these associations and meanings are formed on a daily basis in music classrooms as well as in other settings within the school. The impulse to connect is a strong and powerful tendency, vividly apparent in early childhood and primary music classrooms. Young children exhibit voracious enthusiasm for making associations and

111

drawing on any aspect of their lived experience to personalize whatever is being studied at the time. As students spend more time in schools, however, these connections are often kept private. Drawing them out requires intentional planning and sensitive approaches. The extent to which these meanings are made public, and represented in forms that can be shared, examined, appreciated, and developed is fundamental to interdisciplinary instruction and assessment. Greene (1995) encourages arts educators to provide openings in classrooms through which students can engage in acts of communication using multiple meanings of the arts to establish "communities of the wide-awake." Through classroom encounters with the arts, their "languages can be explored; the reasons given; the moments of epiphany celebrated; the differing vantage points articulated" (150).

The meanings that emerge within a classroom community illustrate what the art educator Michael Parsons (2004) sees as the essence of interdisciplinarity: "integration occurs when students make sense for themselves of their varied learning and experiences, when they pull these together to make one view of their world and of their place in it. It takes place in their minds or not at all" (776). To foster this deep integration, music educators are challenged to relax their often tightly coiled classes and rehearsals to allow interpretive and interconnected dialogue to emerge, and to invite the kind of reflective thinking that prompts students to apply related knowledge to the music they are learning. Disciplines, as human constructions, draw from many sources of insight across soft boundaries of knowledge (Detels, 1999); musical understanding is similarly informed by these realms of human experience. Theories of integrated knowledge sustain cognitive views of mind, sociocultural perspectives of understanding, postmodern theories of education, and the artistic process itself (Efland, 2002; Slattery, 2006).

Assessing deeply integrated and contextual knowledge of the arts is particularly challenging, however, as students draw upon their personal storehouses of background knowledge to form interpretations and understandings of art works. Efland (2002) identifies the arts as "complex and ill-structured domains" (160) which involve symbolic forms and ideas that cannot easily be represented by propositional logic. Rules and generalizations do not easily apply in understanding how works of art evoke feeling or convey meaning.

Assessing connections between and among the arts (each art form a complex and ill-structured domain in itself) is even more puzzling. Jane Remer (2007) cautions that it is "devilishly hard to assess the arts as disciplines, let alone isolate the impact of the arts in any correlative or causal way when they mix with other variables" (9). Combining the arts multiplies the number of possible associations, salient perceptions, and diverse connections that any student might form as a result of an instructional encounter with multiple works and domains.

One might be tempted to abandon the idea of assessing relational thinking as just too complicated to warrant our attention. Eisner (2002) speaks to this concern by reminding us that teachers' judgments in the arts play a central role in students' progress. We judge whether students understand ideas, organize instruction so that we can judge how well students comprehend, produce, and respond to the arts, and provide essential guidance through formative comments that emphasize what kinds of thinking (disciplinary or interdisciplinary) are valued. Clearly, we need to come to terms with interdisciplinarity in the music curriculum.

Toward a Model of Relational Thinking

A conceptual model to guide the assessment of students' relational thinking in an interdisciplinary music curriculum is provided in Figure 1. This model assumes that students will engage in the study of closely related works (either within music or across art forms) and will produce evidence of their relational thinking, which can take multiple forms. The model also assumes that teachers will examine the types of connections students form and the kinds of relational thinking students use to generate the evidence.

Musical repertoire is the starting place for developing relational thinking. Whether selected by teachers or chosen by students, musical works provide the contexts for forming meaningful relationships. Teachers might organize the study of two or more musical works to highlight the *intradisciplinary* relationships of musical elements to other elements, musical works to other works, and musical styles to other styles. This is the foundation of analytical and interpretive understandings *within* music as a discipline. The historical and current practice of music is full of possibilities, since musical borrowing is ubiquitous. Think, for example, of tributes to classical works in other genres, as when Mozart's Turkish Rondo is realized in the *Blue Rondo a la Turk* of Dave Brubeck. Consider how many works are settings or arrangements of other works, such as Grainger's *Lincolnshire Posy* as a complex amalgamation of English folk songs. Arrangements are particularly useful for analyzing how works can be understood and performed as similar yet different, as when Duke Ellington rearranged Grieg's *Peer Gynt Suite*. Highlighting the intradisciplinary relationships between musical works in our curriculum provides students with plentiful opportunities to practice relational thinking.

Connections can also underscore the *interdisciplinary* relationships of music to artistic processes and expressions in other media, musical works to expressive works in related arts, and aspects of time and place that reflect historical and cultural contexts and meanings. These influence our perception, analysis, interpretation, and response to music as well. A few examples of music inspired by art will illustrate this idea, although examples could easily be drawn from cultural studies, literature, dance, or history. A very familiar example is Mussorgsky's *Pictures at an Exhibition*, inspired by the paintings of his friend Victor Hartmann. Less well known, perhaps, is a painting by Paul Klee, the *Twittering Machine,* which has inspired at least sixteen musical compositions (Evans, 2002). Inspiration can travel in the other direction, too, as in art works inspired by music—Mondrian's *Broadway Boogie Woogie*, Romare Bearden's art glorifying jazz, or Arthur Dove's expressions of Gershwin's *Rhapsody in Blue.*

Figure 1. Conceptual Model for Assessing Student's Relational Thinking

Assessing the Strength of Connections

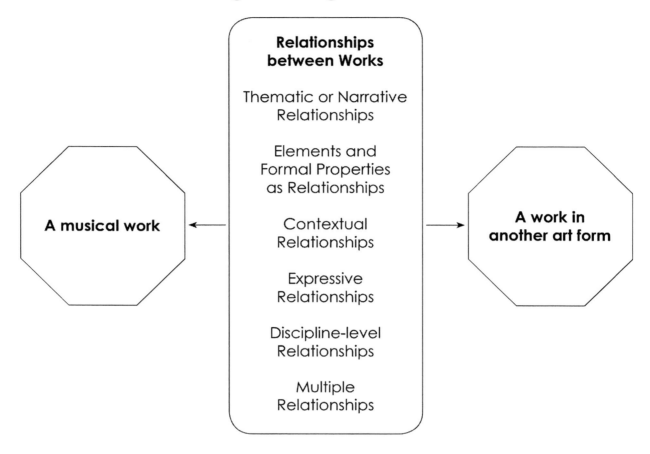

Relationships between Works

Thematic or Narrative Relationships

Elements and Formal Properties as Relationships

Contextual Relationships

Expressive Relationships

Discipline-level Relationships

Multiple Relationships

A musical work

A work in another art form

Assess the types of relationships students form

Evidence of Students' Relational thinking
A description; an analysis; an interpretation; a new work; other responses

Assess the kinds of thinking students use to form these relationships

Fluency   **Credibility or "Fit"**   **Depth**   **Generativity**

If teachers accept the premise that music informs, and in turn is informed by, disciplines outside of the arts, it follows that many musical works have been created and inspired by the times and places in which they were composed and transmitted, and by extramusical sources of inspiration that are reflected in the artistic decisions and characteristics of the work itself (Barrett, McCoy, and Veblen, 1997). Studying works by examining the way they are constructed, the cultures and eras they reflect, and the meanings they represent and evoke often raises questions that benefit from branching out into other domains. This study then folds back into the ways that students perform, interpret, analyze, and respond to the work, laminating understanding as multiple dimensions of the music are layered and strengthened.

Evidence of students' relational thinking could take many forms, including a description, an analysis, an interpretation, a new work, or some other kind of response that makes thinking apparent and tangible. Boix-Mansilla (2005) and her colleagues at Harvard Project Zero have studied the relational thinking of college students who participate in interdisciplinary research centers and educational programs. Their definition of interdisciplinary understanding points strongly toward the synergistic insights that result from combining disciplines (and therefore the criteria used in evaluating such insights) to generate varied responses: "the capacity to integrate knowledge and modes of thinking drawn from two or more disciplines to produce a cognitive advancement—for example, explaining a phenomenon, solving a problem, creating a product, or raising a new question—in ways that would have been unlikely through single disciplinary means" (16). Cognitive advancements such as descriptions, interpretations, new works, and performances allow us to see if the connections have prompted changes in thinking, and whether students have reorganized what they know and feel.

Assessing the strength of connections between music and other disciplines requires the use of at least two interrelated sets of ideas. First, teachers can assess the *types of relationships students form,* which are essentially descriptive categories that center on *relationships between works*—the similarities and distinctive qualities of one work to another and the distinctive attributes of disciplines as well. Six of these categories are described below. The other set of ideas—*criteria for assessing relational thinking*—will follow.

Thematic or narrative ideas are often used by artists in the creation of works that forward some key idea (usually outside of the art form) in sound, image, gesture, or text. Young students often pick up on these topical relationships, and the music curriculum for young children is frequently organized around thematic material as well, such as animals, the seasons, or celebrations. At more advanced levels, themes take on a more abstract nature, such as justice, freedom, metamorphosis, grief, or transformation. Music that is programmatic lends itself to narrative exploration, as anyone who loves to teach Grieg's *In the Hall of the Mountain King* vividly knows. Following the line of a story through the temporal qualities of the music is one way that music can portray extramusical ideas.

Elements and formal properties of a work can be compared and contrasted with the elements and formal properties of another. Such an emphasis requires that students perceive distinct qualities, label those qualities, and then consider how they are manifest across works. When students identify similarities and differences in the use of elements, focusing on sound, image, gesture, and text; focus on general principles of design (unity, variety, emphasis, balance, proportion, contrast); or concentrate on the architectural structures of form, they sharpen their awareness of the way artistic ideas are shaped through the manipulation of elements into satisfying artistic wholes.

115

Relating *contextual connections* in music to contextual connections in other arts and disciplines moves us into regions of culture, style, and historical era. Forming connections goes far beyond merely naming the composer of the work. One can research the history of the work itself as well as the general milieu in which the work was created. Students can situate any particular piece within a family of works connected by style or cultural practice, and act on that knowledge through informed performance practice. Sometimes background stories are uncovered, and those stories change our perceptions and impressions of the work. For the music curriculum, this implies that those who follow the national standards (or their state equivalents) would meld Content Standard 8 (understanding relationships between music, the other arts, and disciplines outside the arts) with Content Standard 9 (understanding music in relation to history and culture).

Affective meanings come into play when teachers and students seek the *expressive characteristics* of the music linked to expressive characteristics of other arts. This is the province of mood, emotion, and feelingful response. The vast realm of expressive meanings of music is inextricably bound to qualities present in the works themselves as well as qualities of the person experiencing the work. When students explore how art works embody feeling, they become more sensitive to the expressive potentials of works and the various interpretive levels of response they evoke.

Discipline-level relationships challenge music teachers to relate music to the characteristics, functions, and uses of other disciplines. This idea is commonly incorporated in state standards, but understanding these relationships fully requires that students be able to think rather abstractly about the fundamental nature of music, art, poetry, dance, and other arts. Beyond useful distinctions such as "music uses sound; poetry uses words; art uses images; dance uses gesture," students must grapple with the distinctive qualities of art forms as complex and complicated disciplines. When standards, for example, ask students to compare and contrast disciplines as school subjects, their answers often reflect how music and the other arts have been separated by time and emphasis within the structure of the school day. In more sophisticated ways, students can be encouraged to identify the properties that define a discipline, the ways that disciplines share common ideas, the ways they are distinct, and instances of work at the borders where disciplinary conceptions have been challenged or expanded. Seeking to understand these discipline-level relationships requires nuances of thought and many examples to draw from in generalizing about abstract relationships.

Synthesizing *multiple relationships among music and other disciplines*. Of course, this descriptive area gives us the most territory for interpretive play, since students can draw upon all of the categories above to show how these multidimensional aspects of art works cohere and interact in the experience of two or more works. Students can describe how the relationships between music and another art or art forms influence the performance, creation, analysis, interpretation, or evaluation of the work or works. It is important, however, to note that not all works relate meaningfully across these dimensions. These categories must be used descriptively to draw attention to the types of relationships that are worth pursuing and ways we could encourage students to connect works within music or between music and other disciplines.

Assessing the kinds of thinking students use to form these relationships involve criteria that capture the extent and quality of relational thinking. Applying these criteria to students' interdisciplinary work gives us evidence of students' overall facility in drawing authentic, meaningful connections across works or disciplines, and allows teachers to evaluate the relational thinking of particular students through the development of their work (parallels to the creative thinking literature and especially the evaluation of divergent thinking will be apparent). These include fluency, credibility or "fit," depth, and generativity. Each will be described in turn.

Students demonstrate *fluency* in their relational thinking when they can make multiple connections between works or disciplines, and when they make numerous connections with ease. Teachers can attend to fluency by asking, "How extensive are the connections students incorporate in their work?" With practice, relational thinking should become more fluent as students develop facility in thinking about multiple relationships and contexts.

Evaluating *credibility or "fit"* is a matter of evaluating the quality of the connections, and the bases students use to form associations. The key idea here is that student work should be supported by evidence. We typically think of evidence as citing details that show how relational thinking is informed by contextual knowledge of the work—who created them, for what reasons, and in what times and places. Relational thinking is also informed by the evidence that stems from students' perceptions of the works and how they articulate those perceptions. Teachers can attend to credibility or fit when they ask, "Do the connections make sense? Can students articulate the bases on which they draw associations between and among works?"

Depth is a matter of moving from the superficial to the sophisticated. Some connections are more straightforward than others (prominent themes, for example), but others require that students look beyond the obvious to deeper levels of thinking. We have not really developed a taxonomy of relationships, but we can recognize when students' products and responses prompt meaningful connections to their lives.

Finally, student thinking can be evaluated according to its *generativity,* or its capacity to lead to further exploration of the works at hand and also works and ideas beyond the immediate context. This criterion has roots in Bruner's notion that "the first object of any act of learning . . . is that it should serve us in the future. Learning should not only take us somewhere; it should allow us to go further more easily" (1960, 17). Teachers attend to generativity when they ask how the connections formed by students lead to meaning beyond the moment and the particular instance of relational thinking. How do students draw upon connections to form new knowledge, products, and explanations, or to conduct inquiry across the disciplines? What is the significance of this educational experience for the next encounter students have with multidimensional works? Unlike the other three criteria of fluency, credibility, and depth, which can be captured by examining the evidence of students' relational thinking in the products and processes of their work, generativity is more elusive to pin down, but fundamentally important to deep understanding.

Moving Toward Meaningful Assessment of Meaningful Connections

Interdisciplinary activity in the music classroom should strengthen, complement, and extend students' musical understanding while stretching interdisciplinary curiosities in areas related to music. Teaching for connections also sets music apart as a distinct form of human expression, and can heighten the way students value music and participate in the pleasures and challenges it affords. Unless we are able to see interdisciplinary approaches as congruent with a comprehensive music curriculum, such work risks being seen as peripheral to our primary purposes and aims. Starting with multidimensional works and studying fewer of them more comprehensively will also allow the instructional space for the interpretation of those works, and for the germination of meaningful relationships. The model presented in this paper attempts to clarify the nature and dimensions of those relationships, which could lead to strategies that would be useful in classroom practice. In addition to focusing on the quality of students' relational thinking, music teacher educators and professional development providers need to attend to the development of music teachers' inter- and intracurricular expertise, assisting them to gain both depth and breadth of understanding as they relate music to the rest of the curriculum, so they in turn can help students relate music to the diverse realms of their lives.

References

Barrett, J. R. 2006. Highways and byways: Interdisciplinarity, teacher knowledge, and the comprehensive music curriculum. *The Mountain Lake Reader: Conversations on the Study and Practice of Music Teaching, IV*: 24–37.

Barrett, J. R., C. W. McCoy, and K. K. Veblen. 1997. *Sound ways of knowing: Music in the interdisciplinary curriculum.* New York: Schirmer Books.

Boix-Mansilla, V. 2005. Assessing student work at disciplinary crossroads. *Change,* 37(1):14–21.

Bruner, J. 1960. *The process of education.* Cambridge, MA: Harvard University Press.

Burton, J. M., R. Horowitz, and H. Abeles. 2000. Learning in and through the arts: The question of transfer. *Studies in Art Education: A Journal of Issues and Research,* 41(3):228–257.

Consortium of National Arts Education Associations. 2002. *Authentic connections.* Reston, VA: Author.

Detels, C. 1999. *Soft boundaries: Re-visioning the arts and aesthetics in American education.* Westport, CT: Bergin and Garvey.

Efland, A. D. 2002. *Art and cognition: Integrating the visual arts in the curriculum.* New York: Teachers College Press.

Eisner, E. 2002. *The arts and the creation of mind.* New Haven, CT: Yale University Press.

Evans, G. 2002. *Music inspired by art: A guide to recordings.* Lanham, MD: Scarecrow Press.

Greene, M. 1995. Releasing the imagination: Essays on education, the arts, and social change. San Francisco: Jossey-Bass.

Hargreaves, A., L. Earl, S. Moore, and S. Manning. 2001. Learning to change: Teaching beyond subjects and standards. San Francisco: Jossey-Bass.

Parsons, M. 2004. Art and integrated curriculum. In E. W. Eisner and M. D. Day, eds., Handbook of research and policy in art education: 775–794. Mahwah, NJ: Lawrence Erlbaum.

Reimer, B. 2003. A philosophy of music education: Advancing the vision, 3rd ed. Upper Saddle River, NJ: Prentice Hall.

Remer, J. 2007. The arts for art's sake vs. integration: A false dichotomy for schools. Arts and Learning Review, 2(1):9.

Russell, J., and M. Zembylas. 2007. Arts integration in the curriculum: A review of research and implications for teaching and learning. In L. Bresler, ed., International handbook of research in arts education: 287–302. Dordrecht, Netherlands: Springer.

Slattery, P. 2006. Curriculum development in the postmodern era, 2nd ed. New York: Routledge.

Zenker, R. 2002. The dynamic and complex nature of musical understanding. In B. Hanley and T. Goolsby, eds., Musical understanding: Perspectives in theory and practice: 27–50. Victoria, BC: Canadian Music Educators Association.

PART 3

Large-Scale Music Assessment

Large-Scale Assessment of Music Performance: Some Whys and Hows for Today's Data-Driven Educational Environment

Special Guest Presentation

Scott C. Shuler
Connecticut Department of Education

Abstract

This paper highlights the need for music educators to develop large-scale assessment systems and provides suggestions for the design of such systems. The opening section outlines the accountability-driven educational context that has emerged over the past decade or so, due in part to the impact of the federal legislation known as No Child Left Behind (NCLB). The second section presents a few of the reasons why it is important to develop and implement large-scale assessment of music learning. The third section, which refers to the Artistic Process model used by the 1997 National Assessment of Education Progress (NAEP) in the Arts and the author's subsequent revision of that model, explains why authenticity in the assessment of K–12 music programs demands the measurement of students' performance achievement. The final section presents common issues that arise when designing large-scale assessment of music performance, and outlines the relative advantages and challenges presented by alternative solutions to those issues.

NCLB and Data-Driven Systems

Many American music educators, having worked since 2002 in schools increasingly affected by the federal education legislation known as No Child Left Behind (NCLB) (H. Res. 1, 2002), have come to blame NCLB for narrowing school curricula and jeopardizing support for arts education. Although the text of the law names the arts officially among the core subjects, NCLB attaches such dire consequences to low test scores in reading, mathematics, and science that it has intensified schools' traditional focus on those few subject areas. This relapse into yet another of America's periodic frenzies about narrowly defined "basics" has drawn attention and resources away from non-tested core subjects, including the arts (Center on Education Policy [CEP], 2005). As a result, music educators and other arts advocates are forced to invest even more of their energy than usual in justifying and defending music programs.

Concomitant to the increased national obsession with test scores in a *narrow* range of subjects is its logical corollary: a heightened interest in accountability for student learning across the *full* range of curriculum areas. NCLB may not have caused, but has certainly deepened, the trend toward focusing school improvement efforts on building systems to measure, analyze, and improve student achievement. Education journals feature articles and conferences feature workshops devoted to data-driven decision-making, and—more predictive of the longevity of this trend—higher education programs are training future school administrators to implement assessment-oriented systems developed by education gurus such as Doug Reeves (Reeves, 2004) and Richard Stiggins (Stiggins, 2002). A recent Google web search on the words "data-based education" yielded 963,000 hits; a search on "data-driven education" yielded 1,020,000.

Individual teachers' contribution to schools, and potentially even their salaries, are being measured by the extent to which they improve student learning (Keller, 2007), a contribution that is sometimes referred to using the business expression "value added." Because standardized test scores are generally reliable and readily available, many music teachers report being pressured by administrators to improve scores on state assessments in the 3Rs and science. Unfortunately, most music teachers lack sufficient instructional time and resources to teach *musical* outcomes, much less to teach 3Rs content for which they lack training or disposition. Although students can and arguably should learn other content through the arts, music teachers know that their first responsibility is to cultivate music learning.

In today's "data or die" system, which demands evidence of the extent to which teachers' efforts are helping students master the curriculum, music educators who want to focus on teaching music must develop and implement systems to measure, analyze, and improve music achievement. While some may view such assessment systems as unwarranted concessions to political pressure, the reality is that they are important, if not essential, to improve music teaching and learning.

What to Assess

The first prerequisite to creating quality assessment systems is to be clear about what should be learned. When Richard Colwell created the *Music Achievement Tests* in 1969, to find the closest available approximation to a consensus about what students should learn in music he was forced to turn to a review of published music textbook series (Colwell, 1969). In 1994 the publication of the National Standards in Arts Education provided the first truly nationwide attempt to codify the key components of what students should know and be able to do (Consortium of National Arts Education Organizations [CNAEO], 1994). This document identified content and achievement standards for grades 4, 8, and 12, but avoided dictating content, such as the specific repertoire or even the general styles of repertoire that all students should study. The National Standards fed and largely guided a concurrent movement among states to develop arts standards, as many states based their standards on or articulated their standards with the national.

The 1997 National Assessment of Education Progress (NAEP) in the Arts provided another centralizing influence on arts content and assessment (National Assessment Governing Board [NAGB], 1997). The development of the framework for NAEP overlapped with the development of the National Standards and, because of ongoing communication between and some common membership on the committees that were developing these two documents, work on each project influenced the other (Shuler, 1996). The NAEP development team was given the charge to develop a framework that would provide common ground among the standards in the four arts disciplines: dance, music, theatre, and visual arts. After considerable discussion, and eventual rejection, of a proposal to organize both the standards and NAEP around the four disciplines of Discipline-Based Arts Education—production, criticism, arts history, and aesthetics—Scott Shuler proposed, and the NAEP design team ultimately adopted as its central model, the three Artistic Processes (Shuler and Connealy, 1998).

Shuler took the original NAEP model back to Connecticut, where teams of teachers applied and refined it through their work in curriculum and assessment (Connecticut State Department of Education [CSDE], 2002) and in portfolio-based teacher assessment. The copyrighted version that was subsequently developed (see Table 1) became the basis not only for Connecticut's Beginning Educator Support and Training (BEST) program, but also for curriculum and assessment work in other states. For example, the State Collaborative on Assessment and Student Standards (SCASS) project, a multi-state collaborative effort under the umbrella of the Council of Chief State School Officers, adopted and has continued to use this revised model as a way of organizing and focusing its work on embedded performance and on-demand assessment tasks (SCASS, 1999). Arts leaders in several state education agencies, including those in Kentucky and Washington, have chosen to use the model to organize their curriculum and assessment efforts (Kentucky Department of Education [KDE], 1999; Washington Office of the Superintendent of Public Instruction [WOSPI], 2007). Educators working for the New Jersey's department of education are currently reworking that state's arts standards to align with the model (Dale Schmid, New Jersey Department of Education Visual and Performing Arts Coordinator, personal communication May 2007), and a group of teachers working under the auspices of the Near East South Asian Council of Overseas Schools (NESA) and the U.S. State Department chose to base new international music standards on the model (NESA, 2007).

Importance of Music Performance

Of the three artistic processes, American school music programs place the greatest emphasis on *performing*. Authentic assessment of music learning therefore requires the measurement of performance achievement. Measuring student attainment in this artistic process is more expensive than in the process of responding, because most aspects of performance do not lend themselves to selected-response and other efficient formats. Nevertheless, in a 2007 survey of state assessment projects, eleven of the sixteen states that reported ongoing work on arts assessment indicated that they already had developed or were planning assessment of music performance (Shuler, 2007).

Although contemporary general music curricula are more varied than during the mid-20th century, when many elementary programs focused primarily on singing, learning to sing—appropriately positioned in the National Standards as content standard number 1—is still arguably *the* foundational musical skill. The voice is the instrument everyone carries around, and the most personal of instruments. Singing also enables students to demonstrate their internalization of sound, sometimes referred to as audiation. Any system designed to measure elementary music learning must therefore measure student achievement, and ideally monitor progress, in singing. At the secondary level, by which time many students have chosen to focus on an instrument, the most sensible approach to performance assessment is to ask students to perform on their "instrument of choice," which might be voice.

Pivotal Design Questions

The fact that large-scale assessment of student musical performance requires a substantial investment in time and technology makes it all the more important to weigh priorities carefully when making a number of key design decisions. The following questions are among those that must be considered.

1. Will students prepare repertoire for performance in advance or sightread?

One important decision assessors must make in assessing performance is whether those performances should be "on demand"—i.e., produced impromptu in response to a task that is first encountered at the assessment site—or prepared in advance. In the early grades, singing for assessment will appropriately occur from memory, which means that the pieces will be prepared. As students progress through the grades, state and national music standards call for them to learn to read and perform from music notation. For most students performance is, in fact, the most common application of notational knowledge. Hence, a case can be made for assessing performance through on-demand tasks, otherwise known to musicians as sightreading.

On the other hand, sightreading introduces a separate set of challenges that impact student performance. Sightreading usually creates an additional layer of assessment anxiety, thereby making it more difficult to determine whether any deficiencies exhibited in a performance are related to singing or to reading. Sightreading is not an appropriate context for measuring expressiveness, which is a key indicator of musical understanding, and therefore arguably the most important attribute of successful performance. Although most students are capable of exhibiting expressiveness in prepared music, few can do so while sightreading. Sightreading is also not a context in which students can showcase their highest-level work. Literature selected for sightreading generally must be less advanced than the literature that students could perform if given time to prepare.

Table 1. The Three Artistic Processes

Creating	Performing	Responding
Imagining Developing idea(s) (concepts, ideas, feelings)	*Selecting* Choosing an artistic work (repertoire) to perform	*Selecting* Choosing an artistic work and/or performance to experience
Planning Experimenting, researching, and designing ways of presenting the idea(s) through artistic materials	*Analyzing* Analyzing structure and researching background of work	*Analyzing* Seeing/hearing and comprehending visual/aural features of the work and performance Mentally assembling what is seen/heard into a whole
	Interpreting Developing a personal interpretation of work (an idea of its expressive intent or potential)	*Interpreting* Developing a personal response to (constructing meaning from) the expressive ideas of both the creator(s) and performer(s)
Making, Evaluating, Refining Applying knowledge and skills/technique to bring idea(s) to life through artistic work Evaluating quality and refining successive versions ("drafts") of the work	*Rehearsing, Evaluating, Refining* Applying knowledge and skills/technique to bring personal interpretation to life through performance Evaluating quality and refining successive versions of the performance	*Evaluating* Evaluating quality of artistic work and its performance
Presenting Presenting in performance or exhibiting completed work for others	*Presenting* Performing work for others	

© 1993 Scott C. Shuler; Revised, 10/11/02

Relying exclusively on sightreading raises some question of authenticity. Being able to read music quickly at sight is useful in a variety of life situations, from singing hymns at church to having a successful first rehearsal in a community ensemble. However, it is an equally important and satisfying independent life skill for students to be able to prepare a performance on their own, from notation or sound, given enough time to work at their own pace. The assessment distinction between sightreading and prepared performance is parallel to that between requiring students to solve math problems quickly on an "on demand," timed, standardized exam and allowing them to solve those problems at their own pace. Relying solely on sightreading therefore does not provide a whole picture of a student's achievement in relation to notation.

One challenge when assessing prepared performances to determine the level of musical *independence* is factoring in the extent to which students have been coached, which might vary considerably from one classroom to another. As has often been noted in relation to traditional large festivals, pre-selecting repertoire for assessment can also lead teachers to focus on teaching that music—often by rote—to the exclusion of other important musical learning. To avoid that problem, many festivals require ensembles to sightread one work in addition to performing their prepared selections.

Although choosing to collect both prepared and sightread performances increases the complexity of assessment, it is the best solution to ensure an accurate picture of students' performance as well as their notational achievement. This is the solution selected by developers of the New York music assessment (New York Department of Education [NYDE], 2007).

Regardless of whether performances are prepared or sightread, judges must be provided with a correctly notated score of any piece performed so that they can judge the accuracy of the performance.

2. *How should repertoire be selected for performance?*

The national standards call for students to perform a variety of music, and that variety is further explained to mean music from a variety of styles and historical periods.

Consistency (reliability) of assessment is enhanced by having students perform identical repertoire. For district-level assessment it is certainly possible to dictate the repertoire students will perform. For state-level assessment it is also possible to specify works that students will prepare for performance—for example, South Carolina's elementary singing assessment currently requires students to sing "Twinkle, Twinkle Little Star" on the neutral syllable "du" (South Carolina Department of Education [SCDE], 2007). When assessing large numbers of students, particularly at the younger grade levels, it is often sufficient to hear just a phrase or two of prepared music to gain an accurate sense of their performance skills.

At the upper grade levels, students will likely perform on different instruments, and will have achieved widely varying levels of achievement. It is probably impossible to select one piece of music that is of equal difficulty to perform on every instrument. Large scale assessors might choose to provide a list of alternative pieces for each instrument, from which students might choose a work to prepare, perhaps in consultation with their teacher. Scoring could take into account the difficulty level of a selection performed, much as scorers of diving and ice skating consider degree of difficulty. Some state standards followed the national standards in specifying grades (difficulty levels) of repertoire for students to perform based on the New York State School Music Association (NYSSMA) list (New York State School Music Association [NYSSMA], 2006).

Table 2. Large-Scale Assessment of Musical Performance: Content Considerations

	Importance and Advantages	Challenges
Prepared Performance: Work Prepared with Assistance (rote song, coached performance)	Essential component of elementary music program assessment Demonstrates students' highest achievement level, given coaching and time	Amount and effectiveness of coaching and practice time provided by teacher can vary considerably from classroom to classroom Specifying works in advance could lead teacher to focus instruction on narrow range of repertoire for assessment
Prepared Performance: Independently Prepared by Student from Notated Score (i.e., teacher coaching limited or prohibited)	Performance demonstrates students' independent reading skills, musicality, and motivation Provides students who need time to master pieces with opportunity to prepare at their own pace Might be able to use existing systems, such as solo and ensemble, to monitor the performance of some subgroups of students	Difficult to control the amount of coaching
On-Demand Performance: Sightreading	Performance demonstrates important notational literacy life skill Conditions can be controlled for fairness: every student has exactly the same amount of time and preparation Can sometimes create hybrid assessment scenario, providing students with substantial time in isolation to prepare a work from notation, if facilities and other aspects of the testing situation permit	Does not reveal students' top level of performance achievement, particularly if reading is a weakness Level of literature difficulty must necessarily be lower than what students can perform with preparation Sightreading does not provide a useful measure of musicality Students who respond poorly to pressure will not showcase their best work
Ability to Self-Evaluate	Essential skill for musical independence Relatively simple to assess by comparing student's self-evaluation to expert judge's evaluation	Difficult to measure students' ability to prescribe successful solutions to performance defects

3. *Will students perform individually, in ensembles, or as one part against a recorded background?*

Some music educators argue that the most important performance context to assess is how well students perform within an ensemble, rather than individually. They point out that students spend most or all of their in-school performance time in an ensemble context, and that assessing ensembles is more efficient and therefore more practical than listening to each student perform individually. Those who adopt the most extreme position suggest not assessing individual students at all, but rather relying on ensemble ratings as a general measure of how well students are learning to perform.

National and many state standards call for students to be able to perform both independently and in ensembles. It is true that students are often more comfortable performing in groups. Piloting for the 1997 NAEP assessment revealed that some eighth graders became upset when asked to sing unaccompanied, so the task was changed to provide a karaoke background and microphone, a format which proved much more comfortable for participants. Accompanied and ensemble performances make it easier to judge students' ensemble skills, such as balance and intonation. If, on the other hand, one purpose of an assessment is to judge the students' level of independent mastery, then unaccompanied solo performance clearly provides a better indication of whether the student can, for example, maintain a steady beat or pitch center.

To assess the full range of performance skills, the ideal design would measure students' performance both unaccompanied *and* within the context of an accompaniment or "music minus one" ensemble setting.

4. *Who should score student performances?*

Teachers must be able to score their students' work consistently in real time to provide students with prompt and accurate feedback in the classroom. The achievement of truly common standards within a district or state requires that teachers share similar expectations, the best evidence of which is their ability to arrive independently at the same scores for the same work. On the other hand, the best way to ensure reliability is to preserve student work for later scoring and training, including the comparison and calibration of scoring by different judges. A combination approach is therefore ideal—i.e., asking music teachers on site to score the performances and provide feedback to students, but recording the work for later review.

One option available to facilitate reliable scoring is collective scoring by trained judges, either in intensive settings such as a summer institute or remotely online. Another option is the use of one of a group of techniques collectively referred to as "moderation." One form of moderation that is potentially useful for states—because it promotes reliability while providing professional development—is that of bringing teachers together who have pre-scored their students' work to cross-check and calibrate their ratings under the guidance of expert scorers (Wynne, 1994).

The collection and scoring of student performances, which once required the cumbersome management of recording media such as reel-to-reel or cassette tape, is greatly expedited by new technologies. The rate of improvement in technology is such that mentioning specific examples would almost guarantee that this article would soon become dated. In general, however, the emergence of digital recording devices that are compact, affordable, and capable of storing large amounts of high-fidelity sound provide teachers with an unparalleled opportunity to collect and store students' musical work.

While the capacity to record and preserve sound has improved dramatically, management and retrieval remain a challenge, although emerging technology promises to help with these tasks as well. SmartMusic (MakeMusic, 2007) is a commercial product that allows students to record multiple performances of the same piece, then select and upload the performance they deem best; teachers can then access the performances for scoring, and students can instantly access and review their scores. Connecticut's www.CTcurriculum.org site was one of the first dynamic sites that allowed teachers to design units and common assessments online, then upload and score student work (CSDE). South Carolina and Rhode Island are among the states that have developed their own online systems designed to facilitate uploading student work for centralized scoring, thereby facilitating large-scale assessment of performances (SCDE, 2007; Rhode Island Department of Education [RIDE], 2007).

5. *Which if any other steps in the artistic process of performing should be assessed?*

The artistic process of performance involves several steps (see Table 1). The first of these is *selection of literature.* The cultivation of students' ability to choose appropriate literature is an important part of the curriculum, and should therefore be assessed over time. However, such an assessment requires an accurate understanding of variables such as the student's technical and musical development that are difficult to measure and factor into a large-scale assessment, and therefore should be left to the classroom.

One important extension of literature selection is students' ability to *construct programs* consisting of works they or their ensemble can perform. Asking students to construct and justify such programs, using musical vocabulary, is a valuable classroom outcome, and one that I have seen measured successfully as a high school ensemble written exam. Again, this seems like a better assessment for the classroom than for large-scale measurement. For one, the music education profession has not yet developed and published a common set of criteria for program selection, although a case could be made for developing such a consensus. More important, the assessment of the appropriateness of such a program depends on knowledge of the level of achievement level of the ensemble, which again is beyond the scope of large-scale assessment.

Another important step—some would argue *the* most important step—in the performing process is students' ability to *self-evaluate and prescribe successful solutions* or strategies for improvement. Ultimately this capacity is the key to independence as a musician, because it weans the student from the teacher. Evaluating the student's ability to self-evaluate in a large-scale assessment is relatively straightforward, as it ultimately boils down to the extent to which students' scoring of their own performances matches expert judges' scores of those same performances. Ideally the student should have an opportunity to listen at least once to a recording of their performance before completing and submitting their self-evaluation.

The ability to prescribe solutions to performance problems, on the other hand, is more difficult to assess on a large-scale basis. First, because each performance is different, the difficulty of correcting each performance will vary widely from student to student. At least in theory, a student who performs poorly should have an easier time identifying errors to correct or phrases to refine than a student who performs almost flawlessly, although the fact that those defects are present might suggest that the student is unable to hear or unwilling to correct them. Just as problematic, in the typical large-scale assessment setting the scorer does not remain on the scene long enough to be able to determine whether the solution(s) identified by a student are implemented and prove successful.

At the district or classroom level it might be possible to design a common, extended task in which students record a performance, perhaps by sightreading; self-evaluate that performance, perhaps after listening to a recording; identify possible solutions to problems in the performance; then have time to implement those solutions before once again recording the performance. For the assessment to truly reflect the students' ability to self-correct, there would have to be strict controls to prevent coaching by the teacher or others. In practice, that would probably mean administering the entire task on-demand and in a single session.

All in all, measuring the ability to recommend solutions might be accomplished more reliably and efficiently as part of a responding assessment, in which all students critique and recommend solutions for the same recorded performance(s).

6. For efficiency, why not assess two artistic processes—i.e., both performing and creating—at once, by having students perform their own compositions?

Student composition is a key outcome of school music programs, and asking students to prepare performances of their own compositions is a very appropriate instructional strategy to integrate two important musical activities. The student work produced by such a task is not, however, appropriate for reliable large-scale assessment, precisely because the task confounds two distinct, complex musical outcomes. Students who create challenging compositions would be at a disadvantage when performing, in comparison to those who create works that are easy to perform. The most sophisticated student composers might therefore appear to be the least proficient performers. In other words, when the two tasks are combined, the students' level of composition is limited by their level of performance, and vice versa. Hence, although having students perform and/or conduct their own compositions is an effective project in a comprehensive curriculum, this combination is not an appropriate task for summative assessment.

7. Which students should be included in large-scale assessment?

The purpose of large-scale assessment necessarily plays a key role in determining which students should be measured, but music program design should also be taken into consideration. Although there are numerous potential "right answers" to the question of whom to assess, it is possible to identify some general principles.

The final grade level at which music instruction is required for all students is a critical level for assessment. Such an assessment offers the opportunity to summarize the learning that all students receive, thereby providing a basis for program improvement. It also establishes a baseline for teachers of music electives in subsequent grades. A state education agency or consortium of school district designing an assessment system should therefore include this grade level. Ideally, the assessment would occur near the end of the grade level, when students have completed most of their music instruction.

As the final grade in many common or general arts curricula, Grade 8 is a critical level for assessment. National Opportunity-to-Learn Standards in the Arts (CNAEO, 1995) recommend that required art and music instruction continue at least through grade 8. Such a delivery system is highly desirable, in part because it provides a continuous and common foundation of musical learning on which high school music electives can build. This fact influenced the selection of the population measured in the 1997 Arts NAEP. Costs associated with administering and scoring performance tasks forced NAEP developers to choose one grade level for the full assessment from among the three grade levels—4, 8, and 12—in which items had been piloted. After weighing considerations such as those outlined above, they ultimately chose to implement the assessment at grade 8 (U. S. Department of Education Office of Educational Research and Improvement [USDOE-OERI], 1998).

Unfortunately, patterns of delivery for music education vary considerably from state to state and district to district, and often fall short of the ideal recommended in the standards. Even in programs where music *is* required through grade 8, schools sometimes excuse students who are in ensembles from taking general music. Such variations in course requirements and curricula present a challenge to those designing assessment.

Given the elective nature of high school music programs, variation in the content and amount of student learning is even greater at this level than in grade 8. The current, nationwide interest in high school reform has caused states to consider alternatives to traditional high school graduation requirements, which have historically been based on Carnegie Units. The obvious alternative, and therefore one being pursued by several states, is to define and assess high school exit proficiency requirements. Arts educators, who have been successful in implementing or maintaining traditional high school arts graduation requirements in many states, now face the task of developing assessment tools so that arts expectations are included among the new proficiency requirements.

If there is any good news in the fact that high school music curricula continue to consist primarily of large performing ensembles, and that most high school students who are enrolled in music are therefore taking these courses, it is that ensembles tend to share common learning outcomes, including—of course—the cultivation of performance. Such commonalities in curriculum should theoretically make assessment design easier, but the task must be approached thoughtfully. Focusing large-scale high school proficiency measures too narrowly on traditional performing ensemble outcomes would tend to sustain the primacy of those programs, and inadvertently discourage schools from making the kind of innovative changes in high school music offerings that are arguably needed to increase the number of students who elect music classes.

A case can be made for targeting Grade 4 as a mid-point for assessment between the beginning of K–12 education and grade 8. The development of grade 4 assessment is supported by the existence of national and, in many cases, state standards for this grade level.

An equally valid case can be made for assessing at grade 5, because it is the culminating level in many elementary schools. A fifth grade music assessment would therefore provide a summary of elementary learning and a baseline of learning as students enter middle school. Assessment at the end of the final grade of elementary school is even more important in districts where music is either required only at the elementary level or where students can choose ensembles in lieu of general music at the middle level, because in such districts leaving elementary school also means exiting the common music curriculum.

The developmental span between preschool and grade 5 is a large one, during which students undergo dramatic changes both physically and intellectually. Hence, a case can be made to develop standards for and assess learning in at least one point during this span. Developers of NESA's AERO standards, for example, elected to develop a set of music standards for grade 2 (NESA, 2007).

8. *Which is the most efficient and effective unit of measurement?*

The Holy Grail of assessment systems would measure all students continuously on *all* important learning outcomes, and provide them with instantaneous, reliable analytic feedback designed to improve their performance. Unfortunately, reality invariably dictates compromises. Most district- and state-level assessments in all subject areas are primarily summative in nature rather than analytic. Performance assessments require a relatively large investment of time by students and scorers, which limits the number and scope of such assessments.

When arts assessments exist, they rarely if ever receive the priority or funding accorded to 3Rs assessment, nor are high stakes—such as eligibility for grade level promotion or graduation—often attached to such assessments. Compromises on the scope of arts assessment are therefore almost inevitable. The challenge is to select the most efficient approach that gathers the information necessary to fulfill the purpose of the assessment.

If there is an upside to the lack of accountability or consequences for each individual student of performance on a music assessment, it is the possibility that offers of using random sampling rather than assessing all students.

NCLB holds individual schools accountable for making Adequate Yearly Progress (AYP), and education reform initiatives often emphasize school-based solutions such as school choice and magnet schools. In an era where so much autonomy and responsibility is focused on individual buildings, and where site-based management systems give many principals almost total control over curriculum and budget, the *school* is the key unit of measurement for large-scale music assessment. Measuring the achievement of students in each building is necessary to encourage administrators and policymakers to provide quality, equitable resources for arts education. Information gathered through such assessments should be publicized in each state's version of the "school report card."

Assessing at the school level means that a random sample of students could be measured at one or more target grade levels. A superior alternative would be to involve all students in those grade level(s) in the assessment, but randomly assign subgroups to complete different "forms" of the assessment, thereby collectively permitting the measurement of a more comprehensive scope of student arts learning within the same amount of time.

Kentucky's arts assessment program, one of the earliest state arts assessment systems and the one with the longest record of implementation, requires random sampling in order to report scores and enforce accountability on the school level. Arts achievement counts for a small percentage of each school's overall score. The Kentucky program, which has for the past several years been limited to pencil-and-paper for both stimulus and response, does not currently measure music performance achievement (KDE, 2006).

Conclusion

Music educators need assessment tools appropriate for large-scale assessment, comparison, and improvement of student learning. Regardless of whether the responsibility for such assessments falls on the state or local districts, their development should ideally be at least coordinated, if not spearheaded, by state education agencies. After all, state education agencies take the lead on assessment in most other content areas.

In the absence of such leadership, other institutions that are concerned about the health and quality of arts education should step forward. In Rhode Island, for example, the lack of an arts consultant in the state education agency led an enlightened state arts council to assume the leadership role in laying the groundwork for high school graduation proficiency assessment. In Kentucky, even after more than a decade of assessment implementation, the music educators association continues to take the lead in advocating for, developing, and even funding improvements in the commonwealth's music assessment program.

When resources are tight, as they often are for state and district initiatives in music and the other arts, it is tempting to settle for an inexpensive test. In practical terms, "inexpensive" usually means pencil-and-paper, on-demand testing. Music assessment cannot, however, authentically represent or drive quality instruction without including some measurement of music performance achievement. Hopefully, by sharing their assessment work, states will assemble sufficient resources and expertise to design common music assessment systems for measuring achievement in performing as well as in creating and responding to music. Music educators and concerned citizens should look forward to the day when schools across the country are held accountable for ensuring that all students have access to a quality music education.

References

Center on Education Policy (CEP). 2005, July. NCLB: Narrowing the curriculum? Policy Brief based on *From the capital to the classroom: Year 3 of the No Child Left Behind Act*. Washington, D. C.: Author.

Colwell, R. 1969. *Music achievement tests*. Chicago: Follett Educational Corp.

Connecticut State Department of Education (CSDE). *Curriculum*. Retrieved June 14, 2007, from www.CTcurriculum.org

Connecticut State Department of Education (CSDE). 2002. *Guide to K–12 Program Development in the Arts*. Hartford, CT: Author.

Consortium of National Arts Education Organizations (CNAEO). 1994. *National standards for arts education: What every young American should know and be able to do in the arts*. Reston, VA: MENC—The National Association for Music Education.

Consortium of National Arts Education Organizations (CNAEO). 1995. *Opportunity-to-learn standards for arts education*. Reston, VA: National Art Education Association.

H. Res. 1, 107th Cong., 115 Stat. 1425 2002 (enacted). *Public Law 107–110, No Child Left Behind Act of 2001* (short title) [Electronic Version].

Keller, B. 2007, April 17. Teacher panel calls for overhaul of pay across profession. [Electronic Version]. *Education Week* 26(33):7.

Kentucky Department of Education (KDE). 2006, August. *Core content for arts and humanities assessment* [Version 4.1]. Frankfort, KY: Author.

National Assessment Governing Board (NAGB). 1997. *NAEP arts education assessment framework*. Washington, D. C.: Author.

Near East South Asian Council of Overseas Schools (NESA). 2007. American education reaches out (AERO) music standards project. Athens, Greece: Author. Retrieved June 14, 2007, from http://www.projectaero.org/AERO%2B/music/index.htm

New York State Department of Education (NYDE). *Draft test sampler*. Albany, NY: Author. Retrieved June 14, 2007, from http://www.emsc.nysed.gov/osa/hsart.html

New York State School Music Association (NYSSMA). 2006. *NYSSMA manual*. Westbury, NY: Author.

Reeves, D. B. 2004. *Accountability for learning*. Alexandria, VA: Association for Supervision and Curriculum Development.

Rhode Island Department of Education (RIDE). 2007. *Rhode Island Arts Learning Network*. Providence, RI: Author. Retrieved June 14, 2007, from www.riartslearning.net

SCASS Arts Education Assessment Consortium. 1999, July. *Presentation materials*. Presented at the National Arts Assessment Institute, Hidden Valley, Pennsylvania. Washington, D. C.: Council of Chief State School Officers.

Shuler, S. C. and Connealy, S. 1998, September/October. The evolution of state arts assessment: From Sisyphus to stone soup. *Arts Education Policy Review*, *100*(1):12–19.

Shuler, S. C. 1996. The effect of standards on assessment practices (and vice versa). In *Aiming for excellence: The impact of the standards movement on music education* (no ed.): 81–108. Reston, VA: MENC—The National Association for Music Education.

Shuler, S. C. 2007. [Survey of State Education Agency Directors of Arts Education]. Unpublished raw data.

MakeMusic, Inc. 2007. SmartMusic (Version 10.0). [Computer software]. Eden Prairie, MN: Author. Retrieved June 15, 2007 from www.smartmusic.com.

South Carolina Department of Education (SCDE). South Carolina arts assessment project. Columbia, SC: Author. Retrieved June 14, 2007, from http://scaap.ed.sc.edu/currenttests.asp

Stiggins, R. J. 2002. Assessment crisis: The absence of assessment FOR learning. *Phi Delta Kappan, 83*(10):758–765.

U.S. Department of Education Office of Educational Research and Improvement (USDOE-OERI). 1998. *The NAEP 1997 arts report card: Eighth grade findings from the National Assessment of Educational Progress*. Washington, D. C.: Author.

Washington Office of the Superintendent of Public Instruction (WOSPI). *Essential academic learning requirements in the arts*. Olympia, WA: Author. Retrieved June 14, 2007, from http://www.k12.wa.us/curriculumInstruct/Arts/EALRs/EALRs.aspx

Wynne, H. 1994, April. *Concepts of quality in student assessment*. Paper presented at the annual meeting of the American Educational Research Association, New Orleans, LA. ERIC Document Reproduction Service No. ED367712.

The Florida Music Assessment Project: An Association-Driven Model of Large Scale Assessment Development

Keynote Address

Timothy S. Brophy
University of Florida

First, I want to thank all of you for attending this symposium. I am deeply grateful that all of you have participated so fully and enthusiastically the past two days. This morning we begin our third and final day, and I look forward to seeing all of you at our closing session this afternoon.

We are fortunate to have representatives from three states at this symposium who are leading large-scale music assessment initiatives. We have heard from Bret Smith, who has shared with us Washington State's Classroom Performance-Based Assessment project (Smith, 2008). Ching Ching Yap and Tara Pearsall have described the web-based music assessment currently in progress in South Carolina (Yap and Pearsall, 2008). Robyn Swanson and Melanie Wood presented their work on Kentucky's Music Listening Project, one of the longest running state music assessments in the nation (Swanson, Wood, and Shepherd, 2008). These projects are all Department of Education initiatives that involve school- and university-based arts educators and/or music education associations.

In this presentation I will share with you the large-scale, association-driven initiative in music assessment that we have undertaken in Florida. First, I will set the stage for this presentation with a brief review of the historical background, philosophical foundation, and developmental framework of our project. Second, I will describe the development of our model within Pistone's (2002) recommendations for developing large-scale assessments in the arts. I will close with a summary of the lessons we have learned in this process in the form of guidelines for association leaders who may be interested in starting this type of project.

Setting the Stage: Foundations of the Florida Music Assessment

The Minear Initiative

In May 2001, Florida Music Educator's Association (FMEA) president Carolyn Minear formed the Florida Music Assessment Task Force to begin finding a way to account for music learning in Florida classrooms. Congress was deliberating the *No Child Left Behind Act of 2001* (H. Res. 1, 2002), and Minear felt that the FMEA needed to take the lead in developing a way to obtain data on K–12 students' progress toward the *Sunshine State Standards for Music* (Florida Department of Education [FLDOE], n.d.b.). This decision stemmed from her belief that accountability in core subject areas is the responsibility of professional educators, and that music educators in Florida should be responsible for accounting for music learning by Florida students. Minear's initiative was for the FMEA to partner with the Department of Education and state universities to develop a large-scale assessment for music. The Task Force consists of two co-chairs, Al D. Holcomb (University of Central Florida) and me, and a team of ten individuals who represent each of the FMEA component organizations as well as additional supervisors of Florida's largest counties. Several component representatives are in-service music teachers. The Task Force membership has remained unchanged since its development. The organizational chart for the Assessment Task Force is presented in Figure 1.

Figure 1. Organizational Chart for the Florida Music Assessment Task Force

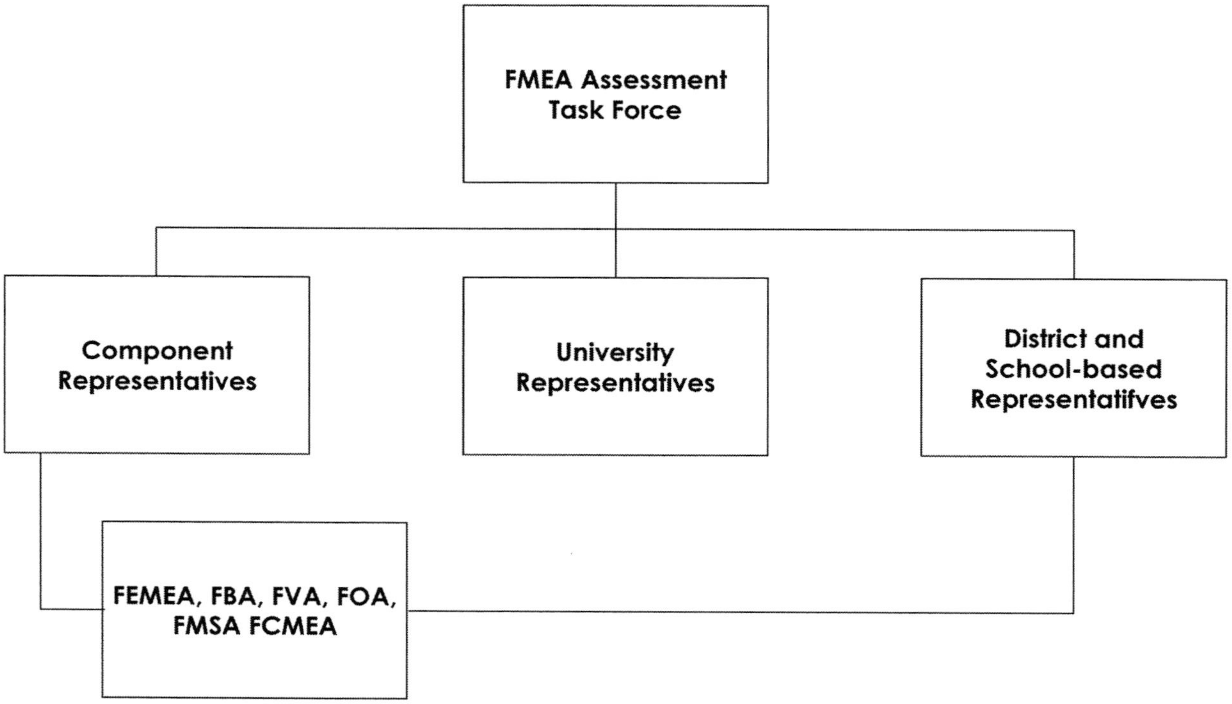

Note. FEMEA – Florida Elementary Music Educators Association; FBA – Florida Bandmasters Association; FVA – Florida Vocal Association; FOA – Florida Orchestra Association; FMSA – Florida Music Supervisors Association; FCMEA – Florida College Music Educators Association

Developing a Philosophical Foundation

The Task Force met for the first time in November of 2001. Our initial efforts focused on the development of a vision, a set of beliefs, and purposes that serve as the foundation for the project. After eighteen months of careful thought and deliberation, the Task Force set forth the following vision for the project:

We envision at the elementary and secondary levels an assessment of students' individual progress toward the Florida Sunshine State Standards for music. The results of these assessments will provide evidence of individual student growth in music and assist in the improvement of student learning and music teaching. (Florida Music Assessment Task Force, March 28, 2003).

At the same time, the Task Force issued the following set of beliefs:

1. The Fine Arts are a core subject, as proclaimed in the Elementary/Secondary Education Act of 2001, commonly referred to as "No Child Left Behind."
2. All Florida students should have equal opportunity to develop a broad background in all of the arts and concentrated study in one arts discipline.
3. There is a depth and breadth of content reflected in the Sunshine State Standards for music that all music students should know and be able to do.
4. Progress toward the Sunshine State Standards for music must be monitored and assessed for all music students in the State of Florida.
5. Assessment of student learning in music will provide an opportunity to monitor student progress and motivate school improvement.

The specific purposes of the Florida Music Assessment were also issued at this time. The purposes of the assessment are to improve K–12 music learning in the State of Florida by:

1. Providing a vehicle for monitoring individual student growth within and among schools, district and the state,
2. Promoting growth toward the comprehensive music knowledge and skills identified in the Sunshine State Standards for Music, thus providing an opportunity to demonstrate academic accountability and credibility,
3. Providing a vehicle for identifying areas to target for future professional development opportunities (e.g., FMEA sessions), and
4. Assisting in the promotion of equitable learning opportunities throughout the state toward the Sunshine State Standards (by identifying factors that prevent schools from offering adequate learning opportunities, e.g., instructional time, equipment, etc.).

Developmental Framework

Pistone (2002) provides a set of recommended steps for developing large-scale arts assessments. These are:

1. Take time.
2. Understand the distinct phases of activity along with the assistance and funding required for each.
3. Apply collaborative strategies from the outset.
4. Link Assessment to the same standards across districts and state schools.

We have developed and maintain important collaborative partnerships as we proceed with our project. School District Testing Directors are our direct contact to the schools. University

141

partners provide consultant expertise as well as academic technology for scoring tests. The Florida Department of Education partnership has been crucial to our success.

Pistone recommends a three-phase plan for developing arts assessments. These are:

1. Phase 1: Plan and Clarify
2. Phase 2: Develop and Generate
3. Phase 3: Implement and Model

While Pistone's recommendations had not been published at the time we initiated the Task Force, we found her recommendations useful and in line with the Task Force's established test development plan. Test item development began in March 2003.

Operationalizing Pistone's Phases in Florida: The Association-Driven Model

Phase 1: Plan and Clarify

The first phase of Pistone's (2002) recommended sequence is to Plan and Clarify. She describes the steps in this phase as follows:

1. Identify the planning and design committee.
2. Establish the purpose of the assessment program.
3. Develop guidelines for the assessment design and implementation.
4. Create a timeline for accomplishing major milestones.
5. Examine and learn from existing large-scale efforts.

Our planning and design committee is the Assessment Task Force. The vision, beliefs, and purposes that guide our project were presented earlier in this paper. We decided that our test would be a "stand alone" music assessment delivered digitally (on CD or via other electronic means), written by trained FMEA members, given during a 4–5 week test window in spring, following the Florida Comprehensive Assessment Test (FCAT), and that we would include special needs and limited English proficiency (LEP) students. We were unable to set definite timelines at the beginning of our project because this was an FMEA-funded initiative, and we were able to meet when the funds allowed. Once the Department of Education began providing grant monies for the project in 2005, our timelines were set in accordance with the schedule for specific deliverables set forth in the grant timelines.

We carefully reviewed available information on large-scale music assessments in other states and the 1997 National Assessment of Educational Progress (NAEP) arts assessment as we began deliberations on the design of our assessment. The *Arts Education Assessment Framework* (National Assessment Governing Board [NAGB], 1994) presents a three-fold model used as the framework for the 1997 National Association of Education Progress (NAEP) arts assessment. The NAEP framework is based on the roles that artists assume when engaged in artistic behaviors. For music, these roles are briefly described here:

1. *Performing.* When performing music, the student is the interpreter of existing music.

2. *Creating*. When creating music, the student improvises, composes, or arranges music.
3. *Responding*. When responding to music, the student assumes the role of audience member, critical listener, and evaluator of musical performances, and engages in musical criticism or analysis.

Our assessment design is based on this model. We are developing our comprehensive assessment in three Phases at the elementary, middle, and high school levels, as follows:

1. Phase 1—Content Knowledge, Listening, and Analysis (Responding).
2. Phase 2—Individual Performance (Performing).
3. Phase 3—Individual Improvisation, Composition, and Arranging (Creating).

At the present time we are field-testing the Phase 1 elementary test, and are planning to pilot the Phase 1 tests for middle school and high school in the 2007–08 school year.

Phase 2: Develop and Generate

The second phase of Pistone's (2002) recommended sequence is to Develop and Generate the assessment. She describes the steps in this phase as follows:

1. Organize Test Development Teams.
2. Create the framework to capture the content in the arts standards.
3. Write test items.
4. Review assessment items.
5. Pilot test items.

The test development teams we have organized consist of teachers, administrators, and district supervisors who are nominated and subsequently approved by the Task Force. We select separate teams of writers and validators for each level of the test: elementary, middle school, and high school. The organizational scheme and selection criteria for the test development teams are shown in Figure 2. One Task Force member serves as a liaison on each of the test development teams.

Figure 2. Test Development Teams for the Florida Music Assessment

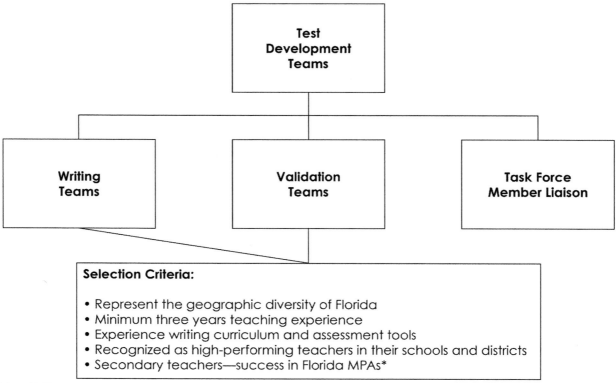

Note. *MPA – Music Performance Assessment, Florida's solo and ensemble event.

Once the test development teams are in place, we proceed to the item writing and review phase. We develop our tests collaboratively over a period of several years. The following describes our test development sequence.

Step 1: Curriculum Review. The Task Force first reviews the Sunshine State Standards, Benchmarks, and Grade Level Expectations (GLEs) for Music (FLDOE, n.d.b.) and identifies those that are best suited for large-scale assessment and those that are best suited for classroom-level assessment. We apply two guiding questions during this: (a) is the Benchmark or GLE assessable, and (b) if it is assessable, can it be effectively developed into questions that provide the response types we determined to be appropriate for music. We then divide the Benchmarks/GLEs into three areas: (a) responding to music (content knowledge, listening, and analysis), (b) musical performance (singing and playing instruments), and (c) musical creativity (composing and improvising).

Step 2: Defining Response Types. The Task Force then reviews the types of responses used in the FCAT (Beech, 2002), and (a) develops musical analogs for these when appropriate, and (b) determines which response types would best be suited for the test phase under development. We developed a set of musical analogs to the structured and open-ended response types used in the FCAT, and determined the response types that best access the skills and knowledge presented in each of the Benchmarks/GLEs of the Sunshine State Standards for Music. Structured response types include:

1. *Short-answer and sentence completion.* Items asking a question that can be answered in a single word or a short sentence are called short-answer items. Items that require students to complete a sentence or fill in a blank are called sentence completion items. By rewording the item, most sentence completion items become short-answer items, and vice versa. Musical applications include (but are not limited to) melodic or rhythmic dictation, and melodic or rhythmic completion.

2. *Selected Response* items consist of a *stem*, often a question or incomplete sentence that introduces the problem. The student selects the response from a set of *options* that follow the stem. Normally, one option is correct, and the remaining options are referred to as *distractors*.

Open-ended response types include:

1. *Essay*: Essay questions use an open-ended response format. Students construct a lengthy response to a question or problem. Essays can be used to assess any skill that can be represented verbally. A musical analog to this type of question is a composition or improvisation, where the student is expected to provide an extended response to a given musical problem.

2. *Performance Assessment*: A performance assessment requires students to produce a product or demonstrate a process, solve a problem involving several steps, or carry out an activity that demonstrates proficiency with a complex skill. For music we defined two specific types of performance: (a) *On-demand Performance*—an unrehearsed performance obtained at the time of the assessment, and (b) *Performance Event*—a rehearsed performance developed over time.

We chose not to pursue portfolio assessment at the state level at this time because of large-scale management issues. The Task Force agreed to encourage portfolio development at the school level, and to consider portfolio assessment at the state level at a later date.

Step 3: Item Specifications. The Task Force members then develop item specifications for the Benchmarks/GLEs selected for large-scale assessment. The specifications are framed to include the following information:

1. The Benchmark/GLE
2. Recommended response type
3. Content/Materials to be covered in the item
4. Procedures/Strategies for implementing the item
5. Recommended scoring procedure
6. Anticipated audio-visual or other equipment

When the Item Specifications are completed, these are presented to the writing team.

Step 4: Writing Teams. Writing teams consist of at least six music educators selected from nominations provided by Task Force members. The criteria for selecting the writers are shown in Figure 2. Because the nominated teachers are active professionally, availability for weekend writing sessions is also a factor in the final selection process. One member is the Task Force liaison.

The writing teams meet three or four times for two-day writing sessions. All writing teams receive item-writing training on the first meeting day before beginning to develop the items. The first two writing events are spent developing the original items, using the item specifications developed by the Task Force as their framework. The third (and fourth, if necessary) writing event is spent revising items based on the Validation Team's comments.

Writers bring State of Florida adopted curriculum materials to each session, and these serve as resources for item content. Writers develop four to eight questions for each Benchmark/GLE included in test phase under development. These items are later divided among the four final forms of the test for piloting and field-testing.

Step 5. Validation Team. A separate team of three to five music educators is appointed by the Task Force to validate the test items. The Validation Team consists of one Task Force liaison, teachers, and supervisors. The selection process and criteria are the same as those for the Writing Team, shown in Figure 2.

The validation team meets for one two-day session to review the content validity of individual items. Because multiple items are developed for each Benchmark/GLE, they also rate the concurrent validity of these items. The Validation team members rate the validity of each item using a Likert-type scale of 1 to 7, with 1 representing "weak validity" and 7 representing "strong validity." In cases where there is interrater disagreement on specific items, the validators include comments that reflect their rationales for their determination. Figure 3 presents the Validation Team Rating Form.

Figure 3. Sample Validation Team Rating Form

VALIDATION TEAM RATING FORM

Instructions: Using the Likert scale below, please rate the content and concurrent validity of the items written for this GLE by circling the number that best coincides with your validation assessment.

GLE MU.C.1.2.2 (1): Explains how use of specific musical elements (for example, rhythm, melody, timbre and expressive devices) is characteristic of music from various world cultures.

Content Validity   1   2   3   4   5   6   7
                      Weak   Strong

Concurrent Validity   1   2   3   4   5   6   7
                      Weak   Strong

Comments on specific items:

Step 6. Item Revisions. Once the Validation Team members complete their review, the Writing Team meets again for two days to revise the items as suggested by the Validation Team. These revised items are then sent to the Task Force members for their review.

Step 7. Task Force Review of Final Items. The Task Force then meets for two days to review all of the validated and revised items. If approved, an item is moved into the Pilot Test Item Bank. If the item requires further revision, the Task Force members may choose to send the items back to the writers, or, in some cases, revise the items at their review meeting.

Once the items are approved for pilot testing, the pilot tests are conducted with a representative sample of students in the target population. Item analyses are completed and reviewed by the Task Force. Based on the Pilot Test results, items are kept, recommended for revision, or deleted. A field test with 10% of the population is the final step of the process. The test development process is summarized in Figure 4.

Phase 3: Implement and Model

The third phase of Pistone's (2002) recommended sequence is to Implement and Model the assessment. She describes the steps in this phase as follows:

1. Build your assessment instrument.
2. Organize and administer your arts assessment.
3. Score student responses and review field test results.
4. Coordinate and administer the assessment district- or state-wide.
5. Analyze test data and report findings.

We have completed item development for the Phase I Middle School and High School tests, and plan to pilot these in the 2007–08 academic year. We have developed, piloted, and field-tested the Elementary Phase I test. Our item bank permitted us to construct four forms of the pilot test, each with twentyitems. All four forms presented five common items and fifteen items unique to that form.

The Pilot test results were examined and the test was revised and expanded for the field test. To improve reliability, the number of items per form was increased from twenty to thirty. The tests were recorded on CD (both the questions and musical examples), and students used a test booklet and answer sheet. Items 1–15 were presented in a test booklet, and items 16–30 were presented on the answer sheet. Items 16–30 were common items on this test. The items were organized in three parts, as follows:

1. Part 1: *Listen, Analyze, and Select.* Students will listen to a musical selection and respond to a question about that selection.
2. Part 2: *Read and Select.* Students respond to written content questions.
3. Part 3: *Symbol identification and Notation Recognition.* Students identify musical symbols and written notation for performed rhythmic and melodic patterns (they hear these patterns twice). These items were common to all four forms of the test.

Lesson Learned: Guidelines for Associations

Any major project requires the cooperation and assistance of many people. I close with a summary of some of the lessons we have learned in the process of developing our assessments as a professional association, and offer some advice to those who might be interested in this process in the future in the form of guidelines for associations.

1. *Strong leadership is essential.* In Florida we are very fortunate to have a strong music educator's association that is led by visionary and competent individuals. Elected association leaders who are committed to the assessment project and a strong executive board are essential to the long-term success of any large-scale assessment.

2. *"It takes a village."* It is wise to capitalize on the strengths of the association membership, seeking members who have expertise in assessment and get them involved. University-based experts, high-performing teachers, top supervisors and administrators, and others are resources that all music educator associations possess.

3. *Stay true to your vision, beliefs, and purposes.* Once your association has developed its vision, beliefs, and purposes, it is important to stay true to them. In Florida we spent eighteen months deliberating these important foundations. We have benefited greatly from this early work over the years of this project, as it has provided a consistent philosophical position and has given us tremendous credibility with our members and our collaborative partners.

4. *Make this a "doable deed."* June Hinckley was a major force behind our work for its first five years, and she always advised us to break this large project down into manageable parts so that it became a "doable deed." Her advice led to the carefully planned sequence we developed for our association-driven model of large-scale assessment development. It is important to keep this in mind as your large-scale assessment becomes large-scale. Managing, delivering, analyzing, and reporting test results for thousands of students is doable when the work is divided and shared appropriately.

5. *Remain flexible in your timeline.* As funding changes, so will your timeline. Professional associations operate on a zero-sum budget, and some years this will mean less financial support is available than others. Expect this until consistent financial support is located and obtained.

6. *Remain responsive to changing political leadership.* State Departments of Education are political entities that serve the public and carry out the policies of the governor, the legislature, and the commissioner. As offices change with elections, policies change to reflect newly elected leadership. In Florida we have remained responsive to these changes and are proactive in our efforts to bring newly elected leaders on board with our ongoing work.

7. *Financial and staff support.* This type of project is expensive for an association. We are fortunate in Florida that we were able to begin the project with a minimal

financial commitment from the association. Through careful advocacy and meetings with Department of Education leaders, we have been able to acquire state grant support for our work. It is important for associations who make the commitment to develop a large-scale assessment to immediately begin seeking grant support for the project. Once adequate funding is acquired, it is important to hire additional office personnel who can be assigned to work on this project either part- or full-time as needed.

8. *Long-term planning.* It is important to periodically reexamine your long-term goals and consider important issues related to the administration and management of large-scale assessments. These plans need to be reviewed by the planning and design committee as well as the entire board. Some of the questions we are deliberating in Florida:

    a. Should the test be voluntary or mandated? In Florida, discussions are that the test will be voluntary with a big "carrot," i.e., schools whose students take the tests and score at a certain level may be eligible for "bonus points" toward the school grade (FLDOE, n.d.a,).
    b. How should a professional association manage testing thousands of students? In Florida, we are considering delivering the test on a three-year rotation. Our plan is to test one-third of the population each year over a period of three years. For example, at the elementary level, this is approximately 65,000 students yearly.
    c. Will test administration be funded by ongoing grants or by a small per-student fee charged to schools that administer the test? We are presently considering charging school districts a small fee per student to cover the costs of the assessment. At the time of this report, there is no final decision on this.

9. *Advocacy takes time.* Pistone (2002) advises that arts assessment developers take time. This has proven true for a number of reasons. First, it takes skill, effort, and time to build and maintain good relationships with stakeholders—including (but not limited to) teachers in the field, district or county testing directors, and Department of Education officials. It is important to keep the lines of communication open, and to communicate positively and consistently with membership and other stakeholders. In Florida we schedule sessions at the annual conference as our primary opportunity for information distribution and updates. Don't stop working to get everyone on the "same page"—just be sure that the page you are on is consistent.

10. *Rumor control is important.* Even when communication is consistent, you can still expect "pushback" from members who are apprehensive about large-scale assessments. These persons can be quite vocal about their feelings. Most often these individuals are operating on rumor instead of fact. Anticipate questions and concerns, and be prepared with positive, accurate information to offset the natural concerns of these individuals. Over time, this strategy has been successful in Florida.

We are pleased with the progress we are making with the Florida Music Assessment. We hope to have all phases of our tests developed, piloted, and field-tested by the 2011–12 academic year. As the project grows, we remain focused on our vision beliefs, and purposes, and maintain complete ownership and management of our tests and the results we obtain.

References

Beech, M. 1997. *Developing Classroom Assessment*. Tallahassee, Florida: Florida State University Center for Performance Technology.

Florida Department of Education (FLDOE) (n.d.a.). *School Grades*. Retrieved January 17, 2007, from http://schoolgrades.fldoe.org/

Florida Department of Education (FLDOE) (n.d.b.). *The Sunshine State Standards*. Retrieved January 16, 2007, from http://www.firn.edu/doe/curric/prek12/index.html

H. Res. 1, 107th Cong, 115 Stat. 1425 2002 (enacted). *Public Law 107–110, No Child Left Behind Act of 2001* (Short Title). [Electronic Version].

National Assessment Governing Board (NAGB). 1994. *The Arts Education Assessment Framework*. Washington, D. C.: Council of Chief State School Officers.

Pistone, N. 2002. *Envisioning arts assessment: A process guide for assessing arts education in school districts and states* [Electronic version]. Washington, D. C.: Arts Education Partnership and Council of Chief State School Officers.

Smith, B. P. 2008. The Development and Implementation of Washington's Classroom-Based Performance Assessments. In T. S. Brophy, ed., *Integrating Curriculum, Theory, and Practice: Proceedings of the 2007 Florida Symposium on Assessment in Music Education*. 153–60. Chicago: GIA Publications.

Swanson, R. K., M. R. Wood, and P. Shepherd. 2008. The Kentucky Music Educators Association (KMEA) and the Kentucky Department of Education (KDE) Music Listening Assessment Pilot Project for Grades 5, 8, and 11. In T. S. Brophy, ed., *Integrating Curriculum, Theory, and Practice: Proceedings of the 2007 Florida Symposium on Assessment in Music Education*. 161–81. Chicago: GIA Publications.

Yap, C. C. andand T. M. Pearsall. 2008. A state-wide web-based music assessment: A collaborative effort. In T. S. Brophy, ed., *Integrating Curriculum, Theory, and Practice: Proceedings of the 2007 Florida Symposium on Assessment in Music Education*. 182–91. Chicago: GIA Publications.

Figure 4. Test Development Process – FMEA's Association-Driven Model

FMEA Assessment Task Force	Develops the initial design, structure, and content for the assessment; aligns the assessment with the standards/benchmarks; determines a possible number of items.
Writing Team	Develops and writes the initial test items.
Content Validation Team	Reviews the initial test items for their validity; accepts, rejects, or requests revision of the initial items, and sends their reviews to the Writing Team.
Writing Team	Reviews the comments of the validation team and accepts or rejects their comments, providing rationale for their decisions; revises the test items and returns these to the Task Force.
FMEA Assessment Task Force	Reviews the revised items—determines if the items adequately cover the initial structure and design of the test. If the test does not meet the initial design, the items will go back to the Writing and Validation teams for additions and revisions.
Pilot	Once the test is determined to be ready, it is piloted for item analysis. A thorough item analysis is conducted, including difficulty level, discrimination indices, point-biserial correlations (r_{pbs}), distractor effectiveness, KR_{20} coefficients.
Pilot Test Analysis	The Task Force reviews the item analysis of the Pilot Test—provides the writers instructions to revise, add, or delete items.
Writing Team	Writers respond to the directives of the Task Force to revise the test according to the Pilot Test results.
Validation Team	Reviews the changes and makes final recommendations to writing team.
Writing Team	Responds to the validators' comments, using the same process as before.
FMEA Assessment Task Force	Review, approval, and recommendation for field testing.
Field Test	Revised test is field tested with approximately 10% of the targeted population.
FMEA Assessment Task Force	Reviews field test statistical analysis, builds final test forms for administration (test construction).

The Development and Implementation of Washington's Classroom-Based Performance Assessments

Bret P. Smith
Central Washington University

Abstract

In 2002, the Office of the Superintendent of Public Instruction (OSPI) in Washington State began a process of developing performance assessment tasks and scoring procedures for music, theater, dance, and visual arts in support of the Essential Academic Learning Requirements. A team of thirty-one people developed items and prompts, piloted in 2003. Under a contract with Riverside Publishing, a second statewide pilot at grades 5, 8, and 10 was conducted, generating 250,000 student samples that were reviewed for the formation of scoring training sets. Anchor responses were selected on a five-point scale (0–4), and were used in multiple in-service training sessions, leading to further revision of items and scoring rubrics. Sixty items are currently available through the OSPI website, with full implementation and reporting targeted for 2009.

Washington State's Office of the Superintendent of Public Instruction (OSPI) has been engaged in a large-scale effort to develop, administer, and collect data from classroom-based performance assessments in the arts (music, dance, theater, and visual arts) since 2002. At present, this project has yielded sixty performance tasks, complete with scoring rubrics and anchor responses, fifteen of these in music (five each at grades 5, 8, and 10—the "benchmarks" as required by state law). This process has involved OSPI employees, in-service teachers, and a test development firm, and was conducted on a statewide basis with representation from urban, suburban, and rural school districts. This process represents one of the most extensive efforts by a state to create an assessment framework that springs from state requirements and is designed to be integrated with classroom instruction. As such, it is important that details of this process of development and implementation be available to those in other regions interested in similar projects. This paper will describe key features of Washington's performance assessment development process, describe some of the items and their scoring, and discuss several issues related to the assessment program.

In 1993, the Washington State Legislature passed House Bill 1209, Washington's Education Reform Act, which included the arts in the areas in which students would have the opportunity to learn to "know and apply...core concepts and principles" (RCW 28A.150.210).

This legislation called for the development of Essential Academic Learning Requirements (EALRs) in these areas, as well as an assessment system that would provide data on student achievement (OSPI, n.d. c).

The Arts EALRs are divided into four areas: 1) the student understands and applies arts knowledge and skills, 2) the student demonstrates thinking skills using artistic processes, 3) the student communicates through the arts, and 4) the student makes connections within and across the arts, to other disciplines of life, cultures, and work. Each of these areas is further elaborated, for example, the second calls for a student to apply creating, performing, and responding processes in the various disciplines (OSPI, n.d. b). The wording and concepts behind the EALRs are based on the framework developed and copyrighted by Shuler (1996) and employed in the 1997 NAEP (see Persky, Sandene, and Askew, 1998); this copyright is acknowledged on OSPI's website.

Following the passage of the federal *No Child Left Behind Elementary and Secondary Education Act* (H. Res. 1, 2002), OSPI designated music, dance, theater, and visual arts as core requirements for all students. An Arts Assessment Leadership Team (AALT) composed of OSPI employees, teachers from all parts of the state and all types of schools, and a parent consultant was formed to develop a total of 60 assessments based on the arts EALRs. In addition, the state contracted with Riverside Publishing Company to assist in the item development and review process. This team, and all assessment work, has been led by AnnRené Joseph, OSPI's Program Supervisor for the Arts (Joseph, 2006).

In early 2003, twelve items were piloted by members of the AALT and reviewed in preparation for a statewide pilot in November 2003. This pilot generated 16,000 samples of student responses that formed the basis for the development of rubrics and scoring training sessions. A second statewide pilot in late 2004 included twenty-six items at the benchmark levels of grades 5, 8, and 10 (music accounted for two items at each level). This pilot generated 250,000 samples, from which Joseph and Riverside Publishing selected 200 samples per item for further range finding, or the establishment of anchors for item scoring. Members of the AALT used these samples to form three training sets, an anchor set, a practice set, and a qualifying set. Each of these contains student samples (on DVD) scored at the 0-, 1-, 2-, 3-, and 4-point levels (Joseph, 2006).

OSPI conducted numerous training sessions in 2005–6 in various parts of the state and the sixty CBPAs were officially released via the OSPI website in February 2006. In March, Joseph and members of the leadership team presented the CBPAs at the National Arts Education Association conference in Chicago. She estimates that the assessment has been presented in 200 districts to approximately 20,000 people (A. Joseph, personal communication).

Future work includes the completion of curriculum frameworks for other grades, the development of reporting guidelines, and program evaluation leading to decisions about the future of the assessment project. In 2007–9 the arts frameworks will become Grade Level Expectations (GLEs). With the 2007–8 school year, high school graduates will be required to complete a full year of study in the arts at Benchmark 3 (10th grade) level. This requirement is significant as state law stipulates that the requirement is non-substitutable and courses must be taught by highly qualified instructors. In 2008–9, schools will be required to implement CBPAs in the arts and the results reported to OSPI.

Examples

To provide an overview of the scope of the music CBPAs, I include the brief descriptions of the five items at the Benchmark 2 (8th grade) level.

1. *All-State All Stars.* Students are asked to perform a sight-singing exercise of four measures of music. Students will be assessed on their understanding of rhythm and steady beat and their ability to perform in the designated key with accurate interval changes, *a cappella.*
2. *Bubble Gum Jingle.* Students are asked to create and perform a jingle, using voice or an instrument, for a brand of bubble gum. Students will be assessed on their understanding of arts concepts, musical form, and arts skills and techniques.
3. *Roller Coaster Fanatic.* Students are asked to create a theme, using voice or an instrument, showing a person's feelings when riding a roller coaster as a theme for a computer game. Students will be assessed on their understanding of notation and arts skills and techniques and their ability to perform their composition.
4. *Music Review.* Students are asked to listen to a musical composition and write a review of the performance. Students will be assessed on their understanding of the elements of music.
5. *Stepping to the Rhythm.* Students are asked to perform a sight-reading exercise of eight measures of music. Students will be assessed on their understanding of rhythm, steady beat, tempo, and dynamics using body percussion (OSPI, n.d. a).

The Bubble Gum Jingle task incorporates elements of musical composition, notation, performance, and the identification and description of musical elements. The item prompt reads as follows:

> *A new brand of bubble gum on the market will help prevent cavities. The bubble gum company is sponsoring a radio show in which students will perform a short jingle about the new gum. Your class has been selected to perform on the radio show. The radio station manager would like each member of your class to write and perform one jingle.*
>
> *The radio station manager requires that you create and perform a jingle that demonstrates an understanding of how tempo, rhythm, dynamics, and timbre relate to the new bubble gum. The radio station manager will give you time to practice before performing the selection. Then you will need to describe your jingle to the radio station manager (OSPI, 2004, p. 41).*

The scoring rubric consists of descriptions of student responses. A four-point response (the highest) in the "creating" area states: "A 4-point response: The student demonstrates a thorough understanding of composition by meeting all four tasks of the task requirements listed below:

1. Uses standard notation, including key and time signature, and correct bar placement;
2. Uses each of the musical elements (tempo, rhythm and dynamics) in the jingle;

3. Creates a jingle with only A and B sections with each section consisting of 4 or 8 measures; and
4. Labels each section of the jingle with the letters A or B.

A three-point response requires achievement of three requirements, a two-point requires two, and so on. Rubrics for the performing and responding components of the task are similar (OSPI, 2004, 50–51). Students are allowed as much time as necessary to complete the task; the suggested timeline requires forty to fifty minutes of class time over four days (OSPI, 2004, pp. 39–40).

An examination of the fifteen available items reveals the several areas of student performance. Grade 5 calls for composing and notating (ABA form, rhythmic rondo), performing on voice or instrument, sight-singing, and listening (to compare and contrast). The eighth-grade items call for sight-singing, composing, performing on voice or instrument, and listening (to critique). The tenth-grade items require composing, notating, performing on voice or instrument, analyzing, sight-reading, and sight-singing. Some tasks at all levels ask students to describe music using appropriate terminology.

Discussion

The development process used in the creation of Washington's Classroom-Based Performance Assessments in the arts appears to conform to that suggested in the Arts Education Partnership and Council of Chief State School Officers' document *Envisioning Arts Assessment* (Pistone, 2002). Items were developed and piloted, revised, and field-tested, and extensive steps have been taken to train evaluators in the scoring process. The assessments are currently voluntary, with schools required to assess and report student achievement in 2008–9. Reading, writing, communication, and mathematics have been required since 1999 as part of the high-stakes Washington Assessment of Student Learning (WASL) process, and various grade levels are currently being developed and introduced.

Any assessment effort will be constrained by matters of time and budget, and the program in Washington is no exception. The current status of the CBPAs represents a significant investment and a substantial achievement; it also raises several questions that can inspire substantive discussions of the aims, usability, and goals of the assessment program. With fifteen items at three grade levels, it seems wise to continue the process of item development and validation with an eye toward creating an item pool containing items of all levels of difficulty that would allow for teachers to select different tasks for pre- and post-test purposes.

A discussion of the items should begin by considering the breadth of skills they require, and the opportunity to learn these skills based on current music teaching in the state of Washington. The four music EALRs preceded the development of the assessments, and the current CBPAs seem to align most strongly with the first three EALRs. EALR number four reads "the student makes connections within and across the arts to other disciplines, life, cultures, and work," and perhaps is the least performance-based of the four. Teachers are expected to address the EALRs in their curriculum and teaching, and with the assessment mandated in two years one can expect teachers to most earnestly address those skills they see emphasized on the tests. If the EALRs do not represent current instructional practices in the state, and in conjunction with the assessment program are intended to expand the scope of music teaching, then it seems that efforts should continue to ensure close alignment between the EALRs and the CBPAs.

As Colwell (1999) noted with regard to the 1997 NAEP, it is instructive to consider the purpose of a test as well as the quality of its items; with regard to the 1997 test, he concluded that "its purpose was not to assess what students knew and could do, but to determine to what extent the voluntary national standards in arts education for music had been implemented and to promote selected instructional objectives." In the case of Washington's CBPAs, various statements on the OSPI website indicate that beyond measuring what students know and are able to do, the music assessments are intended to further the goal of implementing arts instruction as basic education and ensuring instruction will be provide by highly qualified and certified teachers. They also exhibit the desire of state leadership to provide opportunities for staff development through district, regional, and statewide training events. The fact that these tasks are classroom-based also shows a view of assessment as a vehicle for changing curriculum and teaching by its very presence; in this case, the term "classroom-based" seems to refer to the fact that the assessment will be conducted by the teacher in the classroom and is intended to guide instruction, rather than the assessments' being a reflection of current classroom practices.

Whether or not a single assessment can accomplish all these goals is an open question. A predictable difficulty in the face of top-down change is the inertia of tradition, particularly in secondary school music programs where the emphasis has traditionally been on performance of quality music literature in groups. One would doubt, even fifteen years after the publications of the National Standards for Arts Education (Consortium of National Arts Education Associations, 1994), that many ensemble-driven programs in the state devote much time to sequential development of students' compositional skills. An examination of the student examples from grade 10 give an indication of this—an informed guess would be that some of the most detailed and accomplished compositions owed more to the composers' private instrumental study than to typical school instruction. It will be instructive to examine data from the pilot studies and rubric development process—were items rejected as too-difficult based on current practices? When the 0–4 scale was anchored, what was the distribution of responses? In other words, as an instrument for instructional change, it might be hoped that there were more low-scoring responses in the pilots to provide an accurate starting-point and room to grow. Scores can also be difficult to interpret: a student who does not use standard notation in the Bubble Gum jingle would receive the same score as a student who forgets to label the A and B sections: a score of 3.

Data on reliability and validity are not currently available to the public; it is to be hoped that they will be made so. Of particular interest would be inter-rater reliability, especially to document the impact of the scoring training. Ideally, acceptable reliability would be obtainable with minimum expense. If, as is stated in one document, "Teachers will be able to use the items as they are, revise items to tailor the demographic and course needs in their schools, and 'ratcheted [sic] up and/or down' the items at higher and lower grades to give them more options" (Joseph, 2006, p. 2), questions will emerge about validity, and invite caution when interpreting scores from state-wide reporting. At the very least, scores from modified items should be reported separately. Also unclear are plans for modifications to accommodate special learners or non-English-speaking students; the WASL does provide guidance for this in the form of the Washington Alternate Assessment System (WAAS, Riverside Publishing, 2004).

An additional challenge is the imminent graduation requirement: one year of instruction at the Benchmark 3 (grade 10) level. Current band, orchestra, and choir programs may not be equipped to serve students who have not participated in the programs for years, and it seems doubtful that one could expect a fifteen-year-old beginning clarinet player to perform at a defensible sophomore level after a year of instruction. If we are to provide music opportunities in high schools that truly satisfy the spirit of the requirement, it would seem that serious efforts to develop new curriculum and course offerings must be made.

References

Colwell, R. 1999. The 1997 assessment in music: Red flags in the sunset [Electronic version]. *Arts Education Policy Review, 100*(6):33–39.

Consortium of National Arts Education Associations. 1994. *National standards for arts education*. Reston, VA: MENC—The National Association for Music Education.

H. Res. 1, 107th Cong, 115 Stat. 1425 2002 (enacted). *Public Law 107–110, No Child Left Behind Act of 2001* (Short Title). [Electronic Version].

Joseph, A. 2006. Arts assessments for Washington State Classroom-Based Performance Assessments (CBPAs): The journey in progress. Retrieved September 28, 2006, from http://www.k12.wa.us/assessment/WASL/Arts/pubdocs/ ArtsAssessmentsJourney.pdf

OSPI (n.d. a). The arts classroom-based performance assessments (CBPAs): Full and limited training sets and single task items. Retrieved September 26, 2006 from http://www.k12.wa.us/assessment/WASL/Arts/CBPAentireset.aspx

OSPI (n.d. b). The arts—Essential Academic Learning Requirements. Available from http://www.k12.wa.us/curriculumInstruct/Arts/EALRs/EALRs.aspx

OSPI (n.d. c). Implementing arts education and Classroom-Based Performance Assessments in Washington State—OSPI timeline of events. Retrieved September 26, 2006, from www.k12.wa.us/assessment/WASL/ Arts/pubdocs/ArtsEducationTimeline.doc

OSPI 2004. *WCBPA—Washington Classroom-Based Performance Assessment. The arts—music: Exemplar papers*. Retrieved September 26, 2006, from http://www.k12.wa.us/ Assessment/WASL/Arts/CBAs/MusicLimitedPart1.pdf

Persky, H. R., B. A. Sandene, and J. M. Askew. 1998. *The NAEP 1997 arts report card. Washington*, D. C.: U. S. Department of Education, Office of Educational Research and Improvement, National Center for Education Statistics.

Pistone, N. 2002. *Envisioning arts assessment: A process guide for assessing arts education in school districts and states* [Electronic version]. Washington, D. C.: Arts Education Partnership and Council of Chief State School Officers.

Riverside Publishing Company, and C. S. Taylor. 2002. *Washington Assessment of Student Learning: Grade 10 technical report*. Olympia, WA: OSPI. Retrieved September 28, 2006, from http://www.k12.wa.us/assessment/TestAdministration/DataReports.aspx

Riverside Publishing Company. 2004. *Washington Assessment of Student Learning: Washington Alternate Assessment System (WAAS) 2004 technical report*. Retrieved September 30, 2006, from http://www.k12.wa.us/assessment/pubdocs/ Technical%20ReportWAAS2004Final.doc

Shuler, S. C. 1996. Assessment in general music: An overview. The Orff Echo, 28(2):10–12.

Washington State Legislature 1993. Basic education act—Goal. Available online at http://apps.leg.wa.gov/RCW/default.aspx?cite=28A.150.210s

The Kentucky Music Educators Association (KMEA) and the Kentucky Department of Education (KDE) Music Listening Assessment Pilot Project for Grades 5, 8, and 11

Robyn Swanson
Western Kentucky University

Philip Shepherd
Kentucky Department of Education

Melanie Wood
Kentucky Music Educators Association

Abstract

The purpose of the Kentucky Music Education Association (KMEA) and the Kentucky Department of Education (KDE) Music Listening Assessment Project was to design an authentic type of music test in compliance with Commonwealth Accountability Testing System (CATS) regulations, and compare the tests results to existing CATS music test scores for possible inclusion in the statewide tests. From 2002–2006, 1,114 high school, 694 middle school, and 519 elementary school students were administered the pilot music listening exams. The test format included multiple-choice and open-response questions, each with a music listening example. Test results of the pilot study exams for grades 5 and 8, both question formats, and the high-school-level open-response question are in positive correlation with the CATS 2004, 2005, and 2006 music test scores. Additional study will be conducted regarding the test statistics and CATS implementation.

Since 1990, systemic reform has been ongoing with the Kentucky Primary–12 Curriculum-Instruction-Assessment Practices. The Kentucky Education Reform Act of 1990 (KERA), (KRS 158.645) identified Learning Goals with Academic Expectations as the centerpiece for transforming what all Kentucky students should know and be able to demonstrate at high levels of achievement in an ever-changing world (Kentucky Department of Education, 2006d, i).

The arts and humanities, specifically dance, music, drama/theatre, and visual art, were established as core content disciplines in KRS 158.645 (KDE, 2006d, i). All four arts disciplines became part of the high stakes accountability assessment for the benchmark grade levels of 5, 8, and 11 (KDE, 1999). It was administrative regulation that assessment be aligned to the academic expectations specifically for the arts and humanities disciplines (KDE, 1999, 2005c, 2006c). Therefore, Kentucky became a state whereby the arts scores count in each school's overall accountability academic index (score) (KDE, 1999, 2005c, 2006c). Currently, the arts and humanities accountability weight is 4.75% at the elementary level, 7.13% at the middle and high school levels (KDE, 2006a).

Throughout the past sixteen years, revisions have occurred with the original statute (KRS 158.645) and what Kentucky educators use to design curriculum-instruction-assessment. The administrative regulation 704 KAR 3:303 (June, 2006) stated the *Program of Studies for Kentucky Schools Primary–12* is what Kentucky schools will use as a *minimal guideline* for teaching and assessing content disciplines (KDE, 2006d, iii). The Kentucky Department of Education (KDE) released, in August 2006, the Kentucky Core Content for Assessment 4.1 (CCA 4.1) (KDE, 2006c). The core content, which represents Kentucky's Academic Expectations, is a subset of the content standards in the Program of Studies (KDE, 2006c). Beginning in spring 2007, statewide assessment in all content areas, referred to as Commonwealth Accountability Testing System (CATS), will be aligned to the CCA 4.1 version (KDE, 2006c, 2).

The Arts and Humanities music section of the CCA 4.1 is a marginal revision of the 2005 assessment contractor's version CCA 4.0. The format and the content of what will be assessed in the new generation of CCA (4.0–4.1) differ significantly from the 1999 CCA 3.0 (KDE, 2005c, 2006c). The 1999 CCA 3.0 infused what students should know and be able to do in music from the *National Standards for the Arts* (Consortium of National Arts Education Associations, 1994) and was organized in a three-part matrix, labeled performing, creating, and responding. Two content strands, musical elements, and the historical/cultural context of musical styles, were identified as content for statewide assessment. The responding category of content was the only artistic behavior assessed via paper stimulus-paper response on the CATS exams. Performing and creating behaviors were evaluated through multimedia stimulus-paper response and multimedia stimulus-performance response within the instructional settings (KDE, 1999). CCA 4.0 and 4.1, organized by sub-domains, includes the *National Standards for the Arts* (1994), and Webb's (2002) Depths of Knowledge (DOK) (KDE, 2006c, 3–5). These sub-domains are Structures in the Arts, Humanity in the Arts, Purposes for Creating the Arts, and Processes in the Arts for primary through grade 8. At the high school level, another sub-domain, Interrelationships Among the Arts, is added (KDE, 2006c, 3). Currently, the sub-domain of Processes (performing and creating) in the Arts is not included in the CATS exams (KDE, 2006c, 4).

Webb (1997) acknowledged there should be a cognitive match with what is taught and what is assessed. In 2002, Webb defined DOK as a theory, labeling levels of the expected cognitive understanding in relationship to the demands of the assessment (Shepherd and Harmon, 2006, 2). DOK labels 1, 2, and 3 are included with each CCA 4.1 content item (KDE, 2006c).

To date, the CATS Arts and Humanities exams are in twelve different test forms with specific percentages of questions per art form. These are *Dance*: Grade 5, 8, 11: 20%; *Drama/Theatre*: Grade 5, 8, 11: 20%; *Music*: Grade 5: 30%, Grades 8 and 11: 25%; *Visual Art*: Grade 5: 30%, Grades 8 and 11: 25%; and *Literature*: Grades 8 and 11: 10% (KDE, 2004a, 2005a, 2006b). Each CATS test form consists of twelve multiple choice and one open response test items in a paper stimulus-paper response assessment format and are distributed randomly to the students (KDE, 2004a, 2005a, 2006b). (Refer to Appendices A [Grade 5], B [Grade 8] and C [Grade 11] for sample CATS Released Items, KDE, 2004b). The academic performance of Kentucky's students is reported by achievement levels: Novice = 1, Apprentice = 2, Proficient = 3, and Distinguished = 4 (KDE, 2004a, 2005a, 2006b). CATS open-response items are scored by teams of teachers who compare the student's answers to the scoring guide's criteria and a pre-determined example of student's work (anchor set of scores) for each level 0–4, with 4 being the highest score (KDE, 2004a, 2005a, 2006b). The scoring team must reach consensus regarding the score of each test (KDE, 2004a, 2005a, 2006b). The Kentucky accountability weight for a school's arts and humanities (music score) is factored at two-thirds for open-response questions and one-third for multiple-choice questions (KDE, 2006a).

In the fall of 2002, the Kentucky Music Educators Association (KMEA) leadership presented to the Kentucky Department of Education (KDE) Assessment and Accountability Commissioners and its National Technical Advisory Panel on Assessment and Accountability (NTAPAA) a proposal to experiment with authentic types of music assessment item construct, in which students could demonstrate what they know and can do via the artistic behaviors of performing, creating, and responding to music, for possible inclusion in the statewide accountability and assessment system CATS (KDE, 2006a, Swanson, 2003). Brophy (2000), The National Standards in the Arts (1994), and the National Assessment Governing Board (NAGB) (1997) National Assessment of Educational Progress (NAEP), *Arts Education Assessment Framework* (Figure 1, 9), provided the premise for devising authentic performing, creating, and responding to, music assessment. NTAPAA supported the KMEA authentic music assessment proposal (Swanson, 2003). The KDE Assessment Commissioner requested that the KDE Arts and Humanities Curriculum Consultant assist KMEA and its project director, with development of a music assessment pilot study.

Purpose

The purpose of the KMEA and the KDE Music Listening Assessment Project was to design a more authentic type of responding to the music test (multimedia stimulus-paper response) in compliance with Commonwealth Accountability Testing System (CATS) regulations and compare the results of the music listening items to CATS music test scores for possible inclusion in the statewide assessment system (Swanson, 2003).

The KMEA/KDE Music Listening Assessment Pilot Study Project evolved into two phases. The first phase was to design and administer the high-school-level music listening pilot exam aligned to 1999 CCA 3.0 (2002–2004) and re-test the high school music listening multiple-choice questions at the middle school level (2005) (Swanson, 2004, 2006b). During the second phase (2005–2006), the process for constructing music listening items was refined. Music listening test items were developed in alignment with the new CCA 4.0–41 for grades 5 and 8 and the pilot tests were administered to grades 5 and 8 students (Swanson, 2006b).

Item Design Process

Since developing multimedia stimulus-paper response items elicited a revised CATS format, direction was gleaned from listening to music test items that are part of the Education Testing Service (ETS) (2003) *Praxis II Music Content Knowledge Exam*, and the *Highlights of the NAEP 1997 Arts Assessment Report Card* (Office of Educational Research

163

and Improvement, (1998). The process regarding how to design authentic responding to music items in conjunction with the Kentucky music CCA was synthesized from *Critical Thinking in Music: A Trilateral Model* (Brophy, 2000, Fig. 5–3, 235), *The Summary of Steps and Guiding Questions for Developing Standards Based Assessment in Music* (Lindeman, 2003, Fig. 6, 13) and the NAGB (1997), (NAEP) *Arts Education Assessment Framework*.

The fifty Kentucky music educators who served as music listening item writers for the assessment project (grades 5, 8 and 11 levels) were trained in how to develop CATS music items by the KDE Arts and Humanities Consultant (Swanson, 2004, 2006b). A majority had served on the Kentucky Core Content Advisory Committee (CAC) (2003, 2005b). Members of the Kentucky CAC meet annually to design new test items, review, revise, and/or delete released test items for the CATS testing cycle (KDE, 1996). In compliance with CATS regulation, the item writers prepared matrices for each music multiple-choice and open-response test item (question and music listening example) to identify connections with the arts and humanities academic expectations and music content items (KDE, 2003, 2005b). DOK alignment was necessitated for Grade 5 and 8 music listening items (KDE, 2005b). Copyright clearances were obtained so that musical examples could be recorded for pilot test experimentation (Swanson 2004, 2006b).

The music listening item writers unanimously agreed that adding aural stimuli to the question authenticated the paper response assessment. However, developing music listening items required critical analysis of the listening excerpt and reflective thinking. The writers believed developing multiple-choice items with musical examples was more difficult than creating open-response items. The following questions guided the multiple-choice item design process. Does the music content within the musical example match the question? What should be the appropriate length of the excerpt to ensure students? Have adequate time to select the answer? And, could there be more than one plausible answer? The writers developed the test items independently, posted them on the wall of the meeting room, and the committee reviewed each question and its accompanying musical example for item validity (Swanson, 2006b).

After the music listening test items were written, six Kentucky university and college music education professors reviewed each question, selected, and validated the items for the pilot tests (Swanson, 2004, 2006b). The pilot music-listening exams included one form, twelve multiple-choice and one open-response test questions, an answer sheet, and a CD consisting of narrated test directions, all questions, multiple-choice answer responses, and the musical examples (Swanson, 2004, 2006b. Refer to Appendices D–J for Music Listening Assessment Test Items).

Testing, Results and Discussion, Phase 1

The KMEA project director prepared and presented the technical report for the design of the high-school-level music listening test items and pilot test data to NTAPAA and KDE in September 2004 (Swanson, 2004). The music listening pilot assessments were administered to 1,114 Kentucky high school students from twenty-five schools representing diverse demographics and geographic locations from January through March, 2004. The open-response music listening item (sample) score mean was 2.2 (Swanson, 2004. Refer to Appendix J for the High-School-Level Open-Response Question). The 2004 CATS music open response score mean was 1.9 (KDE, 2004a). NTAPAA and KDE viewed the open-response music listening data as positive (Swanson, 2006a). The high-school-level multiple-choice music listening item (sample) score mean was 0.87 (Swanson, 2004). The 2004 CATS music multiple-choice items score mean was 0.60 (KDE, 2004a). NTAPPA recommended that the high school items be tested at the eighth-grade level and the project should be expanded to include music listening items for Grade 5 and Grade 8 (Swanson, 2006a).

In November of 2005, 948 students from four demographically diverse middle schools were administered the 2004 high-school-level multiple-choice music listening assessment questions. The music listening multiple-choice questions (sample) score mean was 0.76, compared to the 2005 CATS score mean of 0.63 and the 2006c ATS score mean of 0.59 (KDE, 2005a, 2006b, Swanson, 2006b). Item analyses infer the questions align with the eighth-grade core content more congruently than the Grade 11 core content (Swanson, 2006b).

Testing, Results and Discussion, Phase 2

Throughout 2005–2006, KDE has been restructuring the music content, defining DOK levels of assessment (2005–2006), and experimenting with technology generated CATS tests (KDE, 2006b, 2006c). All facets of the Grades 5 and 8 music listening assessment pilot project reflect experimentation with those changes (Swanson, 2006b).

Based on previous CATS statistics, demographics and geographic locations, in 2005, the KDE Office of Accountability and Assessment selected ten Grade 5 and ten Grade 8 schools as pilot music listening assessment sites (Swanson, 2006b). The music listening pilot exams were administered in May 2006, approximately two weeks after the 2006 Music CATS testing, by trained test administrators (Swanson, 2006b).

Ten elementary schools, (519) students, were involved in the music listening pilot study. The sample open response score mean was 1.94 (Refer to Table 1, Swanson, 2006b). The 2005 state music open response score mean was 1.9 and the 2006 state score mean was 1.8 (KDE, 2005a, 2006b). The sample score mean is in positive correlation with the 2005 and 2006 state score means. It can be concluded that the pilot study Grade 5 music listening open response item is a viable statewide measurement tool for music content. (Refer to Appendices E for Grade 5: Music Listening Test Open-Response Item, and F for Item Analysis).

Table 1. Grade 5 Music Listening Open Response Question Data (N = 519)

School	N	M	4	3	2	1	0
1	62	1.6	1	9	27	15	10
2	56	1.9	0	18	20	10	8
3	54	1.6	1	4	26	19	4
4	32	1.6	3	2	12	10	5
5	54	2.2	4	16	27	3	4
6	59	2.4	3	28	23	2	3
7	77	1.7	6	8	27	29	7
8	67	1.9	7	10	25	17	8
9	32	2.5	2	14	15	0	1
10	26	2.0	0	7	15	2	2
Total M		**1.94**					

The multiple-choice portion of the exam consisted of twelve multiple-choice questions. The 2005 CATS music multiple-choice score mean was 0.70 and the 2006c ATS score mean was 0.68 (KDE, 2005a, 2006b). The sample score mean was 0.51 (Refer to Table 2, Swanson, 2006b).

Table 2. Grade 5 Music Listening Multiple-Choice Question Data (N = 519)

Sites	N	M	1	2	3	4	5	6	7	8	9	10	11	12
1	62	0.41	34	15	16	60	32	31	21	40	9	5	20	21
2	56	0.57	37	21	26	53	44	48	26	39	26	2	17	40
3	54	0.46	29	3	14	34	28	22	16	29	11	8	18	29
4	32	0.38	14	1	4	30	10	15	20	20	8	1	14	11
5	54	0.5	27	32	34	6	20	26	25	29	41	44	34	5
6	59	0.67	42	52	29	58	55	44	43	35	19	9	40	50
7	77	0.59	55	26	27	75	51	48	38	31	36	28	39	57
8	67	0.53	38	18	32	61	37	47	32	46	22	19	28	40
9	32	0.52	28	13	18	25	18	15	13	14	5	5	15	29
10	26	0.47	16	11	11	26	19	13	13	13	4	4	4	15
Total M		0.51	0.62	0.37	0.41	0.88	0.61	0.60	0.48	0.57	0.35	0.29	0.44	0.57

After critical review of the twelve multiple-choice test items in relationship to the CCA 4.1, music terminology in items 1, 3, and 10 is not included in CCA 4.1. Test item 2 refers to terminology in CCA 4.1 but those terms have not been included on previous CATS music tests. If questions 1, 2, 3, and 10 were deleted, the overall sample mean would in all probability correlate at a higher level to the 2005 and 2006c ATS multiple-choice means (Swanson, 2006b). The DOK level on the multiple-choice music listening items ranged from simple term identification, DOK 1, to analysis of the excerpt, DOK 2, to analysis-synthesis of the function of music elements within historical periods/cultures, DOK 3(Shepherd and Harmon, 2006). (Refer to Appendix D for Grade 5: Music Listening Test Sample Multiple-Choice Items).

Six middle schools, 694 students, were involved in the music listening pilot study. Due to end of the year time constraints, only six of the ten middle schools could participate, and in school 1, only band and orchestra students were tested (Swanson, 2006b).

The music listening open-response scores ranged from 1.7–2.4. The overall sample score mean was 1.9 (Refer to Table 3, Swanson, 2006b). The 2005 CATS Grade 8 music open response score mean was 1.7 and the 2006c ATS score mean was 1.9 (KDE, 2005a, 2006b). The sample mean in correlation to the 2005 and 2006 state mean is positive. It can be concluded that the Grade 8 music listening open-response item is a viable statewide measurement tool for music (Swanson, 2006b). (Refer to Appendices H for the Grade 8: Music Listening Test Open Response Item and I for Item Analysis).

Table 3. Grade 8 Music Listening Open Response Question Data (N = 694)

School	N	M	4	3	2	1	0
1	70	2.4	2	30	34	4	0
2	37	1.7	0	8	14	11	4
3	51	1.9	0	7	34	7	3
4	139	1.7	1	16	70	43	9
5	164	2.1	5	42	82	32	3
6	233	1.8	5	38	114	48	28
Total M		1.9					

The multiple-choice portion of the exam consisted of twelve multiple-choice questions. The 2005 CATS music multiple-choice score mean was 0.63 and the 2006c ATS score mean was 0.59 (KDE, 2005a, 2006b). The sample mean was 0.67 (Refer to Table 4, Swanson, 2006b).

Table 4. Grade 8 Music Listening Multiple Choice Question Data (N = 694)

School	N	M	1	2	3	4	5	6	7	8	9	10	11	12
1	70	0.76	57	59	57	58	46	23	57	60	57	55	59	56
2	37	0.64	12	30	25	30	23	14	12	27	28	30	27	28
3	51	0.61	27	35	36	41	24	14	21	41	33	31	38	36
4	139	0.62	62	109	95	85	80	30	66	101	102	105	103	101
5	164	0.76	104	142	132	105	130	110	133	123	99	142	157	121
6	233	0.61	178	148	123	142	138	85	97	176	147	181	163	139
Total M		0.67	0.63	0.75	0.67	0.66	0.64	0.4	0.56	0.76	0.67	0.78	0.79	0.69

By analyzing the twelve multiple-choice exam responses, questions 6 and 7 yielded the highest number of incorrect answers. The music terminology in item 6 is in the CCA 4.1, but the answer required a high level of aural discrimination and synthesis of music knowledge. Question 7 included Italian tempo terms that are in the CCA 4.1 (Swanson, 2006b). (Refer to Appendix G Grade 8: Music Listening Test Sample Multiple-Choice Items).

Grade 8 Music Test Preference Survey

As an added dimension to the Grade 8 music listening assessment, the 694 students were surveyed about which music-testing format they preferred, the music listening format or the traditional CATS pencil-paper format. Survey results report 92% (641) selected the music listening version and 8% (53) selected the traditional CATS format (Swanson, 2006b).

Future Directions

This type of music listening exam could easily be administered via computer. Because the music and narration of test items are on a CD, the test format could be technology-designed as user-friendly, whereby the students could touch the screen for their answer selection. Such a computer-generated music listening format would allow students opportunity to go back and individually listen to an item. Currently the exam is administered to an entire group at one time and the questions and musical example are heard only once.

Conclusion

From 2002–2006, 3,275 Kentucky students were administered the music listening pilot exams. Over three-hundred Kentucky music educators served as members of the project's task force, item writing and scoring committees, item validation teams, test administrators and pilot site coordinators (Swanson, 2004, 2006b).

In summation, music listening is an effective mode to test the CCA 4.1 and would authenticate the traditional pencil-paper test formats. The scope and depth of the KMEA/KDE Music Listening Assessment Project typifies a partnership that is committed to advance the cause of music education across the Commonwealth of Kentucky.

Efforts are underway by KDE with the assistance of their Arts and Humanities Task Force (personal communication, September 21, 2006) to build an accountability system for all the art forms (dance, drama/theatre, music, visual art) that would include the other two authentic assessment domains, creating and performing in the arts. Such progress in developing a more authentic Kentucky assessment system for music is a direct outcome of the KMEA 2002 proposal.

References

Brophy, T. S. 2000. *Assessing the developing child musician: A guide for general music teachers.* Chicago: GIA Publications, Inc.

Consortium of National Arts Education Associations. 1994. *National standards for arts education: What every child should know and be able to do in the arts.* Reston, VA: MENC—The National Association for Music Education.

Education Testing Service (ETS). 2003. The music content knowledge test. In *The Praxis series: Music study guide—Concepts and processes, analysis, and content knowledge,* 17–75. Princeton: Author.

Kentucky Department of Education. 1996. *Kentucky Department of Education advisory groups.* Retrieved August 30, 2006 from http://www.education.ky.gov/KDE/Administrative+Resources/Testing+and+Reporting+/CATS/Advisory+Groups/default.htm?IMAGE=Search

Kentucky Department of Education. 1999. *Kentucky core content for assessment, CCA version 3.0.* Retrieved September 26, 2006 from http://www.education.ky.gov/cgi-bin/MsmFind.exe?QUERY=core+contentandImage=Search

Kentucky Department of Education. 2003. *Core content advisory committee item development training for the Kentucky core content test CCA 3.0.* Unpublished manuscript.

Kentucky Department of Education. 2004a. *Commonwealth Accountability Testing System (CATS) 2004 test scores.* Retrieved August 4, 2006 from http://www.education.ky.gov/KDE/Administrative+Resources/Testing+and+Reporting+/default.htm

Kentucky Department of Education. 2004b. *2004 Released test items.* Retrieved August 4, 2006 from http://www.education.ky.gov/KDE/Instructional+Resources/Curriculum+Documents+and+Resources/ Released+Test+Items/default.htm

Kentucky Department of Education. 2005a. *Commonwealth Accountability Testing System (CATS) 2005 test scores.* Retrieved August 4, 2006 from http://www.education.ky.gov/KDE/Administrative+Resources/Testing+and+Reporting+/default.htm

Kentucky Department of Education. 2005b. *Kentucky core content advisory committee (CAC) item development training for the Kentucky core content test 4.0 (contractor's version).* Unpublished manuscript.

Kentucky Department of Education. 2005c. *Kentucky core content for assessment, CCA version 4.0 (contractor's version).* Retrieved September 26, 2006 from http://www.education.ky.gov/cgi-bin/MsmFind.exe?QUERY=core+contentandImage=Search

Kentucky Department of Education. 2006a. *Accountability weights for the CATS 2007 test.* Retrieved September, 27, 2006 from: http://www.education.ky.gov/KDE/Administrative+Resources/Testing+and+Reporting+/CATS/Accountability+System/Blueprint+for+Kentucky+Core+Content+Test.htm?SUBMIT=Search

Kentucky Department of Education. 2006b. *Commonwealth Accountability Testing System (CATS) 2006 Test score media release.* Retrieved September 21, 2006 from http://apps.kde.state.ky.us/secure_cats_reports_06/index.cfm

Kentucky Department of Education. 2006c. *Kentucky core content for assessment, CCA version, 4.1.* Retrieved September 26, 2006 from http://www.education.ky.gov/cgibin/MsmFind.exe?QUERY=core+contentandImage=Search

Kentucky Department of Education. 2006d. *Kentucky program of studies*. Retrieved September 26, 2006 from http://www.education.ky.gov/KDE/Instructional+Resources/Curriculum+Documents+and+Resources/Program+of+Studies/default.htm

Kentucky Music Educators Association (KMEA). 2006a. *KMEA music listening pilot assessment exam, Grade 5*. Unpublished manuscript.

Kentucky Music Educators Association. 2006b. *KMEA music listening pilot assessment exam, Grade 8*. Unpublished manuscript.

Lindeman, C.A. Ed.. 2003. *Benchmarks in action: A guide to standards-based assessment in music*. Reston, VA: MENC—The National Association for Music Education.

National Assessment Governing Board. 1997. *NAEP arts education assessment framework*. Washington, D. C.: Author.

Office of Educational Research and Improvement. 1998. *Arts education: Highlights of the NAEP 1997 arts report card*. Washington, D. C.: National Center for Education Statistics (NCES).

Shepherd, P. and J. Harmon. 2006. *Support materials for Kentucky core content for arts and humanities assessment CCA Version 4.0*. Unpublished manuscript.

Swanson, R. K. 2003. Music listening assessment update. *Bluegrass Music News, 55*(2):29.

Swanson, R. K. 2004, September. *KMEA high school music listening assessment pilot study report for the National Technical Advisory Panel on Assessment and Accountability (NTAPAA) and the Kentucky Department of Education (KDE)*. Paper presented at the quarterly meeting of NTAPAA and KDE, Frankfort, KY.

Swanson, R. K. 2006a. Music assessment update. *Bluegrass Music News, 57*(4):43.

Swanson, R. K. 2006b. *KMEA music listening assessment, grade 5 and 8 pilot study report to the National Technical Advisory Panel on Assessment and Accountability (NTAPAA) and the Kentucky Department of Education (KDE)*. Manuscript in progress.

Webb, N. L. 1997. *Criteria for alignment of expectations and assessments in mathematics and science education*. [Monograph No. 6)]. Washington, D. C.: Council of Chief State School Officers.

Appendix A

2004 Sample Released CATS Items: Grade 5

Music Multiple-Choice Question: Grade 5

Use the music below to answer question 1.

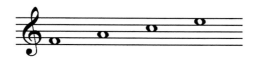

1. The notes in the spaces of the treble clef music staff shown above from bottom to top are
    ☐ FACE
    ☐ FGAB
    ☐ CAGE
    ☐ EGBD

(KDE, 2004b, Arts and Humanities, Grade 5, 30)

Music Open-Response Question: Grade 5

Instrument Families

5. Instruments make different sounds and are grouped together into families based on how these sounds are produced. The four instrument families are strings, woodwinds, brass, and percussion.

    a. Name TWO of the families of instruments and identify ONE instrument from EACH family.

    b. Explain how sound is produced by EACH of the two instruments.

(KDE, 2004b, Arts and Humanities, Grade 5, 32)
For additional test item data analyses and annotated scoring guides refer to Grade 5 Released Items go to):
http://www.education.ky.gov/KDE/ Instructional+Resources/Curriculum+Documents+and+Resources/
Released+Test+Items/default.htm

Appendix B

2004 Sample Released CATS Items: Grade 8

Music Multiple-Choice Question: Grade 8

1. Which instrument belongs in the woodwind family?
   - ☐ trumpet
   - ☐ clarinet
   - ☐ cello
   - ☐ xylophone

(KDE, 2004b, Arts and Humanities, Grade 8, 26)

Music Open Response Question: Grade 8

New Musical Instruments

Imagine that you have designed a new musical instrument that is capable of producing delicate, high pitches.

a. Explain how the instrument works (produces sounds).

b. Explain how it would be used in a musical ensemble or performing group.

c. Tell what existing instrument influenced your design.

(KDE, 2004b, Arts and Humanities, Grade 8, 76)
For additional test item data analyses and annotated scoring guides refer to Grade 8 Released Items go to:
http://www.education.ky.gov/KDE/Instructional+Resources/Curriculum+Documents+and+Resources/Released+Test+Items/default.htm

Appendix C

2004 Sample Released CATS Items: Grade 11

Music Multiple Choice Question: Grade 11

1. The Renaissance period was an important period in music history. The term <u>Renaissance</u> means:
   ☐ recovery
   ☐ rebirth
   ☐ illumination
   ☐ exploration

(KDE, 2004b, Arts and Humanities, Grade 11, 42)

Music Open Response Question: Grade 11

Time Machine to the 60s

You are able to travel through time via a time machine. You choose to travel to the decade of the 1960s because you have a report due for your humanities class. Since your report is about music of that decade, you visit several years during the 1960s to listen to music of that period.

a. Describe TWO ways that the issues and/or events of the 1960s (for example, the Civil Rights movement, the Vietnam War) affected the music of that time period.

b. Describe TWO effects that music had on social change and/or people's beliefs in the 1960s.

(KDE, 2004b, Arts and Humanities, Grade 11, 44)
For additional test item data analyses and annotated scoring guides refer to Grade 11 Released Items go to:
http://www.education.ky.gov/KDE/Instructional+Resources/Curriculum+Documents+and+Resources/Released+Test+Items/default.htm

Grade 5: Music Listening Test Sample Multiple Choice Items

All directions and test questions on the Grade 5 Music Listening Exam are narrated on a CD. Students receive the test questions and an answer booklet. The testing time for twelve multiple-choice questions is fifteen minutes and thirty minutes is allowed for the open-response question. The actual test question number is provided.

Example of the Testing Directions

- Read the question.
- Listen to the musical example.
- Select only one answer per question.

Selected Listening Examples: Multiple Choice Grade 5

Question No. 2

The form of the following musical examples is:

A. call-and-response
B. round
C. two-part (AB)
D. three-part (ABA)

Aligns to 4.1 CCA, DOK 2
Musical Example: Round: *Make New Friends* (Traditional Song) (B)
Item Statistic: M = 0.37

Question No. 12

Choose the dynamics which you hear in the musical example.

A. *forte (f)*
B. *forte (f), piano (p)*
C. *piano (p)*
D. *piano (p), forte (f)*

Aligns to CCA, DOK 1
Musical Example: Theme from the Surprise Symphony by Franz Joseph Haydn (D)
Item Statistic: M = 0.57   CATS 2005 MC M = 0.70   CATS 2006 MC M = 0.68   Pilot MC M = 0.51
(Swanson, 2006b)

Appendix E

Grade 5: Music Listening Test Open Response Item

Open Response Question

Title: *Music in a Ballet*

Prompt: Composers use instruments to represent characters in a ballet.

Instructions: Listen to the following example.

Answer: A. Identify the musical instruments you hear which represents the characters.
                 B. Identify the instrument's family.
                 C. Tell how the instrument's timbre or sound describes the character.

Aligns to 4.1 CCA, DOK 3
Musical Example: *Dance of the Sugarplum Fairy* by Pyotr Tchaikovsky
Statistics: CATS 2005 OR M = 1.9   CATS 2006 M = 1.8   Pilot OR M = 1.94

Scoring Guide

SCORE	DESCRIPTION
4	Student names three instruments and identifies their family of instruments. Student appropriately explains with detail how the instrument's timbre or tone color describes the selected characters for each instrument.
3	Student names two instruments and identifies their family of instruments. Student generally describes how the instrument's timbre or tone color describes the selected characters for each instrument.
2	Student names two instruments and identifies their family of instruments. Student provides a limited explanation of how the instrument's timbre or tone color describes the selected characters for each instrument.
1	Student demonstrates a minimal understanding of the instruments and their families and describes irrelevant characters.
0	Student's response is totally incorrect or irrelevant.

(Swanson, 2006b)

Grade 5: Music Listening Test Open-Response Item Analysis

The open response question, a DOK 3 level, aligned with the CCA 4.1, asked students to identify tone colors (timbre) of instruments, match the tone colors heard with the respective families of orchestral instruments, and how the sound of the instrument's tone color describes character(s) in a ballet. The open-response scoring guide for the question outlines qualitative descriptions for expected levels of written response with 4 as the highest score to 0, no or minimal response (Kentucky Music Education Association, 2006a, 2006b; Shepherd and Harmon, 2006). The music example used for the test question for students in seven of the ten schools (schools 1, 2, 3, 4, 7, 8, and 9) was *Dance of the Flutes* from the ballet, *The Nutcracker Suite,* by Peter Tchaikovsky. The scores ranged from 1.6–2.5 (Refer to Table 1). Students in the other three schools (schools 5, 6, and 10) were tested using the same question but with the *Dance of the Sugarplum Fairy* from *The Nutcracker* Suite by Tchaikovsky. The scores ranged form 2.2–2.4 (Refer to Table 1). According to the scoring team's comments regarding student's answers, the instrumental tone colors in the *Dance of the Sugarplum Fairy* excerpt was more appropriate for describing details about the characters in a ballet and allowed students more opportunity to demonstrate a higher level of creative thought than with the other musical example (Swanson, 2006b). Since the test item does implicate dance and drama/theatre content, item writers in those content areas may benefit by studying its construct and the student's answers.

(Swanson, 2006b)

Grade 8: Music Listening Test Sample Multiple Choice Items

All directions and test questions on the Grade 8 Music Listening Exam are narrated on a CD. Students receive the test questions and an answer booklet. The testing time for twelve multiple-choice questions is fifteen minutes and thirty minutes is allowed for the open-response question. The original pilot test question number is provided. (Refer to Table 4 for item analysis).

Example of the Testing Directions

- Read the question.
- Listen to the musical example.
- Select only one answer per question.

Selected Listening Examples: Multiple Choice Grade 8

Question No. 1

The dynamic level best illustrated by this musical example is:

A. *pp pianissimo*
B. *mf mezzo forte*
C. *mp mezzo piano*
D. *ff fortissimo*

Aligns to 4.1 CCA, DOK 2
Musical Example: *O Fortuna* from *Carmina Burana* by Carl Orff (D)
Item Statistic: M = 0.63

Question No. 7

The tempo that best describes this music is:

A. *Adagio*
B. *Allegro*
C. *Moderato*
D. *Presto*

Aligns to 4.1 CCA, DOK 2
Musical Example: *Adagio for Strings* by Samuel Barber (A)
Item Statistic: M = 0.56   CATS 2005 MC M = 0.63   CATS 2006 MC M = 0.59   Pilot MC M = 0.67
(Swanson, 2006b)

Grade 8: Music Listening Test Open-Response Item

Open-Response Question

Title: *Music is Stylin'*

Prompt: Music is all around us, created for different purposes.

Instructions: Listen to the following musical example.

Musical Example *It Don't Mean A Thing If You Don't Have That Swing* by Duke Ellington

Answer:
    A. Identify the style of music from the listening example.
    B. List 3 instruments you hear that are common to this style.
    C. For what purpose do you think this music was written? Explain your answer.

Scoring Guide

SCORE	DESCRIPTION
3	Student correctly identifies style, three instruments used and one purpose. Student included in depth and insightful discussion.
3	Student correctly identifies style, two instruments used and one purpose. Student included an adequate description of the purpose.
2	Student correctly identifies style, one or two instruments, or one purpose. Student demonstrated a limited understanding of the purpose.
1	Student demonstrates a minimal understanding of the question or the prompt.
0	Student's response is totally incorrect or irrelevant.

(Swanson, 2006b)

Grade 8: Music Listening Test Open-Response Item Analysis

The music listening open-response question aligns to CCA 4.1, a DOK 3 level, and asked students to identify the style of music within the musical excerpt, list three instruments that are common to this specific style of music, and describe the purpose why this music was created. The listening example was: *It Don't Mean A Thing If You Don't Have That Swing* by Duke Ellington. The scoring guide outlined expected qualitative descriptions for all three parts of the question, ranging from a 4, complete, relevant answers, to a minimal or 0, no response (Kentucky Music Education Association, 2006a, 2006b). Unlike the grade 5 open response question, all Grade 8 students listened to the same musical example. The scoring team reported 540 students provided partial (level 2), some (level 1), or no (level 0) relevant descriptions about what they heard in the musical example. The other 154 students answered all parts of the question. Thirteen (13) of the 154 students scored a 4 and provided appropriate responses that illustrated a high level of critical and creative thought.

(Swanson, 2006b)

2004 High School Music Listening Test Open-Response Question

Performance Ensembles

Prompt: Music composers create differences in timbres by using different types of performing ensembles to perform their music.

Instructions: A. Listen to the two listening examples.
                       B. Describe the differences in timbre between the two examples.
                       C. Describe how the differences in timbre define the performing ensemble in each example.

Musical Examples   *Ode to Joy* (German text) from the *Ninth Symphony* by Ludwig Van Beethoven

                             String Quartet in D (The Lark) by Franz Joseph Haydn

Scoring Guide

SCORE	DESCRIPTION
4	The student compares the differences in timbre in the two music examples providing in depth and insightful details in the comparison. The student completely and accurately describes how the differences in timbre and the use of musical instruments/voices define the performance ensemble.
3	The student compares the differences in timbre in the two music examples providing adequate details in the comparison. The student describes how the differences in timbre and the use of musical instruments/voices define the performance ensemble but may be incomplete or include some incorrect information in the description.
0	The student compares the differences in timbre in the two music examples providing little or no supporting details in the comparison. The student provides a minimal description of how the differences in timbre and the use of musical instruments/voices define the performance ensemble and is incomplete and /or includes incorrect information in the description.
1	The student compares the differences in timbre in the two music examples providing no details to support the comparison. The student is unable to provide a relevant description of how the differences in timbre and the use of musical instruments/voices define the performance ensemble.
0	The student is unable to address any part of the directions in a relevant manner.

2004 CATS M = 1.9   Sample M = 1.9
(Swanson, 2004)

A Statewide Web-Based Music Assessment: A Collaborative Effort

Ching Ching Yap
Tara Pearsall
University of South Carolina

Abstract

The development of the statewidestatewide music assessment was a collaborative effort among the state department of education, the college of education at the state university, and local music educators. The collaboration utilized a bottom-up approach that included extensive involvement of music educators at each state of development. To date, that assessment has completed two years of field-testing and is in the third year of implementation at several schools throughout the state in conjunction with a state arts grant. All assessment items and the assessment framework were developed by trained music educators and included both multiple-choice and performance tasks. Throughout the development, music educators provided constant feedback regarding implementation process and recommendation for modification. Using this bottom-up approach, this assessment was able to achieve high teacher buy-in and hence, produce a successful statewidestatewide music assessment that has the potential to increase student achievement and unify instructional objective throughout the state.

To address the state Education Accountability Act in 2000, the state department of education and the educational oversight committee developed an arts indicator for the school report card designed to reflect each school's overall performance with regard to providing opportunities to learn in the arts. Because that indicator addresses only arts opportunities, the policy makers, assessment consultants, and arts educators involved in its development see the indicator as a temporary solution. The present lack of an arts assessment deemphasizes the value of the arts curriculum standards and allows implementation of instructional objectives that may not be aligned to those standards. Without a valid and reliable assessment tool, arts instruction suffers because arts educators do not have a tool to assess their students' level of achievement in relation to the arts curriculum standards and administrators do not have the information to address the educational needs of their students. To accomplish the challenging task of developing a statewidestatewide arts assessment, a collaboration effort was launched among the state department of education personnel, assessment and measurement specialists, and most importantly, arts educators. The focus of this paper is to describe the development and implementation of the music portion of the 4th-grade statewide arts assessment. Because the assessment is a secured state test, specific information regarding test items is not included in the description.

First Field Test: The Beginning

In Year One, the arts assessment collaborators began development of music and visual arts assessment for statewide use at the elementary level. Initially, the collaborators focused the assessment on 4th-grade students because most schools in the state included music and visual arts instruction in 4th-grade curricula. The first step in developing the statewide arts assessment was to convene a meeting among collaborators that included experienced arts educators with training in assessment, music faculty members from a university, and an assessment specialist. The objectives of this meeting were to determine the assessment format and select content and achievement standards appropriate for large-scale assessment from the state's visual and performing arts curriculum standards, which closely corresponded to the *National Standards for Arts Education* (Consortium of National Arts Education Associations, 1994). As a result of the meeting, the participants decided to design an assessment that included both multiple-choice test items and performance tasks. In addition, the collaborators formed a Music Advisory Committee that consisted of a select group of practicing elementary music educators with arts assessment training to oversee the development of the assessment and provide continuous content area guidance to a team of assessment specialists at a university. The Music Advisory Committee then finalized a table of specifications[1] for the assessment that outlines the percentages of items to be developed for each standard.

Once the format was determined and the table of specifications developed, the assessment specialists convened an item writing session to develop multiple-choice and performance task items. In addition, state department of education offered a professional development course to train additional item writers in assessment. For the multiple-choice portion, the item writers developed sufficient items to compile three parallel paper-and-pencil music multiple-choice test forms, each with forty items. Items were digitally stored on a website to build an item bank. Each multiple-choice test item was associated with a standard and a Bloom's Taxonomy Level and adhered to the item writing guidelines suggested by Kuh, Johnson, Agruso, and Monrad (2001). All items were then reviewed by a panel from the Music Advisory Committee for standards alignment and adherence to item-writing guidelines.

The item writers also developed two performance tasks: a singing task that required students to sing a familiar melody on a neutral syllable and a rhythm task that required students to improvise a rhythm pattern in a given meter. The multiple-choice test forms included a CD with music examples as interpretative materials for specific items and the performance tasks included a performance task CD and booklet to standardize administration.

The assessment was administered to approximately 1,853 students at twelve schools that were involved in arts reform projects. Classes were randomly assigned to test forms and fifty randomly selected students from each school completed the music performance tasks. Test administrators were trained in the assessment administration procedures, especially in the recording of student performance tasks. After test administration was completed, the test administrators completed a feedback form regarding their experiences with the test

---

[1] The table of specifications for the music assessment is available in the technical documentations of the assessment on the website http://scaap.ed.sc.edu/documents.asp.

administration process; that feedback was used to inform the subsequent year's test administration.

Students' multiple-choice answers were recorded on answer sheets and electronically scored. The assessment specialists conducted statistical analyses including Differential Item Functioning (DIF) analysis using classical test theory to evaluate the quality of the assessment and of individual test items. Reliability indices of the music multiple-choice test forms ranged between 0.58 to 0.71. Students' performance tasks were recorded using a tape recorder, digitized by the assessment specialists, and rated by trained raters.

Prior to rating the performance tasks, a validation committee was formed and student performances were benchmarked based on holistic rubrics developed by the validation committee members. A group of music educators were then trained using the benchmarked performances to rate the items at a central location and completed the rating over three days. Those music educators were either graduates from the annual Arts Assessment Institute, a professional development course sponsored by the State Department of Education, or had experiences with assessment and rating of performance tasks. The interrater reliability indices for two raters, calculated using generalizability theory, ranged between 0.82 and 0.93.

Second Field Test

In Year Two, the assessment specialists conducted an item review session with the Music Advisory Committee to revise or remove multiple-choice items based on the item statistics from the first year's field test that did not meet the rigorous standards for large-scale assessments. Then, with assistance of the committee, the assessment specialists compiled two paper-and-pencil music multiple-choice test forms with forty-five instead of forty items to increase the reliability. In addition to selecting the items, the assessment team also produced music prompts and music performance tasks instructions using music and recording software. The music assessments including the performance tasks were administered to approximately 710 4th-grade students at ten of the elementary schools that participated in the first year's field test.

To simplify the time-consuming task of digitizing and preparing the performance recordings for rating, and to minimize the difficulties associated with playing interpretive material for the multiple-choice test forms, the state department of education initiated the development of a web-based assessment prototype. The web-design process was a collaborative effort among the state department of education, the assessment specialists, and a university web-designer. The assessment specialist pilot-tested the web-based assessment prototypes at one of the ten participating schools during Year Two. The assessment specialist observed and partially administered the assessment to evaluate the feasibility of implementing a statewide web-based music assessment.

To begin the process of using advanced technology and transitioning to a web-based assessment, the second field test also required the test administrators to record student performances on their computers, burn the recorded performances onto a CD, and send them to the assessment specialist to be prepared for subsequent rating. The schools that did not have a CD burner, however, continued using the tape recorder for the performance tasks. At the test administrator training session, the assessment specialists demonstrated using the technology and provided the test administrators with instructions on how to use the computer for recording student performances.

Similar to first year, multiple-choice answer sheets were scored electronically and performance recordings were rated by trained raters after a validation session that benchmarked student performances for that year using the holistic rubrics developed in the previous year. Although the interrater reliability was high using the holistic rubrics, the Music Advisory Committee felt that additional information could be obtained by using analytic rubrics. Analytic rubrics can provide detailed feedback to music educators regarding student achievement based on specific music criteria. To investigate the effectiveness of using analytic rubrics versus holistic rubrics, additional groups of raters were employed to score the performance tasks using the analytic rubrics while the other groups continued to use the holistic rubrics. The hierarchical analytic rubric is based on the rating scale developed by Gordon (2002). Each criterion ranged from 0–4 points. The singing tasks rubric included three criteria: tonal, rhythm, and vocal quality; the rhythm task rubric included two criteria: rhythm and improvisation.

In-depth statistical analyses including DIF analysis using classical test theory were conducted again to evaluate the quality of the assessments. For Year Two, reliability indices for the music multiple-choice test forms ranged from 0.76 to 0.80 for both the paper-and-pencil test forms and the web-based prototype. The interrater reliability indices for two raters, calculated using generalizability theory, ranged between 0.84 and 0.95 for the holistic rubric and between 0.57 and 0.92 for the analytic rubrics. The lowest interrater reliability of 0.57 was for the rhythm dimension on the analytic rubric for the second performance task, which was expected based on the perceptual difficulty associated with making temporal judgments. Based on the feedback from the raters, the Music Advisory Committee decided to modify the task by requiring students to perform the rhythm task using rhythm syllables to improve the interrater reliability. Other modifications to the test administration procedure were also made based on the recommendation from test administration feedback forms.

Third Year Assessment

For Year Three, the state department of education, based on the recommendations from the assessment specialists, decided to implement the web-based assessment at schools that received state arts grants. The web-based assessment was implemented with the understanding that results from participating schools would only be used for diagnostic and research purposes. Similar to the previous year, two forty-five-item test forms were compiled by using the item statistics as guidelines when selecting items. Several poorly functioning items were revised by the Music Advisory Committee for inclusion in this year's test forms. Moreover, a three-item sample test was compiled for students to practice the web-based test taking procedure prior to taking the actual test. Sample items are available on the assessment website http://scaap.ed.sc.edu/sampletest. Performance task one was the same as the previous year while performance task two was modified to include the use of rhythm syllables.

Approximately 5,200 students from a total of sixty-six elementary schools in the state participated in the Year Three music assessment. Multiple test administration training sessions were provided in computer labs throughout the state. The assessment specialists conducted hands-on, test administrator training sessions using an administration manual that included instructions for registering students and assigning usernames and passwords to students. During the training session, test administrators also practiced recording and uploading sound files to the website.

After the completion of the assessment at all schools, the assessment specialists retrieved the multiple-choice test results from the website for conducting statistical analysis. In addition to computing item statistics using classical test theory and DIF analysis, the assessment specialists used Item Response Theory (IRT) to equate the test forms and compute equated test scores for individual schools. The classical reliability indices for both test forms ranged from 0.77 to 0.78, while the empirical reliability index for the equated test form was 0.81. Detailed descriptions of specific statistical analyses conducted are available in the technical documentations on the assessment website http://scaap.ed.sc.edu/documents.asp.

A group of music educators was then employed to score student performances using the web-based rating system programmed by the university web designer. The main purpose of a web-based rating is to reduce the cost of gathering raters at a central location for the duration of the rating period. In this year, all training and monitoring processes were web-based. Raters were not required to meet at a central location during the rating period. The web-based training required the raters to first listen to the benchmarked performances and then take a qualifying test that consisted of fifteen randomly-generated items from a bank of student performances rated by the validation committee. Passing the qualifying test allowed the raters to begin scoring student performances. The assessment specialists and the Music Advisory Committee members were available via e-mail or phone to discuss the benchmarked items with the raters during the rating process. A web-based rating system included a monitoring procedure that required raters to pass a refresher test after rating each 100 performances. The refresher tests also included fifteen randomly-generated student performances from the bank of performances rated by the validation committee.

For Year Three, the Music Advisory Committee decided to use only the analytic rubrics because the interrater reliability indices using the analytic rubrics and the time required to score the items were comparable to using holistic rubrics. The committee asserted that analytic rubrics are better suited for providing diagnostic information to state music educators. Using generalizability theory, the interrater reliability indices for two raters ranged between 0.75 and 0.92.

With the lowest reliability index at 0.75, the assessment specialists were confident that the music assessment was adequate for making medium stake decisions at the school level (with more than twenty-five students) but not at the individual student level (Phillips, 2000; Herman, Ashbacher, and Winters, 1992; Thorndike, Cunningham, Thorndike, and Hagen, 1991). School level results were generated by the website for individual schools. Each school administrator received a username and a password that enabled access to his/her school's results. Combined means and standard deviations for all schools were also provided on that site. Teachers' feedback regarding the new web-based test administration procedure was analyzed and modifications were made based on those recommendations.

Year Four Assessment

In Year Four, the review of multiple-choice items and compilation of test forms continued without major changes. The acceptable interrater reliability indices indicated that the performance tasks did not require modification. A total of fifty-one elementary schools with approximately 3,732 students from around the state participated in music assessment. To analyze student results from Year Four, the assessment specialists conducted statistical analyses using both classical test theory and IRT. School level results provided were based on equated test scores across Year Three and Year Four.

After viewing student test results on the web, the music educators at participating schools wanted standards-based information from the assessment. As a result, an additional feature was added to the school results pages in which school administrators were able to view the percentages of students that correctly answered individual items and the standard associated with each item. By analyzing those results for trends, teachers can obtain a general impression of their students' standards-based music achievement. This method of presenting standards-based results was used because each test form does not include sufficient items to report reliable results for individual standards. For standards-based results to be reliable, approximately forty items are needed for each standard. Although stratified sampling used by the National Assessment of Educational Progress (2003) could reduce the number of items administered to each student, that method require many items and complex sampling procedure. Due to limited funding, the state department of education decided to continue the established assessment format.

Based on the raters' feedback, a major change was made to the web-based rating procedure. All raters were required to attend a one-day rating training session at a central location. During this session, the raters discussed the score of all benchmark performances, and then practiced scoring with a ten-item practice test. This practice test provides the raters with immediate feedback regarding their level of agreement with the validated scores. After the practice test, raters were required to pass the qualifying test prior to leaving the central location and scoring student performances. The Music Advisory Committee and the assessment specialists facilitated the training session and were available to answer rater questions. Raters were given one month to complete scoring all student performances after the training session.

The classical reliability indices for the Year Four test forms ranged from 0.76 to 0.86, while the empirical reliability index for the equated test form was 0.81. The interrater reliability indices, (i.e., G-coefficients) for two raters ranged between 0.75 and 0.92. Again, the criterion that received the lowest interrater reliability was rhythm. The assessment specialists and the Music Advisory Committee strongly suggested revising the rubric for the rhythm criterion for subsequent year's rating.

Summary of Current Music Assessment Design

To date, the music assessment is entirely web-based through a secure website and includes multiple-choice and performance tasks. The multiple-choice section of the music assessment consisted of two parallel test forms, each with forty-five multiple-choice items. Students demonstrate their knowledge of and skills in (a) music vocabulary, (b) notation, (c) music listening, (d) evaluation of performance problems, and (e) performance of music skills. Each test form was divided into two sections: "Understanding Music" and "Listening to Music." Most items included multimedia interpretive materials (i.e., digital pictures and audio prompts) to authentically measure music achievement. Approximately one hour was allocated for completing each multiple-choice test form. Student answers were stored in a web-based database that generates online results accessible by the school administrators using username and passwords.

The two performance tasks require students to demonstrate a specified skill on demand in content areas chosen from the state's visual and performing arts curriculum standards. Music Performance Task One required students to individually perform a familiar song on a neutral syllable ("du"), while Music Performance Task Two required students to individually perform a rhythm improvisation using rhythm syllables. Each student was required to listen to the instructions on a CD and perform the task when prompted. Students' music performance recordings were digitally recorded and uploaded to the server for subsequent rating.

All performance tasks were scored by music educators using hierarchical analytic rubrics in which each criterion ranged from 0–4 points. The hierarchical analytic rubric is based on the rating scale developed by Gordon (2002). Music Performance Task One was scored using a hierarchical analytic rubric with three criteria; (a) tonal, (b) rhythm, and (c) vocal quality. Music Performance Task Two was scored using another hierarchical analytic rubric with two criteria: (a) rhythm and (b) improvisation.

Prior to rating the students responses, a validation committee was formed to review and finalize the rubrics, and select student responses representative of each performance level described in the rubrics. Those representative responses were benchmarked and used for training and monitoring raters. Raters were randomly assigned in pairs so that each student's response is scored by two raters. The score resolution method for nonadjacent scores utilizes expert raters, a widely accepted rating practice (Johnson, Penny, Fisher, and Kuh, 2003; Johnson, Penny, and Gordon, 2001; and Johnson, Penny, and Gordon, 2000). All raters are required to attend a one-day rater training session at a central location. After passing the qualifying tests that consists of fifteen randomly-generated student performances that were validated, the raters then begin rating student performances at home. A stringent monitoring procedure that includes using multiple-refresher tests and seed items were used. School administrators were then notified when the results are available. Each principal will receive a username and password to access the school result.

Conclusions

The development of a statewide music assessment requires collaboration among state agencies, assessment specialists, and music educators. The bottom-up approach, used in the development of this state assessment, was successful because of the extensive involvement of music educators at each stage of development. In the initial stages, the music educators were provided assessment training that enabled them to serve as experts and assist in item development. Throughout the development, the music educators provided constant feedback regarding the implementation process and recommendations for modifications. In addition, this bottom-up approach may potentially achieve high teacher buy-in, and hence produce a successful statewide music assessment.

References

Consortium of National Arts Education Associations. 1994. *National standards for arts education: What every child should know and be able to do in the arts*. Reston, VA: MENC—The National Association for Music Education.

Gordon, E. E. 2002. *Rating scales and their uses for measuring and evaluating achievement in music performances*. Chicago: GIA Publications.

Herman, J., P. Ashbacher, and L. Winters. 1992. *A practical guide to alternative assessment*. Alexandria, VA: Association for Supervision and Curriculum Development.

Johnson, R. L., J. Penny, S. Fisher, and T. Kuhs. 2003. Score resolution: Investigation of the reliability and validity of resolved scores. *Applied Measurement in Education, 16*(4):299–322.

Johnson, R. L., J. Penny, S. Fisher, and T. Kuhs. 2000. The relationship between score resolution methods and interrater reliability: An empirical study of an analytic scoring rubric. *Applied Measurement in Education, 13*(2):121–138.

Johnson, R. L., J. Penny, and B. Gordon. 2001. Score resolution and the interrater reliability of holistic scores in rating essays. *Written Communication, 18*(2):229–249.

Kuhs, T., R. Johnson, S. Agruso, and D. Monrad. 2001. *Put to the test: Tools and techniques for classroom assessment*. Portsmouth: Heinemann.

National Assessment of Educational Progress. 2003. *Selecting the samples for the NAEP arts assessment*. Retrieved December 10, 2006 from http://nces.ed.gov/nationsreportcard/arts/sampledesign.asp.

Phillips, S. E. April, 2000. Legal Corner: GI Forum v TEA. *NCME Newsletter 8*(2):n.p.

Thorndike, R., G. Cunningham, R. Thorndike. and E. Hagen. 1991. *Measurement and evaluation in psychology and education*, 5th ed. New York: MacMillan.

PART 4

Facilitating Music Assessment Practice

Section A

Facilitating Practice in K–12 Music Classrooms

Assessing Creativity: An Oxymoron?

Special Guest Presentation
Maud Hickey
Northwestern University

One of the most important yet confounding issues that teachers face when dealing with music composition in the classroom is that of assessment. Prominent art educator Viktor Lowenfeld described the art classroom as the one place in school where the teacher should not evaluate students. "There should be one place in the school system where marks do not count. The art room should be a sanctuary against school regulations, where youngsters are free to be themselves and to put down their ideas and feelings and emotions without censorship, where they can evaluate their own progress toward their own goals without the imposition of an arbitrary grading system" (Lowenfeld and Brittain, 1987, 176). On the other hand, music educator Rena Upitis warns: "Some compositions are simply not as successful as others, and children know this as well as the adults who teach them. Just as some paintings or stories show more imagination than others, so, too, do the musical creations of children. It would be a mistake to treat all compositions in the same way, and this is apparent to children as well as to the adults with whom they may share their works" (Upitis, 1992, 32).

For the purposes of this paper I will offer cautions as well as suggestions for providing assessment to children's compositions in light of the contradicting opinions of the scholars quoted above. In composition, where there are possibilities for multiple answers—not one right or wrong way—and when judgment must be so subjective, I hope to offer ideas for providing feedback to children in the fairest manner. I will begin by clarifying the terms that I will use throughout the paper, and then follow with suggestions for an assessment process. My conclusion offers thoughts about how teachers might help themselves in determining benchmarks for children's compositions and improvisations.

Terminology

In this current and crazy time of tests and evaluation in education, terms are loosely bantered about without careful thought of the meaning behind these terms. Words such as measurement, assessment, evaluation, standards, etc., can and often do carry several different meanings. Therefore, for the purposes of this paper I will define what I mean by these terms in order to keep my ideas in context for the reader. By defining the terms for this paper, however, I am in no way saying that they are the "right" or only definitions—that argument is for another paper.

I will use Boyle and Radocy's definition of *evaluation* which is that "it usually involves or at least implies the use of tests and measurements, but in addition involves making some judgment or decision regarding the worth, quality, or value of experiences, procedures, activities, or individual or group performances as they relate to some educational endeavor" (1987, 7). In other words, there is a focus on the "value" of something; there is an implication that a judgment of some sort will be given. In education, this could be in the form of a numerical score (a percentage out of 100) or a letter grade, and is often used in relation to peer performance or a set criterion. A rating of a clarinet solo at a solo-and-ensemble festival is an example of an evaluation, and in fact is a relatively easy one to give, because we have a pretty good idea of what a clarinet solo should sound like at our pre-determined levels. This is not so easy to do when evaluating a 3rd-grade child's musical composition, however. First of all, we do not know enough about what a 3rd-grade child is capable of producing as a musical composition, and because of this, we often have to make a very subjective decision. (I will return to this idea of "benchmarks" at the conclusion of this paper).

For this paper I will use *assessment* as a broad term that might include a value judgment, but for my purposes will generally mean non-evaluative feedback. As a feedback tool, non-evaluative assessment is used to clarify and comment on what is heard (or saw) in order to understand the intentions of the student. Both evaluation and assessment can be used not only to give feedback to students, but also for teacher improvement as well as program improvement and comparison. For this paper I will not be addressing the use of evaluation and assessment of composition for program improvement, nor in the context of the recent state and national "high-stakes" testing movement, but rather as a tool for student feedback in order to affect student achievement in music composition.

Why Are You Composing in Your Classroom?

The most essential question that must be answered before considering either the assessment or evaluation of children's musical composition is this: Why are you asking your students to compose? Classroom activities must be inextricably linked to classroom goals and objectives, and by logic, then, assessment or evaluation. Are you having children compose in your classroom in order to be more creative musicians? Or to be better composers? Or both? Or are you having children compose in order to learn about key signatures and time signatures? Or to improve their notation skills? All of these are legitimate and fine reasons for composing and improvising in your classroom; whichever you choose, however, should directly affect your evaluation procedures. And, in fact, I hope to show that knowing the purpose for composing may help solve the conundrum presented by the opposing views of Lowenfeld and Brittan vs. Upitis. Keep the purpose for composing in mind as I offer suggestions in the next section about the assessment and evaluation of both the process as well as product of children's musical compositions.

Assessment and Feedback of the Composition Process

As in all educational endeavors, and especially in more subjective areas such as visual art, creative writing, or music composition, appraising the process toward a goal can be as

196

enlightening as evaluating the final product. In creative writing, several typologies for the writing process have been developed to aid teachers in stimulating and guiding students' creative products. One useful process typology, utilized by Tsisserev (1997) to analyze music composition processes of high school students, was borrowed from the creative writing literature (Hillocks, 1975), and may prove useful for teachers to use when assessing the process of music composition (see Figure 1).

The process categories that Tsisserev applies to music composition (shown in Figure 1) are idea generation, idea development/expansion, idea organization, and idea expression. The composer begins by generating her ideas, inspired by any myriad of stimuli (including teacher instruction). The idea may be a simple and small musical motif, or it might be a grand soundscape inspired by a sunset. At this starting point, a teacher may help by offering prompts for a composition. Or, a teacher might assess whether the student is able to generate ideas on his own. The idea for a composition then moves on to the next stage, where it is expanded upon and developed into longer and more complex ideas. Teachers may aid at this point by providing or commenting on choices for development or variation, or by helping the composer reflect on the development process she chooses. The composer then organizes her ideas by creating patterns, repeating motifs, transposing, and re-arranging into a more complete whole. Students who struggle at this point can be aided by teacher guidance on more technical matters such as notation or theoretical concepts. Finally, the composer applies her final touches to a composition in order to help communicate the expressive qualities that are intended. It is at this final stage, Tsisserev points out, that the composer relies most on her overall musical knowledge and decision-making ability. Perhaps this is the stage, too, which separates the most successful composers from others (and this is directly related to product assessment and evaluation). Teacher awareness of each of these stages of the composition process may help make feedback to, and assessment of, student composers' as helpful as commenting on the final product.

Another useful model for assessing the process of composition can be borrowed from the creative writing literature, and specifically the writing workshop model developed and refined by Lucy Calkins and colleagues (Calkins, 1983; Calkins, Hartman, and White, 2005). In this approach, every step of the process of creative writing is carefully observed, but through a cooperative effort worked out between student and teacher. It involves a four-step process of research (learn the intent of the project), decide (what to teach), teach (to aid the student), and link (to the original objective [Calkins, et al, 2005]). This takes time and a dedicated effort on the part of teachers. Music composition in the classroom, if treated like creative writing, would not simply be giving one or two short composition tasks over the course of a year (because it is in the standards) but approached as a process that takes time to develop[1].

---

[1] For more information about the writer's workshop model as a model for teaching music composition I recommend the writings of Calkins (1983) and Calkins, et al. (2005).

Figure 1. Music composition process points for teacher response

Composition Process:

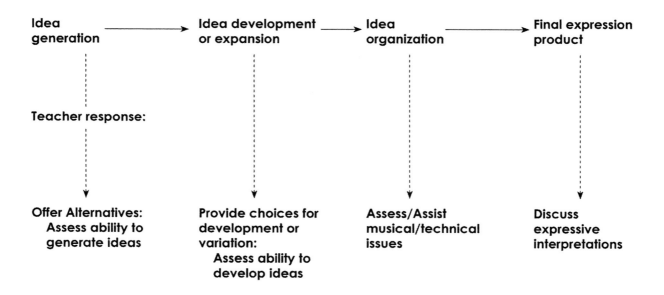

Assessment and Evaluation of the Composition Product

Assessment has the most impact on learning when objectives are clear to both students and teachers (Colwell, 2002). Assessment and evaluation must be linked to the goals of teaching, especially when dealing with a task as subjective as music composition. An assessment or evaluation of a child's music composition should depend upon the reason for having the child compose, and this should affect the type of composition task that is given. I view this as a three-step process. The first step is to decide the purpose for asking children to compose in your classroom; in other words, how does any composition task link to your classroom goals and objectives? The second step to consider, and one that should rely on the answer to the first, is what kind of composition task will be given and how open or closed this task should be. In musical performance, the task parameters are often closed: the composer has written the notes and dynamic markings and expression marks, etc., for us. With music composition however, the teacher has the control as to how many of these decisions will be made by the child or by the teacher. An open task will have few parameters or rules to follow, while a closed task will have many. Finally, and depending on decisions made in the first two steps, one must decide upon the evaluation or assessment stakes for the assignment. Will the assignment be evaluated or graded? And if so, how much weight will it carry for an overall evaluation of a students' achievement in the music class? Or, will there be non-evaluative feedback, or student self-assessment, or both? These decisions have shown to have an interesting effect on the creativity and intrinsic motivation of children, and so before I offer

198

specific examples of this three-step process, I move to the research literature that highlights the importance of these decisions.

Creativity and Motivation

One of the goals for doing music composition in our classrooms should be to enhance the creativity of our students. However this goal toward creativity adds a twist to the assessment picture. Literature on intrinsic motivation and its role in creativity presents a complex array of factors involved in establishing the most conducive environments for creative output. Researchers have found an interesting interaction between the parameters of a creative task and the assessment method; this interaction affects the creativity and intrinsic motivation of students. One finding seems consistent: giving a reward for a task (such as a grade) can be detrimental to the intrinsic motivation for the task (Deci, Koestner, and Ryan, 2001; Kohn, 1993) as well as the creativity of the resulting product (Amabile, 1996; Hennessey and Amabile, 1988; Hennessey, 2000). Lowenfeld's aversion toward evaluating children's art may be fair, and the lesson may be that teachers who want to encourage the most creative output from their students should try to avoid always giving rewards or evaluative marks for creative work. The interaction between instructional sets and types of reward and its effect upon motivation and creativity is illustrated in Figure 2[2].

Figure 2. The interaction between instructional set and levels of external reward and its effect upon creative output and intrinsic motivation

| | | Reward | |
		Low External Reward	**High External Reward**
Instructional Set	**Closed Task**	Low creativity High intrinsic motivation	High creativity Low intrinsic motivation
	Open Task	High creativity High intrinsic motivation	Low creativity Low intrinsic motivation

In Figure 3 I have set up four possibilities of the interaction of assignment parameters with evaluation stakes from the viewpoint of the teacher and the student. One can see from both Figures 2 and 3 that there is much more at stake when evaluating a product that has open-ended task parameters than for one that is being created for more specific purposes with pre-defined (closed) parameters given. Imagine how anxious students would feel if they were asked to compose a piece of music, with no other guidelines except that it be something good, but that the assignment will be graded (open task, high evaluation; Lower-right

---

[2] This is an over-simplification of very complex phenomena, used here to illustrate the basic idea.

199

quadrant in Figures 2 and 3). This is not only unfair to students, but also very difficult for teachers to do. On the other hand, if an assignment is to write an eight-measure composition in 6/8 time using eighth, quarter, and dotted-quarter notes, it is easy to evaluate students' ability to compose using these parameters. Giving a grade (or any evaluation) on this closed-task assignment makes perfect sense (closed task, high evaluation; upper right quadrant in Figures 2 and 3). A closed task assignment (many parameters) with low reward value may set up high intrinsic motivation on the part of students (This is easy to do!), but may ultimately feel more like busywork and less like creative work (Why are we doing it?). (Upper left quadrant.)

Figure 3. Four possibilities for the interaction of assignment task and evaluation

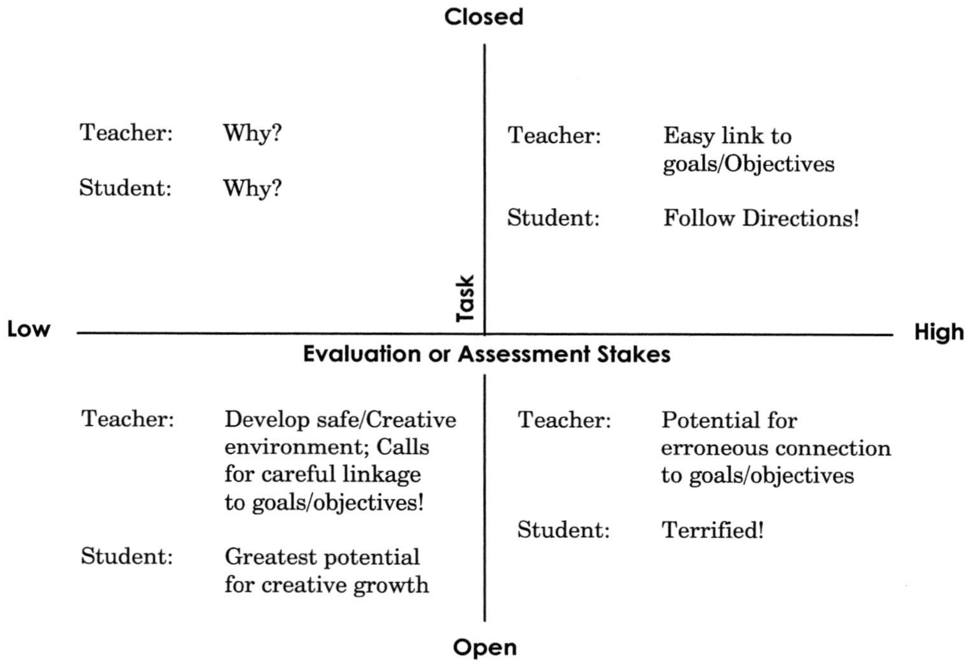

The Three Step Process

Let's look more closely at two specific examples using the three-step process to determine an assessment or an evaluation approach to a music composition keeping in mind the relationship between task parameters relationship and the type of assessment.

1. *The Goal.* By the end of their 5th-grade year, students will be able compose music that shows awareness of the different musical forms learned during the school year. In addition, they will be able to notate their compositions using standard notation.

200

2. *A Task*. Compose a melody (or rhythm) for your instrument that is in rondo form. Your "A" theme should be at least two measures long. Create at least two other themes. Be sure that you can play your melody, and that it is interesting and something that you like when you are finished. You should revise it as often as necessary until you are satisfied with your melody. Your completed composition should be at least twelve measures long. Notate your composition using standard notation and include expressive markings.

3. *Evaluation*. This task contains relatively defined—or closed—parameters, and therefore an evaluation of this product is fairly easy, as well as appropriate. There are several objective factors that can be measured. These are:

   • An A theme that is two measures long
   • The presence of B and C themes
   • Correct Rondo form
   • The composition is at least twelve measures long
   • Legibly notated in standard notation
   • Includes expressive markings
   • Optional: Student ability to perform the composition expressively

Within this final step, one must then choose an appropriate evaluation tool, such as a rubric, rating form or even a simple checksheet that would allow the student and teacher to know whether the goal was met, and to what extent it was met.

A second example of this three-step process involves an assignment that requires fewer parameters (an open task), and therefore more freedom for the student to be creative. This particular example is an assignment that I often give to students early on in a composition class and it encourages experimentation and exploration of sounds. It is an assignment that would have no right answer.

The Goal. By the end of their 5th-grade year, students will be able organize sounds in imaginative and expressive ways through music composition.

A Task. Compose a "Musical Scenery." Imagine a place that is special to you. It can be real or pretend. What sounds are in this space? Using GarageBand,[3] compose a music composition that organizes sounds in a way that depicts your musical place. Use appropriate timbres and expressive elements to make this musical place come alive!

Assessment. Most appropriate in this case, and to encourage the most creative thinking, is to provide thoughtful feedback on the composition rather than to give it an evaluative mark. This is not to imply that there is no record of the child's composition. A record of whether the child completed the composition along with prose of both teacher and student reflections would suffice.

---

[3] Using a software program such as GarageBand is one possibility. This assignment could also be easily done with a variety of classroom instruments and children working alone or in groups.

In cases where there are few task parameters, one should begin by determining the composer's intent. Here again we can learn from teachers of visual art and creative writing. In the process of working with creative writers, Calkins, et. al (2005) insist that the first step for teachers is to research. That is to "observe and interview to understand what the child is trying to do as a writer. Probe to glean more about the child's intentions" (7). Reese (2003) captures ideas from creative writing and visual artists for music teachers and offers helpful suggestions for providing feedback to a students' composition:

- Observe carefully, and know students' music well before offering critiques.
- Encourage students to find solutions to musical problems on their own. Help them discover how other composers may have addressed problems similar to ones they are having.
- Use a systematic approach to description of the work and delay interpretation or judgment.
- When changing or adding to a student's music, offer incremental changes based directly on the student's musical ideas.
- Help students who are stuck by varying one of their ideas or by offering incomplete portions of music to extend.
- Validate students' work through genuine responses, because these are inherently valuable, even when they do not contain detailed comments.
- Use a facilitative approach to help students find their own composing interests in addition to a didactic approach which gives direct suggestions on changes that could or should be made in the music.

Conclusion

Which goals and tasks are more appropriate? All of them are appropriate when the goals and tasks are linked to the assessments. Composition should be used in music classrooms both as a tool for getting better at understanding music as well as a tool for the development of creative musical thinking. The ideal condition for supporting high intrinsic motivation and high creative output is one in which students perceive that external rewards are low, and the tasks involved are relatively open (i.e., the lower-left box in Figure 2). When offering composition tasks with strict parameters, then it is appropriate to evaluate the outcomes.

The realities of teaching remind us that student personalities, among many other factors, confound the issue of task parameters, assessment, intrinsic motivation, and creativity. Children come to the classroom with a multitude of personality traits that may inhibit or contribute to their creative and motivational approach toward learning. Different students have varying thresholds for ambiguity. Some students will have an easier time with strict parameters, while others will prefer the freedom of few parameters. We also know that setting up closed assignments is necessary for achieving specific teaching goals. Too much of either extreme for too long is not educational. We need to be doing both kinds of composition and both assessment and evaluation in our music classrooms. Both Lowenfeld and Upitis are right!

But What's Good?

One problem still confronting us, however, and perhaps a reason that we don't see a lot of composition in schools, is that we simply don't have a sense of what is a "good" composition. What should a proficient level composition sound like for a ten-year-old child? We have standards, but are short on benchmarks.[4] We still need to know what is "good," or constitutes meeting a standard at an acceptable level. In music performance this is easy. We have pretty reliable rating systems and a relatively solid sense of levels of difficulty. We don't have this for music composition. It's a vicious circle: we don't compose because we don't know what constitutes "good," but we don't know what is "good" because we don't compose. The profession needs models and benchmarks of children's compositions. I would suggest that teachers could help themselves here by beginning in their own classrooms as well as school districts. Compose with students and compose a lot! Keep compositions in order to develop a sense of proficiency for children at each grade level as well as to provide models of "good" and "bad" to students as well as other teachers.

Beauty is in the ear of the listener. But that should not stop teachers from utilizing music composition and improvisation tasks in the classroom for multiple purposes (including the development of creative musical thinking), in multiple ways, and with thoughtful consideration of assessment.

---

[4] The MENC publication of benchmarks for composition and improvisation is a start (Rinehart, 2002), but we need more!

References

Amabile, T. M. 1996. Creativity in context: update to The social psychology of creativity. Boulder, CO: Westview Press.

Boyle, J. D. , and R. E. Radocy. 1987. Measurement and evaluation of musical experiences. New York: Schirmer Books.

Calkins, L. M. 1983. Lessons from a child. On the teaching and learning of writing. Portsmouth, N. H.: Heinemann.

Calkins, L. M., A. Hartman, and Z. R. White. 2005. One to one: The art of conferring with young writers. Portsmouth, NH: Heinemann.

Colwell, R. 2002. Assessment's potential in music education. In R. Colwell and C. Richardson, eds. The new handbook of research on music teaching and learning, 1128–1158. New York: Oxford University Press.

Deci, E. L., R. Koestner, and R. M. Ryan. 2001. Extrinsic Rewards and Intrinsic Motivation in Education: Reconsidered Once Again. Review of Educational Research, 71(1):1–29.

Hennessey, B. A. and T. M. Amabile. 1988. The conditions of creativity. In R. J. Sternberg, ed., The nature of creativity, 11–38. New York: Cambridge.

Hennessey, B. A. 2000. Rewards and creativity. In C. Sansone, and J. M. Harackiewicz, eds., Intrinsic and extrinsic motivation: The search for optimal motivation and performance, 55–78. San Diego: Academic Press.

Hillocks, G. 1975. Observing and writing. Urbana, IL: National Council of Teachers of English (ERIC Document Reproduction Services No. ED102574).

Kohn, A. 1993. Punished by rewards: The trouble with gold stars, incentive plans, A's, praise, and other bribes. Boston: Houghton Mifflin.

Lowenfeld, V. and W. L. Brittain. 1987. Creative and mental growth, 8th ed. NJ: Prentice Hall.

Reese, S. 2003. Responding to Student Compositions. In, M. Hickey, ed., Music Composition in the Schools: A New Horizon for Music Education, 211–232. Reston, VA: MENC.

Rinehart, C., ed. 2002. Composing and arranging. Standard 4 benchmarks. Reston, VA: MENC—The National Association for Music Education

Tsisserev, A. 1997. An ethnography of secondary school student composition in music: A study of personal involvement within the compositional process. Unpublished doctoral dissertation, University of British Columbia, Vancouver, British Columbia, Canada.

Upitis, R. 1992. Can I play you my song? The compositions and invented notations of children. Portsmouth, NH: Heinemann.

Assessment: How It Works In the Elementary General Music Classroom

Special Guest Presentation

Sandra K. (Tena) Whiston
Beattie Elementary School
Lincoln Public Schools, Lincoln, Nebraska

Two words that generally create a discord with music educators are *assessment* and *evaluation*. In this paper I would like to focus on these terms and how we can connect them to the instruction that is already taking place within our elementary general music classrooms. By fitting these puzzle pieces together and planning for them, we can make viable connections between instruction, assessment, and evaluation which will in turn strengthen our curriculum, change and challenge our teaching strategies, and benefit our individual students.

First of all, I do not have all of the answers. Over the years I have read the current research and articles (Brophy; 2000, Brummett and Haywood, 1997; Colwell, 2002; Guskey and Bailey, 2000; Miller, 2005) which pertain to assessment and evaluation and applied them to my own general music classroom. This has included a lot of trial and error on my part and flexibility on the part of my students as we entered into this process together. My goal for my students was to infuse assessment and evaluation into my teaching in such a way that it was non-threatening for them and encouraged them to always be a part of the music-making process. We have worked together and achieved some milestones, but we are still at the threshold of this process. In order to begin this journey with you, I would like to take the time to define these terms and look at ways in which we can infuse assessment and evaluation into our daily teaching and lesson planning. As we work through this process, I hope that you will see that the application and end results of including these techniques into our daily lesson plans does benefit both you and your students.

Defining the Terms

Assessment

Assessment is the ongoing teacher observation of student progress toward a goal or concept that will be evaluated after an appropriate time for student practice has been allowed within the music classroom setting. Assessment also drives the ongoing adjustment and planning of our daily curriculum. Because this is an ongoing process, individual student data is recorded at selected intervals only. Assessment assists the teacher in planning future curriculum expectations, modifying long-range planning, organizing appropriate lesson planning, adjusting daily teaching strategies, and in meeting individual student learning needs.

Evaluation

Evaluation is the process of synthesizing testing (summative data) and formative data (ongoing documentation) for the purpose of reporting progress to parents and students through grading and/or other reporting methods. Written assessment data are recorded both in the curriculum content areas of instruction as well as the effort and participation skills of the individual students. Evaluation facilitates data collection on student learning, documenting student learning, and reporting progress to parents, and in preparing future curriculum plans.

About My Music Classroom

Currently, I see my students once a week for fifty minutes of music instruction. Our quarters are nine weeks in length. This requires that I spend my time wisely, teaching during the lesson so that the content/benchmark goals can be adequately covered for assessment and evaluation. It also means that I need to allow time for the students to practice the assessment skills during the lessons prior to the actual evaluation. While some terms and skills are easy to teach and assess, it is the practice time for the students that I need to keep in the forefront for those more difficult and advanced skills in order to be able to evaluate them during the quarter.

In the Lincoln, Nebraska school district we use a four-point scale for recording our student grades on their report cards:

> 4 = Exceeds District Standards
> 3 = Meets District Standards
> 2 = Approaches District Standards
> 1 = Does Not Meet District Standards
> # = Not Taught/Assessed this Quarter

I firmly believe that to evaluate students, you need to have a concrete recording system. Therefore, I have set up seating charts (Figure 1), which contain individual blocks for daily participation grades as well as larger blocks for skills that will be evaluated during each quarter. I believe that it is important to limit the amount of notations that you need to make on the daily seating charts. For instance, for participation grades during class, I will mark only those students who have received a 2 (approaches) or a 4 (exceeds) on my chart right after class. At lunch, I will go back to the chart and fill in the 3s for the rest of the class. This evaluation can be done during passing time as we have five minutes built into our schedules between each class. I usually target three skills from the benchmarks during the course of each quarter. One of those skills is always a singing skill. It is important that I know where each student is in their vocal development process and what I need to do to help them become more independent singers. By having this information in front of me every day, it helps me to use the students who have already mastered certain strategies in a leadership role and to focus on the individuals who need more guided practice.

The Assessment Puzzle

Puzzle Piece No. 1: The Music Curriculum

The first piece of this puzzle requires that you have an established music curriculum with specific goals for each quarter by grade level for the entire school year, which is used consistently throughout your school district. Assessment and evaluation cannot take place unless you have a content specific curriculum in place. If you do not have an established quarterly curriculum, then this would be your first step in moving forward on the assessment and evaluation scale. The good news is that you do not have to start this process from scratch, as there are many curriculum guides available from MENC, different school districts, scholarly publications, and websites.

Figure 1. Seating Chart Used for Recording Assessment Data

Sample Seating and Recording Chart

Class _____ Time _____ Rotation Day _____ Quarter_____

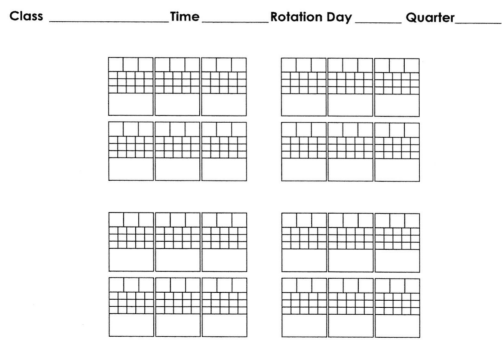

When planning for my individual classes, I begin with the quarterly list of content terms for each grade level. I *publish* (print) these benchmark terms (Figure 2) on the walls of my music room. At the beginning of the quarter, I take some time to talk with each one of the classes to let them know what our focus terms are for the upcoming quarter. The students like the idea of the Word Wall and know that they will need to refer to it often during the course of the quarter.

Once we have covered the benchmark terms for the quarter, my goal is to use them frequently throughout the lesson and encourage the students to do the same. When planning for individual lessons, I use the indices created by the music publishing companies to help me locate songs, listening activities, dances, and other materials that would be the best examples for teaching our target terms. When selecting an activity, it needs to be musical, a good (not marginal) example of the target benchmark, and one that I would not mind repeating many times. My goal is to find the best examples for my classes. I also browse through many personal resources, books, and workshop handouts to help me collect the very best musical examples. I personally believe that by adding new pieces to my repertoire for teaching that it helps me to grow as a musician.

Figure 2. Grade 3 Third Quarter Benchmarks—Lincoln Public Schools (in progress)

| A cappella unison and solo singing |
| Partner Songs and Rounds |
| Rondo Form: Rhythmic Rondo |
| Introduce the single eighth note (♪): Improvisation, Dotted Rhythms |
| Fermata |
| Coda: Interlude |
| Staccato and Legato |
| Identifying Orchestral Instruments: the Brass Family |
| Conducting Patterns |
| Instrumental techniques |

Puzzle Piece No. 2: Plan for Implementation

The second piece of this puzzle is to start with a plan of implementation for assessing and evaluating your students. Assessment procedures should be designed to provide students with an opportunity to demonstrate their progress *often* in a safe and structured manner within the classroom setting, which is integrated into the instructional process. Assessment groupings can consist of solo, small group, and/or large group demonstrations of the concept being measured. Assessment design should include auditory, verbal (singing), visual, kinesthetic, and written responses in order to adapt to individual student learning needs and strengths. Figure 3 presents a list of activities that isolate components that music teachers can easily assess during regular classroom instruction.

There are several different types of assessment tools (Brophy, 2000) which we can use routinely in our daily instructional plans:

1. Performance-based assessment
2. Student Self-Assessment
3. Group Assessment
4. Written Tests
5. Portfolios

The advantage of performance-based assessments is that they allow for evaluation in a musical context where a real connection can be made between instruction and evaluation. Performance-based assessment allows the teacher to evaluate the process as well as the end result. The disadvantages of performance-based assessments are that the scoring can be subject to teacher bias, students may not perform consistently, and (of course) record-keeping. Student self-assessment is a valuable tool, as they are usually honest and often much harder on themselves. I like to make my students be responsible for their own learning, so self-assessment to me is an important tool to use. Group assessment through the use of a "thumbs up or down" process holds everyone accountable for what the large group is doing. I have found that this is a useful way to keep the entire group in check with the concept that is being taught. They just never know when they might need to signal their assessment of what is happening in the classroom.

Figure 3. Sample Activities for Classroom Music Assessment

Auditory	Rhythmic notation
	Melodic notation
	Drawing phrases while listening to a piece of music
	Arranging letters to create the form of musical works
Verbal/ Singing	Using mallets as microphones to facilitate individual and group singing
	Call-and-response songs
	Assign student leaders for an individual song or for the entire music period
	Have students sing a song as the teacher plays an ostinato pattern on an Orff instrument
	Reading rhythmic patterns using syllables
	Discuss, analyze, compare, and contrast
Visual	Use individual staff boards for notation
	Use long strings for writing/creating melodies (Place the string on the floor in front of you; work from left to right shape the string into a melodic shape or pattern)
	Bubbles:follow the movement of the bubble in the air with your voice
	Identify instrument pictures
Kinesthetic	Trace musical phrases in the air as they are heard or sung
	Performing rhythmic patterns on instruments (pitched or unpitched)
	Show musical form through movement
	Perform a melody or ostinato pattern while singing
	Compose or improvise a melody
Written	Use individual staff boards for notation
	Use long strings for writing/creating melodies (For younger children, place a long string on the floor and have them create a shape which moves from left to right that they can sing)
	Use popsicle or craft sticks for rhythmic notation
	Have students develop a rubric for a specific activity or concept
Tools and Strategies	Develop and use seating charts with spaces for record-keeping
	Publish and/or print your rubrics prior to using them
	Plan activities that involve active music-making for all during the assessment
	Mark only those students who are above or below expectations
	Plan activities that allow for repetition
	Plan activities that specifically isolate the objective or concept being measured
	Provide positive feedback as well as instruction for improvement
	Develop individual student or class portfolios
	Develop and utilize individual assessment stations[1]
	Design lesson plans that approach musical concepts in multiple ways to facilitate mastery

---

[1] I have developed stations where the student can independently get more practice on a particular concept. In one station they might be working on sight and sound recognition of instruments and then take a pre-recorded listening test. Another station might provide practice in rhythm writing or building chords.

Puzzle Piece No. 3: Lesson Planning

The next step in connecting assessment and evaluation to instruction is to plan for individual class lessons. Lesson planning is so much easier when you have clearly defined objectives to teach for each lesson. When planning, take the time to include the National Standards in your plans in order to make sure that you are covering all of them, not just your personal favorites. I often include the concept that I am teaching with the title of the activity to keep my teaching focused. Always make sure that you include a variety of levels of activities within each lesson including: singing, moving, listening, playing instruments, creating, and notating. Only choose quality literature to do with your students. You can never sing enough folk songs!

When structuring my classes, I usually begin with a listening piece at the beginning of the lesson (see Figure 4). In quarter three for third grade, our benchmark terms include: Brass, Rondo, Duple or Triple Meter, Accent, Staccato, Legato, Fermata, Coda, Solo, Tutti, and Brass Quintet. These terms help me to focus on finding listening examples which will include as many of these terms as possible and to allow for a variety of listening experiences throughout the quarter. I start my lessons in this manner to let the students (and teachers) know that our music class begins when they walk into my room. My students understand that they will need to either find the beat (moving in groups of two's or three's) or the conducting pattern for the selected listening piece and be prepared to use the benchmark terms to discuss what they are listening to on the CD player. With this activity, I can easily evaluate whether or not they can find the beat or perform the conducting pattern. I then notate the students on my seating chart that need more work on these skills.

Once I have targeted the goals for the lesson, then I begin to plan different activities that will allow us to experience the benchmark terms in many different ways throughout the lesson. It is important to teach the benchmark in as many different ways as possible in order to reach each individual child in your classroom. In this sample lesson plan, I have utilized listening, singing, playing instruments, movement, and body percussion in order to focus on the Rondo concept.

Puzzle Piece No. 4: Reflection After the Lesson

The last piece in this puzzle occurs after you have taught the lesson and done the assessment and evaluation of your students. These questions guide my post-lesson reflection:

1. Were your students able to meet the criteria you published?
2. Did your evaluation tool match your provided student practice activities?
3. Did the rubric accurately reflect your benchmark target goal?
4. How will what you have learned affect your planning for instruction and assessment in the next lesson?
5. When you were recording the evaluation, was everyone in the classroom involved in a music-making activity?

To facilitate involvement I make sure that students have the opportunity for guided practice within the lesson. Every student is a part of the music making activity, not just the students being evaluated for that day.

Assessment and evaluation become less threatening words to the student (and teacher) if they happen in a performance-based setting with everyone involved in the music-making. Finding great examples of this type of activity can be the challenge, but it also becomes the reward because everyone grows in their own musicianship skills the more we are involved in the making and performing of music. If you make assessment and evaluation a regular part of your classroom activities it will strengthen your curriculum and allow your students to become better musicians and consumers of music.

Final Thoughts

I close with some guiding thoughts to get started with assessment in your classroom.

1. Keep your goals in mind when writing assessments.
2. Be as clear as possible about what you want your students to be able to do on any given task.
3. Publish your objectives for the students.
4. Provide many ways for the students to succeed (visual, aural, kinesthetic, and tactile).
5. Use your assessments to refine instruction and improve learning.
6. There are a million "right" ways to assess and evaluate.
7. Find a way to report your assessment information to students, parents, and administrators.

The time to begin assessing and evaluating our students is now in this era of accountability. I would suggest starting small by targeting one concept at a certain grade level as a place to begin. The hardest part is recording the data and keeping it accessible so that we can use it for improving our lesson plans. Once you start to make assessments, you will begin to see that it gets easier and easier to include them in your lesson plans. A well-thought-out lesson plan that utilizes many different modalities of learning (aural, visual, tactile, and kinesthetic) coupled with outstanding examples of music taught using a variety of skills (singing, moving, playing instruments, notating, creating and improvising) will immerse students in musical knowledge. It will also allow them to become independent musical thinkers and creators.

References

Brophy, T. S. 2000. *Assessing the developing child musician: A guide for general music teachers*. Chicago: GIA Publications, Inc.

Brummett, V. M., and J. Haywood. 1997. Authentic assessment in school music: Implementing a framework. *General Music Today, 11*(1):4–10.

Colwell, R. 2002. *The New Handbook of Research on Music Teaching and Learning*. New York, NY. Oxford University Press.

Guskey, T. R. and J. M. Bailey. 2000. *Developing grading and reporting systems for student learning*. Thousand Oaks, CA: Corwin Press

Lincoln Public Schools (in progress). *Curriculum for K–12 Music*. Lincoln, NE: Author.

Lindeman, C. A., ed. 2003. *Benchmarks in action: A guide to standards-based assessment in music*. Reston, VA: MENC—The National Association for Music Education.

Miller, C. C. 2005. *Assessment in the Music Classroom*. Milwaukee: Hal Leonard Corporation.

Figure 4. Third Grade Lesson Plan (S.K. Whiston)

Third Grade Lesson Plan

National Standard No. 6

Listening: "Mouret" by The Canadian Brass: Bolero and Other Classical Blockbusters, CD 09026-68109-2.

Have the music playing while the students enter the room. Find the meter (4). Start the music again and play a game of Fudge. (To play Fudge, the teacher finds a place to keep the beat in groups of two or four. The students watch until the teacher says "Fudge." Then the teacher moves to a new pattern of four while the students start the old pattern. The game continues with the students always one pattern behind the teacher. My students like to take turns being the leader as well as being the follower.)

The student should begin to realize that there is a repeated melody in this piece.

Assessment: Are the students able to copy your pattern of four beats with 80% accuracy? If yes, make the patterns more difficult by increasing the levels of body percussion. If no, choose one pattern as an A section and then alternate: A, something different, A, something different.

No. 4, 5

Review: Have four rhythms displayed on the board in a meter of four.

Read and clap through each of the patterns twice. Then ask the students to clap their favorite pattern four times while you or selected students keep a steady pulse on the drums. Next, choose their second-favorite rhythm to clap, and then their third-favorite rhythm. Set it up in Rondo form (ABACA) for the final clapping performance. (You could transfer to instruments of the students' choice here as well, and then perform.)

Assessment/ Evaluation: Have the four students being assessed that day share their rhythmic Rondo patterns with the class

- Did they perform with a steady beat?
- Use the appropriate form?
- Clap the rhythmic patterns correctly?

Warm-ups: Fireworks sounds (ooh—ahh!), puppy whines, and lip trills. Set these patterns up in a Rondo form (ABACA), your choice or the students' choir as to which pattern is A, B, or C.

No. 1, 9

Sing: "Skip to My Lou," "Bow Belinda," "Paw Paw Patch," and "Sandy Land" with an autoharp or guitar. (Key of F; chords are F and C^7.)

Have the students decide which song should be the A, B, and C section. Sing in Rondo Form (ABACA). You could extend the form here to ABACADA if you would like. My students also enjoy singing these songs as partner songs, since their chord structure is the same—an easy step into harmony.

Assessment: As a class, could we sing each song using a steady tempo and good singing technique? Did we create a Rondo form?

No. 1, 3 Orff Activity/ Singing Game: New: "Listen" from Strike it Rich by Jeff Kriske and Randy DeLelles. This song is perfect to reinforce the Rondo concept (ABACADA). Teach the refrain, then chant the B, C, and D sections, which refer to the differently pitched Orff instruments. I adapt their process by:

1. Transposing the piece to the key of F.

2. Transferring the triangle part to tone clusters on the Orff instruments.

3. Adding eight beats for improvisation on the specific instruments for each chanted section.

We improvise as a group first. When they are comfortable with the concept, I will ask for volunteers to share their creations.

Note: If you do not have Orff instruments, create some words which describe the instruments that you have in your room so you can sing, chant, and then play.

Assessment/ Evaluation: Were the students using correct mallet technique? Were they students creating a melody which lasted for eight beats and ended on "Do"?

Closure: Today we experienced the form Rondo through movement, body percussion, singing, and playing instruments. The form is ABACA.

Extension: Play the singing games which accompany the songs in Rondo form. Listen to:

- Für Elise
- A Little Night Music
- Tanz from Carmina Burana
- Viennese Musical Clock from Hary Janos Suite by Zoltán Kodály.

Create additional rhythmic Rondo creations using different rhythm patterns.

Primary Students' Singing Achievement: Assessment Data Comparisons and Conclusions

James D. Merrill
Milton Terrace Primary School
Ballston Spa Central School District, New York

Abstract

The purpose of this paper is to present assessment data comparisons of singing achievement for K–2 students and conclusions about their singing development obtained in my classroom. Six years of second grade assessment data for five song phrases were collected and analyzed to demonstrate how assessment data can improve instruction and student achievement. Kindergarten achievement on one song over several years is compared to the achievement of first graders. A comprehensive singing assessment program for first graders with twenty-two assessments is presented, and achievement for four years at specific singing tasks is analyzed and discussed. Singing assessment seating charts and Singing Voice Evaluation rubrics are provided.

Music teachers know in general when their students as a group are singing well, but individual assessment is necessary to know and foster each child's vocal development. In this paper, I show how a music teacher can also be a researcher in the music classroom, and how comparisons and conclusions from singing assessment data can improve instruction and the student learning. This ongoing study is guided by the following questions:

1. How do music teachers know that all of their students are improving their singing and provide evidence of this improvement?
1. What kinds of assessments should be used?
1. Are primary students more successful on certain kinds of assessments?
1. Can music teachers assess and teach for improvement at the same time?

I have found the best way to help young children become better singers is through working with them one-on-one. The data collected from this individualized process and from monitoring their singing in a group provide answers to these questions. The primary purpose for using singing assessments is to help children improve their singing; improvement in instruction results from interpreting the assessment data and from reflecting on the student-teacher interactions.

The data were collected for each student in a class by using a Singing Assessment Seating Chart (see Figure 1). In most of the assessments, the teacher modeled the singing task and the child echoed. If the child did not respond correctly, the teacher used various techniques such as verbal feedback, modeling again, and light/head voice tasks to help the child improve. The final result was marked on the seating chart using the rating scale developed by the teacher (see Figure 2). The data for each class was tallied on a spreadsheet (see Figure 3). The class results at one grade level were tallied and percentages for each rating were recorded. The rating percentages for each singing task are reported across several years.

Figure 1. Singing Assessment Seating Chart

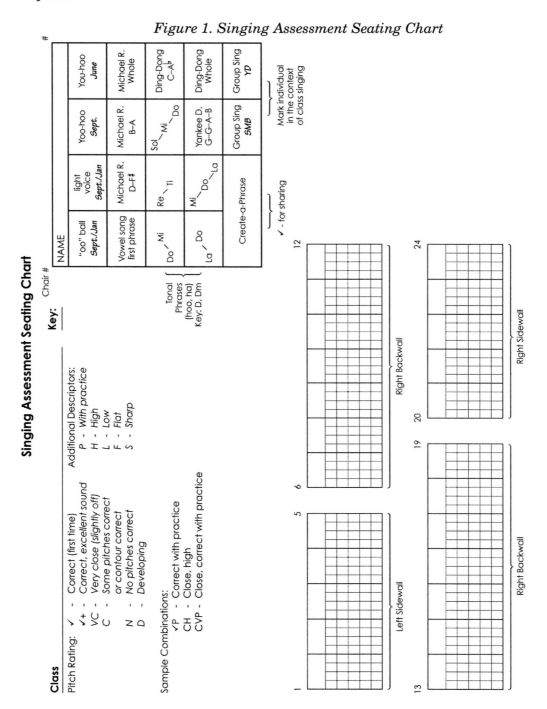

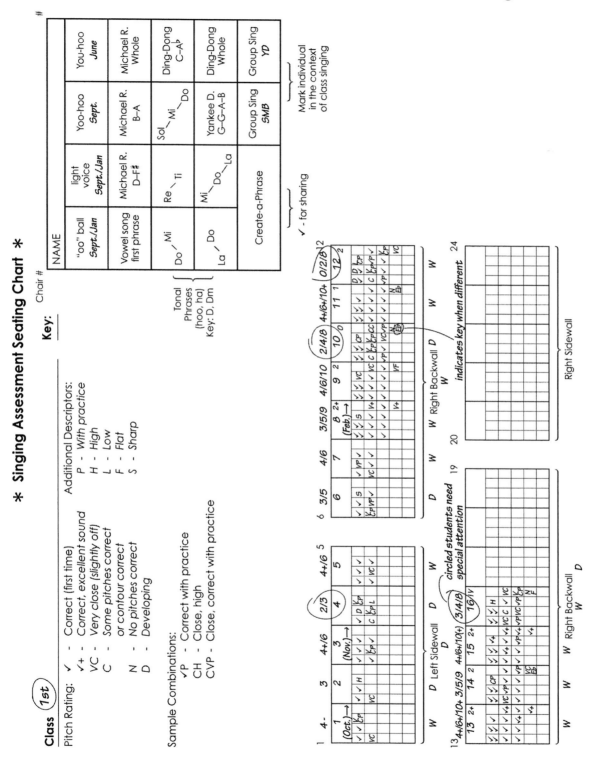

Figure 2. Singing Assessment Seating Chart with Markings

219

Figure 3. Singing Assessment Spreadsheet-sample

Key

First letter
- b = ball
- l = light voice

Second letter
- r = correct
- d = developing
- l = low

Gr. 1 "Oo" Singing Ball and Light Voice Sept. 2003								
Gronau	Montessano	Scalzo	Sitterly	Smith	Raw Total	RC Total (Raw Combined)		Total %
br-17	br-18	br-17	br-19	br-19	90		r	97%
	bd-2		bd-1		3		d	3%
					Total 93			
lr-13	lr-17	lr-16	lr-17	lr-19	82		r	88%
ld-4	ld-1	ld-2	ld-2	ld-1	10		d	11%
		ll-1			1		l	1%

Key

First letter
- y = Yoo-hoo
- v = vowel song

Second letter
- r = correct
- rp = correct with practice
- v = very close
- c = close
- l = low

Gr. 1 Yoo-hoo a–f♯ Sept. 2003								
yr-7	yr-5	yr-6	yr-8	yr-8	34		r	37%
yrp-2	yrp-4	yrp-1	yrp-1	yrp-6	14		rp	15%
yv-5	yv-8	yv-4	yv-5	yv-5	27	r/v 75	r/v	81%
yc-2	yc-1	yc-8	yc-4		15			
yl-1			yl-1	yl-1	c	c/l 18	c/l	19%
Total 17	Total 18	Total 19	Total 19	Total 20	Total 93			

Gr. 1 The Vowel Song f♯–g–a–g–f♯ Oct. 2003								
vr-5	vr-10	vr-8	vr-8	vr-10	41		r	44%
vrp-4			vrp-3		7		rp	8%
vv-4	vv-1	vv-8	vv-6	vv-4	23	r/v 71	r/v	76%
vc-2	vc-6	vc-3	vc-5	vc-3	19			
vl-2	vl-1				3	c/l 22	c/l	24%
Total 17	Total 18	Total 19	Total 19	Total 20	Total 93			

It is hoped from the information presented that elementary music teachers and researchers will gain a better knowledge of what primary students are capable of doing in terms of using their singing voices and singing in tune, as well as gain practical knowledge for assessing singing and teaching young children to sing.

Grade 2, Six Years of Assessment Data

The first assessment results presented are of second graders echoing two short phrases in an "Echo Blues." Students first sing the song as a group, echoing many phrases using nonsense syllables and then take a solo turn. The lower-pitched phrase was sung "Bah-dop-bah" and the higher-pitched phrase was sung "Bah-dop-bah-dah" ascending, and "Noo-noo-nah-nah" descending in the last two years. Over six years 865 children were assessed in September of second grade; the pitches for each phrase are shown in Table 1.

The rating criteria are as follows: *Correct* means the phrase was sung with the correct pitches the first time without practice. *Correct w/practice* means, with the teacher's help, the student echoed the phrase correctly. *Very Close* means it was sung within a quarter step of the correct pitch, slightly flat or sharp on one or two notes; this rating also includes a student who improved with practice. *Close* means that at least one note was incorrect or the response was similar at a different pitch level. *Low* means that the child used a much lower voice, sometimes more like a speaking voice. The ratings are recorded on the Singing Assessment Seating Chart (see Figure 1).

The second graders were much more successful at the three-note phrase in a low range than the four-note ascending phrase into the upper range. Sixty-eight to 78% sang the low three-note phrase correctly the first time compared to 34–43% on the four-note ascending phrase, and 59–61% on the four-note descending phrase. Correct, Correct w/practice and Very Close are considered acceptable achievement responses. Eighty-seven to 95% had acceptable achievement on the low three-note phrase compared to 65–79% on the four-note ascending phrase, and 87.5–88% on the four-note descending phrase. In the last two years to improve instruction, the second phrase was sung descending from the upper range resulting in a significant increase in achievement; this supports the common premise that children are more successful descending from the light/head voice than ascending to the light/head voice.

Correct w/practice ranges from 2–19%. Typically assessment does not include practice, but because the objective is to help children improve their singing, practice during the assessment process gave those who needed it an opportunity to improve their performance, resulting in higher achievement. Considering the limited time available to teach children, I feel that if they were assessed without practice, a great opportunity to learn would have been lost. Nevertheless, the data shows clearly the percentage of students that responded correctly the first time.

The second assessment results presented are of second graders answering a singing question in "Who has the Penny?" The words are "Who has the penny? Who has the key? Who has the nickel?" The first phrase is low, the second is mid-range, and the third is high, making this an excellent assessment of the singing voice range; the pitches for each phrase are indicated on Table 2. Over six years, 865 children were assessed in February or March of second grade except for the first year, which was in October. In the second year, when the assessment was done later in the year, the children were more successful, especially on the high descending phrase, so the song and assessment were done later each year thereafter.

The four-note ascending phrase in the mid-range was the easiest for students to sing correctly the first time. Ninety-one to 100% had acceptable achievement on the two phrases in the lower and mid-range compared to 82–98.5% on the high descending phrase (excluding the October assessment). Correct w/practice ranges from 4–37%; sometimes students improved on their second turn singing the same phrase without any help from the teacher, but were still rated as correct w/practice.

Table 1. "Echo Blues" Second Grade Assessment Results (N = 865)

Phrase (Pitches)	Month/Year Assessed	N	Correct	Correct w/practice	Very Close	Close or Low**	*Correct and Very Close
1 (e–c#–e)	9/2000	181	78%	5%	9%	8%	92%
	9/2001	161	71%	8%	8%	13%	87%
	9/2002	184	72%	8%	11%	8%	92%
	9/2003	98	68%	19%	7%	5%	95%
	9/2004	72	68%	12.5%	14%	5.5%	94.5%
	9/2005	169	73%	8%	12%	6.5%	93.5%
2 (e–g–a–b)	9/2000	181	39%	5%	21%	35%	65%
	9/2001	161	42%	2%	30%	26%	74%
	9/2002	184	43%	7%	27%	22%	78%
	9/2003	98	34%	4%	41%	21%	79%
3 (b–a–g–e)	9/2004	72	61%	14%	12.5%	12.5%	87.5%
	9/2005	169	59%	12%	16%	12%	88%

* Correct, Correct w/practice and Very Close are considered acceptable achievement responses.
** Close and low are *not* considered acceptable achievement responses.

Table 2. "Who Has the Penny?" Second Grade Assessment Results (N = 865)

Phrase (Pitches)	Month/Year Assessed	N	Correct	Correct w/practice	Very Close	Close or Low	Correct and Very Close
1 (d–d–e–f#–d)	10/2000	181	51%	7%	26%	16%	84%
	3/2002	161	61%	11%	22%	6%	94%
	2/2003	184	53%	22%	20%	4%	96%
	3/2004	98	51%	37%	11%	1%	99%
	2/2005	72	58%	32%	10%	0%	100%
	2/2006	169	61.5%	24%	14%	1%	99%
2 (f#–f#–g–a)	10/2000	181	56%	4%	19%	21%	79%
	3/2002	161	72%	11%	8%	9%	91%
	2/2003	184	61%	27%	9%	3%	97%
	3/2004	98	68%	25%	5%	2%	98%
	2/2005	72	85%	11%	4%	0%	100%
	2/2006	169	69%	18%	9%	3.5%	96.5%
3 (d–c#–b–a–f#)	10/2000	181	34%	11%	16%	39%	61%
	3/2002	161	53%	9%	19%	18%	82%
	2/2003	184	47%	24%	18%	11%	89%
	3/2004	98	46.5%	30%	17%	6%	94%
	2/2005	72	62.5%	18%	18%	1.5%	98.5%
	2/2006	169	50%	27%	15%	8%	92%

Kindergarten and Grade 1, "Yoo-hoo" Assessment Data

Tables 3 and 4 show singing achievement for kindergarteners and first graders, respectively, on the song "Yoo-hoo." Individual students echo the teacher singing "yoo-hoo" on the pitches A to F♯. The assessment was given early in the year for baseline data and then repeated near the end of the year to show what improvement had been made over the year.

Only 18–44% of kindergarteners were able to echo this simple phrase correctly the first time; acceptable achievement ranges from 53–78%. Improvement is shown later in the year, but varies in each year. Only 37–49% of first graders were able to echo the phrase correctly the first time in September, but a big improvement is shown in June: 61–69%. Acceptable achievement in September ranges from 71–91%, much higher than kindergarteners in October/November, 53–78%. In June, acceptable achievement for first graders ranges from 93–99% with no Low singers; correct w/practice ranges from 11–25%.

The difference in achievement between kindergarteners and first graders may be attributed to (a) age, (b) prior music instruction for first graders, (c) music twice a week for first graders, once a week for kindergarteners, (d) focused singing instruction for first graders including twenty-two assessments, less-focused singing instruction for kindergarteners, only 6six to ten assessments, and (e) singing in the kindergarten classroom that can sometimes have a negative effect on the use of a lighter voice.

Table 3. "Yoo-hoo" Kindergarten Assessment Results on the Pitches A–F♯ (N = 723*)

Month/Year Assessed	N	Correct	Correct w/practice	Very Close	Close or Low	Correct and Very Close
10/2000	149	39%	n/a	14%	47%	53%
10/2001	134	40%	10.5%	16%	33.5%	66.5%
10/2002	50	44%	4%	30%	22%	78%
10/2003	253	41%	18%	19%	22%	78%
10/2004	87	22%	17%	18%	42.5%	57.5%
10/2005	50	18%	18%	24%	40%	60%
5/2001	140	59%	n/a	18%	23%	77%
5/2002	132	39%	19%	25%	17%	83%
5/2003	50	40%	28%	16%	16%	84%
6/2004	249	45%	17%	15%	22.5%	77.5%
6/2005	91	34%	15%	22%	28.5%	71.5%
5/2006	50	36%	16%	18%	30%	70%

*N is lower (712) in the second assessment (May/June) because of students moving out of the district or being absent.

223

Table 4. "Yoo-hoo" Grade 1 Assessment Results on the Pitches A–F♯ (N = 467)

Month/Year Assessed	N	Correct	Correct w/practice	Very Close	Close or Low	Correct and Very Close
9/2001	155	47%	13%	11%	29%	71%
9/2002	99	49%	18%	14%	18%	82%
9/2003	91	37%	15%	29%	19%	81%
9/2004	122	46%	18%	27%	9%	91%
6/2002	155	61%	19%	13%	7%*	93%
6/2003	99	69%	11%	15%	4% *	96%
6/2004	91	67%	25%	7%	1% *	99%
6/2005	122	62%	23.5%	10%	4% *	96%

*There were no students who were assessed as "Low."

Grade 1, Comprehensive Singing Assessment Program

First grade is an ideal age to give children explicit instruction and practice in learning to sing songs and phrases. In the 2001–2002 school year, I developed a comprehensive singing assessment program for first grade based on assessments done the prior year. Seventeen different assessments were done, one was done twice, and two were repeated three times for comparison purposes resulting in a total of twenty-two assessments. Six conclusions were drawn from the singing data and the same assessments were made for the next three years to see if they were valid. The conclusions from the first year were:

1. In general, first graders are more successful at shorter echo singing tasks than at remembering and singing longer phrases or short songs.
2. In general, first graders are more successful at singing alone on shorter echo singing tasks than at singing a song in a group.
3. Success at singing a whole short song alone or in a group seems to be about equal for first graders.
4. Children improve over time with music instruction.
5. Practice improves achievement and can be part of an assessment.
6. The ability to use a light voice has a direct effect on achievement.

Singing data comparison tables for four years are presented as well as a description of the assessments. The data are then used to see if the conclusions are supported.

In the beginning of each year, first grade students were assessed on their ability to use their light/head voices while throwing a make-believe "Oo" singing ball (like the second half of a siren) and to sing "light voice" in a high range gradually dropping in pitch while throwing a make-believe feather in the air. A correct response had to be above the pitch "A" using a light voice; occasionally the teacher helped a child improve. Both tasks were repeated in January and June (see Tables 5 and 6). Ninety-six to 100% of the children were able to sing "Oo" above the pitch "A" throughout the year with the exception of September, 2001 (not done the prior year in kindergarten). Ninety-six to 98% of the children were able to sing "light voice" above the pitch "A" by June, showing an improvement from September.

224

Table 5. "Oo Ball" Grade 1 Assessment Results (N = 467)

Month/Year Assessed	N	Correct	Correct w/practice	Very Close	Close or Low	Correct and Very Close
9/2001	155	88%	0	0	12%	88%
9/2002	99	98%	0	0	2%	98%
9/2003	91	97%	0	0	3%	97%
9/2004	122	98%	0	0	2%	98%
1/2002	155	96%	0	0	4%	96%
1/2003	99	100%	0	0	0	100%
1/2004	91	99%	0	0	1%	99%
1/2005	122	100%	0	0	0	100%
6/2002	155	98%	0	0	2%	98%
6/2003	99	100%	0	0	0	100%
6/2004	91	100%	0	0	0	100%
6/2005	122	99%	0	0	1%	99%

Table 6. "Light Voice" Grade 1 Assessment Results (N = 467)

Month/Year Assessed	N	Correct	Correct w/practice	Very Close	Close or Low	Correct and Very Close
9/2001	155	88%	0	0	12%	88%
9/2002	99	86%	0	0	14%	86%
9/2003	91	88%	0	0	12%	88%
9/2004	122	95%	0	0	5%	95%
1/2002	155	92%	0	0	8%	92%
1/2003	99	100%	0	0	0	100%
1/2004	91	98%	0	0	2%	98%
1/2005	122	98%	0	0	2%	98%
6/2002	155	97%	0	0	3%	97%
6/2003	99	98%	0	0	2%	98%
6/2004	91	96%	0	0	4%	96%
6/2005	122	97.5%	0	0	2.5%	97.5%

Knowing that a child can use a light voice or throw an "Oo" singing ball in a high voice is very helpful in the practicing and improvement process when working on songs or short phrases. The "Oo" singing ball was used frequently in helping children improve on the song "Yoo-hoo" which was the next assessment in September (see Table 4); correct w/practice ranges from 11–25%.

The results of the next four assessments of partial song phrases are presented in Table 7 followed by results of five assessments for short tonal phrases in Table 8. The first song is the "Vowel Song," where students had to remember a longer phrase containing long notes sung on the five vowels A–E–I–O–U. "Michael, Row the Boat Ashore" has a two-note phrase in a low range on the word "Michael" and a two-note phrase in the light/head voice on the syllables...*Lu-Yah*. "Ding-Dong" is a short two-note phrase sung on the words *Ding-Dong* that requires the light/head voice; the pitch was raised a half-step after the first year so a chest voice could not be used. These assessments were all done by echoing the teacher and included practice as needed. All the tonal phrases were sung using a combination of the neutral syllables *Ha* or *Hoo* after an audiation pause. *Ha* was always used on the low "D" and *Hoo* was always used on the higher pitch "A" because it helped the children to find the lower or higher voice respectively.

In October, the longer phrase in the "Vowel Song" was more difficult than the other shorter assessments. In November, for "Michael, Row the Boat Ashore," students' mastery (correct rating) on the B–A phrase which requires the use of the light voice was higher than the D– F♯ phrase; this was a bit surprising because often students who have trouble singing sing too low. The use of the "Oo" singing ball in particular on ...*Lu-Yah* helped each child to open up the range of his or her voice. In December, *Ding-Dong* was a little more difficult than the "Michael, Row the Boat Ashore" phrases.

For the tonal phrases, 62–81% sang the two-note phrases in the low range correctly the first time compared to 45–58% on the three-note phrases in the low-mid range. Ninety-six to 99% had acceptable achievement on the two-note phrases in the low range compared to 90–95.5% on the three-note phrases in the low-mid range; Correct w/practice ranges from 11–29%. The children were more successful singing the D– F♯ phrase using the neutral syllables in the context of tonal phrases than singing "Michael" in the song context. Achievement in November-January on major phrases was similar to minor phrases in March-April; the leading tone approached by skip presented no problems for singing in tune.

In May, each child sang the first four notes of "Yankee Doodle." This phrase required the children to ascend into the light/head voice. Interestingly, one reason some students had to practice was to repeat the pitch "G" correctly, the tendency was to go up on the second pitch; correct w/practice ranges from 12–25% (see Table 9). Forty-nine to 60% sang correctly the first time and 91–94% had acceptable achievement.

Table 7. *"Vowel Song," (VS) "Michael, Row the Boat Ashore" (MR), and "Ding-Dong" (DD),
Grade 1 Assessment Results (N = 467)*

Song (Pitches)	Month/Year Assessed	N	Correct	Correct w/practice	Very Close	Close or Low	Correct and Very Close
VS (f♯–g–a–g–f♯)	10/2001	155	40%	5%	21%	34%	66%
	10/2002	99	38%	5%	26%	30%	70%
	10/2003	91	44%	8%	24%	24%	76%
	10/2004	122	37%	11%	24%	28%	72%
MR (d–f♯)	11/2001	155	61%	18%	11%	10%	90%
	11/2002	99	56%	15%	21%	8%	92%
	11/2003	91	60%	18%	16.5%	5.5%	94.5%
	11/2004	122	56.5%	23%	14%	6.5%	93.5%
MR (b–a)	11/2001	155	64%	7%	20%	9%	91%
	11/2002	99	72%	5%	14%	9%	91%
	11/2003	91	65%	16.5%	12%	6.5%	93.5%
	11/2004	122	65.5%	16%	9%	9%	91%
DD (b–g) DD (c–a)	12/2001	155	50%	19%	10%	21%	79%
	12/2002	99	45%	22%	18%	16%	84%
	12/2003	91	60%	21%	10%	10%	90%
	12/2004	122	55%	19%	13%	13%	87%

Table 8. Tonal Phrases Grade 1 Assessment Results (N = 467)

Tonal Phrase Pitches	Month/Year Assessed	N	Correct	Correct w/practice	Very Close	Close or Low	Correct and Very Close
d–f♯	11/2001*	155	63%	21%	12%	4%	96%
	11/2002	99	68%	17%	11%	4%	96%
	11/2003	91	67%	25%	5.5%	2%	98%
	11/2004	122	72%	13%	11%	4%	96%
e–c♯	11/2001	155	69%	24%	5%	2%	98%
	11/2002	99	76%	18%	3%	3%	97%
	11/2003	91	77%	19%	1%	3%	97%
	11/2004	122	65.5%	29%	2.5%	3%	97%
a–f♯–d	11/2001	155	50%	18%	22%	10%	90%
	11/2002	99	52%	29%	14%	5%	95%
	11/2003	91	58%	25%	11%	5.5%	94.5%
	11/2004	122	52%	22%	19%	7%	93%
d–f	3/2002**	155	62%	21%	14%	3%	97%
	3/2003	99	69%	18%	9%	4%	96%
	3/2004	91	81%	11%	7%	1%	99%
	3/2005	122	72%	15%	9%	4%	96%
a–f–d	3/2002	155	45%	25%	23%	7%	93%
	3/2003	99	54%	22%	16%	8%	92%
	3/2004	91	52%	28%	16%	4.5%	95.5%
	3/2005	122	53%	18%	19%	10%	90%

*Each year all phrases were assessed over three months November-January.
**Each year all phrases were assessed over two months March-April.

Table 9. "Yankee Doodle" Grade 1 Assessment Results on the Pitches G-G–A–B (N = 467)

Month/Year Assessed	N	Correct	Correct w/practice	Very Close	Close or Low	Correct and Very Close
5/2002	155	58%	17%	17%	8%	92%
5/2003	99	60%	12%	18%	9%	91%
5/2004	91	53%	25%	17%	6%	94%
5/2005	122	49%	20%	23%	8%	92%

The final assessments in June were the repetition of the "Oo" singing ball, "light voice" and "Yoo-hoo" (See Tables 4, 5, and 6).

In contrast to the short phrase assessments, in February each child sang two short songs; "Michael, Row the Boat Ashore" and "Ding-Dong." For these assessments, the class sings the song together with no accompaniment and then one child sings alone; there is no individual practice. The class plays a guessing game where the child who sang the song alone guesses who is singing. The rating criterion Very Close is also used instead of Close to indicate when the song was sung correctly or very close at a different pitch level (see Table 10).

Table 10. "Ding-Dong" and "Michael, Row the Boat Ashore" Whole Song Grade 1 Assessment Results (N = 467)

Song (Range/Key)	Month/Year Assessed	N	Correct	Very Close (correct pitch level)	Very Close (different pitch level)	Close or Low	Correct and Very Close
Ding Dong (e♭–c/A♭ major)	2/2002	155	15%	16%	35%	34%	66%
	2/2003	99	28%	10%	43%	18%	82%
	2/2004	91	31.5%	10%	41.5%	17%	83%
	2/2005	122	26.5%	9%	45%	20%	80%
Michael Row (d–b/D major)	2/2002	155	28%	12%	34%	25.5%	74.5%
	2/2003	99	27%	8%	46%	18%	82%
	2/2004	91	30%	18%	42%	10%	90%
	2/2005	122	27%	20.5%	39%	13%	87%

Note. None of the students were assessed as "Correct w/practice"

Only 26.5–31.5% sang the songs perfectly or almost perfectly (marked as Correct) except on "Ding-Dong" in 2002. Interestingly, 34–46% sang the songs correctly or very close at a different pitch level. Except for 2002, 80–90% had acceptable achievement.

The vast majority of students who sang at a different pitch level sang lower even though the class was just singing at the correct pitch level; this is probably because many children tend to sing lower on their own. It's important to realize that a child is not a non-singer just because they aren't used to singing in a higher range; that is why it is important for music teachers to teach children how to use their light/head voice and work with them individually.

Two "singing with the group" assessments were done, in March with the song "See Me Beautiful," range C♯–B in D major, and in May with "Yankee Doodle," range low B–high C in G major (see Table 11). Some children sing differently in a group as compared to singing alone, usually lower; the teacher walks around in front of the children and listens for each child's voice. Fifty-seven to 81% sang the two songs correctly and 67–84% had acceptable achievement.

Table 11. "See Me Beautiful" and "Yankee Doodle" Individual in Group Grade 1 Assessment Results (N = 467)

Song (Range/Key)	Month/Year Assessed	N	Correct	Very Close	Close or Low	Correct and Very Close
See Me Beautiful (c♯–b/D major)	3/2002	155	62%	10%	28%	72%
	3/2003	99	79%	5%	16%	84%
	3/2004	91	81%	3%	16%	84%
	3/2005	122	80%	0%	20%	80%
Yankee Doodle (b–c/G major)	5/2002	155	59%	8%	33%	67%
	5/2003	99	57%	11%	32%	68%
	5/2004	91	76%	3%	20%	80%
	5/2005	122	78%	0%	22%	78%

Note. None of the students were assessed as "Correct w/practice"

All individual data is recorded on the Singing Assessment Seating Chart. The assessments are used cumulatively to evaluate the child's singing voice using a Singing Voice Evaluation Rubric and then marked on the seating chart (see Figure 1). Four years of voice rating statistics are presented in Table 12. The rubrics used for evaluating the singing results for Grade 1 are shown in Figures 4, 5, 6, 7, and 8. The assessments are listed at the top of each rubric and the rating is additive for correct or very close, except for the June rubric. The student is judged as Sings Well, Developing Singer, or Beginning Singer.

Table 12. Singing Voice Evaluation Statistics Grade 1 (N = 467)

Month/Year Evaluated	N	Sings Well	Developing Singer	Beginning Singer
2/2002	155	64%	31%	5%
2/2003	99	73%	27%	0%
2/2004	91	80%	18%	2%
2/2005	122	75%	21%	3%
6/2002	155	68%	29%	3%
6/2003	99	70%	30%	0%
6/2004	91	80%	19%	1%
6/2005	122	78%	19%	3%

Note. See Figures 6 and 7 for the singer's rating criteria. Student evaluation criteria varied slightly in the first two years from the evaluation criteria shown in the rubrics.

Figure 4. Singing Voice Evaluation Rubric—Grade 1, October

Rating ↓ Criteria →	4 Assessments: "Oo" singing ball, "Light" voice, "Yoo-hoo," "The Vowel Song"
4—Sings Well	4 correct or very close
3—Developing Singer	3 correct or very close
2—Developing Singer	2 correct or very close
1—Beginning Singer	1 correct or very close
0—Beginning Singer	0 correct or very close

Figure 5. Singing Voice Evaluation Rubric—Grade 1 November

Rating ↓ Criteria →	6 Assessments:	"Oo" singing ball "Light" voice "Yoo-hoo" "The Vowel Song" "Michael Row" (d–f♯) "Michael Row" (b–a)
6—Sings Well	6 correct or very close	
5—Developing Singer	5 correct or very close	
4—Developing Singer	4 correct or very close	
3—Developing Singer	3 correct or very close	
2—Beginning Singer	2 correct or very close	
1—Beginning Singer	1 correct or very close	
0—Beginning Singer	0 correct or very close	

Figure 6. Singing Voice Evaluation Rubric—Grade 1 February

Rating ↓ Criteria →	12 Assessments:	10 phrases: "Oo" singing ball "Light" voice "Yoo-hoo" "The Vowel Song" "Michael Row (2) Tonal phrases (3) "Ding Dong" 2 short songs: "Michael Row" "Ding Dong"
8–10+(1 or 2) Sings Well	8–10 phrases Correct or Very Close and 1 or 2 short songs Correct (any key) or 2 short songs Very Close (any key)	
8–10+(0) Developing Singer	8–10 phrases Correct or Very close, no short songs Correct (any key) and 1 or 0 Very Close	
6–7 Developing Singer	6–7 phrases Correct or Very Close and 0–2 short songs Correct or Very Close (any key)	
5+(2) Developing Singer	5 phrases Correct or Very Close and 2 short songs Correct or Very Close (any key)	
5 or below+(1 or 0) Beginning Singer	5 or less phrases Correct or Very Close and 1 or 0 short songs Correct or Very Close (any key)	

Figure 7. Singing Voice Evaluation Rubric—Grade 1 June

Rating ↓ Criteria →	4 Phrase Assessments: Tonal phrases (2) "Yankee Doodle" "Yoo-hoo"	2 Group Singing Assessments: "See Me Beautiful" "Yankee Doodle"
Maintain Sings Well	3–4 correct or very close	1–2 correct or very close
New Sings Well	4 correct or very close	2 correct or very close
Looses Sings Well Developing Singer	2–4 correct or very close	0 correct or very close
Developing Singer	3–4 correct or very close	0–1 correct or very close
Stays a Beginning Singer	0–3 correct or very close	0 correct or very close

232

Figure 8. Singing Voice Evaluation Rubric-Grade 1 February (2007 Revision)

Rating ↓ Criteria →	12 Assessments:	9 phrases:
		   "Oo" singing ball
		   "Light" voice
		   "Yoo-hoo"
		   "Michael Row (2)"
		   Tonal phrases (3)
		   "Ding Dong"
		1 short song:
		   "Michael Row"
		2 group singing:
		   "The Vowel Song"
		   "Michael Row"

12—Sings Well		9 phrases, 1 short song (any key), and 2 group singing tasks: All Correct or Very Close
10–11—Sings Well		7–9 phrases, 1 short song (any key), and 1–2 group singing tasks: All Correct or Very Close
6–11—Developing Singer		3–9 phrases, 0–1 short song, and 0–2 group singing tasks: All Correct or Very Close
5 or below—Beginning Singer		5 or less Correct or Very Close on phrases, the short song, and group singing tasks

Note. This revision provides a more comprehensive evaluation of singing ability because it includes the group singing assessment which came after February in the other rubric.

Conclusions

The conclusions about first graders from the first year of data collection were then evaluated for their validity using the data collected over four years. The acceptable achievement data (ratings of Correct, Correct w/practice, and Very Close) are cited to compare student success on the various singing tasks.

1. *In general, first graders are more successful at shorter echo singing tasks than at remembering and singing longer phrases or short songs.* TRUE.
   - The success rate for the ten short phrases ("Yoo-hoo" June assessment) was 90–99% except for "Ding-Dong," 79–90%.
   - Only 66–76% had success on the long phrase in the "Vowel Song" and 66–83% had success on the short song "Ding-Dong"; 74.5–90% had success on the short song "Michael, Row the Boat Ashore."

233

2. *In general, first graders are more successful at singing alone on shorter echo singing tasks than at singing a song in a group.* TRUE with modification: "Shorter echo singing tasks w/practice."
   - The success rate for the ten short phrases ("Yoo-hoo" June assessment) was 90–99% except for "Ding-Dong," 79–90%.
   - Only 72–84% had success singing in a group on the song "See Me Beautiful" and 67–80% had success on "Yankee Doodle."
   - The validity of this conclusion is very clear when comparing the 91–94% success rate on the first four notes of "Yankee Doodle" to the 67–80% success rate when singing "Yankee Doodle" in a group.

3. *Success at singing a whole short song alone or in a group seems to be about equal for first graders.* MOSTLY TRUE. (Assessing the same song would yield a much better comparison.)
   - Except for "Michael, Row the Boat Ashore" in 2004 and 2005, the percentages are in the same range for singing a short song alone or in a group, 67–84%. It should be noted that on the short song solos approximately half (sometimes less, sometimes more) of the students who were successful, sang in a different key than the original, usually lower.

4. *Children improve over time with music instruction.* TRUE for these assessments, but much more comparative assessment data is needed (i.e., assessing the same song at different times).
   - The children showed significant improvement on the song "Yoo-hoo." Acceptable achievement in September ranges from 71–91% compared to 93–99% in June with No Low singers.
   - For the "Light voice" assessment, 86–95% were successful in September compared to 96–98% in June.

5. *Practice improves achievement and can be part of an assessment.* TRUE.
   - Correct w/practice ranges from 5–29%. Only five assessments are below 10% for correct w/practice compared to thirty-seven assessments that are 15% or more.
   - All the assessment data shows clearly the percentage of students who responded correctly the first time

6. *The ability to use a Light voice has a direct effect on achievement.* TRUE.
   - Acceptable achievement percentages for phrases requiring the "Light voice" (high "B" or "C") were as follows: "Yankee Doodle": 91–94%, "Michael, Row the Boat Ashore": 91–93.5%, and "Ding-Dong": 84–90% three years out of four.
   - For the song "Michael, Row the Boat Ashore," students' mastery (Correct rating) on the B–A phrase, which requires the use of the Light voice was higher than the D–F♯ phrase, 64–72% compared to 56–61%, respectively.

The conclusions and observations in this paper are substantiated by the data collected and do inform instruction. Further research using the same songs for comparisons of different tasks and the same songs for comparisons at different times would make conclusions three and four stronger. In the endeavor to help young children become successful singers, individual assessment including practice will ensure that every child will improve as a singer and provide the proof that it is indeed happening.

Assess for Success

Denese Odegaard
Fargo Public Schools
Fargo, North Dakota

Abstract

Music educators need to acquire tools for formative and summative assessment to allow all students to realize their ultimate musical potential. This paper is based on my personal experience with curriculum and assessment in the beginning, middle school, and high school orchestra classroom, and presents ways to write, record, and report assessments based on my classroom experience as a string educator. Through assessment, teachers determine what students have learned and use assessment results to make decisions to re-teach or to move on based on student response. Students' desire to learn and do well is heightened when they receive frequent and specific feedback. They are also capable of assessing themselves. When students know what is expected of them, they take ownership of their learning. By using the national standards and benchmarks to write a school music curriculum, a teacher can determine what to assess and when. It is also important to share the music curriculum and assessments with administrators, students and parents, so that everyone understands the scope and rigor of the subject.

The introduction of the national standards for music education in 1994 (Consortium of National Arts Education Associations, 1994) was a turning point in instruction and student motivation in music classes. The new standards provided a framework for music curricula and corresponding assessments, motivating teachers to guide students to excel in their musical training and become independent thinkers as a result of specific and timely feedback. Granted, it takes time to develop a successful system of curriculum and assessment, but the benefits reaped are well worth the time spent. In this paper, I share my process for developing standards-based assessments.

Developing a Foundation for Assessment

The foundation for successful assessment is a well-organized, sequential, standards-based curriculum. To develop this, begin with the National Music Standards (Consortium of Arts Education Associations, 1994), which defines K–4, 5–8 and 9–12 benchmarks, as a guideline. Curriculum should be written for each area of study (i.e., band, orchestra, choir, and general music), keeping all nine standards separate in order to write a detailed, spiraling curriculum for each grade level. If desired, write separate curricula for jazz band, jazz choir, special learner music programs, or other special classes.

Curriculum should be written within the following framework:

- Standard—: the nine national music standards
- Benchmark—: the benchmarks provided in the standards document
- Learning Targets: the specific knowledge students should know at that grade level
- Performance Tasks: the activities implemented to teach these targets or concepts

A sample curriculum framework for National Content Standard 3, Improvisation (Consortium of National Arts Education Associations, 1994), is shown in Figure 1. From this curriculum, decide what specific learning targets should be assessed and by which methods (e.g., checklist, rubric, observation, self-evaluation, and evaluation of others). This list may be used to create a knowledge base or a list of what the student should learn at that grade level (see Figure 2 for a sample knowledge base for 5th-grade violin). The knowledge base can be given to older students at the beginning of the year as a preview to what will be learned and referred to periodically throughout the year. Giving younger students a copy mid-year shows them what they have already learned and what they still need to learn. This reference for teachers reminds them what they have taught and still need to teach. This list may also serve as a progress report or portfolio page for reporting student achievement. By keeping the standards listed on any reporting device, administrators, teachers, students, and parents are aware of the standards.

Figure 1. Sample Curriculum Framework for Standard 3—Improvisation

Standard 3: Improvisation. Students improvise melodies, variations, and accompaniments.
Benchmark 3.8.1: Improvise simple harmonic accompaniments.
(Consortium of National Arts Education Associations, 1994)

Grade	Learning Target	Performance Task
5	Listens and determines when the chord changes from tonic to dominant in a basic accompaniment.	Student listens to an accompaniment, raising the index finger for tonic chords and all five fingers for the dominant chord.
6	Improvises an accompaniment based on the root tone of the tonic and dominant chords.	Student determines the root tone of the tonic and dominant chords for an accompaniment to a simple melody and makes the proper chord changes using a rhythmic pattern of his choice.
7	Improvises an accompaniment based on the root of the tonic, subdominant, and dominant chords.	Student determines the root tone of the tonic, subdominant, and dominant chords for an accompaniment to a simple melody and makes the proper chord changes using a rhythmic pattern of his choice.
8	Improvises an accompaniment based on the triads of the tonic, subdominant, and dominant chords.	Student determines the triads of the tonic, subdominant, and dominant chords for an accompaniment to a simple melody and makes the proper chord changes using a rhythmic pattern of his choice.

Research suggests that feedback should be corrective in nature, timely, criterion-specific, and that students can effectively provide some of their own feedback. Assessment *for* student learning (formative assessment) is the number one reason students become engaged learners and desire to do their best.

Students should understand what is being assessed before the assessment and learn to receive feedback (what is done well and what needs improvement) in order to accomplish goals set forth by the curriculum to build skills. Assessment focuses the teacher's and student's attention on specific goals. Figure 2 presents an example of an information sheet that I use to inform 5th-grade violin students of what will be assessed during the school year.

When teaching a new concept, it is important to constantly check for understanding. In order to leave no child left behind, assess each student frequently. It is better to discover that a student is struggling at the beginning stages of learning a new concept than during summative assessment (final assessment) when it is too late.

Create a trusting atmosphere of trial and error in your classroom where students feel comfortable to experiment. Let them know it is okay to make mistakes in order to improve and always allow them to try again in order to perfect something. Students are rarely given this opportunity in their education.

Developing Assessments for Classroom Use

There are several reasons to assess students in the music classroom. Some of these are:

- To check for student understanding.
- To inform students of their progress—what do they do well and what they need to do to improve.
- To guide teachers in making decisions about teaching—moving on or re-teaching concepts.
- To report student progress to others.

Assessment entails observing, recording, and reporting information. Music instructors spend a large part of the class period observing what the students are able to do. Oftentimes we fall short in the area of recording because it takes time. By imbedding assessment into the learning targets, assessment is seamless. In order to be less interruptive during class, students perform a short excerpt of music that includes a new concept instead of the entire piece. Clap and count four to eight measures instead of a whole piece. Less is better when it comes to assessment. Assess a few students each day in the middle or at the end of a class period. In large performing groups, record student performances and listen to them outside of the class period.

To maximize success, develop assessments that:

- Align with the standards.
- Are fair and free from bias.
- Clearly define criteria for assessment.
- Can be shared with students prior to the assessment.
- Provide students with multiple opportunities to demonstrate their learning.

- Provide students with flexibility in how they demonstrate their learning.
- Provide students with opportunities to self-assess and assess others.

Figure 2. Sample Information Sheet for Fifth-grade Violin Students

Violin

5th Grade Knowledge Base

key signature - key of D - F# and C#

D Major Scale

whole note	whole rest	half note	half rest	quarter note	quarter rest	eighth notes	
1-2-3-4	1-2-3-4	1-2	1-2	1	1	1	and

4=number of beats per measures
4=quarter note receives one beat

down bow up bow   ledger line   bar line   repeat sign   double bar

TERMS
Violin - GDAE
Orchestra
Music staff - 5 lines/4 spaces
Bar lines - divide the music staff into measures
Measures -the space between bar lines. Each measure has the number of beats found
    in the top number of the time signature
Ledger lines - notes with lines above or below the staff that extend the music staff
    higher or lower
Double bar -the end of the piece of music
Repeat sign - go back to the beginning and play the music again
Key Signature - tells what notes to play with sharps and flats
Down bow - move the bow away from your body (to the right)
Up bow - move the bow toward your body (to the left)
Pizzicato (pizz) - pluck the strings
Arco - play with the bow on the string
Bow lift - ' lift the bow and return to its starting point
Left hand pizzicato - plucking the strings with the fingers of the left hand
Staccato - short notes produced by stopping the bow between notes
Legato- smooth bow strokes with no space between notes
Allegro - fast tempo
Moderato - medium tempo
Andante - walking tempo
C - Common time - same as 4/4
Tie - a curved line that connects the same pitch
Slur - more than one note in a bow direction
Plus any terms used in the music we are playing

241

When developing these assessments, remember to:

- Provide multiple ways to teach students and multiple ways for students to succeed, accommodating multiple intelligences, learning styles and special needs.
- Share with students what is exemplary work and what is not acceptable by collecting samples of student work.
- Clarify to the students what is expected of them.
- Assign weight to criteria commensurate with their importance to your program, particularly when designing point-based rubrics (Brophy, 2000).

Suggestions for Facilitating Assessment in Music Classes

Modeling assessment during class teaches students to assess themselves and others. One tool to help students evaluate music is a vocabulary of musical terms. Students should be able to pronounce, spell, and know the definitions of terms in order to put specific evaluation into words. Offer time for students to reflect on their work and time management. Have students create self-assessments with guidance. Give students the opportunity to explain why things did or did not go well and ask them what they would change if the assessment were given again.

The biggest roadblock for music teachers is the time it takes to assess. One solution is to integrate multiple standards into a learning activity or lesson, which allows students to practice concepts in many different ways. In a beginning string class, students may learn the new notes G, A, B. They practice by saying the notes, singing the note names, singing in solfege, reading the rhythms of a song, and finally playing the song. Playing these three new notes in several songs or exercises allows a student to practice reading these new notes in different combinations. Improvise short phrases using the new notes to allow students to be creative. Compose, by hand, a twelve-measure piece with these three notes in ABA form and now students are able to place the notes on the staff. When completed, the composition can be entered into a music-writing software program and printed so that the song can be played by other students. The student's composition can also be recorded for a portfolio and sent home via email for parents to enjoy. When recording the song, students should listen to their performance and determine if it is done to their satisfaction or if improvement is needed. Have them verbalize what needs to be corrected and record the song again. It is always amazing how students know how to evaluate their performance right from the beginning stages of playing. By using all of these standards, music embraces the student. Assessments can be executed for note and rhythm reading, performance, improvisation, composition, technology, and self-evaluation.

Assessments should be created so that many tasks may be assessed with the same tool. A partial sample assessment tool is shown in Figure 3. By creating a rubric for performance, any exercise, piece, or excerpt may be assessed. A rubric for performance includes a vertical list of criteria that are assessed. Horizontally to the right of each criterion list statements of varying degrees for the levels of mastery with Level 4 on the left going to Level 1 on the right. Level 3 is where the majority of students of that grade or experience level will fall. Level 4 would be the exceptional student, Level 2 is for developing skills, and Level 1 is beginning stages of proficiency. Create an initial master list of criteria for high school and the middle school and elementary assessments can be crafted from this list by eliminating criteria not used and simplifying statements that younger students understand. It is also possible to weight each criterion by assigning points commensurate with the importance of that criterion in the overall score.

Suggestions for Developing Classroom Assessment Tools for the National Standards

Choosing Criteria for Assessment

A performance rubric for Standards 1 (Singing) and 2 (Instrumental Performance) must include all of the criteria for performing (e.g., a performance rubric may include 1) tone, 2) notes, 3) rhythmic accuracy, 4) articulation, etc.). By numbering the criteria, an instructor may choose as many or as few criteria as desired to assess on a performance assessment. For example, 1) tone, 2) notes, and 4) articulation may be the three criteria for one assessment and on another, the teacher may just want to assess 4) articulation.

Standards 3 (Improvisation) and 4 (Composition) deal with creativity within certain guidelines. These rubrics can be written similarly from grade level to grade level and for all areas because they deal with the same issues. Improvisation criteria can be rhythmic, melodic, or both, and should include harmonic structure with older students. Composition addresses accuracy of note placement, use of rhythms, harmonic structure, neatness, alignment, and use of markings in the music.

Standard 5 (Reading Music) encompasses reading, labeling, sight-reading, and standard notation symbols.

Standard 6 (Listening) and Standard 7 (Evaluating) both require a knowledge base of terms and their definitions, styles of music, elements of music, and aesthetic value of music in order to describe and evaluate music either written or verbally. Teaching students to make specific statements about music on a daily basis, building a word bank and comparing and contrasting pieces as a group enables students to do this individually.

Standard 8 (Music and other Disciplines) and Standard 9 (Music, History, and Culture) relate music to other arts, the world around them, history, and other cultures. It helps students better understand of how music fits into their lives and the lives of people throughout history. Activities for these standards may include projects such as PowerPoint presentations, videos, or demonstrations. Presenting a rubric based on one of these projects prior to students beginning the task will give the students a clear picture of expectations. This may be a rubric on presentations or cooperative learning.

Developing Rubrics

Rubrics are detailed scoring guides that are designed to capture the variability of student performance with clearly defined assessment criteria. Some of the benefits of using rubrics are:

- Students know what is expected of them.
- Concrete evidence of student learning without bias.

- Students are responsible and held accountable for the work they do.
- General rubrics for each standard can be used for many tasks.

Rubrics present descriptions of levels of achievement for the selected assessment criteria. Some general rubric level descriptors are:

Level 4   Student shows exceptional ease or creativity/advanced.
Level 3   Student performs at grade level expectation/mastery of skill/proficient.
Level 2   Student understands and is working on the learning target but has not mastered it yet.
Level 1   Student is at beginning stages of mastery of a skill or concept.

Here are some tips for writing rubrics:

- Write the most-assessed criteria toward the top of the rubric and the less-often-assessed criteria lower in the left column.
- Number each criterion so that you can inform students which criteria you will be assessing prior to the assessment.
- Write positive statements that encourage lower-level students to reach proficiency.
- Avoid counting mistakes—use words like some, few, and many as descriptors.
- Avoid subjective words such as good, acceptable, or poor.

Figure 3. Sample Assessment Tool (Rubric) for Tone, Notes and Intonation, and Articulation

Criterion	Level 4	Level 3	Level 2	Level 1	Weight	Score
Tone	Student uses bow placement, speed, and weight appropriate for the musical selection. Demonstrates advanced bow techniques to play expressively.	Student uses bow placement, speed, and weight appropriate for the musical selection.	Student generally uses bow placement, speed, and weight appropriate for the musical selection.	Student begins to understand bow placement, speed, and weight appropriate for the musical selection.	20 points	60 (Level 3 times 20 points = 60)
Notes and Intonation	Student plays all notes with precisions and fluency in a steady tempo.	Student plays all notes accurately in a steady tempo.	Student plays most notes accurately, occasionally altering the tempo to accommodate unfamiliar sections.	Student plays most notes accurately, frequently altering tempo to accommodate unfamiliar sections.	10 points	20 (Level 2 times 10 points = 20)
Articulation	Student plays all articulations correctly, making smooth transitions from one to the other in a musical manner.	Student plays all articulations correctly.	Student plays most of the articulations correctly.	Student plays some of the articulations correctly.	20 points	60 (Level 3 times 20 points = 60)
					TOTAL POINTS	140

Note. The shaded areas represent the student's achievement level. Each level is worth a certain number of points (the *weight*), and this weight is multiplied by the number of the achievement level to earn points for that criterion. This student received 140 points out of 150 points, or 93%.

Checklists

A simple checklist is another way to assess playing positions or posture. Simply list the criteria down the left side of the page and create columns in which you can insert the date and check what areas need improvement. Over time, it is usually evident to the student what needs to be corrected. For quick checks, only mark the areas that need fixing.

Recording Student Assessments

Recording student assessments is most burdensome to teachers, but can be done quickly and easily using a spreadsheet in which the names of students can be pasted down the left side and the name of the assessment or criteria for an assessment written in columns across the top. If teaching a large class, assess a few students each day at the middle or end of the class period, while the others students have a specific activity to do or complete, and keep track of it on a quick assessment chart. This can then be transferred to a grade book or grading program.

Occasionally having students assess themselves and others strongly imbeds criteria set forth in the assessments. Assessing themselves puts the responsibility on the student to do things correctly and excel. Education today focuses on students being actively involved in their learning. By giving the students the assessment criteria, they know what is expected of them and will know exactly what they did well and need to improve.

Recording assessments varies as much as the number of school districts in the nation. Each school district uses different grading programs and documenting and transferring grades from the grade book to the program is inevitable. There are several ways to document assessments.

The most common way is a grade book listing the names of students down the side and inserting grades to the right of the student's name. Try using one grading page per student, listing assessed tasks down the left side and columns for recording scores to the right. Label each task with the standard number such as singing (1), dictation (5), music listening, (6) and so on. This is a great tool to use at parent-teacher conferences. It is easier to display, confidential, and parents become aware of the presence of standards.

In a beginning instrumental class where a progress report may be filled in by hand, standard 2 is assessed more than the other standards. Create a grading page for standard 2 listing all of the performance criteria across the top horizontally and student names down the left side. Input a rubric score for each item as a performance assessment is completed. All of the other standards can be listed across the top horizontally on another recording page with student names down the side. The difference is that the standard 2 record page has very specific criteria listed and the other standards page may just have final scores from a rubric given to the student prior to the assessment. If you have specific assessments in which you would like to list the criteria, make a separate grading page for that standard as well.

Spreadsheets are great for creating recording documents. Create a fill-in assessment report with students' names down the left and columns to the right to fill in the title of the assessment. Another way is to group standards across the top: vocal, instrumental, create, read/write, listen/analyze, and history/culture. Leave columns for three assessment scores per category and in the fourth column insert the formula to average the three columns prior to it. This saves you time in averaging scores.

Reporting Student Progress to Parents

Reporting assessments is also varied from one school district to another. If using a standards-based report card, be sure to include the standard number and descriptor such as singing, playing, improvising, etc. Combining standards in the categories mentioned above may be a necessity for space constraints. If there are any district initiatives, such as writing across the curriculum, include assessment scores for these activities. If your district has a strategic plan you can incorporate into your reporting, this strengthens your program's validity with the administrators. An example of tying into a strategic plan is listing items that relate to items such as character (attendance and lesson preparation), life skills (materials and instrument present or attendance at large group rehearsals), and academic performance (lesson preparation).

Progress reports are best if the learning targets are listed by standards. Conferences are a great time to show parents the individual grade sheet and to play student audio or visual recordings for them. Email comments or student recordings to parents once a quarter. Several school districts have on-line grading systems that can be viewed by parents, which should be kept current. If there is a need to transfer rubric scores to a letter grade, calculate the percentage of points earned on the assessment (divide the points earned by the total possible points) and apply that percentage to the letter grading scale (see Figure 3).

Final Thoughts

Some additional considerations for teachers when writing a standards-based curriculum and assessments are:

- Determine what kinds of resources are needed to carry out effective assessments.
- Hire floating music instructors to run middle and high school performing group rehearsals so that the regular teachers can assesses individual students or groups.
- Determine what kind of professional development is needed for music educators.
- Work with instruction supervisors to incorporate time for all music instructors to meet and work on curriculum and assessments together by grade level or groups of grade levels. By working together, everyone understands first hand what is expected. Sharing expertise is a great benefit to this time together.
- Take time to bring in student assessments and evaluate them together. This improves the ability of some teachers to evaluate more accurately and effectively.
- Determine what kind of technology and technology training is needed.
- Once your curriculum is written, view it grade to grade and from standard to standard within each grade level to look for gaps in instruction and/or repetitions.
- Share curricula from area to area (general music, band, orchestra, and choir).
- Put all of the documents your staff uses on the web or in a district shared folder for easy access.
- Once the curriculum is completed, write your own classroom-specific curriculum.
- Develop accountability of teachers.
- Have teachers observe each other.

A teacher's top priorities for assessment are (a) to improve instruction and (b) show student growth over time, while making assessments relevant to what the students are studying. Standards and assessments have improved the way teachers teach and students learn. Take the time to write a detailed curriculum based on the standards, determine ways to include standards in everyday instruction, and administer assessments that flow from the curriculum. This is meaningful instruction with the rigor that the students require.

References

Brophy, T. S. 2000. *Assessing the developing child musician: A guide for general music teachers*. Chicago: GIA Publications.

Consortium of National Arts Education Associations. 1994. *National standards for arts education: What every young American should know and be able to do in the arts*. Reston, VA: MENC—The National Association for Music Education.

Standards and Tools of Assessment in the Elementary Music Classroom

Sarah Hearn
Dorothy Pullen Elementary School, Rowlett, Texas

Abstract

In this day of high-stakes accountability testing, the place of assessment in music education has come under scrutiny. Educators everywhere are considering the best methods for evaluating the arts subjects. While all would agree assessment is necessary to hold teachers and students accountable, the methods of evaluating progress vary. A fair number of researchers hold to the belief that measuring the arts with pencil and paper tests is a very limited way to represent growth and learning. The same researchers believe that authentic assessment tools are a much more appropriate means for evaluating the arts. The tools of assessment discussed in this paper include: portfolios, rubrics, checklists, rating scales, observation journals, student surveys, video and audio taping, and peer assessments. The creative nature of the arts compels us to develop methods of assessment that are innovative, imaginative, and more effective than standard pencil and paper tests.

The field of education has drastically changed since the National Assessment of Educational Progress (NAEP) began in 1969. According to a study by Guthrie and Wynne (as cited by Eisner, 2002, 182), the NAEP was established to determine the health of America's schools. When it was determined that schools in the United States were falling behind in the areas of mathematics and science as compared to European and Asian countries, legislation was enacted to change the situation. The outcry has been get "back to the basics" ever since. The affect on arts education has been a mixed bag.

Since the No Child Left Behind Legislation was passed in 2001, America has been called upon to scrutinize its system of education. Every state in the nation has had to establish higher learning standards in both foundation and enrichment areas. Texas has adopted a bill which mandates what is required of all schools. According to the Center for Educator Development in Fine Arts (CEDFA), the State Bill 815 (2003) requires both foundation and enrichment subjects be taught in all districts.

SB 815 mandates that the Texas Essential Knowledge and Skills (TEKS) are now required of all Texas school districts as a condition of accreditation in providing instruction in all of the required curriculum—foundation and enrichment subject areas. There are two categories of the state-approved required curriculum that all school districts in Texas must offer: foundation and enrichment. The foundation content areas consist of English language arts, mathematics, science, and social studies. The enrichment content areas consist of fine arts, languages other than English, health, physical education, economics, career and technology education, and technology applications.

The passage of SB 815 was indeed a step in the right direction for Texas. However, certain statements within the legislative document pose concern regarding the quality of instruction. Although it is required that students be educated in the areas of music, art, and theatre on the elementary level, the State falls short of requiring certified specialists in the arts to actually be in place in each district. It also does not mandate the amount of time for instruction or the methodologies to be taught. According to the Texas State Board of Education (SBOE), *all* elementary teachers are certified to teach all subjects in both the foundation and enrichment areas. Therefore, any district may elect to require generalist teachers to include the arts in the curriculum they teach rather than hire specialists. According to the Education Commission of the States (2005), Texas is not the only state in the union that allows this on the elementary level. Most states, including Texas, require certified specialists on the secondary level.

The disparity between foundation and enrichment subjects is great in Texas. The foundation subjects take precedence. Part of the reason for the inequity is TAKS (Texas Assessment of Knowledge and Skills) testing. Districts are held accountable for student performance on the tests beginning in third grade. The high-stakes testing environment greatly influences how state funds are dispersed. Very often, the lowest-performing districts cut enrichment programs in order to fund special tutoring programs to boost student achievement on the tests. In theory, the TAKS test ensures that all children are given an equal education in the foundation subjects. Because there is no such accountability required in enrichment areas, they are often relegated to a lower status in the education of children. Not having a standard of accountability in the arts causes one to wonder whether all children are being given an equal education in these disciplines.

One point to be considered is whether a subject like music should be assessed in a similar manner as is being done with foundation subjects. In other words, should there be a pencil-and-paper music standardized test? Author Eisner (2002) agrees that testing scores are a visual representation of the learning which takes place in schools.

When it comes to standardized testing, individual scores are provided for each student and are also often aggregated for grade, school, school district, and state. Why does the public display a keen interest in test scores? One answer is that there is precious little else provided with which the public can assess the quality of its schools (Eisner, 2002, 182).

This statement is interesting to consider from the standpoint of music education. The evidence that learning is taking place should be obvious to parents when they see their child perform in public. Vocal, instrumental, and theatrical skills can all be plainly ascertained during a school performance. In fact, the arts have probably always led the way in showing evidence of mastery of skills. So, should there be a statewide administration of a music TAKS test at certain grade levels? Noted author Eric Jensen (2001) makes this strong declaration:

The measuring of arts may or may not destroy any explicit learning available from them, but it will miss the more subtle but powerful way which arts enhance seven neurobiological systems. And we may kill off the joy, the love, the sense of wonder and discovery that must go hand in hand with art-making. (Jensen, 2001, 107)

250

David Henry Feldman (1998) is a noted researcher with Harvard Project Zero. Feldman believes "If we overlook the broad range of human abilities to concentrate on those few that show up on paper-and-pencil tests, we are dooming many children to years of frustration and disappointment, if not outright failure" (Gardner, Feldman, andand Krechevsky, 1998, 2).

Nierman makes a very important assertion about developing a proper means of authentic assessment:

> It is not enough to meet this challenge by simply vowing to give at least one "pencil and paper" test and/or use one standardized test in music so that there will be some "objective" information to discuss with parents. If this is all we do, we fall prey to the same criticisms which have been leveled against education in general. (MENC, 2001, 42)

Still, there are other researchers who believe, "in the absence of assessment, we are unable to determine if our students are actually improving their musical skills and knowledge about music" (MENC, 2001, 13).

The evidence that non-standard measures of assessment are more effective in the area of the arts is compelling. All of the above-mentioned researchers would agree that assessment is a vital element to hold both teachers and students accountable. But they would also agree that there are many ways to determine progress that allow for creative processes to develop unhampered by assessment methods.

Elementary Music Tools for Assessment

Effective educators agree that assessment measures are necessary to ensure students understand and internalize what is being taught. Assessment is also a way for teachers to maintain focus when teaching the required elements. Given the creative nature of the arts, it behooves us to develop methods of assessment that are more innovative and imaginative than standard pencil and paper tests.

The following methods have been suggested by music educators across the country as excellent techniques for assessment in music: portfolio assessment, rubric assessment, checklist, rating scale assessment, observation journals, student surveys, video and audio taping, and peer assessment.

Portfolio Assessment

Portfolio assessment chronicles the progress a student has made throughout a given period of time. It is an authentic assessment tool that allows parents to see what their child has learned throughout the year. Kelly has suggested, "The purpose of the musical portfolio is to provide a sample of a student's achievement and overall musical behavior and to gain indicators of program quality" (MENC, 2001, 26). The pros of using portfolio assessment are not unlike those in a regular classroom. In theory, this appears to be a useable method. The cons of portfolio assessment include the sheer volume of work to maintain such a system. Most elementary music teachers see every student in their school. If a school is large, having more than 600 students, the task of maintaining portfolios could become overwhelming and ineffective. Nierman suggests that students do the work of creating and maintaining their own portfolios, thereby making them more accountable for their own progress in learning (MENC, 2001, 50). This appears more doable, provided students are responsible and the system actually works. Perhaps limiting it to certain grade levels would cut down on the maintenance aspect of this method and make it more feasible as well. Another manner of portfolio assessment might be focusing on a performance to chronicle the progress of a particular grade level as a program is prepared and presented.

Rubric Assessment

A rubric is an assessment instrument with variables that is created to determine levels of achievement in a given task. Rubrics often include a numbered scale between 1 and 5. The rubric clearly states what elements show superior, excellent, good, fair, or poor work on a particular project. Each required element is listed on a grid with specific standards of achievement to be reached. If a student desires to obtain the highest grade, the requirements are clearly spelled out. Lopez made a strong case for rubric assessment by stating, "Because all students were being judged using the same criteria, there was no room for teacher bias. The second was the fact that, void of criteria, we really cannot make reliable, fair, and valid judgments" (MENC, 2001, 34). For an assessment tool to be valid, it needs to be fair and free from teacher bias. Since creative expression requires a judgment call on the part of the teacher, having clear standards to judge by ensures fairness toward students.

Checklist Assessment

This form of assessment may be the easiest to administer provided the checklist is not overly complicated. A teacher-prepared grid is used with students listed on the left. Columns to the right list what areas of mastery the teacher is looking for in each student. The checklist can be placed in a notebook or folder and saved for parent conferences to show whether a student has obtained mastery in certain areas. The checklist assessment is actually an observation tool and one that can be easily utilized by any teacher. Ease of use is the most attractive feature of this method.

Rating Scale Assessment

Rating scales can be effective assessment tools in the music classroom. Nierman uses the rating scale in combination with the checklist. First of all, he uses the checklist to determine if a particular skill had been mastered, then he uses the rating scale to ascertain the quality of the performance (MENC, 2001, 46). The purpose of using both in combination is to give more detailed feedback to a student. It is also an effective tool for determining a student's grade for a specific time period during the year.

Observation Journal

The teacher observation journal can be one of the most effective ways to assess children. The thing about an observation instrument is that it offers ease of use. Teachers can focus their observations on one or several skills and make quick notations about the progress of each student. The observation journal is similar to a checklist. It is the preferred method of the author of this paper for cooperative group work. The author uses observation journals in conjunction with rubric assessment. Figure 1 shows an example of a cooperative group observation journal. In this case, the journal was used for the purpose of determining: 1) the level of cooperation among students; 2) whether all students were on task and contributing to the group; 3) if processes and procedures were being followed; 4) how students were developing their final products; and, 5) the performance element at the completion of a product. Students were supplied with a detailed rubric to prepare their products by and the observation criteria with which the teacher judged each group while they were working. Figure 2 shows an example of a rubric which can be given to students. It is not for the purpose of determining products or performances; rather, it compliments the teacher's observation journal and gives students the boundaries concerning group interaction.

Figure 1. Cooperative Group Observation Log

COOPERATIVE GROUP OBSERVATION LOG

Date: _____

Class: _____   **Grade Level:** _____

Group 1	☐ On Task	☐ Off Task	☐ Conflict/ Resolution	☐ Process	☐ Procedure	☐ Product	☐ Performance
Observation Notes:					Daily Grade:		
Group 2	☐ On Task	☐ Off Task	☐ Conflict/ Resolution	☐ Process	☐ Procedure	☐ Product	☐ Performance
Observation Notes:					Daily Grade:		
Group 3	☐ On Task	☐ Off Task	☐ Conflict/ Resolution	☐ Process	☐ Procedure	☐ Product	☐ Performance
Observation Notes:					Daily Grade:		
Group 4	☐ On Task	☐ Off Task	☐ Conflict/ Resolution	☐ Process	☐ Procedure	☐ Product	☐ Performance
Observation Notes:					Daily Grade:		
Group 5	☐ On Task	☐ Off Task	☐ Conflict/ Resolution	☐ Process	☐ Procedure	☐ Product	☐ Performance
Observation Notes:					Daily Grade:		
Group 6	☐ On Task	☐ Off Task	☐ Conflict/ Resolution	☐ Process	☐ Procedure	☐ Product	☐ Performance
Observation Notes:					Daily Grade:		

Figure 2. Cooperative Group Rubric.

COOPERATIVE GROUP RUBRIC

✓ ++ (95–100)	✓ + (90–94)	✓ (85–89)	✓ – (80–84)	✓ – – (70–79)
On Task	On Task	1 or 2 off task	Majority off task	All off task
No Conflicts	Minor Conflict with full resolution	Conflict with partial resolution	Conflict with brief teacher visit and partial resolution	Conflict with teacher intervention and no resolution
Processes followed	Processes followed	Processes partially followed	Processes not followed or partially followed	Processes not followed, no progress made
Procedures Followed	Procedures followed	Procedures partially followed	Procedures not followed or partially followed	Procedures not followed, no progress made
Products in development with progress made	Products in development with some progress made	Products partially developed	Products not in development, conflicts impede progress	Products not in development, extreme conflicts impede progress
Performance in development and tied to products	Performance in development and partially tied to products	Performance partially developed	Performance not in development, conflicts impede progress	Performance not in development, extreme conflicts impede progress

GRADING PROCEDURES

1. Grades assigned on a daily basis.

   ✓ ++ (95–100) = All on task, no conflicts, processes and procedures evident, end products in development.

   ✓ + (90–94) = Some conflicts, but resolved by the end of class, processes and procedures evident, end products in development.

   ✓ (85–89) = One or two students off task, some conflicts with partial resolution, processes and procedures not completely followed, end products not in development or only partially developed.

   ✓ – (80–84) = Majority of the group off task, conflicts evident with teacher brief visit, processes and procedures not completely followed, end products not developed or only partially developed.

   ✓ – (70–79) = Majority of the group off task, conflicts evident with teacher intervention needed, processes and procedures not followed, end products not discussed or evident.

2. Feedback to students at the end of each class will include revealing the group grade for the day and observation notes by the teacher.

3. Final grade will be based on a final average of daily grades and the quality of the product or performance created by each group.

Student Surveys

A student survey is usually conducted before and/or after a class project. Teachers can use surveys to determine how much information a class already knows before beginning a large-scale project. The direction of the project can be altered or modified to meet the needs of a particular group of students before it even begins enhancing the chance of success. Surveys can also be an effective means of closure at the end of a project to measure what knowledge was gained. It also allows students to assess themselves, which is a useful tool in their own self-development.

Video and Audio Taping

Taping children while they are performing or working cooperatively is an effective means of assessment that allows teachers to revisit the student's performance later. This method is an authentic assessment tool. It is standard practice to obtain a consent form from parents before conducting this type of assessment. One of the pros of using a consent form is parents are informed about what students are studying in music and that you will be monitoring their progress. Having a tape of a child's performance is solid evidence about their ability to sing or work cooperatively in a group. The equipment to do cassette-taped assessments is not costly. Very often schools have video equipment that can be accessed by music teachers if one wishes to do a video assessment. A con might be the storage of consent forms or tapes of multiple classes. Consent forms can be hole-punched and placed in notebooks or filed in class folders and placed in an out-of-the-way location. One way of getting around the tape issue is to send videotaped footage to a computer and save the performance on a writeable CD using Windows Movie Maker. CDs are easier to store, are less bulky, and can hold an entire class or grade level of performances. Tapes can then be re-used for the next assessment.

Peer Assessment

In one research text, Soep (as cited by Eisner, 2002, 183) suggests a method of peer assessment that appears to have good merit. In this method, "crits" are used for the purpose of creating reciprocal relations between students as they evaluate each other's work. "Crits" are positive suggestions for improving technique. Since each one knows their turn to receive suggestions is coming, they are careful to choose their words wisely and with care. Being able to give useful and encouraging evaluations is a life-skill students will be able to use in whatever career they pursue.

The Future of Music Assessment

Teaching has changed over the past six years due to high stakes accountability testing. Generalist teachers are judged by the success or failure of students on state-mandated assessment tests. So far, most states have not required the same level of accountability in the arts. Solid assessment practices will validate the place of fine arts in the education of our nation's children. Now is the time for every teacher of the arts to develop superior methods of assessment. Being able to validate fine arts education through effective and unobtrusive appraisals may be the most important issue in the future. Music educators can lead the way toward authentic assessment and perhaps change the way testing student knowledge and skills is measured. In the long run, if schools graduate creative, thinking individuals, our society will be greatly enriched.

References

Center for Educator Development in Fine Arts. 2003. Senate Bill 815 requires the fine arts TEKS. Retrieved on July 16, 2006, from http://www.cedfa.org

Education Commission of the States. 2005. State policies regarding arts in education. Retrieved on July 16, 2006, from http://www.ecs.org/Artscan

Eisner, Elliot. 2002. *The arts and the creation of mind.* New Haven, Connecticut: Yale University Press.

Gardner, H., D. Feldman, and M. Krechevsky. 1998. *Building on children's strengths: the experience of project spectrum.* New York: Teachers College Press.

Jensen, Eric. 2001. *Arts with the brain in mind.* Alexandria, VA: Association for Supervision and Curriculum Development.

MENC—The National Association for Music Education. 2001. *Spotlight on assessment in music education.* Reston, VA: Author.

258

A Class Portfolio Can Be Feasible in General Music Classes

Ming-Jen Chuang
National Taichung University, Taichung City, Taiwan

Abstract

In music education, the collection of data about classroom activities as the basis for reflective planning is especially important. A process that enables the systematic collection of diverse classroom data and provides structure for teacher reflection and planning is the assembling of a portfolio. The process of collecting, managing and reflection on data from portfolios may be challenging for general music teachers who are expected to work with several hundred students each week, but the results of doing so are worth the effort.

Thompson (2003a) has proposed the class portfolio for use by general music teachers. A teacher has an individual class portfolio for each class. Through reviewing a class portfolio, the teacher improves his or her reflection, adjusts appropriate teaching activities and strategies, and plans appropriate instruction for the particular students in a particular class (Chuang, 2004).

In 2003, the author asked three music teachers in Taiwan to compile class portfolios. The definition and concept of class portfolios, possible contents of a class portfolio, and weaknesses and advantages of using a class portfolio provided by the three music teachers, and recommendations are discussed.

The primary responsibility of a teacher is to provide opportunities for student learning. Certainly, if a teacher wants to know about his or her students' growth, data about the students' growth should be collected (Dahlberg, Moss, and Pence, 2002). Meaningful and useful collection of data about students' growth should include information about both the processes through which learning occurs and the products that provide evidence of the skill or knowledge students have acquired (Dirth, 2000; Tarnowski, Knutson, Gleason, Gleason, and Songer, 1998). A review of students' learning processes and products will enable the teacher to revise his or her goals, plan instruction, and adjust teaching appropriately (Vani, 2000). Therefore, monitoring of student activities will become an important part of effective teaching to ensure that the anticipated learning did indeed occur (Sonnier, 1999; Turner-Bisset, 2001).

Dahlberg, et al. (2002) pointed out that when teachers collect data about their students' learning and their own teaching, they are able to integrate their assumptions about their own teaching effectiveness. Thus, teachers will better understand what is going on in their own classrooms. Collecting and reviewing the data will enable teachers to reflect on prior actions and find new inspiration (Fu, Stremmel, and Hill, 2002). They will become more involved in their teaching, carefully plan what their students should learn, and use appropriate strategies to facilitate that learning (Wolf, Whinery, and Hagerty, 1995).

Challenges for General Music Teachers

In music education, the collection of data about classroom activities as the basis for reflective planning may be especially challenging. Not only do general music teachers work with a large number of students, but the learning goals in most general music classes are quite diverse, ranging from the acquisition of skills for musical performance, to the acquisition of knowledge about the structure and style of music, and also to the development of an appreciation for the value that music adds to human life (Hackett and Lindeman, 2001). Consequently, general music teachers will need to collect large amounts of diverse types of data if they are to effectively assess students' progress toward these goals and their own teaching behaviors. Given these varied goals, it seems that a single medium, such as tests, evaluations of musical performances, or written reports, would be inadequate as a record of classroom activities and as an indicator of student progress. Furthermore, collecting and managing data from hundreds of students presents a big challenge for general music teachers (Goolsby, 1995; Smith, 1995; Thompson, 2003b). General music teachers need their own system for collecting data about student learning in order to facilitate ongoing analysis that will lead to improved practice. Such analysis may enable general music teachers to become more reflective about their teaching practice.

The nature of data collected in general music classrooms should include the full range of learning experiences in which students are engaged (Brophy, 2000; Winner, Davidson, and Scripp, 1992). Music teachers may design activities to develop a broad range of skills, such as singing, playing instruments, reading notation, or composing (Hackett and Lindeman, 2001; Spruce, 2002). Teachers may structure activities to facilitate acquisition of musical knowledge, such as student reports on composers, worksheets on musical style, and various types of guided listening activities (Dura, 2002). General music teachers may also plan activities designed to develop awareness of the relationship between music and other arts, between music and history, and between music and culture (Gelineau, 1995; Swanwick, 1999).

In addition to data about the general music activities identified above, general music teachers may also need to compile repertoire lists of songs sung, music used for movement and listening, lists of works of visual arts literature examined in relationship to music listening, student compositions in a particular style, and projects developed in collaboration with classroom teachers that integrate music with other subject areas (Glover and Ward, 1993; Hackett and Lindeman, 2001). In short, teachers need data on students' involvement with the full range of learning activities in the general music classroom if they are to thoughtfully reflect on student learning and effectively plan successive learning experiences (Doerksen, 1990).

Portfolios are Receiving Increasing Attention from Educators

A process that enables the systematic collection of diverse classroom data and provides structure for teacher reflection and planning is the assembling of portfolios. Portfolios are receiving increasing attention from educators in many subjects and at various levels (Brummet and Haywood, 1997; Gray, 1993; Klenowski, 2002). Recent studies have analyzed the use of portfolios in different disciplines (McLaughlin and Vogt, 1998; Smith, 1995), with researchers indicating several advantages of the use of portfolios in classroom settings (Brophy, 2000; Klenowski, 2002). A portfolio provides opportunities to include many kinds of data from the teacher and the students, ranging from print to multimedia sources. A portfolio can receive data at any time, thus offering schedule flexibility to meet both the limited time general music teachers have with students and the irregular and changing schedules under which many general music teachers function. A portfolio can also contain both individual student and class data (Brummett and Haywood, 1997; Thompson, 2003a).

For general music teachers, Brophy (2000) defined portfolios as "a collection of a student's work that he or she feels best represents his or her progress in a particular subject area; it contains examples of the student's work to show the range of skills and abilities possessed by the individual in each area" (307). Thompson (2003b) stated that a portfolio is a collection of artifacts, selected to provide evidence of specific accomplishment, collected over time, documenting process and final product, as well as authentic data for evaluation. The primary purpose of portfolios, according to both Brophy (2000) and Thompson (2003b) is to provide a basis for the assessment of student learning. However, different kinds of portfolios have been developed for different contexts and purposes.

Portfolios Provide a Basis for Teacher Reflection

Portfolios designed to support learning and teaching should provide a basis for teacher reflection. Reflection is one of the most important functions of using portfolios (Winner, et al., 1992). Bengier (2000) stated that reflective thinking can help teachers improve aspects of their teaching. Developing portfolios encourages them to engage in purposeful reflection (Senne, 1997). As teachers develop portfolios that systematically include data about a variety of classroom learning activities, they will have more opportunities for reflection (Beck, 1996; Vani, 2000). Portfolios provide opportunities for teachers to review their teaching process critically and reflectively (Klenowski, 2002; Richert, 1987). Moreover, portfolios containing data about teaching and learning systematically collected over time feature the unique potential to provide evidence of change in the work of both teachers and students (Brown, 1996). Therefore, teachers using portfolios have opportunities to analyze what they and their students have done. By monitoring students' growth and progress, teachers are able to rethink teaching strategies and plan instruction for improving teaching (Bengier, 2000).

Issues with the Use of Portfolios

While it seems that portfolios offer a very good means for teachers to collect data about classroom activities and provide a basis for meaningful reflection that can lead to increased teaching effectiveness, there are a number of issues surrounding the use of portfolios that must be considered, such as lack of teacher training in portfolio development, management of portfolios, and reliability of portfolio data. Goolsby (1995) pointed out that teachers must have sufficient training to make informed interpretations and judgments about student work. Whether using portfolio data for planning future instruction or for evaluating student achievement, it is important that teachers make accurate and insightful interpretations of the work contained in the portfolios. There is little evidence that such training is part of traditional teacher preparation or in-service programs (Goolsby, 1995; Thompson, 2003a). Therefore, teachers cannot be expected to develop and use portfolios effectively without specialized training.

While portfolios may contain many meaningful materials, collecting and storing individual portfolios for a large number of students can present staggering management problems for music teachers. Not only do teachers need space to store the student portfolios, but they also need a lot of time, as creating and reviewing individual portfolios for every student requires a major time commitment from both the music teacher and his or her students (Brummet and Haywood, 1997; Smith, 1995). Some educators, therefore, may be concerned that time devoted to portfolios would be an obstacle for teachers who use them. Barry (1996) confirmed that portfolios can present a problem because of the time it takes to prepare and evaluate them.

Class Portfolios as Viable Alternatives

It seems that portfolios offer an effective means to collect data about student learning and the teaching process and offer a means to encourage teacher reflection and more effective planning. However, the assembling of individual portfolios of the diverse data for the hundreds of students of general music teachers is highly impractical. Thompson (2003a) proposed the class portfolio as an alternative to individual student portfolios. He defined a class portfolio as a collection of artifacts that tell the story of a particular class of students. These artifacts are samples of the work of that class that illustrate both the processes and products of the group's experiences. He pointed out that many learning activities in general music are group activities. Students sing, play instruments, move to music, and even improvise music as part of the group. He also offered the opinion that in the planning process, most music teachers think about group learning rather than the learning of individual students. Thompson indicated that class portfolios do not provide materials that result in grades for individual students, a means of comparing individual students, nor a quick, convenient, easy way to address assessment issues. Although class portfolios have their own weaknesses, Thompson suggested that they may provide a vivid account of students' experiences, a means of charting group progress, a basis for planning future learning experiences, a basis for comparing achievement among classes, a basis for assessing the quality of teaching and programs, as well as a means for demonstrating achievement to administrators, parents, and public (Table 1).

Table 1. Strengths and Weaknesses of a Class Portfolio

Strengths	Weaknesses
A class portfolio is a collection of artifacts that tell the story of a particular class of students.	Class portfolios do not provide materials that result in grades for individual students.
These artifacts are samples of the work of that class that illustrate both the processes and products of the group's experience.	Not a means of comparing individual students.
Class portfolios may provide a vivid account of students' experiences.	Not a quick, convenient, easy way to address assessment issues.
A means of charting group progress.	
A basis for planning future learning experiences.	
A basis for comparing achievement among classes.	
A basis for assessing the quality of teaching and programs.	
A means for demonstrating achievement to administrators, parents, and the public.	

Exploring the Feasibility of General Music Class Portfolios

Theoretically, class portfolios appear to offer a viable means for general music teachers to collect and analyze data about student learning and engage in reflective planning for future class activities. However, there was no evidence to support this theory. I decided to systematically examine the feasibility of class portfolios in general music classes.

In 2003, I asked three music teachers in Taiwan to compile class portfolios. I analyzed the process through which they worked and the class portfolios they developed as part of my doctoral research.

The questions that guided my research were:

1. What are the three music teachers' concepts of a class portfolio at the end of the semester?
2. What contents do the three music teachers include in their class portfolios?
3. What problems do the three music teachers encounter in compiling class portfolios?
4. How do the three music teachers feel about developing and using class portfolios?

I provided a brief training session on portfolios for these general music teachers and communicated with them bi-weekly by telephone or e-mail throughout the Spring semester of 2003, during which they developed and used class portfolios for one of their general music classes. I analyzed transcripts of our communications, the portfolios they developed, and their responses to questions asked at the end of the semester to answer these questions. The following is a summary of my findings.

The three music teachers reported their concepts of class portfolios (Table 2). Their concepts of class portfolios revealed similarities. The goals for the class will determine the content for the portfolio. Furthermore, the portfolio content should show differences among classes. For instance, if a music teacher has two fourth-grade general music classes, the portfolio for each class should somehow reflect the different learning, achievement, and uniqueness of these two classes.

Contents of Class Portfolios

One goal of this project was to find out what kinds of data general music teachers would collect for class portfolios. The analysis of the content of the three portfolios is summarized in Table 3. Elements common to all three portfolios as well as unique items in each teacher's portfolio can be identified in this Table.

It can be seen from these data that the portfolios were more similar than different. One teacher chose to include only what she considered the best work of her students, while the others included the work of all students. Two of the three teachers reported that the inclusion of student's critique sheets would be helpful for their reflective teaching. All teachers included copies of their lesson plans, teacher journals and samples of student work, both in the form of video recordings and worksheets. Some of the similarities might have resulted from the fact that these items were among possibilities discussed during the training session.

At the end of the semester, teachers were asked to identify those items in their respective portfolios that they found most valuable as a basis for their planning. A summary of their responses are given in Table 4.

Table 2. Definitions of a Class Portfolio by Three Music Teachers in Taiwan

	Music Teacher A	Music Teacher B	Music Teacher C
Definitions of a Class Portfolio	A class portfolio includes a record of students' learning activities and teaching process. Using a class portfolio is situational. For example, each class portfolio is developed for particular teaching situations for a particular class. Any teacher's class portfolio is different from other teachers' class portfolios. Each class is unique, so each class portfolio is unique for the particular class.	A class portfolio includes all teaching processes, products, grading, and records of students' learning. A class portfolio not only helps a teacher improve teaching in the class, but also maintains the record of students' learning, such as assessment of music learning in the class and improved musical abilities of students. Through using a class portfolio, teachers can have the records of students' learning processes.	A class portfolio is to improve students' learning and the fact that students make progress during a semester. It is also the process that traces what the teacher did. A class portfolio is to help a teacher have systematic and effective teaching as well as accomplish the goals of teaching and learning. In addition, a class portfolio is the record of the process of a teacher's efforts and devotion to all students in a particular class.

I considered the process through which teachers developed class portfolios and their feelings about that process to be more important than the portfolio materials they collected and developed through this initial experience. Teachers' reactions to the class portfolio process was gathered from the bi-weekly interviews and from the final interview at the end of the semester. A summary of these findings is in the section that follows.

Table 3. List of Contents of the three Music Teachers' Class Portfolios

Items	Teacher A	Teacher B	Teacher C
Lesson Plans	+	+	+
Teacher's Journals	+	+	+
Student's Journals	+	+	−
Video Tape Recordings	+	+	+
Audio Tape Recordings	+	+	−
Checklists/ Assessment Sheets	+	+	+
Photographs	+	−	−
Student's Critique Sheets	−	+	−
Worksheets	+	+	+
Teaching/Anticipated Goals	+	+	+
CD-ROM	−	+	−
Teaching Outlines	+	−	−
Materials Developed by Teachers	+	+	+
Student Best Work	−	−	+

Note. Included: +   Excluded: −

Table 4. A Comparison of the Most Helpful Portfolio Contents

Music Teachers	Items that Helped Participants Reflect
Teacher A	Teacher Journals, Student Journals, Worksheets
Teacher B	Teacher Journals, Student Journals, Videotape Recordings
Teacher C	Teacher Journals, Checklists, Videotape Recordings

Teachers' Response to the Class Portfolio Process

All music teachers felt that class portfolios were useful and helpful for their planning and teaching. In the process of developing class portfolios, the teachers found that it was necessary to design appropriate goals for students, identify different levels of goals for individual students, and adjust their goals to meet students' needs (Table 5).

Table 5. A Teacher's Changes of Goal-Setting Before and During Class Portfolio Development

	Goal Setting
Before	"My teaching goals were based on the Competence Index of the Arts and Humanities (current national curriculum standards in Taiwan) and the content of the textbooks, although I designed my own teaching goals."
During	"My students could meet most goals I designed. Students could meet the goals that were dependent on the different levels of difficulties. Some students could meet easy level goals but some could meet difficult levels."
During	"I adjust the goals for students and urge them to achieve at least easy-level goals."

Teachers' discussions of their planning process and teaching materials selected revealed changes during the semester in which they developed the class portfolios. These changes included the use of materials beyond those offered in the textbooks, exploration of new teaching strategies and student learning activities, greater concern for individualizing instruction to meet the needs of individual students, and greater concern for the learning climate in the classroom.

The analysis of data revealed that the portfolios did influence teachers' thinking about and choice of teaching strategies. In addition, it was apparent that the three music teachers had the desire to identify strategies that would provide solutions to some classroom management problems in their general music classes. The development and use of class portfolios had a positive effect on the music teachers' perception of classroom climate and their interactions with students. Moreover, there was evidence that the use of portfolios positively influenced the three music teachers' approaches to assessment in their general music classes (Table 6).

Problems Teachers Encountered

The three music teachers had logistical and technical difficulties and frustrations as they began to develop class portfolios; however, by the end of semester, they had positive attitudes about the use of class portfolios and had solutions as well as suggestions to overcome the problems they encountered. Three specific sources of frustrations for teachers working with portfolios in general music classes were: (1) time, (2) technology, and (3) confidence.

Table 6. The Use of Class Portfolios Influenced Teachers' Approaches to Assessment

Teacher A	"Before I began to use the class portfolio, I assessed my students by using singing or playing recorder as well as a paper-and-pencil test per semester. Sometimes I informed students the day I would assess them. Some students felt nervous and then did not have good performance in their final assessment. I needed to spend at least five class meetings to complete the assessments, so I could not teach anything in the last three weeks before school closed. When using the class portfolio, I got the idea that assessment is a part of teaching, so I assessed students informally, such as observing students reactions, using checklists, performing in small group with solo in classes. I found that students felt comfortable and did not know they were assessed by me. The change is different from my previous assessment approach that was so boring and sometimes gave students pressure."
Teacher B	"I used checklists, three paper-and-pencil tests, and worksheets to assess my students' learning in music this semester. Before I used the class portfolio, I did not have clear ideas for assessing students. I only depended on the three paper-and-pencil tests or performing a song and then gave students final grades. My assessment was too narrow."
Teacher C	"I had final assessment for students' learning in music before I used the class portfolio. I think that my previous final assessment was like a one-shot assessment, only singing a song or playing a song on recorder. Sometimes, I added a paper-and-pencil test about assessing music knowledge and theory. While using my class portfolio, I changed my assessment approaches from a final assessment to the emphasis on learning process and product."

The three music teachers indicated that the process of developing portfolios required a great deal of time. They reported that time was needed to obtain and learn how to use video equipment to record class activities. One teacher reviewed the video recordings with her class and reported that the process required a lot of class time. Teachers who had students write journals about class activities reported that considerable time was required for that activity. In addition, teachers reported that considerable out-of-class time was required for their management and review of materials and their own reflective thinking. All three music teachers expressed concern about the willingness of other general music teachers, especially those with many classes, to make the time commitment necessary to work with portfolios.

All three music teachers recognized that technology is necessary to collect and organize the data needed for a general music class portfolio. All teachers had some skill using some forms of technology, but felt they needed assistance from others, especially in making and editing video recordings that captured meaningful class experiences. They also recognized the potential of CD technology for the storage of the data they collected, but reportedly did not feel they had sufficient skill with this technology to use it most effectively.

The data suggested that the teachers' lack of confidence in their ability to develop and use class portfolios was initially a frustration. Teachers in Taiwan view themselves as technicians, following a curriculum and implementing learning activities prescribed by a textbook. In this project the participants were given only a general concept of a class portfolio. Initially, teachers were frustrated because there was neither a prescribed structure nor procedures for the development and use of the class portfolios. They expected to be told what to do and how to do it. That did not occur and the teachers displayed a lack of confidence in their ability to work without specific directions. However, as they began to collect materials and use them as a basis for reflection and planning, they realized that they could make better decisions about portfolio structure and content and that they could also use the materials they collected as a basis for planning. By the end of the semester they all were confident that they could develop and use class portfolios and indicated that they intended to continue using them in the future. The frustration and lack of confidence that appear to be a problem at the beginning of the semester changed to confident enthusiasm at the end.

How Teachers Felt about Developing and Using Class Portfolios

The three music teachers expressed the opinion that developing and using class portfolios was very time-consuming, but that the process was beneficial to their teaching. They reported several benefits gained from the use of class portfolios: (1) reflective thinking, (2) effective teaching, and (3) student centeredness.

The three music teachers felt that through the use of portfolios, they became more reflective teachers. As a result they became more effective as they began to make better decisions about teaching content and instructional planning. They also reported that the process of collecting and reviewing student materials for the portfolios made them more aware of students' interests and needs. Additionally, they indicated that they became more student-centered teachers. Because of the benefits of reflective thinking, effective teaching, and student-centeredness, the three music teachers had confidence and clear ideas for planning instruction during the semester and in the future, and they were satisfied with the use of class portfolios.

Conclusions and Recommendations

The three music teachers generously contributed thoughts and feelings about their experiences working with class portfolios. In general, it can be concluded: (1) Class portfolios can be complied and used by general music teachers as a basis for more reflective teaching. (2) Class portfolios are time-consuming to develop and general music teachers initially experience frustration at the process. (3) The three teachers who developed and used class portfolios for one semester reported that the experience was quite valuable and that as a result of working with class portfolios they felt their teaching improved considerably.

It would appear that class portfolios have some potential to improve general music teaching. The trial by three teachers in Taiwan offers data from a very limited and specialized sample; however, the successes of this trial suggest that broader implementation and examination is warranted. On the basis of the limited trial of class portfolios undertaken in the study reported here, I offer the following recommendations:

1. Initially provide teachers with a clear description of a music class portfolio, a suggested list of contents, and a description of the process for compiling and using a class portfolio. Such specifics were purposefully avoided in this study because

269

one goal was to identify the contents that the teachers considered important. The frustration initially experienced by the teachers prevented them for committing to the process early in the semester, resulting in less complete portfolios than might be desirable.

2. Provide technical support for setting up and using audio and video recording equipment.

3. Explore ways that class portfolios can provide data from which to make expected formal assessment of individual students.

4. Explore the use of class portfolios in performance-based music classes, in addition to general music classes.

References

Barry, N. H. 1996. Developing a teacher's portfolio in a university music methods course. *Update: Applications of Research in Music Education, 15*(1):22–27.

Beck, L. W. 1997. *Teacher reflective practice: Documenting reflection in a teacher collaborative group* (Doctoral Dissertation, University of California, 1997). *Dissertation Abstracts International 57*(11):4700A. [UMI No. AAT 9711573].

Bengier, A. L. 2000. *How one middle school began to plan for instruction: An action research journey* (Doctoral Dissertation, Virginia Polytechnic Institute and State University, 2000). *Dissertation Abstracts International 61*(06):2161A. [UMI No. AAT 9974739].

Brown, C. R. 1997. *A case study of the effects of learner-centered portfolio assessment on teachers' and students' views of literacy development* (Doctoral dissertation, The University of North Carolina at Greensboro, 1997). *Dissertation Abstracts International 57*(09):3793A. [UMI No. AAT 9705288].

Brophy, T. S. 2000. *Assessing the developing child musician: A guide for general music teachers.* Chicago: GIA Publications.

Brummett, V. M., and J. Haywood. 1997. Authentic assessment in school music: Implementing a framework. *General Music Today 11*(1):4–10.

Chuang, M. J. 2004. *The experiences of teachers developing and using class portfolios in general music classes in Taiwan Republic of China.* (Doctoral dissertation, The Pennsylvania State University, 2004). *Dissertation Abstracts International 65*(07):2536A. [UMI No. AAT3140000].

Dahlberg, G., P. Moss, and A. Pence. 2002. *Beyond quality in early childhood education and care: Postmodern perspectives.* Philadelphia: Routledge, Falmer, Taylor, and Francis.

Dirth, K. A. 2000. *Implementing portfolio assessment in the music performance classroom* (Doctoral Dissertation, Columbia University Teachers College, 2000). *Dissertation Abstracts International 61*(06):2229A. [UMI No. AAT 9976711].

Doerksen, D. 1990. *Guide to evaluating teachers of music performance groups.* Reston, VA: Music Educators National Conference.

Dura, M. T. 2002. *Music education and the music listening experience.* Lewiston, NY: The Edwin Mellen Press.

Fu, V. R., A. J. Stremmel, and L. T. Hill. 2002. *Teaching and learning: Collaborative exploration of the Reggio Emilia approach.* Upper Saddle River, NJ: Pearson Education.

Gelineau, R. P. 1995. *Experiences in music,* 3rd ed. Englewood Cliffs, NJ: Prentice Hall.

Glover, J., and S. Ward. 1993. Music in the integrated primary curriculum. In J. Glover and S. Ward, eds., *Teaching music in the primary school* (164–183). New York: Cassell.

Goolsby, T. W. 1995. Portfolio assessment for better evaluation. *Music Educators Journal, 82*(3):39–44.

Gray, L. 1993. Portfolio assessment: The Arts Propel project. *General Music Today, 6*(3):9–14.

Hackett, P., and C. A. Lindeman. 2001. *The music classroom: Background, models, and skills for elementary teaching,* 5th ed. Upper Saddle River, NJ: Prentice Hall.

Klenowski, V. 2002. *Developing portfolios for learning and assessment processes and principles.* New York: Routledge Falmer.

McLaughlin, M., and M. E. Vogt. 1998. *Professional portfolio models.* Norwood, MA: Christopher-Gordon.

Richert, A. E. 1988. *Reflex to reflection: Facilitating reflection in novice teachers* (Doctoral Dissertation: Stanford University, 1988). *Dissertation Abstracts International 48*(11):2852A. [UMI No. AAT 8801015].

Senne, T. A. 1997. *The interactive teaching portfolio: A developmental approach to promoting professional development in physical education student teachers,* (Doctoral Dissertation: North Carolina State University, 1997). *Dissertation Abstracts International 58*(02):427A. [UMI No. AAT 9720864].

Smith, J. 1995. Using portfolio assessment in general music. *General Music Today 9*(1):8–12.

Sonnier, C. A. 1999. *Elementary general educators' beliefs, attitudes, and practices of portfolio assessment* (Doctoral Dissertation, The University of Alabama, 1999). *Dissertation Abstracts International 60*(06):1914A. [UMI No. AAT 9935576].

Spruce, G. 2002. Planning for music teaching and learning. In G. Spruce, eds., *Aspects of teaching secondary music: Perspectives on practice* (15–31). New York: Routledge Falmer.

Swanwick, K. 1999. *Teaching music musically*. New York: Routledge.

Tarnowski, S., M. Knutson, E. Gleason, C. Gleason, and E. Songer. 1998. Building a professional portfolio. *Music Educators Journal 81*(1):17–20.

Thompson, K. P. February 10, 2003a. *Student teacher portfolios*. Address to student teachers at The Pennsylvania State University, University Park, PA.

Thompson, K. P. April 12, 2003b. *Class portfolios for assessing general music*. Address to the Pennsylvania Music Educators Association Conference, Hershey, PA.

Turner-Bisset, R. 2001. *Expert teaching: Knowledge and pedagogy to lead the profession*. Ormond House, London: David Fulton.

Vani, L. 2000. *Portfolio: Assessment as transformative learning* (Doctoral Dissertation, Canada: University of Toronto, 2000). *Dissertation Abstracts International 61*(06):2150A. [UMI No. AAT NQ49869].

Winner, E., L. Davidson, and L. Scripp, eds. 1992. *Arts PROPEL: A handbook for music*. Cambridge, MA: Educational Testing Service and Harvard Project Zero.

Wolf, K., B. Whinery, and P. Hagerty. 1995. Teaching portfolios and portfolio conversations for teacher educators and teachers. *Action in Teacher Education, 17*(1):30–39.

Integrating Curriculum, Theory, and Practice: Assessment in Music Education for Students with Disabilities and Impairments

Helen Farrell
Department of Education, Melbourne, Victoria, Australia

Abstract

This paper is a response to national, state and local assessment and reporting practices in music education. The fundamental assumption that underlies this paper is that music education and all of *The Arts* are important for *all* students, including those with disabilities and impairments. The paper presents a discussion of the impact and local implementation of assessment and reporting of musical thinking in students with disabilities and impairments. The focus of this paper is to develop an understanding of the extraordinary complexities that encompass assessment and reporting about musical thinking in students with disabilities and impairments. For most people, an understanding of these extraordinary complexities may reduce fear, unease, and distrust. The phenomenon would seem logical. I debate the economic efficiency, political feasibility and social and cultural effectiveness of recent reforms in Australian and Victorian assessment and reporting policy in special education sectors, i.e., notions of inclusive education in relation to the development and implementation of assessment and reporting practices in music education.

The Issue: Notions of Inclusivity

There have always been children with disabilities and impairments, but there has not always been special education. Children living with disabilities and impairments have been viewed through various lenses throughout history (Ball, 1971; Kauffman, 1976; Lane, 1976). Social and cultural theory suggests that contemporary society and culture is extremely diverse (Derrida, 1978; Lyotard, 1984). Gill (1999) and Seelman (2000) described a paradigm of thinking about disability and impairment that shifts the location of problems with disability and impairment from the individual to environmental responses to disability and impairment that evolved from the legacy of these scholars, activists with disabilities and impairments, and their non-disabled allies. The paradigm frames disability and impairment from the perspective of a social and cultural minority group that is defined as a dimension of human difference and not as a defect. The goal for people with disabilities and impairments is not to eradicate their disability or impairment but to celebrate their distinctiveness, pursue an equal place in society and acknowledge that their different-ness is not defective, but valued.

Current principles of social and cultural theory challenge very powerful, economically efficient, and politically expedient values with social and cultural values centered on equal opportunity and diversity. These principles call for those who advocate social and cultural values to emerge with voices that have produced very positive effects. These notions have had a profound influence on social and cultural attitudes toward people with disabilities and impairments.

Many education systems throughout the world have accepted responsibility for the education of *all* students irrespective of disability or impairment in recent decades. Notions of inclusive education, integration, normalization, and least-restrictive environment for people with disabilities and impairments were espoused by Wolfensberger (1972) and Wolfensberger and Zauha (1973) as far back as the early 1970s. Policy and program initiatives in response to these notions in special education sectors in many world education authorities have led to more inclusive educational systems and improved practice in recent decades. For example, in the USA, such policy and program initiatives include the *Education of All Handicapped Children Act* (S. Res. 6, 1975); *Towards Equity: Education of the Deaf* (Commission on Education of the Deaf 1988), *Procedures Governing Programs and Services for Children with Special Needs* (North Carolina Department of Public Instruction 1993); and *Individuals with Disabilities Education Act* (IDEA—Individuals with Disabilities Education Act, 1997). Visser and Upton (1995) provided insights into the broader impact of such policy and program initiatives in the English education system (Warnock, 1978).

Historically, Australian educators have had a substantial concern with the education of students with disabilities and impairments. Long (1988, 1994) and Ashman (1988) provided insights into the broader impact of such policy and program initiatives in Australian public education systems. In the State of Victoria, policy and program initiatives include *Better Services, Better Outcomes in Victorian Government Schools: A Review of Educational Services for Students with Special Education Needs* (Lake, 2001); *Blueprint for Government Schools: Future Directions in the Victorian Government System* (Department of Education, Employment and Training Victoria, 2003), Collins (1984), Cullen and Brown (1992), and Cullen and Brown (1993); and *Public Education: The Next Generation* (more commonly known as the PENG Review) (Department of Education, Employment and Training Victoria, 2000).

Equal opportunity and diversity has meant increased support for many more students with disabilities and impairments in mainstream primary school and secondary college settings where appropriate, and in specialist school settings. Categories of potential research questions concerning trends and issues affecting special education are numerous. What is the purpose and role of assessment and reporting about musical thinking in students with disabilities and impairments in an increasingly politicized, data-driven, and accountability-focused educational environment? In what ways can assessment and reporting data be most effectively used to improve music learning for such students? In what ways can effective assessment and reporting practices in music education for students with disabilities and impairments be facilitated? What approaches to the planned and systematic process of assessment and reporting about musical thinking in students with disabilities and impairments would be most appropriate?

Social and cultural theorists appear to offer a discourse with which to liberate and empower pedagogy: the science of thinking and learning (Aronowitz and Giroux, 1991; Giroux and McLaren, 1989; Giroux, 1988, 1990). These views have allowed such people to emerge with a voice in the shaping of assessment and reporting practices in music education

274

for students with disabilities and impairments. For example, adopting Derrida's approach, special educators and music educators can attempt to deconstruct the role of language that is used to influence these assessment and reporting practices and take the side of those with disability or impairment.

Assessment and Reporting Practices in Music Education for Students with Disabilities and Impairments: The Teacher-Researcher

Assessment and reporting is understood as the planned and systematic process of gathering information about learning in relation to curriculum focuses and learning outcomes. Traditional quantitative approaches in the general psychological research and theory literature have had the most profound influence on music research and theory (Boyle, 1992; Boyle and Radocy, 1987; Colwell, 1970). For example, historically important quantitative approaches to measurement of creative musical thinking include those by Baltzer (1988, 1990), Barron (1969), Guilford (1957), McPherson (1995), and Webster (1983a, 1987b, 1989, 1992). Quantitative measurements of musical aptitude and achievement have been designed to capture the breadth and diversity of responses to music that reflect a value hierarchy (Bentley, 1966a, 1966b; Bergendal and Talo, 1969; Colwell, 1969a, 1969b, 1970, 1979; Gordon, 1965, 1979, 1982, 1987, 1989, 1991; Seashore, Lewis and Saetveit, 1960; Wing, 1961). Trehub, Thorpe, and Trainor (1990) investigated infants' perception of good and bad musical melodies. Flowers and Jellinson (1990), Kuhn, Sims, and Shehan (1981), and LeBlanc (1982) suggested a relationship between listening time and like-dislike rating scales in students with disabilities and impairments. However, quantitative measures of musical preference are apparently notoriously imperfect (Flowers, 1981; Kuhn, 1980; LeBlanc, 1986).

Assessment and Accommodations for Students with Disabilities and Impairments

Thurlow, Ysseldyke, and Silverstein (1993, 3) suggested that "...there does not [currently] exist a set of guidelines about acceptable accommodations in testing students with disabilities and impairments that is based on comprehensive, empirical research...." Pitoniak and Royer (2001) provided a review of nearly 100 published articles related to this issue since 1993. Some accommodations indeed may be inappropriate. Applebaum, Engle, Koegel, and Imhoff (1979), Bennett and Ragosta (1988), Bixler (1968), Ellis (1982), Heim (1963), Ianocone (1977), McLeish and Higgs (1982), and Nocera (1981) have adapted various test protocols in traditional quantitative approaches to measurement of musical achievement for students with disabilities and impairments.

One direction for future research and theory may be the establishment of norms for students with disabilities and impairments for pre-existing measures of aptitude and achievement. Another option is the construction of new test protocols designed specifically for children with disabilities and impairments (Kaplan 1977). Time and funding are generally not available to develop such protocols.

Assessment and reporting about musical thinking in students with disabilities and impairments is regarded as far more than test scores alone. Extensive reviews of knowledge, continued interest in multiple intelligence theory, and a growing desire to know more about the generative processes in music have been published (Deutsch, 1999; Hargreaves, 1986; Hodges, 1996; Radocy and Boyle, 2003; Reimer, 2003; Sloboda, 1985). However, there appears to be a paucity of music research and theory literature relating to musical generative processes in students with disabilities and impairments. It does appear that musical thinking in such students is more similar to that of non-disabled children of comparable mental age than chronological age. Adamek and Darrow (2005), Davis, Gfeller and Thaut (1992), and Lathom-Radocy (2002) describe the characteristics of these students, the educational implications of disabilities and impairments, appropriate adaptations as well as approaches to music education, and music therapy programs with such students.

Approaches to Assessment of Students with Disabilities and Impairments

In a small-scale qualitative inquiry and evaluation, Farrell (2006) examined national and international research and theory relating to qualitative inquiry and evaluation. Topics explored included The Research Context, History and Research Traditions, Theoretical Paradigms and Perspectives, Criteria for Judging Quality and Credibility, and Case Study and Action Research Strategies. Approaches to the collection, display, and analysis of qualitative data were examined. Ethical and political issues were explored. This work was guided by methodologies designed specifically for researchers who study those with disabilities and impairments (Mertens and McLaughlin, 2004; Standley and Prickett, 1994; Wheeler, 1995). Farrell's findings are discussed here.

Qualitative approaches to assessment and reporting about musical thinking in students with disabilities and impairments by definition relied on multiple ways of capturing as much of reality as possible. Such approaches are "...inherently multi-method in focus..." (Flick, 1992, 1998; Louis, 1982; Yin, 1993, 2003). The use of multiple types and sources of data reflected and attempted to secure an in-depth understanding about musical thinking in students with disabilities and impairments (Guba, 1990; Denzin, 1989a, 1989b; Eisner, 1998; Richardson, 2000).

There has been growing interest in the collection and analysis of multiple types and sources of data (assessment and reporting tools) in the special education context, i.e., the planned and systematic process of gathering information about what students with disabilities and impairments can do rather than exclusive reliance on single scores on traditional quantitative approaches (Thompson and Thurlow 2001). Such an approach assists to craft a montage of images that surround an understanding of musical thinking in students with disabilities and impairments. The montage is not crafted from sequential images, one at a time, but rather from multiple images about the context that are reflected and refracted simultaneously. Readers and audiences were invited to become immersed in and comprehend competing images. The many ways in which such students responded to a musical activity or experience were recorded, however particular, irrational, or even unnatural the behavior may have seemed. Behaviors were difficult to interpret. No single behavioral indicator could possibly fully illustrate musical achievement, nor could achievement be fully demonstrated by engaging in just one musical activity or experience.

No single type or source of data was trusted to provide a comprehensive perspective. Each type and source of data had strengths and weaknesses. Each type and source of data enabled information to be gathered from a range of teaching and learning contexts. This combination of types and sources of data enhanced quality and credibility as the strengths of one approach compensated for the weaknesses of another (Bradshaw, 1999; Goetz and LeCompte, 1984; Keating and Krumholz, 1999; Kirk and Miller, 1986; Patton, 2002; Smith and Robbins, 1984; Yin, 2003).

Multiple types and sources of data assisted to produce generally coherent findings (Campbell and Stanley, 1966; Cook and Campbell, 1979; Kvale, 1989). LeCompte and Preissle (1993) argued that descriptive assessment and reporting should be consistent with readers' experience. Multiple types and sources of data were used to corroborate, support, or indeed contradict interpretation and presentation of findings. Rich and thick and meaningful narrative was important (Connelly and Clandinin, 1990; Denzin, 1989b; Geertz, 1973; Van Maanen, 1988).

Multiple types and sources of data (assessment and reporting tools) were collected and analyzed in Farrell's (2006) study:

- *Documents and records* (LeCompte and Preissle, 1993; Lincoln and Guba, 1985; Merriam, 1998; Patton, 2002).

- *Participant observation* (Adler and Adler, 1987; Ashcroft, 1963; Atkin, 1992; Barr, 2000; Berg, 1989; Britsch, 1995; Bruyn, 1966; Davis and Ferguson, 1992; Denzin, 1989a; Douglas, 1976; Eisner, 1986; Fetterman, 1989; Glesne and Peshkin, 1992; Gold, 1958; Hammersley andAtkinson 1983, Holly 1987, Jorgensen 1989, Keller 1993, Lincoln and Guba, 1985; Loftland and Loftland, 1984; Mertens and McLaughlin, 1995; Mertens and McLaughlin, 2004; Mertens, 1991a; Peshkin, 1986; Phillips, 1985; Spradley, 1980; Wagner, 1990; Whyte, 1955; Wiley, 1987; Woods, 1985).

- *Folios, visual images and work samples* (Brandt, 1987; Gold, 1989; Harper, 2005; Prosser, 1998; Reimer, 2003; Wolf, 1986, 1987, 1989; Zessoules, 1988).

There appears to be no hard-and-fast rule that defines how long a teacher-researcher should stay in a field setting to collect data. Prolonged observation provides scope. Persistent observation provides depth. The teacher-researcher observes for a period sufficient to highlight key issues about the musical thinking in individual students. When key issues about the musical thinking in individual students appear to repeat instead of extend, it may be the time to discontinue (Guba, 1978; Lincoln and Guba, 1981, 1985; LeCompte and Goetz, 1982; Schwandt and Halpern, 1988). Data for Farrell's (2006) study was collected over the period of a ten-week teaching term.

The teacher-researcher seeks to demonstrate patterns in the data relating to students' musical thinking. Matrices of codes assist in the complex task of demonstrating patterns in the data relating to the musical thinking in individual students from the extraordinary amounts of data collected (Miles and Huberman, 1994, 59). Patterns in the data are greatly assisted by the inclusion of data displays (Armstrong, 1994; Brant, 1987; Miles and Huberman, 1994; Zerull, 1990).

Assessment and reporting of students' musical thinking is rigorous and demanding work (Kvale, 1988; Loftland, 1971). The analysis of data involves creativity, intellectual discipline, analytical rigor and many hours of work. A large range of diverse tasks for the collection of data was performed. Large amounts of data from a multiplicity of types and sources were compiled, organized and analyzed to make sense of what was learned about the students' musical thinking (Atkinson, 1990; Plath, 1990; Sanjek, 1990). Careful data management was implemented to facilitate (a) a systematic, coherent process of data collection, storage and retrieval aimed at ensuring high quality and readily accessible data, (b) documentation of completed analyses, and (c) retention of data and associated analyses after the study was complete. The information and communication technology available that supported this work continues to emerge (Fielding and Lee, 1991; Gibbs, 2002; Miles and Huberman, 1984, 1994; Pfaffenberger, 1988; Pool, 1959; Richards and Richards, 1994; Sieber 1976; Tesch, 1990, 1991; Weitzman and Miles, 1994).

Quality and credibility in assessment and reporting are judged according to certain logical concepts, including trustworthiness, confirmability, and dependability (Denzin, 1989a, 1989b; Eisner, 1998; Guba, 1981; Kidder and Judd, 1986; Miles and Huberman, 1994; Patton, 2002; U. S. General Accounting Office, 1990; Yin, 2003). Quality and credibility come about to the extent to which a reader is able to see what they would have missed without the teacher-researcher's observations. The style of narrative in assessment and reporting draws the reader closely into the world of individual students and contain a high degree of internal coherence, plausibility, and correspondence with what the reader would recognize from their own experiences. The teacher-researcher's responsibility was to provide sufficient detail to enable the reader to make such a judgment about students' musical thinking through extensive and careful *thick description* of time, place, context, and culture (Guba and Lincoln, 1989).

Narrative had to rely on *persuasiveness* and *utility* rather than proof. The goodness and quality of the inquiry would be judged on *trustworthiness* and *authenticity*. The concept of *authenticity* to enhance quality and credibility referred to interpretation and presentation with a balanced view of all perspectives, values, and beliefs. Has the teacher-researcher been fair in presenting views? *Fairness* was the extent to which different constructions and their underlying value structures are solicited and honored in the assessment and reporting process (Flippen, 2001; Guba and Lincoln, 1989; Lincoln and Guba, 1995; Mertens and McLaughlin, 1995; Miles and Huberman, 1994). The objective was a meaningful understanding of students' musical thinking.

Emergent Insights and Conclusions: The Continuing Challenge into the New Millennium

Farrell's (2006) review of the public laws, reports, and reviews in response to notions of inclusive education, integration, normalization, and least-restrictive environment for people with disabilities and impairments highlighted a key challenge: the development and implementation of assessment and reporting practices in music education initiatives, including those with the most severe, profound, and multiple disabilities and impairments, who are unlikely to achieve at or beyond the initial key level or stage of standards-based music curriculum frameworks. Assessment of special learners in the music classroom is a concern for many teachers. The overarching concept is to assess and report musical learning in increments that are specific to the student and observable and recordable for the teacher. Farrell's (2006) study suggested that teachers create very specific and detailed checklists, rubrics, and rating scales that can show the steps toward mastery of a skill or concept as well as the measure of that student's success over time.

Because of the variability of skills and cognitive levels within the special education population, emergent insights and conclusions can only be true for a specific context at a particular time. Emergent insights and conclusions cannot be true for all contexts at all times. The development and implementation of assessment and reporting practices for *all* students should provide relevant and accessible information about what a student knows and can do and how future learning will be supported and extended, including those with disabilities and impairments. For example, Farrell's (2006) study suggests that assessment and reporting provides substantiation for the comprehensiveness and validity of program content for such students. Assessment and reporting assist teacher monitoring and reflect on the effectiveness of activities in relation to curriculum focuses and learning outcomes for such students.

Farrell (2006) argues the careful development and implementation of reliable, valid, and fair assessment and reporting practices for students with disabilities and impairments. Continued research is necessary to provide further development and implementation of reliable, valid, and fair practices for such students.

References

Adamek, M. S. and A. A. Darrow. 2005. *Music in special education*. Silver Spring, MD: The American Music Therapy Association.

Adler, P. A. and P. Adler. 1987. *Membership roles in field research*. Newbury Park, CA: Sage.

Applebaum, E., A. L. Engle, R. L. Koegel, and B. Imhoff. 1979. Measuring musical abilities of autistic children. *Journal of Autism and Developmental Disorders*, 3(9):279–285.

Armstrong, C. L. 1994. *Designing assessment in art*. Reston VA: National Art Education Association,

Aronowitz, S. and H. A. Giroux. 1991. *Postmodern education: Politics, culture, and social criticism*. Minneapolis: University of Minnesota Press.

Ashman, A. F., ed. 1988. Integration 25 years on. *The Exceptional Child* (Monograph Number 1). Brisbane, Queensland: University of Queensland, Australia.

Atkin, J. M. 1992. Teaching as research: An essay. *Teaching and Teacher Education*, 8(4).

Atkinson, P. 1990. *The ethnographic imagination*. London: Routledge.

Ball, T. S. 1971. *Itard, Seguin and Kephart—sensory education—A learning interpretation*. Columbus, OH: Charles E. Merrill.

Baltzer, S. 1988. A validation study of a measure of musical creativity. *Journal of Research in Music Education*, 36(4):232–249.

Baltzer, S. 1990. *A factor analytical study of musical creativity in children*. Unpublished doctoral dissertation, Indiana University, Bloomington.

Barron, F. 1969. *Creative person and creative process*. New York: Holt, Rinehart and Winston.

Bennett, R. E. and M. Ragosta. 1988. Handicapped people. In W. W. Willingham, M. Ragosta, R. E. Bennett, H. Braun, D. A. Rock, and D. A. Powers, eds., *Testing handicapped people*, 17–36. Boston: Allyn and Bacon.

Bentley, A. 1966a. *Measures of musical abilities*. New York: October House.

Bentley, A. 1966b. *Musical ability in children and its measurement*. New York: October House.

Berg, B. 1989. *Qualitative research methods for the social sciences*. Boston: Allyn and Bacon.

Bergendal, B. and Talo, S. 1969. The response of children with reduced phoneme systems to the Seashore Measures of Musical Talents. *Folio Phoniatrica, 21*, 20–38.

Bixler, J. 1968. Musical aptitude in the educable mentally retarded child. *Journal of Music Therapy*, 5(2):41–43.

Board of Studies. 1995. *Curriculum and standards framework: The arts*. Carlton, Victoria: Author.

Boyle, J. D. 1992. Evaluation of musical ability. In R.Colwell (Ed.), *Handbook of research on music teaching and learning*, 247–265. New York: Schirmer.

Boyle, J. D. and Radocy, R. E. 1987. *Measurement and evaluation of musical experiences*. New York: Schirmer.

Bradshaw, T. K. 1999. Communities not fazed: Why military base closures may not be catastrophic. *Journal of the American Planning Association, 65,* 193–206.

Brandt, R. 1987. On assessment in the arts: A conversation with Howard Gardner. *Educational Leadership, 45,* 30–34.

Britsch, S. J. 1995. The researcher as teacher: Constructing one's place in the story of events of preschoolers. *International Journal of Qualitative Studies in Education, 8*(3):297–309.

Bruyn, S. T. 1966. *The human perspective in sociology*. Englewood Cliffs NJ: Prentice-Hall.

Campbell, D. T. and Stanley, J. 1966. *Experimental and quasi-experimental designs for research*. Chicago: Rand McNally.

Cook, T. and Campbell, D. T. 1979. *Quasi-Experimentation*: *Design and analysis issues for field settings*. Chicago: Rand McNally.

Collins, M. K. 1984. *Integration in Victorian education*: *Report of the ministerial review of educational services for the disabled*. Melbourne, Australia: Education Department of Victoria.

Colwell, R. 1969a. *Music achievement tests 1 and 2*. Chicago: Follett Educational Corporation.

Colwell, R. 1969a. *Music Achievement Tests 3 a n d 4*. Chicago: Follett Educational Corporation

Colwell, R. 1970. *The evaluation of music teaching and learning*. Englewood Cliffs NJ: Prentice-Hall.

Colwell, R. 1979. *Silver Burdett music competency tests*. Morristown: Silver Burdett.

Commission on Education of the Deaf. 1988. *Towards equity*: *Education of the deaf*. Washington D. C.: Author.

Connelly, F. M. and Claudinin, D. J. 1990. Stories of experience and narrative inquiry. *Educational Researcher*, 19(4):2–14.

Cullen, R. and Brown, N. 1992. *Integration and special education in Victorian schools*: *A Program Effectiveness Review*. Education Department of Victoria, Melbourne.

Cullen, R. and Brown, N. 1993. *Cullen-Brown implementation advisory committee*: *Report*. Education Department of Victoria, Melbourne.

Davis, W.B., Gfeller, K. E. and Thaut, M. H. 1992. *An introduction to music therapy, theory and practice*. William Brown Publishers, IA.

Department of Education, Employment and Training Victoria. 2000. *Public education*: *The next generation*. Retrieved April 7, 2001 from http://www.sofweb.vic.edu.au/publiced/pdfs/PubEd.pdf

Department of Education, Employment and Training Victoria. 2003. *Blueprint for government schools*: *Future directions in the Victorian government system*. Retrieved February 20, 2004 from http://www.sofweb.vic.edu.au

Department of Education, Science and Training. 2004. *National review of school music education*. Retrieved December 12, 2004 from http://www.schoolmusicreview.edu.au

Denzin, N.K. 1989a. *The research act*, 3rd ed. Englewood Cliffs NJ: Prentice Hall.

Denzin, N.K. 1989b. *Interpretive interactionism*. Newbury Park CA: Sage.

Derrida, J. 1978. *L'écriture et la différence* [Writing and difference]. Routledge and Kegan Paul: London.

Deutsch, D., ed. 1999. *The psychology of music*, 2nd edition. New York: Academic Press.

Douglas, J.D. 1976. *Investigative social research*. Beverly Hills CA: Sage.

Eisner, E. W. 1998. *The Enlightened eye*: *Qualitative inquiry and the enhancement of educational practice*. Upper Saddle River NJ: Merrill.

Ellis, D. 1982. *Differences in music achievement among gifted and talented, average and educable mentally handicapped, fifth- and sixth-grade students*. Unpublished doctoral dissertation, The University of North Carolina.

Farrell, H. J. 2006. *The impact and local implementation of standards-based curriculum policy frameworks and music education programs for students with disabilities and impairments in Victoria*: *A qualitative evaluation*. Unpublished doctoral dissertation, The University of Melbourne.

281

Fetterman, D. M. 1989. *Ethnography*: *Step by step*. Newbury Park, CA: Sage.

Flick, U. 1992. Triangulation revisited: Strategy of validation or alternative. *Journal for the Theory of Social Behaviour*, *22*, 175–198.

Flick, U. 1998. *An introduction to qualitative research*: *Theory*, method and applications, London: Sage Publications.

Flowers, P. J. and Jellinson, J. A. 1990. *The measurement of music behaviour in music therapy and education*. Paper presented at the Annual Meeting of the National Association of Music Therapists, Washington D. C.

Flowers, P. J. 1981. Relationship between two measures of music preference. *Contributions to Music Education*, *8*, 47–54.

Gaylord-Ross, R., ed. 1990–1992. *Issues and research in special education* (two volumes). New York: Teachers College Press.

Geertz, C. 1973. Thick description: Toward an interpretive theory of culture. In C. Geertz, ed. *The interpretation of cultures*, 3–32. New York: Basic Books.

Gibbs, G. R. 2002. *Qualitative data analysis*: *Explorations with NVivo*. Buckingham: Open University.

Gill, C. 1999. Invisible ubiquity: The surprising relevance of disability issues in evaluation. *American Journal of Evaluation*, *29*(2):279–287

Giroux, H. A. and McLaren, P. 1989. *Teachers as intellectuals*: *Toward a critical pedagogy of learning*. Granby, MA: Bergin and Garvey.

Giroux, H. A. 1988. *Schooling and the struggle for public life*: *Critical pedagogy in the modern age*. Minneapolis: University of Minnesota Press.

Giroux, H. A. 1990. *Curriculum discourse as postmodernist critical practice*. Geelong, Victoria: Deakin University.

Glesne, C. and Peshkin, A. 1992. *Becoming qualitative researchers*. White Plains, NY: Longman.

Goetz, J. P. and LeCompte, M. D. 1984. *Ethnography and qualitative design in educational research*. New York: Academic Press.

Gold, R. L. 1958. Roles in sociological field observations. *Social Forces*, *36*, 217–223.

Gold, S. J. 1989. Ethical issues in visual fieldwork. In G Blank, ed., *New Technology in Sociology*: *Practical Applications Research and Work*, 99–112. New Brunswick, NJ: Transaction Books.

Gordon, E. E. 1965. *Musical Aptitude Profile*, Houghton Mifflin, Boston.

Gordon, E. E. 1979. *Primary measures of music audiation*. Chicago: G.I.A. Publications, Inc.

Gordon, E. E. 1982. *Intermediate measures of music audiation*. Chicago: G.I.A. Publications, Inc.

Gordon, E. E. 1987. *The nature, description, measurement and evaluation of music aptitudes*. Chicago: G.I.A. Publications, Inc.

Gordon, E. E. 1989. *Advanced measures of music audiation*. Chicago: G.I.A. Publications, Inc.

Gordon, E. E. 1991. *Iowa tests of musical literacy*, 2nd edition. Chicago: G.I.A. Publications, Inc.

Guba, E. G. and Y. S. Lincoln. 1981. *Effective evaluation*: *Improving the usefulness of evaluation results through responsiveness and naturalistic approaches*, San Francisco: Jossey-Bass.

Guba, E. G. 1978. *Toward a methodology of naturalistic inquiry in educational evaluation.* CSE Monograph Series in Evaluation No 8, Center for the Study of Evaluation, University of California, Los Angeles.

Guba, E. G. 1990. The alternative paradigm dialog. In E.G. Guba, ed., *The Paradigm Dialog,* 17–30. Newbury Park, CA: Sage.

Guilford, J. P. 1957. Creative abilities in the arts. *Psychological Review, 64,* 110–118.

Hammersley, M. and Atkinson, P. 1983. *Ethnography: Principles in practice.* London: Tavistock.

Hargreaves, D. J. 1986. *The developmental psychology of music.* Cambridge University Press, Cambridge, MA.

Harper, D. 2005. What's new visually. In N. K. Denzin and Y. S. Lincoln, eds., *The sage handbook of qualitative research,* 3rd edition, 747–762. Thousand Oaks, CA: Sage Publications.

Heim, K. E. 1963. *Musical aptitude of seven high school students in residential schools for the blind as measured by the wing-standardized test of musical intelligence.* Unpublished masters' thesis, University of Kansas, Lawrence.

Hodges, D. A., ed. 1996. *Handbook of music psychology,* 2nd ed. San Antonio, TX: IMR Press.

Holly, M. L. 1987. *Keeping a personal professional journal.* Burwood, Victoria: Deakin University Press.

Ianacone, R. N. 1977. *The measurement of music aptitude for the mentally retarded.* Unpublished doctoral dissertation, The University of Florida, Gainesville.

Individuals with disabilities education act (I.D.E.A). 1997. Retrieved from http://www.ed.gov/offices/OSERS/IDEA

Jorgensen, D. L. 1989. *Participant observation: A methodology for human studies.* Newbury Park, CA: Sage Publications.

Kaplan, P. R. 1977. *A criterion-referenced comparison of rhythmic responsiveness in normal and educable mentally retarded children.* Unpublished doctoral dissertation, The University of Michigan, Ann Arbor, MI.

Kauffman, J. M. 1976. Nineteenth century views of children's behaviour disorders. *Journal of Special Education, 10,* 335–349.

Keating, W. D. and Krumholz, N., eds. 1999. *Rebuilding urban neighborhoods: Achievements, opportunities and limits.* Thousand Oaks, CA: Sage.

Kirk, J. and M. L. Miller. 1986. *Reliability and validity in qualitative research.* Beverly Hills, CA: Sage.

Kuhn, T. L., Sims, W. L. and Shehan, P. K. 1981. Relationship between listening time and like-dislike ratings on three music selections. *Journal of Music Therapy, 18,* 181–192.

Kuhn, T. L. 1980. Instrumentation for the measurement of music attitudes. *Contributions to Music Education, 8,* 2–38.

Kvale, S. 1988. The 1000-page question. *Phenomenology and Pedagogy, 6(2):*90–106.

Kvale, S. 1989. To validate is to question. In S. Kvale, ed., *Issues of Validity in Qualitative Research,* 73–92. Lund, Sweden: Studentlitterture.

Lake, J. 2001. *Better services, better outcomes in victorian government schools: A review of educational services for students with special educational needs.* Melbourne, Australia: Department of Education, Employment and Training.

Lane, H. 1976. *The wild boy of aveyron.* Boston, MA: Harvard University Press.

Lathom-Radocy, W. B. 2002. *Paediatric music therapy.* Springfield, IL: Charles C. Thomas.

LeBlanc, A. 1982. An interactive theory of music preference. *Journal of Music Therapy, 19,* 28–45.

LeBlanc, A. 1986. Effects of vocal vibrato and performer sex on children's music preference. *Journal of Research in Music Education, 34,* 222–237.

LeCompte, M. D. and J. P. Goetz. 1982. Problems of reliability and validity in ethnographic research. *Review of Educational Research, 52*(1):31–60.

LeCompte, M. D. and J. Preissle. with R. Tesch. 1993. *Ethnography and qualitative design in educational research,* 2nd ed. NY: Academic Press.

Lincoln, Y. S. and E. G. Guba. 1985. *Naturalistic inquiry.* Beverly Hills, CA: Sage.

Loftland, J. and L. H. Loftland. 1984. *Analyzing social settings: A guide to qualitative observation and analysis,* 2nd ed. Belmont, CA: Wadsworth.

Loftland, J. 1971. *Analyzing social settings.* Belmont, CA: Wadsworth.

Long, P. C., ed. 1988. *"The Continuing Challenge: Special Education and Effective Integration,"* selected papers from the Australian Association of Special Education XII National Conference, Melbourne.

Long, P. C., ed. 1994. *Quality outcomes for all learners.* Selected papers from the Australian Association of Special Education XVII National Conference, Melbourne.

Louis, K. S. 1982. Multisite/multimethod studies. *American Behavioural Scientist, 26*(1):6-22.

Lyotard, J. 1984. *The postmodern condition: A report on knowledge.* Translation of *La condition postmoderne* by Geoff Bennington and Brian Massumi. Minneapolis: University of Minnesota Press.

McLeish, J. and G. Higgs. 1982. Musical ability and mental subnormality: An experimental investigation. *British Journal of Educational Psychology, 52,* 370–373.

McPherson, G. E. 1995. The assessment of musical performance: Development and validation of five new measures. *Psychology of Music, 23*(2):142–161.

Merriam, S. B. 1998. *Qualitative research and case study applications in education,* 2nd ed. San Francisco: Jossey-Bass Publishers.

Mertens, D. M. and McLaughlin, J. A. 2004. *Research and evaluation methods in special education,* 2nd ed. Thousand Oaks, CA: Corwin Press (Sage Publications).

Miles, M. B. and A. M. Huberman. 1984. *Qualitative data analysis: A sourcebook of new methods.* Beverly Hills, CA: Sage Publications.

Miles, M. B. and Huberman, A. M. 1994. *Qualitative data analysis: An expanded sourcebook,* 2nd ed. Thousand Oaks, CA: Sage Publications.

Miller, C. August 7th, 2005. Help promised for students with disabilities. *The Sunday Age,* 2.

Nocera, S. D. 1981. *A descriptive analysis of the attainment of selective musical learnings by normal children and by educable mentally retarded children mainstreamed in music classes at the second grade and fifth Grade Level.* Unpublished doctoral dissertation, The University of Wisconsin, Madison.

North Carolina Department of Public Instruction. 1993. *Procedures governing programs and services for children with special needs.* Raleigh, NC.

Patton, M. Q. 2002. *Qualitative research and evaluation methods,* 3rd ed. Thousand Oaks CA: Sage Publications.

Peshkin, A. 1986. *God's choice* Chicago: University of Chicago Press.

Pfaffenberger, B. 1988. *Microcomputer applications with qualitative research.* Newbury Park, CA: Sage Publications.

Pitoniak, M. J. and J. M. Royer. 2001. Testing accommodations for examinees with disabilities: A review of psychometric, legal and social policy issues. *Review of Educational Research*, 71(1):53–104.

Plath, D. 1990. Fieldnotes, filed notes and the conferring of notes. In R. Sanjek, ed., *Fieldnotes: The makings of anthropology*. Albany: State University of New York Press.

Pool, I., ed. 1959. *Trends in content analysis*. Urbana: University of Illinois Press.

Prosser, J., ed. 1998. *Image based research: A sourcebook for qualitative researchers*. London: Falmer Press.

Radocy, R. E. and J. D. Boyle. 2003. *The psychological foundations of musical behaviour*, 4th ed. Springfield IL: Charles C Thomas.

Ray, M. 1990. *Report of the music education committee of review*. Melbourne: Corporate Relations Division, Western Metropolitan Region, Ministry of Education.

Reimer B. 2003. *A philosophy of music education: Advancing the vision*, 3rd ed. Englewood Cliffs, NJ: Prentice-Hall.

Sanjek, R., ed. 1990. *Fieldnotes: The makings of anthropology*. Albany: State University of New York Press.

Schwandt, T. A. and E. S. Halpern. 1988. *Linking auditing and metaevalution: Enhancing Quality in applied research*. Newbury Park, CA: Sage.

Seashore, C. E., D. L. Lewis, and J. G. Saetveit. 1960. *Seashore measures of musical talents*, rev. Initially appeared in 1919; extensively rev. in 1939; out of print by 1994. NY: The Psychological Corporation.

Seelman, K. D. 2000. *The new paradigm on disability: Research issues and approaches*. Washington, D. C.: National Institute for Disability and Rehabilitative Research.

Sieber, S. D. 1976. *A synopsis and critique of guidelines for qualitative analysis contained in selected textbooks*. NY: Center for Policy Research, Project on Social Architecture in Education.

Sloboda, J. 1985. *The musical mind: An introduction to the cognitive psychology of music*. NY: Oxford University Press.

Smith, A. G. and A. E. Robbins. 1984. Multimethod policy research: A case study of structure and flexibility in D. Fetterman, ed., *Ethnography in Educational Evaluation*, 115–132. Beverly Hills, CA: Sage.

Spradley, J. P. 1980. *Participant observation*. New York: Holt, Rinehart and Winston.

S. Res. 6, 94th Cong., Public Law 94–142 (enacted). 1975. *Education of all handicapped children act* (Short Title). [Electronic version.] Retrieved December 12, 2004, from www.scn.org/~bk269/94–142.html

Standley, J. M. and C. Prickett, eds. 1994. *Research in music therapy: A tradition of excellence*. Silver Spring, MD: National Association for Music Therapy.

Switzky, H. N. and W. L. Heal. 1990. Research in speech education methods in R. Gaylord-Ross, ed., *Issues and Research in Special Education*, 1, 1–81.

Tesch, R. 1990. *Qualitative research: Analysis types and software tools*. New York: Falmer.

Tesch, R., ed. 1991. Computers and qualitative data, special focus issues, *Qualitative Sociology*, 14, 3–4.

Thompson, S. and Thurlow, M. L. 2001. *2001 State special education outcomes: A report on state activities at the beginning of a new decade*. National Center on Educational Outcomes. Minneapolis: University of Minnesota.

Thurlow, M. L., J. E. Ysseldyke, and B. Silverstein. 1993. *Testing accommodations for students with disabilities*, National Center on Educational Outcomes. Minneapolis: University of Minnesota.

Trehub S. E., L. A. Thorpe, and L. J. Trainor. 1990. Infant's perception of good and bad melodies. *Psychomusicology*, 9(1):5–19.

U. S. General Accounting Office (Program, Evaluation and Methodology Division). 1990. *Case study evaluations*. Washington, D. C.: Government Printing Office.

Van Mannen, J. 1988. *Tales of the field: On writing ethnography*. Chicago: University of Chicago Press.

Visser, J. and G. Upton, eds. 1993. *Special education in Britain after Warnock*. London: David Fulton Publishers.

Wagner, J. 1990. *Field research as full participant in schools and other settings*. Paper presented at the annual meeting of the American Education Research Association, Boston.

Warnock, H. M. (Chair). 1978. *Special educational needs: Report of the committee of enquiry into the education of handicapped children and young people*. London: H.M.S.O.

Webster, P. R. 1983a. *An assessment of musical imagination in young children*. Paper presented to Bowling Green State University Symposium on Music Teaching and Research, Bowling Green State University, Bowling Green, Ohio.

Webster, P. R. 1987b. Refinement of a measure of creative thinking in music. In C. K. Madsen and C. A. Prickett, eds., *Applications of Research in Music Behaviour*, 257–271. Tuscaloosa, AL: The University of Alabama Press.

Webster, P. R. 1989. Creative thinking in music: The assessment question. In *The Proceedings of the Suncoast Music Education Forum on Creativity*. University of South Florida, Tampa.

Webster, P. R. 1992. Research on creative thinking in music: The assessment literature. In R. Colwell, ed., *Handbook of research on music teaching and learning*, 266–280. NY: Schirmer.

Weitzman, E. A. and M. B. Miles. 1994. *Computer programs for qualitative data analysis: A software sourcebook*. Thousand Oaks, CA: Sage Publications.

Wolf, D. P. 1986. All the pieces that go into it: The multiple sources of arts education. In A. Hurwitz, ed., Ae*sthetics in education: The missing dimension*. Mattituck, MD: Amercon Press.

Wolf, D. P. 1987. Artistic learning: What and where is it? *Journal of Aesthetic Education*, 22(1):144–155.

Wolf, D. P. 1989. Portfolio assessment: Sampling student work . *Educational Leadership*, 46(7):35–39.

Wheeler, B., ed. 1995. *Music therapy research*. Phoenixville, PA: Barcelona Publishers.

Whyte, W. F. 1955. *Street corner society: The social structure of an Italian slum*. Chicago: University of Chicago Press.

Wing, H. D. 1961. *Standardized tests of musical intelligence*. The Mere, England: National Foundation for Education Research.

Woods, P. 1985. Sociology, ethnography, and teacher practice. *Teaching and Teaching Education*, 1(1):51–62.

Wolfensberger, W. and Zauha, H., eds. 1973. *Citizen advocacy and protective services for the impaired and handicapped*. Toronto, Canada: National Institute on Mental Retardation.

Wolfensberger, W. 1972. *The principle of normalization in human services*. Toronto, Canada: National Institute on Mental Retardation.

Wiley, J. 1987. The shock of unrecognition as a problem in participant observation. *Qualitative Sociology*, 10(1):78–83.

Yin, R. K. 1993. *Applications of case study research*. Newbury Park, CA: Sage Publications.

Yin, R. K. 2003. *Case study research: Design and methods*, 3rd ed. Thousand Oaks, CA: Sage Publications.

Zerull, D. S. 1990. Evaluation in arts education: Building and using an effective assessment strategy. *Design for Arts in Education*, 92(1):19–24.

Zessoules, R. 1988. A better balance. In J. Burton, A. Lederman and P. London, eds., *Beyond DBAE: The case for multiple visions of art education*. North Dartmouth, MA: Southeastern Massachusetts University.

The Development and Validation of a Measurement Tool for Assessing Students' Ability to Keep a Steady Beat

Glenn E. Nierman
University of Nebraska—Lincoln

Abstract

The purpose of this study was to develop a valid and reliable way to assess nine-through fourteen-year-old students' ability to maintain a steady tempo of regular pulses given at different tempos in a group setting. One hundred and sixty-seven fifth- and sixth-grade students were asked to count six sounded tones silently and to continue counting at the same tempo established by the six tones during a subsequent period of silence until they heard a major chord sounded. Then they were to mark on their answer sheet the number that had been reached in their silent counting when the chord was sounded. After adjustments, a second version of the Steady Beat Exercise (SBE) was found to be internally consistent ($\alpha = 0.7532$) and item analysis revealed all items indices were within an acceptable range. Criterion-related validity was assessed by correlating teacher ratings with SBE scores using the point-biserial technique.

Choosing the right instrument for beginning instrumental music study is an important decision faced by young students and their parents. Information about students' musical aptitude, timbre preferences, eye-hand coordination, etc. could help students, parents, and teachers to reach a decision about which instrument to play that could result in fewer dropouts from the instrumental music program, and ultimately, a lifetime of enjoyable musical encounters for students. Several years ago, the *Student Musical Instrument Compatibility Test (SMICT)* (Nierman and Pearson, in progress) was designed to provide relevant information for this important decision[1]. The tasks (subtests) included in the SMICT consisted of the assessment of (a) the ability to keep a steady beat, (b) tone color preferences, (c) musical aptitude, and (d) eye-hand coordination. In this study we focused on the development and validation of a tool to assess students' ability to keep a steady beat (or described another way, "to audiate" a steady beat at different tempos), a component which has been identified in the literature as a key component of success in instrumental study.

Assessing rhythmic ability has been a topic of interest to authors of standardized music aptitude and achievement tests since Carl Seashore devised his *Measures of Musical Talent* in 1919. The rhythmic aspect of particular concern for this study was how to assess

---

1 The author gratefully acknowledges the work of Bruce Pearson, co-researcher and developer of the SMICT.

students' ability to keep a steady beat or pulse. Although this aspect of rhythmic ability has received far less attention from researchers than other temporal areas, some studies investigating this area were found. Gordon and Martin (1993–94), for example, used keyboards to determine that one-third to one-half of the subjects (ages 12 to 14) were unable to play consistently in time. Some, such as Parncutt (1994) and Fraisse (1982), looked theoretically at the matter of pulse salience. Others (Geringer, Madsen, and Duke, 1993–94; Geringer, Duke, and Madsen, 1992; and Duke, Geringer, and Madsen, 1991) examined the perception of beat note within varying contexts such as tempo changes. Thackray's (1969) steady beat exercise asked students to join in tapping the pulse at various tempos and then to continue tapping for an additional eight pulses at exactly the same speed (22). This task, however, is very time-consuming, requiring students to be assessed individually. John Flohr (2003) had a similar idea in mind for assessing steady beat. Flohr's (2006) *Rhythm Performance Test Revised (RPT-R)* is a standardized, norm-referenced instrument that measures rhythmic performance to the nearest millisecond. The RPT assesses skills across two domains: (1) matching the steady beat of recorded examples and (2) listening to and repeating rhythm patterns.

The purpose of this study was to develop a valid and reliable way to assess nine-through fourteen-year-old students' ability to maintain a steady tempo of regular pulses given at different tempos in a group setting.

Procedure

The researcher-designed Steady Beat Exercise (SBE) was constructed and validated to determine how well students' inner pulse or sense of a steady beat has developed. There were two administrations of the SBE, a pilot study followed by the primary study. Subjects for the pilot study were 82 fifth grade students, 10–11 years of age, from a suburban school district in the Midwest. Subjects for the primary study were 167 fifth- and sixth-grade students, ages 10–12, again from a suburban school district in the Midwest.

The pilot study was revised for the present study. The total time for administration of the revised 12–item SBE was seven minutes, forty-two seconds. The SBE items were written using Finale™ notation software, which allowed the metronomic markings to be specified exactly, and were then realized for recording on a cassette tape using a Yamaha DX100 synthesizer.

We determined the number of test items and the range of individual test item parameters using the following rationale. Based on research by Geringer, Madsen, and Duke (1993–94), we varied the metronome markings (MM) by twelve beats within a range of MM = 60–120, reasoning that anything less than a difference of twelve may not be perceived by students as significantly different. This resulted in six possible tempos: 60, 72, 84, 96, 108, and 120. It was decided to list beat numbers (BN) 7–16 on the answer sheet, but place the sounded chord only on beats 9–14. This produced a range of six possible beat numbers (9, 10, 11, 12, 13, and 14) on which the chord could be sounded. Placing the sounded chord on beat 7 or 8 would have been too easy and would have perhaps hindered discrimination power. Similarly, placing the chord on beats 15 or 16 at slow tempi was found to be too difficult for children in this age group. To utilize all of the possible MM/BN combinations for the pilot test, thirty-six test items (six MMs times six BNs) were constructed. These items began in the middle range of both MM and BN and then alternated from fast tempo/most delay of sounded chord to slow tempo/least delay of sounded chord until all possible combinations of MM/BN were utilized.

The directions for the revised SBE were modified based on item analysis of the pilot study and observations of those administering the pilot study. The revised directions are noted below:

> In this exercise we are interested in determining how well your inner pulse (P) or sense of a steady beat has developed. For each item you will hear a series of six tones sounded at different speeds—sometimes fast, [P1: sound six beats at MM = 120] sometimes slow [P2: sound six beats at MM = 60]. Count each of these six tones beginning with the number "1" silently to yourself as they are sounded [P3: sound six beats at MM = 96 with whispered counts 1–6]. Continue counting to yourself at the same speed using the numbers (7–8–9–10, etc.) during the period of silence following the tones until you hear a chord that sounds like this: [sound chord alone]. The number you reached in your silent counting when the chord is sounded is the answer we are seeking.

Results

In addition to face validity, construct validity and criterion-related validity were considered relevant to the measure's development. Internal reliability, examined by computing coefficient alpha, and item analysis (computing difficulty and discrimination indices) were further examined in the primary study ($N = 167$).

The construct validity of the SBE, defined as the degree to which the ability to keep a steady beat is a unique aspect or dimension of rhythmic ability, was examined through a review of the literature. Thackray's (1969) study of the relationship between rhythmic perception and rhythmic performance was particularly relevant to construct validity considerations. He concluded in his analysis of his combined rhythmic performance batteries that although there was "...considerable evidence for a substantial factor of 'general rhythmic ability' running through the tests" (34), "the general low correlations between the [rhythmic perception] tests suggest a fairly high degree of specificity, which supports the hypothesis that rhythmic ability is complex and many-sided" (18).

It was considered desirable to assess students' ability to maintain a steady tempo of regular pulses given at different tempi using less time and fewer test items. Therefore, using information from face validity reviews by a panel of experts, from item analysis, and from SPSS Reliability Analysis–Scale (Alpha) of the pilot study, the SBE was revised for a second administration.

The revision of the SBE began by making adjustments in the directions based on the review of the panel of experts and resulted in the changes previously noted in the Procedure section of this report. Then, using the SPSS Reliability Analysis–Scale (Alpha), various SBE items with the most damaging effects to coefficient alpha were discarded. This resulted in the elimination all but twelve of the original thirty-six items. With attention to keeping items with acceptable difficulty and discriminating indices, a table of specifications was then created to ascertain that all six tempo groups (MM = 60, 72, 84, 96, 108, and 120) and all six beats (beats 9 through 14) on which the major chord was sounded were represented in the revised item pool. An examination of this table showed that all of the beats on which the major chord was sounded were represented twice within the twelve-item pool, but no items at MM = 108 were represented. An examination of the pilot data showed that all MM = 108 items not selected were in the last half of the test, suggesting that fatigue might have been a factor in poor reliability coefficients for these items. Pilot item 34 (MM = 108) was then selected to replace an item in the table of specifications so that this tempo group would be represented. These changes resulted in the twelve-item version of the SBE which had an acceptable reliability coefficient (α = 0.7921). Each of the six beats on which the major chord was sounded represented twice, and each of the six tempo groupings represented at least once (MM = 60—1 item; MM = 72—2 items; MM = 84—3 items; MM = 96—3 items; MM = 108—1 item; and MM = 120—1 item).

The mean of the revised twelve-item SBE given to 167 subjects was 7.907 (*SD* = 2.869), with an overall reliability coefficient of α = 0.7532. The difficulty and discrimination indices for each item are shown in Table 1.

A criterion-related validity coefficient was obtained by using teacher ratings of students' abilities to keep a steady beat according to a format used by Colwell (1969) in designing the *Music Achievement Tests* (23–24). Teachers in each of the nine classes were asked to list the three students who they thought would score highest and the three students who they thought would score lowest on the SBE. This process imposes an artificial dichotomy upon a truly continuous variable. To eliminate any possible contamination, teachers were not furnished SBE test scores. The results of the biserial technique used to correlate the dichotomous variable (e.g., high/low achievers) with the continuous dependent variable (SBE scores) are shown in Table 2.

Table 1. Item Analysis of SBE (Second Administration)

Item Number (MM/Beat)	Difficulty	Discrimination
1 (84/9)	.705	.333
2 (96/13)	.513	.433
3 (60/11)	.777	.278
4 (120/12)	.534	.441
5 (84/13)	.746	.336
6 (72/24)	.632	.248
7 (96/9)	.762	.519
8 (108/10)	.705	.490
9 (84/11)	.720	.452
10 (108/12)	.570	.472
11 (72/10)	.813	.357
12 (96/14)	.430	.303

Table 2. Correlations of Teacher Ratings (High/Low) with SBE Scores (Second Administration)

Class (n)	r
1 (20)	.705
2 (23)	.580
3 (22)	.830
4 (22)	.742
5 (22)	.532
6 (26)	.424
7 (29)	.274

Discussion

The purpose of this study was to develop a valid and reliable way to assess nine-through fourteen-year-old students' ability to maintain a steady tempo of regular pulses given at different tempos. The essence of the discussion, then, should focus on the validity and reliability of the instrument.

The information supplied from item analysis statistics can provide useful guidelines for construction and interpretation of the data-gathering instrument. Colwell (1970) offers the following guidelines for the difficulty value:

> ...there should be no question that everyone answers correctly and no question that everyone misses; all those taking the test should be able to correctly answer some of the items, but no one should be able to make a perfect score. Test makers often strive for a range of difficulty from 0.20 to 0.80, with most of the items from 0.40 to 0.70 (65).

Item discrimination may be misleading and requires careful scrutiny of the questions themselves. Colwell interprets this value as follows: "The higher the item discrimination, the more fair the measurement. With the previous exceptions, item discrimination should be above 0.20" (Colwell, 1970, 66).

With these criteria in mind, an examination of Table 1 shows that in terms of the difficulty index, the SBE items are all within the acceptable ranges indicated by Colwell, although there were two students who got a perfect score on the exercise. Likewise, all of the discrimination values are acceptable in terms of the criteria given by Colwell. The highest discrimination value was only 0.519, however.

In the interpretation and evaluation of a reliability coefficient, it should be remembered that factors such as length, objectivity, heterogeneity of the group, clarity and conciseness of directions and test items, conditions of administration, independence of items, order of items, and scope contribute in varying degrees to the reliability of a test (Lehman, 1968, 14). However, in criteria discussed by Nunnally (1978, 245), the SBE correlation coefficient ($\alpha = 0.7532$) would seem to be acceptable for measuring an area where a wide range of abilities exist.

Just as SBE reliability was found to be acceptable, so the validity of the SBE was found to be suitable for assessment of student's ability to keep a steady beat. Face and construct validity were probed as part of the pilot study, and appropriate revisions were made before the second administration of the exercise. Of particular interest are the point biserial correlations between teacher rankings and SBE scores from the revised version of the exercise found in Table 2. The majority of the correlations are moderately high, i.e., the correlation is equal to or greater than 0.50. However, one of the correlations (0.274 for class 7) showed a very low correlation between teacher rankings and SBE scores. Perhaps the teacher rankings for class 7 were made more difficult by the fact that several students new to the district were enrolled in that class.

In conclusion, the twelve-item version of the SBE was found to have an acceptable reliability coefficient, verifying the internal consistency of the test. Construct validity was supported by a review of the literature, which confirmed that the ability to keep a steady beat is a unique aspect or dimension of rhythmic ability; and criterion-related validity was shown by the correlations between SBE scores and teacher ratings of ability to keep a steady beat. It seems plausible, then, that the SBE is a valid and reliable tool that could assist music educators and researchers in assessing students' ability to maintain a steady tempo of regular pulses given at different tempos.

References

Colwell, R. 1968–70. *Music achievement test manuals.* Chicago: Follett Educational Corporation.

Duke, R., J. Geringer, and C. Madsen. 1991. Performance of perceived beat in relation to age and music training. *Journal of Research in Music Education, 39*(1):35–45.

Flohr, J. 2006. *Rhythm performance test-revised.* Champaign, IL: Electronic Courseware Systems.

Fraisse, P. 1982. Rhythm and tempo. In D. Deutsch, ed., *The psychology of music,* 149–177. Orlando, FL: Academic Press, Inc.

Geringer, J., Duke, R., and Madsen, C. 1992. Musicians' perception of beat note: Regions of beat change in modulating tempos. *Bulletin of the Council of Research in Music Education, 114,* 21–33.

Geringer, J., Madsen, C., and Duke, R. 1993–94. Perception of beat change in modulating tempos. *Bulletin of the Council of Research in Music Education, 119,* 49–57.

Gordon, A., and Martin, P. 1993–94. A study of the rhythmic skills of musically unsophisticated secondary school students when playing the electronic keyboard with a drum machine. *Bulletin of the Council of Research in Music Education, 119,* 59–64.

Parncutt, R. 1994. A perceptual model of pulse salience and metrical accent in musical rhythms. *Music Perception: An Interdisciplinary Journal, 11,* 409–464.

Nierman, G., and Pearson, B. *Student Musical Instrument Compatibility Test (SMICT).* In progress.

Thackray, R. 1969. *An investigation into rhythmic abilities.* London: Novello and Company Limited.

PART 4

Facilitating Music Assessment Practice

Section B

Facilitating Practice in Music Teacher Education

Assessing the Effectiveness of a Music Teacher Professional Development Program

Al D. Holcomb
University of Central Florida

Colleen Conway
University of Michigan

Mary Palmer
University of Central Florida

Abstract

The purpose of this paper is to discuss the perceived effectiveness of evaluation techniques created for a four-year professional development program for music teachers. Varied and ongoing formative assessments, including observation, external evaluation, interviews, surveys, and examination of teacher created artifacts were found to be helpful in improving professional development activities. Summative program assessments, such as external evaluation and teacher-created electronic portfolios, provided meaningful data for evaluating project effectiveness, although portfolios lacked valid and reliable scoring procedures. Further investigations are needed to develop more effective strategies for assessing changes in teacher practice and student achievement.

Those involved in professional development for music teachers recognize the challenges in meeting professional development needs and assessing program effectiveness. There is very little published research on the professional development of the music teacher in general (Bauer [2007]; Conway [2007]) and no research on music teacher professional development program evaluation specifically. The small body of research that there is suggests that music teachers need music specific professional development and time and space to interact with one another to share best practices and strategies (Conway, in press b). The purpose of this paper is to describe the program goals, project components, assessments, and program evaluation information gathered throughout a four-year professional development project for music teachers.

Between 2001 and 2005, a federally-funded professional development program for music teachers was implemented in a large school district in Florida. With an over-arching goal of improving music teaching and learning, project leaders designed a program to help participants improve their personal musicianship and their ability to plan, teach, assess, and reflect on music teaching. Throughout the project, program leaders addressed the following assessment questions:

1. How should program effectiveness be assessed?
2. How should teacher growth assessed?
3. How can assessment data be used to improve development activities?

Project Overview

Initial Development

The project was initiated when the Orange County Public Schools[1] (OCPS) Fine Arts Coordinator[2] approached two University of Central Florida music education faculty members to assist in designing a professional development program for music teachers employed by Title I schools in Orange County. Working with the Fine Arts Coordinator, the university faculty members crafted a proposal for a federal grant, the Professional Development for Music Educators Project (CFDA No. 84.351C). The following five objectives were specified in the application (Orange County Public Schools):

1. To develop high quality in-service professional development modules for music teachers.
2. To provide teachers with up to date research based information to better prepare them to teach music.
3. To establish sustained and on-going collaboration between teachers, cohort groups, mentors, local universities, and arts organizations.
4. To implement use of technology into the daily instructional routine.
5. To create materials and models to be easily replicated.

In accordance with the grant rationale, the proposal supported the strengthening of music education toward Florida Sunshine State Music Standards (Florida Department of Education, 1996). The development experience was designed to reflect a variety of best practices in professional development, including the National Staff Development Council Standards (National Staff Development Council, 2001) for Staff Development and the National Board for Professional Teaching Standards Certification Process (National Board for Professional Teaching Standards, 2001). Once the grant was received, the Fine Arts Coordinator and two university music education faculty members served as project leaders who met regularly to plan project experiences during the four-year period.

---

1 Orange County Public Schools (OCPS) encompasses the Orlando, Florida area.
2 The Program Coordinator is Carolyn Minear.

Project Components

Primary project components included monthly seminars with related assignments, ongoing support through mentoring and cohort group interactions, collaborative curriculum and assessment development, artist-in-residence projects, technology resources, and funding for conference attendance and summer study. At the conclusion of the project, teachers constructed electronic portfolios to demonstrate achievement toward prescribed music teaching competencies addressed during content seminars.

Participant Demographics

The cohort of twenty-five teachers participating in this project during 2004–2005 was drawn from among an original pool of thirty-nine teachers from culturally diverse, lower socioeconomic schools. Twenty percent of the participants were Hispanic, 48% black, and 32% white. Forty-seven percent of the cohort had been teaching in their schools for one year or less, while 48% had served for four or more years. Eighty-three percent were returning to the same school in which they had taught the previous school year. The teachers, predominantly elementary music specialists (92%) participated in the program over a four-year period.

Seminars

Throughout the four-year period, monthly seminars provided regular opportunities for training and collaborations among participants. During the first three years, the primary focus areas of the project consisted of modules targeting building community and trust among participants, enhancing teacher musicianship, and improving skills related to planning, teaching, assessing, and reflecting on music learning. Nationally recognized music educators and curriculum specialists presented seminars in targeted areas, while school district and university personnel developed seminars designed to engage teachers in regular reflection on teaching and collaboration with others to improve their craft and develop and implement action research skills in their daily work. The original framework for the seminars focused on critical areas of need for teacher development as identified by the program leaders. These areas, if improved, would have a significant impact on teaching and upon student learning outcomes. In addition, participants received instructional resources for each seminar topic, completed relevant individual and group assignments, completed seminar evaluations, and discussed instructional process and techniques used by each presenter.

Technology Resources and Training

Teachers focused for two-years on best practices related to planning, teaching, and reflecting on teaching. During the third and fourth years, the focus shifted to incorporating technology into the daily instructional routines of participating teachers. In the spring of 2004, each participant received a music technology workstation, including a computer, printer, keyboard, video camera, and a variety of music software applications. National and local experts provided training and ongoing support to assist teachers in developing skills for notating compositions and arrangements, making accompaniment tracks, recording video and audio tracks, and for providing music instruction. OCPS technology staff provided district-wide training and site support for computer and web-based projects. Upon request, project participants with technological expertise provided individual support to their colleagues. The training sessions also provided teachers with the skills for capturing and editing video excerpts of teaching and learning and for creating class compositions, accompaniments, and arrangements for student performance. By the end of the fourth year, approximately twenty-one of the participating teachers and mentors had created a web page to communicate information about their music program and educate readers about the role of quality arts education.

Mentoring

Music teachers who taught similar grade levels in non-Title I schools were selected to mentor three to five teachers assigned to a cohort group. Criteria for mentor selection included teaching assignment, experience, ethnic representation, recognition, such as National Board Certification and/or teacher of the year, and effectiveness in the classroom observed by project leaders. Mentors were asked to provide support to mentees through regular communication (phone calls, email, meetings) and to assist the mentees in developing and demonstrating specific practices related to planning, teaching, assessing, and reflecting on music teaching.

Between 2001 and 2003, selected mentors were asked to engage in discussions about improving teaching with assigned mentees as well as observe their teaching through on-site observations and teaching captured on video. We provided mentor development workshops at the beginning of 2004 and 2005 academic years. In the fall of 2004, ten elementary/general music teachers and one secondary/choral teacher attended the training session. In 2005, eight elementary/general and three secondary teachers (two instrumental and one choral) attended the mentor development session.

Formative Assessments

Various formative assessment strategies were developed and used to gather of information to assist in assessing project objectives and activities. These included seminar evaluations, written assignments, teaching observations, electronic portfolios, external evaluation reports, and mentor interviews.

Seminar Evaluations

To assess the effectiveness of the individual seminars, program leaders developed seminar evaluation surveys (Appendix A) for participants to complete following the seminars. They asked the participants to rate their pre- and post-seminar knowledge and skill relative to the seminar content on a Likert-type scale ranging from 1 "Not knowledgeable at all" to 5 "Expert." In addition, they asked participants to note highlights, things they would change, usefulness of the seminar content, and whether they would like to study more about the subject, and, if so, what they would like to know. Program coordinators also asked teachers to identify the highlights of each seminar.

Written Assignments

Project leaders and mentors evaluated teacher understanding of seminar content through written assignments, including planning, assessment, and reflection documents. Written artifacts were reviewed by mentors and project leaders to assess teacher ability to incorporate seminar content.

Teaching Observations

Project leaders and mentors evaluated teacher understanding of seminar content via review of videotapes of participants' teaching and site visitations. An observation form was used to capture specific evidence of seminar content and specified best practices in music teacher (Appendix B).

E-portfolios

Electronic portfolios were developed to provide evidence of teacher understanding and growth toward their ability to plan, teach, and assess toward specific objectives. In addition, the portfolio was used to provide evidence of teacher musicianship, technology integration, and the teacher's ability to reflect (see Appendix C).

External Evaluation Reports

In 2002 and 2005, two subject experts were hired to conduct outside evaluations toward attainment of project objectives and overall effectiveness. Prior to conducting the first site visit, the grant evaluators submitted a brief questionnaire to be completed by the participants *via* email or hard copy (Appendix D). The questionnaire (Currie and Perry, 2002, 6) consisted of five questions addressing the following:

1. Initial fears or skepticism of the project.
2. Positive and/or negative "surprises" encountered during participation.
3. Personal growth as a teacher and/or musician as a result of the project.
4. Areas of growth in their students throughout the project.
5. What is needed to ensure that student growth continues.

During the initial site visit, the grant evaluators conducted an additional survey (Appendix E) to assess participants' perceptions (Currie and Perry, 2002, 6). The questionnaire included questions based on the following categories:

External Evaluation Survey Question Categories

1. Building administrator and faculty support and encouragement.
2. Conversation with colleagues concerning collaboration, reflective practice, teaching and learning.
3. Actual collaboration with the five major component groups involved: participating teachers, cohort groups, mentors, university faculty/students, arts organizations.
4. Perceived value of collaboration with the aforementioned groups.
5. Current plans to continue collaboration efforts.
6. Number of times teacher met *individually* with mentor or university personnel.
7. Perception of the amount of time spent on the five identified activities: workshops, mentor teacher feedback/observations, reflection, technology, and university faculty and student technical assistance.
8. Percent of time teachers incorporate new learning from this project into their teaching.
9. Future professional development needs.

In addition to the written feedback, participants met informally with the grant evaluators to discuss their thoughts about the project and its effect on their work. Common themes emerged throughout and will be discussed in the findings section.

Mentor Interviews

The project included a separate evaluation of the mentor development workshops. The first mentor development session was held in October, 2004. At that meeting, the mentors ($N = 11$) were asked to answer the following questions on index cards:

1. What do you believe to be the characteristics of a good mentor?
2. What do you think you have to offer as a mentor?
3. What will help you to help your mentee(s)?

As displayed in Table 1, participant responses were collected and kept for use in planning the second year workshop and for the study.

Table 1. Mentor Development Session Initial Responses.

What do you believe to be the characteristics of a good mentor?

Response	No. of similar responses	Participant No.
Good/Reflective Listener	6	5, 8, 9, 10, 11, 12
Knowledgeable	5	6, 7, 8, 9, 12
Experience	4	1, 2, 4, 5
Open to other's ideas	4	1, 2, 3, 4
Humble	3	1, 3, 11
Flexible/Available	3	1, 2, 4
Quality Teaching Skills	3	4, 7, 12
Communication Skills	3	4, 6, 10
Approachability	2	3, 10
Compassionate/Sensitive	2	4, 6
Strong Musicianship	2	6, 9
Patience	1	5
Love for children	1	6
Understanding value of music in children's lives	1	6
Supportive/Thoughtful	1	7
Good evaluator of mentee's needs	1	8
Eagerness	1	2

What do you think you have to offer as a mentor?

Response	No. of similar responses	Participant No.
Experience	10	1, 2, 3, 5, 7, 8, 9, 10, 11, 12
New Ideas/Resources	4	1, 5, 7, 8
Share/Exchange Ideas	4	2, 4, 9, 12
Strong Knowledge Base	3	6, 7, 8
Eagerness	3	2, 4, 10
Communication Skills	3	4, 6, 9
Compassion	3	6, 8, 12
Strong Musicianship	3	6, 7, 12
Availability	2	2, 3
Easy-going Nature	2	3, 6
Understanding the value of music in children's lives	2	6, 12
Knowledge/Love for children	2	6, 8
Management	1	1
Quality Teaching Skills	1	4
Commitment to Professional Growth	1	7
Interest in Developing Sequential Teaching	1	3

What will help you to help your mentee(s)?

Responses	No. of Similar Responses	Participant No.
Time Management	4	1, 4, 7, 12
Skills for Observing	Total—3	
In general	1	11
Communicating what is observed	1	9
For more experienced teachers	1	9
Mentoring Experienced Teachers	Total—2	
Approach	1	10
How to Observe	1	9
Non-Threatening Approach	2	6, 8
Develop Resources	1	1
Learn New Techniques	1	2
Keep-up relationship	1	6
Effective use of e-mail, telephones, etc.	1	7
Help in gauging what mentee's needs are	1	8
Getting Started	1	11
Strategies for Intervention	1	3

What are your mentor challenges?

Response	No. of Similar Responses	Participant No.
Time Management	3	1, 2, 3
Mentoring Experienced Teachers (not open to new ideas)	2	1, 6
Using Non-Threatening Approach	2	3, 8
Observing	1	5
Getting Started	1	6
Maintaining Informal Mentoring relationships alongside ones that are formal	1	8
Developing the next generation of teachers	1	8
How to be proactive	1	3
Mentoring someone from a Title 1 school	1	4
Standards	1	7

Topics covered in the second year workshop included (a) an overview of research on mentoring in music, (b) strategies for communication with mentees, (c) techniques for observation, and (d) common problems faced by mentees. We kept and saved notes regarding participants' interactions as well.

In August 2005, the mentors ($N = 11$) returned for a second mentor development session that included (a) group discussion of experiences; (b) a mentoring styles activity in which teachers generated mentor scenarios and then used mentor styles and characteristics description from Smith (2003) to discuss approaches to the scenarios; (c) a focus on reflecting in and reflecting on action in teaching; and (d) a focus on action research and process documentation. Information from this workshop also included notes that were made from the small group work that captured the interaction of participants. The assessment tool for the mentor component included individual interviews with eight of the experienced music mentors in May 2006 (see Appendix F for the interview protocol).

Data reveal that the most important aspects of effective mentoring include:

1. Clear goals and a continuous focus toward those goals.
2. Establishing community and cohort groups.
3. Mentor training and support.
4. Ongoing opportunities for content application and technology training.
5. Administrative support.
6. Flexible experiences that meet the diverse needs of music teachers.

The interviews with mentors revealed that music mentors perceive themselves to be more effective when they receive instruction in mentoring and have opportunities to discuss mentoring challenges and strategies with other mentors. Several participants suggested that mentoring might be a valuable professional development activity for the mentors. The following sample data support this key finding:

1. As a result of my mentoring experience, I play recorder every week with other teachers. Mentoring taught me that I like to teach teachers. Even another mentor called me for help (final interview, mentor 4).
2. I really learned a lot about myself in this program. I became a better teacher by observing another mentor – I took 10 pages of notes! (final interview, mentor 8).
3. I know that I am a better teacher (final interview, mentor 3).

Conclusions

Various informal assessments, including surveys, interviews, and observations by leaders provided data that assisted in the evaluation of professional development goals and related indicators of project effectiveness, such as changes in teacher attitudes and practices. We noted that observations became more authentic and meaningful when teachers established a sense of community. Interviewing mentors provided insights for assisting with improvements in mentor development. Interviews revealed that preparation, support, and clear goals were needed for mentors to feel effective in their role as mentors. Teacher-created artifacts, including planning and assessment documents, written reflections, websites and e-portfolios provided additional evidence to assess teacher ability to implement content of instructional modules. Formative and summative evaluation by external evaluators functioned to communicate progress toward stated goals as well as recommendations to for improvement.

Although a completed portfolio is a valuable product for evaluating teaching effectiveness, we believe that the collaborative process of planning, developing, and reviewing portfolios provides an invaluable learning opportunity for music teachers. Engaging participants in portfolio development was one of the most challenging aspects of the program. While the majority of the teachers had started or completed their portfolios by the end of the fourth year, those not completing the portfolio reported a lack of time as their main reason for not starting portfolio development. It is also possible that these participants were not comfortable sharing lesson plans or video excerpts with their colleagues or they have lacked technology skills.

We acknowledge that the assessment strategies used in this project provided useful information for program development and assessment. However, it is evident that additional strategies are needed to better examine the impact on changes in teacher practice and student learning. Further investigations are needed to develop valid assessment techniques and tools for measuring changes in teacher practice.

References

Bauer, W. (2007). Research on the professional development of experienced teachers. *Journal of Music Teacher Education*, 17(1):12–21.

Conway, C. M. (2007). Setting an agenda for professional development policy, practice, and research in music education. *Journal of Music Teacher Education*, 17(1):56–61.

Conway, C.M. (in press). Experienced music teacher perceptions of professional development throughout their careers. *Bulletin of the Council for Research in Music Education, 174.*

Currie, J., and P. Perry. 2002. *Music: Personal, cultural, universal—The professional development of music educators program—Orange County Public Schools, Orlando, Florida external evaluation report.* Unpublished manuscript.

Florida State Department of Education (1996). *Florida sunshine state standards for music.* Tallahassee, FL: Author.

National Board for Professional Teaching Standards 2001. *Music standards.* Washington, D. C.: Author.

National Staff Development Council. 2001. *National staff development council standards.* Washington, D. C.: Author.

Orange County Public Schools. 2001. *Application for Federal education assistance.* Unpublished document.

Smith, M. V. 2003. Making mentoring work. In C. M. Conway, ed., *Great beginnings for music teachers: Mentoring and supporting new teachers.* Reston, VA: MENC—The National Association for Music Education.

Seminar Evaluation Form

Name _____

1. Rate your **pre-seminar knowledge and skill** of the content from this seminar.

    5   Expert
    4   Very knowledgeable
    3   Somewhat knowledgeable
    2   Barely knowledgeable
    1   Not knowledgeable at all

2. Rate your **post-session knowledge and skill** of the content from this seminar.

    5   Expert
    4   Very knowledgeable
    3   Somewhat knowledgeable
    2   Barely knowledgeable
    1   Not knowledgeable at all

3. List the **highlights** of this seminar.

4. What things would you **change** about this seminar?

5. In your teaching, can you **implement** information, ideas, materials, and/or strategies from this session? If yes, what and how?

6. Would you like to study **more** on this topic?

    Yes
    No

What further things would you like to know about this topic?

Classroom Observation Form – Year 1

Teacher _____ Grade Level_____

Date _____ Type of Class: Ensemble   General Music   Other

1. Which **seminar module topics** are reflected in the lesson(s) observed? Include all that you observe.

    __ music of Ghana (Karen Howard)
    __ integration of music and the total curriculum (Sue Snyder)
    __ music of South Africa (Kathy Robinson)
    __ music of Latin American cultures (Carlos Rodriguez)
    __ brain development (Sarah Sprinkle)

    Comments on lesson content:

2. Did the lesson(s) observed include:

    __ use of technology? If so, explain.
    __ development of music literacy? If so, explain.
    __ specific efforts to assess individual student learning? If so, explain.
    __ evidence of the teacher's ability to establish and sustain a positive learning environment? If so, explain.
    __ other content from seminar module topics? If so, explain.

3. Was **alignment** of lesson planning (including Standards), teaching (including sequential steps in the process), and assessing learning evident?

    Comments:

4. Comment on the teachers' ability to analyze his/her teaching success (i.e. the **reflective practitioner**).

5. List the **teacher's strengths.**

6. List **challenges** facing this teacher.

7. List suggestions for **future development** for this teacher.

8. Other observations/comments:

Electronic Portfolio Development

What is a Music Teaching ePortfolio?

Your music-teaching ePortfolio is a collection of artifacts (e.g., video clips, planning documents, lesson reflections, teaching materials, student work) that demonstrate two things:

1. Best practices in music teaching (a high level of **musicianship** and your ability to effectively **plan, teach, assess individual student learning**, and **reflect** on your teaching.
2. Evidence of student learning.

Why Develop a Music Teaching ePortfolio?

1. A music-teaching ePortfolio demonstrates your accountability for providing quality music learning experiences. In the current climate, it is becoming increasingly important for music teachers to demonstrate accountability for pursuing the highest levels of teaching and learning.
2. The process of collaboratively developing and reviewing music teaching portfolios contributes to enhanced music teaching and learning. As is the case with most music learning, the process is as valuable as the product.
3. The development of an ePortfolio should be incredibly helpful to those of you who may want to apply for National Board Certification. We want you to lead the way for the rest of the district.
4. We recognize that effective models of great music teaching would be helpful to all music teachers. An OCPS Music Teaching Resource Website that includes great lesson plans, assessment tools, and video clips taken from portfolios would be incredibly valuable to you and your colleagues.

How do I Create a Music Teaching ePortfolio?

The music-teaching ePortfolio is developed **over time**, in collaboration with other music teachers. Portfolio development requires that you:

1. **Understand** the look of great music teaching (see *The Look of Best Practice in Music Teaching*).
2. **Pursue it and demonstrate it** in your classes.
3. **Collect evidence** best practices and of student learning (growth).
4. Work with other teachers to **select artifacts** that effectively portray best practices and student learning.
5. **Construct** the portfolio.

What Do I Need in Order to Create a Music Teaching Portfolio?

You need the following in order to create a portfolio:

1. Digital video camera with accessories (tapes, tripod, fire wire cable).
2. Macintosh computer.

E-Portfolio Contents

We are asking that post some evidence for each the following categories:

1. **Evidence of Teacher Musicianship** (e.g., demonstration of accurate/expressive conducting/gesture, modeling, accompanying; accurate descriptions and analyses of music, compositions/ arrangements).
2. **Evidence of Effective Planning** (evidence of appropriate curriculum and assessment development, including planning documents, a series of sequential lesson plans that show linkage to OCPS benchmarks and essential skills).
3. **Evidence of Effective Teaching** (teaching demonstrations, technology applications, assessment applications, that reflect *Best Practices In Music Teaching*).
4. **Evidence of Reflective Practice** (written documents that describe your thoughts as you taught a lesson, what you learned about yourself and your students as a result of teaching a lesson or a series of lessons and watching the videos, and areas you will target for future growth).
5. **Evidence of Individual Student Achievement** (brief video clips of students that demonstrate individual growth/improvement toward identified objectives over time).

Portfolio Development

1. Design a series of lesson plans (with the help of your colleagues) that will help students develop appropriate musical knowledge and skills (essential skills?) for a single class that you can video tape over a series of classes.
2. Capture some teaching and learning on video.
3. Write down your thoughts (reflections) after teaching classes.
4. Work with your colleagues to select some video clips, lesson plans, and reflections.
5. Post the artifacts in your portfolio.

Tips for How to Create a Music Teaching Portfolio

1. **Capturing effective teaching on video.** Record as many classes as possible on video so you have lots to material to choose from when you begin to edit and select brief video clips (2–3 minute clips) you want to

include in your portfolio. This also helps you and the students get used to having a video camera in the room.

2. **Collecting artifacts that demonstrate effective music teaching.** Collect documents that help to demonstrate your ability to effectively plan, teach, assess, and reflect on music teaching. When appropriate to your objectives, try to include teaching knowledge and skills that were included in any of our seminars. *Make sure that any documents that you include in your portfolio are word-processed (not handwritten). Develop and include a series of (at least three) sequential lesson plans that demonstrate an effective teaching/learning process over time (across lessons) toward appropriate objectives (identified OCPS benchmarks and/or essential outcomes) and any relevant assessment tools.*

3. **Capturing your musicianship.** Your musicianship can demonstrated in several ways in the classroom, including:
   a. How you select music that is worthy, varied and appropriate for the students (written commentary).
   b. How you describe, analyze and evaluate music (e.g., video, lesson plan, written commentary).
   c. How you perform, model, use gestures/conducting, and accompany to enhance accuracy and expression in student performance.
   d. How you create music (improvise, compose, arrange).

4. *Note: It is preferred that you capture your musicianship through your teaching. However, you may also include brief video clips and other documents that help to document your musicianship outside of the classroom.*

5. **Technology applications.** It is desirable for you to show how you have used technology to enhance teaching and learning (worksheets, arrangements, accompaniment tracks, etc.). Compositions, audio files, arrangements you have created may also be used to provided evidence of your musicianship.

6. **Capturing student growth over time on video.** Please make sure that it is not a problem to capture any students on video in your classroom. *Note: It is your responsibility to check with your principal about any restrictions on taping students. Remember, this video is not intended for public access and will only be shared with other music teachers if you choose to post contents on your public website.* Select a few (two to three) students in a class to track their growth over time toward one of your identified objectives. Try to pick diverse students to help show that you can be effective with different types of students. *It would be ideal if these students were positioned next to each other so you capture their progress without having to move the camera.* **Provide a written commentary that helps guide the viewer to what is intended to be seen.** For example: "Notice how the tall boy in the green shirt (student 1) is not singing in tune in this excerpt." Avoid referring to students by name in the written commentary. With brief video clips (thirty seconds each might be enough) and written commentary, help the viewer understand where the students started,

how far they have come, and where you want them to go in terms of their progress toward your identified objectives and goals.

7. **Student work**. Please remove all identifying information (name, class, etc.) from any student work you are including in your portfolio.

8. **Reflecting on your teaching**. After watching the video clips, create written lesson reflections that describe
   a. **How** and **why** you modified the lesson (e.g., why you changed what you thought you were going to do as a result of student responses; why you added a step or took out a step—*reflecting in action*)
   b. What you learned about your students and yourself as a result of teaching a lesson and/or watching the video (e.g., assumptions you made about the students, insights into how the students learn; how you could have taught the lesson better, what you did really well; what you wish you had done better—*reflecting on action*).
   c. What areas you may want to target for future growth to become a better music teacher.

Examples of artifacts we might expect to see in your portfolio:

1. A video excerpt of your teaching that demonstrates your ability to do any or all of the following:
   a. Provide an appropriate vocal or instrumental model.
   b. Accompany, conduct, use gesture, or describe music in a way that enhances accurate and artistic student performance.
   c. Choose appropriate literature (diverse, worthy of study, appropriate to objectives).
2. A series of sequential lesson plans (three or more) that show direct linkage to OCPS benchmarks/essential outcome and logical process (across lessons) toward the objective(s).
   a. Written commentary, lesson plan, or video that shows how you address individual differences (personalities, disabilities, learning styles, different achievement levels) in a class.
   b. Assessment tools or strategies that demonstrate how you effectively collect information on individual student progress, provide meaningful feedback to students, and communicate results.
3. Worksheets or arrangements that you created using any of the music software applications.
4. Video excerpt that demonstrates a positive learning environment (organization, efficiency, enthusiasm for music and music learning, effective classroom management, effective motivational strategies).
5. Video excerpts demonstrate individual student growth over time toward the identified objective(s) in the series of lessons (*If you can't get to everything this spring, this would be the one to work on in the fall*).
6. Written commentaries that help to explain the context or to clarify what is being demonstrated in a video excerpt.

7. Video excerpt that demonstrates any of the best practices in music, including students engaged in analytical thinking, the development of a musical vocabulary.
8. Written lesson reflections that describe what you learned as a result of teaching each lesson.

Grant team Questionnaire

Please respond briefly to the questions below. Complete sentences or paragraphs are not necessary.

1. Describe the biggest fears or areas of skepticism you had at the beginning of this project.

2. Describe the surprises you have had throughout this project, both positive and negative.

3. Describe your professional growth as a teacher and/or musician as a result of this project.

4. Describe the areas of growth you have observed in your students throughout this project. What do you need so that you can be sure this student growth continues?

Orange County Public Schools
Grant Evaluation Process

Teacher Perceptions Survey

1. At the start of the 2001–02 school year, how long had you taught at your school?

1	2	3	4
Zero	One year	Two to Three years	Four or more years

2. Are you teaching in the same school *this year* in which you taught *last year*?

   Yes   No

3. My building administrator has been/was aware of my participation in this project.

   Yes   No

4. Has he/she supported me actively, e.g., encouraging me to collaborate with my colleagues, providing released time for conversations/observations, etc.?

   Yes   No

5. Other faculty members in my school have been aware of my participation in the project.

1	2	3
No One	A few close teachers	Entire Faculty

6. Over the course of the project, I have had ongoing conversations with teachers in my school about my work on the project, e.g. lessons tried, new assessments, etc.

1	2	3
Never	Occasionally	Often

7. Over the course of the project, I have had conversations with teachers in my school about my reflections on my own teaching.

1	2	3
Never	Occasionally	Often

8. Because our subject areas are so different, I do not feel that I can have meaningful conversations with my building-based colleagues about teaching and learning.

  1   2
  True   False

9. Through this project I have found _____ music teachers with whom I feel comfortable taking risks.

  1   2   3   4
  None   One   Two or three   Four or more

10. Indicate *the extent of your collaboration* with each of the following during this project:

Participating Teachers

  1   2   3
  None   Inconsistent   Consistent
             but present   and Ongoing

Cohort Groups

  1   2   3
  None   Inconsistent   Consistent
             but present   and Ongoing

Mentor Teachers

  1   2   3
  None   Inconsistent   Consistent
             but present   and Ongoing

University

  1   2   3
  None   Inconsistent   Consistent
             but present   and Ongoing

Arts Organizations

  1   2   3
  None   Inconsistent   Consistent
             but present   and Ongoing

11. Rate *the value* of your collaboration with each of the following during the project:

Participating Teachers

  1   2   3
  No Value   Some Value   A lot of Value

Cohort Groups

1	2	3
No Value	Some Value	A lot of Value

Mentor Teachers

1	2	3
No Value	Some Value	A lot of Value

University

1	2	3
No Value	Some Value	A lot of Value

Arts Organizations

1	2	3
No Value	Some Value	A lot of Value

12. I have *current* plans to continue collaboration with the following:

Participating Teachers
Yes   No

Cohort Groups
Yes   No

Mentor Teachers
Yes   No

University
Yes   No

Arts Organizations
Yes   No

13. Though I do not have current plans established, I *definitely intend* to continue my collaboration with the following:

Participating Teachers
      Yes   No

Cohort Groups
      Yes   No

Mentor Teachers
      Yes   No

University
      Yes   No

Arts Organizations
      Yes   No

14. How many times did you meet *individually* with a mentor teacher to discuss your teaching, lesson design or other area related to the project?

1	2	3
Never	One	Two or more

15. Rate your perception of the amount time spent on each of the following areas:

Workshops

1	2	3
Not Enough	Just Right	Too Much

Mentor Teacher Feedback/Observations (for those who met individually with mentor or university professor or graduate student)

1	2	3
Not Enough	Just Right	Too Much

Reflection

1	2	3
Not Enough	Just Right	Too Much

Technology

1	2	3
Not Enough	Just Right	Too Much

University faculty and student technical assistance

1	2	3
Not Enough	Just Right	Too Much

16. If the grant were extended for another year, indicate which of the following collaborations that you think should continue.

Participating Teachers

       Yes   No

Cohort Groups

       Yes   No

Mentor Teachers

       Yes   No

University

       Yes   No

Arts Organizations

       Yes   No

17. Indicate the percent of time you incorporate into your daily teaching practices what you have learned in each of the following areas *as a direct result of your participation in the project:*

Planning

       Not at all   20%   60%   80%   100%

Teaching

       Not at all   20%   60%   80%   100%

Assessing

       Not at all   20%   60%   80%   100%

Reflecting

       Not at all   20%   60%   80%   100%

Personal Musicianship

       Not at all   20%   60%   80%   100%

18. In the future, I would like to have more professional development in the area of:

Planning

1	2	3
No More	Some more	A lot more

Teaching

1	2	3
No More	Some more	A lot more

Assessing

1	2	3
No More	Some more	A lot more

Reflecting

1	2	3
No More	Some more	A lot more

Personal Musicianship

1	2	3
No More	Some more	A lot more

Mentor Interview Protocol

Question 1: Tell me about your mentoring experiences over the past two years.

Question 2: Tell me about your grant participation experiences over the past two years.

Question 3: In what ways do you feel the mentor training most contributed to your success as a mentor?

Or

What were the most meaningful mentor development activities during the last two years?

Question 4: What suggestions do you have regarding your preparation for work as a music mentor and/or the preparation of future music teacher mentors?

The Effect of Performance Rubrics on College Level Applied Studio Faculty and Student Attitudes

Kelly A. Parkes
Virginia Polytechnic Institute and State University

Abstract

Grading satisfaction of music performance undergraduates ($n = 44$) and music performance faculty ($n = 11$) were examined to establish whether the use of a performance rubric effected overall grading satisfaction in either students or faculty in college-level applied studios. Three subscales were used to establish satisfaction in (a) jury process, (b) preparedness, and (c) continuous assessment with a researcher-developed survey.

Participants were solicited from three music institutions and were randomly assigned into a control group (no rubric) and an experimental group (rubric use). No statistically significant differences were found in either faculty or student attitudes toward grading between pre- and post-tests. Low participation rates from faculty were a weakness in this study and directions for future research should consider defining applied faculty beliefs about assessment and pursuing a more qualitative approach to understand performance faculty approaches to involvement in educational research.

The applied music studio is a long-standing Western music tradition. Most musicians have had private lessons for much of their musical lives. However, "there is a mystery that often surrounds the applied studio" (Brand, 1992). This mystery usually concerns the studio's instructional processes, which are often ignored by research (Brand, 1992). The applied studio is based on an oral tradition where the student gets advice from the teacher about how to perform repertoire, which in turn is based on how the teacher learned to perform the repertoire from a previous generation of teachers.

There is concern that applied teachers seem reluctant to embrace music education research toward better teaching practice and specifically, better grading practices. Madsen (1963) cautioned the following:

> Many teachers within the profession seem to be unconcerned with anything that cannot be passed on in the privacy of the studio, and most articles, methods, and demonstration-lectures amount to no more than personal 'testimonials' concerning how music should be taught. (63)

Today, this is often still the *modus operandi* for many applied studio teachers at the college level. For performers, artists, and virtuosi, this is the way things have always been and there is no perceived need for change. Teachers will teach the way they were taught so therefore, as Schleuter (1997) succinctly points out, "good, bad, and inefficient methods and techniques of teaching music persist through unquestioned adherence to tradition" (20).

"Good, bad, and inefficient techniques" can also be seen in the grading processes that college applied studio teachers use to grade their students. Grading processes are a common concern at the college level and grading is a topic much discussed by both faculty and students alike. Boyle and Radocy (1987) point out that "the measurement of musical performance is inherently subjective" (171) and over the last twenty years, steps toward providing performance measures have been steadily advancing. The use of the Watkins-Farnum Performance Scale (1954, 1962), Likert scales, semantic differentials, magnitude estimations, criteria specific rating scales, and rank ordering systems have been present in the area of instrumental performance. These techniques have not been used in a consistent way at the college level.

The literature shows empirical research into teaching processes and there are many advances toward improving instruction techniques. The works of Schmidt (1992), Abeles (1973), and most recently Duke (2005) have been influential. This research defines better instructional practices, but it does not define better grading processes and not all college applied teachers read related research about grading (Parkes, 2006).

The literature also shows research about instrumental performance grading at the high school level and this literature provides a solid foundation for establishing such processes at the college level. One salient area is the use of criteria-specific rating scales as part of the instrumental grading process. The work of Saunders and Holahan (1997) has pioneered the development of rating scales for use in the high school setting. It indicates that the use of specific criteria helps judges come to more consistent grading outcomes. Labuta and Smith (1997) concur in their model of behavioral objectives. They argue that there needs to be an assessment standard and they give labels to the criteria and standards of performance (98). They also suggest there should be a specified criterion standard as a musical objective (99). Much of the research regarding rating scales for the high school setting is helpful in designing what is also appropriate for the college level.

Many music instruction theories include "assessment" or "grading" as a means to quantify what has been learned and how. They are, however, different from each other. Duke (2005) describes it clearly as "Assessment measures a learner's performance," whereas grading, or evaluation, "describes the learner's performance in relation to other learners or according to a continuum of graduated labels" (53).

Colwell (2002) states that "assessment is one of the more important issues in education" (1128), yet there is no evidence of major change to the way college applied faculty have been assessing or grading since the beginning of conservatories in the United States. He goes on to say that "Evidence from learning psychology reveals that assessment properly conducted makes a major difference in student learning, and when incorrectly used, a negative effect" (1130). What this means in the applied studio setting is that assessment could be used to guide student learning throughout a semester and the final grading process could also be based on these guidelines. This would mean that the student knows more about what he or she will ultimately be graded for and is not surprised when they receive the grade given at the end of the semester. This is not how most applied studio teachers currently assess or grade their students (Parkes, 2006).

The work of Bergee (1993, 1997, 2003) does examine the use of specific criteria rating scales, or rubrics, in the college applied studio setting. His work supports the concept that the criteria do help the judges grade more consistently and shows that they grade with more reliability. This work is the only research undertaken in the college setting and the present study is based to some degree on Bergee's research. The assumption that criteria-specific rating scales have a superior diagnostic ability is used in the design of the present study.

There is evidence (Schmidt, 1992) to support this view, the view that "relatively little systematic research has addressed the complex nature of one-to-one or tutorial music instruction. This is in marked contrast to the "relatively extensive research base that has accumulated in classroom teaching" (32). Clearly, more research is needed in this area, and most specifically at the higher education level in the applied studio grading processes.

Since there is a lack of literature about systematic grading processes in college applied studio settings, it seemed important to test the use of one. It was expected that the use of the rubrics would improve levels of satisfaction in both faculty and students. The following research questions guided this study:

1. Does the use of criteria specific performance rubrics improve the overall grading satisfaction of faculty and students in the applied studio setting?
2. Does the use of the criteria specific performance rubric improve student and/or faculty level of satisfaction with the jury process?
3. Does the use of criteria specific performance rubrics improve students and/ or faculty levels perceived level of preparedness?
4. Does the use of continuous assessment procedures affect the level of grading satisfaction in either faculty or students in the applied studio setting?

Experimentally testing the use of the performance rubric on the attitudes of student and faculty attitudes about grading was expected to provide answers for these questions.

Method

Participants and Instrumentation

Faculty participants were initially solicited from three universities. Faculty were teaching applied studio in either brass or woodwind areas, from a variety of positions. Tenured faculty, part-time instructors, adjunct, and teaching assistants were all represented. Ten faculty participants were male, and one was female. Table 1 illustrates the percentage of faculty who consented to be involved in both the use of the rubric in their studio and the survey of their perceptions, after initial solicitation. Student participants were then solicited as students of faculty who agreed to be involved. Students were given consent forms and forty-four chose to participate in the survey. Student and faculty survey questions are found in Appendix A. The faculty survey was the same as the student survey, only revised to read from the faculty perspective.

Table 1. Percentage of faculty participation

Site	Number Solicited	Number Agreed	Percentage of Agreement
1	18	7	38
2	16	1	<1
3	15	1	<1

Note. Two faculty teachers who also agreed to participate are not represented here, because they were solicited from two additional universities as additional participants in an effort to raise the number of faculty participants.

Procedure

Once consent was obtained, all participants took the survey to establish pre-test grading satisfaction with scores in the three subscale areas of jury process satisfaction, preparedness, and continuous assessment satisfaction in the author-developed survey. This survey, Grading Attitude Survey (GAS) yielded a GAS score for both faculty and students at the pre-test stage. Faculty in the experimental group were then briefed on how to use the rubrics, which included detailed directions from the researcher that they refer to the rubric during lessons as an indicator of assessment methods to be used in the final juries. Faculty participants in this group were given a log sheet with which they were to record the days they referred to or used the rubric in applied lessons. It was understood by the faculty in the experimental group that they would also use the rubric in the end-of-semester jury exams. Faculty participants in the control group were not given rubrics to use.

Data on faculty rubric use during the one-academic semester experimental period was obtained via phone calls, face-to-face conversations, and email. The researcher regularly supported their use of the rubric in the applied lesson by keeping in contact with faculty participants. Near the end of the semester, participants using the rubric were again briefed individually about how to use the rubric with their colleagues in the jury exams.

The GAS was re-administered at the end of the semester to yield post-test scores for both students and faculty. The only changes in the post-test GAS was an additional section for participants to check a box if they had used the rubric and an area for open responses to comment on the performance rubrics. The data was reviewed, ensuring all pre-test participants had responded as post-test participants in the surveys. Faculty participants in the experimental group were asked to turn in their used rubrics for secondary reliability calculations, and their documentation of how they had used the rubric during the semester[1].

The open-ended responses from both pre- and post-test faculty surveys were coded by hand by the researcher and her assistant, a doctoral student, for inter-coder reliability. Themes were revised and categorized into two areas: positive and negative comments about

---

1 Faculty participants kept logs of their rubric use throughout the semester.

grading. Pre-and post-test open-ended answers from the student surveys held no content written by students.

Results

The first analyses yielded the reliability values for both the faculty survey and the student survey. These can be seen in Table 2. Based on the difference in reported reliabilities, the two groups' data were analyzed separately in relation to the research questions.

Table 2. Internal consistency coefficients
for student and faculty pre-test surveys

Survey	n	Cronbach
Faculty	8	.558
Student	44	.795

Faculty data

The small number of faculty who participated in the pre-test survey ($n = 18$) is likely to have contributed to the survey's low internal consistency coefficient. Eleven participants elected to participate in the entire research project, including pre- and post-testing and random assignment to either the experimental or control group. Of these eleven, five were placed in the experimental group and six were in the control group. Further analysis was deemed unnecessary due to the low numbers of participants (see Table 1).

When following up the use of the rubric, the researcher collated the rubrics used by faculty in the end of semester juries. Only two faculty participants (18%) used the rubrics in the jury setting, despite regular and detailed instructions from the researcher in how to do so. The low incidence of rubric use in jury situations negatively impacted the inter-judge reliabilities. Only two out of five faculty members submitted their rubrics for analysis after the juries and these two participants had a small number of students each. Inter-judge reliabilities calculated from the submitted rubrics yielded similar reliabilities to those obtained in the pilot administration. One brass faculty participant had used the rubrics with two other panel members for five students, and the reliability coefficient for the brass CSPR was 0.93, slightly lower than the pilot reliability coefficient of 0.98. The woodwind faculty participant who had used the rubric with two other panel members returned rubrics had only three students. The reliability coefficient for the woodwind CSPR was 0.93, which was slightly higher than the pilot reliability coefficient of 0.92.

Three out of five faculty participants returned their logs. These indicated a consistent use of the rubric but at various intervals. One participant only used the rubric in the middle of the semester, rather than weekly. The other two faculty participants' logs revealed that they used the rubric on a weekly or bi-weekly basis. Reduced use of the rubric, as evidenced in the logs, is assumed to be part of the reason why no differences were reported in the student attitudes from pre- to post-testing. The four research questions specific to faculty remain unanswered largely due to low participation rates of the faculty, and to some degree, their low use of the rubrics, and logs.

Student and faculty data

Only the first research question could be answered about the students in this research, due to reliability of data. While Cronbach's = 0.795 for the student survey seemed stable, internal alphas were calculated on the three subscales: (a) Grading satisfaction, (b) Preparedness, and (c) Continuous grading satisfaction. The following internal consistencies were reported and shown in Table 3. The pre-determined subscale factors were not stable representations of the factors present in the survey, so the sub-scale items were not examined further. To examine if student attitudes changed with the use of the rubric, either between the control group and the experimental groups, or between pre- and post-tests of either group, a repeated-measures ANOVA was performed using SPSS 14. The results of this analysis are shown in Table 4.

No statistically significant difference was found between the pre- and post-test of either group, nor was there any statistically significant difference found between faculty or students.

Table 3. Internal consistency coefficients for survey subscales

Subscale	Survey items	Cronbach's
Jury process satisfaction	1–8	.59
Level of preparedness	9–14	.68
Continuous assessment satisfaction	15–20	.69

Table 4. Analysis of Variance for student attitudes toward grading

Source	df	MS	F	p
Within subjects				
Pre-Post	1	11.468	0.872	0.356
PrePost*Group	1	22.923	1.743	0.194
Error	42	13.151		
Between subjects				
Intercept	1	284005	4013.781	0.996
Group	1	0.002	0	
Error	42	70.758		

Qualitative data

The small percentage of performance faculty willing to be involved in this research revealed the need for additional data to be examined and the faculty pre- and post-test open-ended survey question revealed more attitudes about grading. Participant number nine reveals frustration in the grading process, in fact, with the whole higher education system.

The wheels of education keep turning, the teachers give acceptable grades, the student graduates, and everybody wins. The student gets the degree he or she paid for. The school gets their money, and the teacher keeps his or her job (Participant 9).

While this is only one opinion, it illustrates how complex the nature of grading within an art-based discipline such as music can be. Some faculty reported positive attitudes toward grading:

Specific guidelines clarify expectations for the students. Knowing exactly which areas need attention guides them more effectively (Participant 5).

As a teacher, I feel grading is a necessary evil. My ultimate goal for my students is 100% comprehension. Unfortunately, many students need the additional motivation exams provide to stimulate their personal learning experience. I do feel grading is an important indicator (Participant 11).

One faculty member, Participant 15, stated exactly why s/he didn't want to participate in this research. The statement, "I do not need these rubrics to help me grade the students," may indicate a broader reason as to why many others also did not participate.

Discussion

There were no observed effects from the use of performance rubrics on applied studio faculty and student attitudes toward grading. The low reliability coefficient obtained for the faculty survey was largely due to the very small size of the sample. The low internal consistency coefficients of the three sub-scales precluded a response to the four research questions. The low faculty participation rate contributed to the overall weakness of the results. This reveals a new research question, one which supports the importance of investigation into this field. Researchers should now ask: "What are the contributing factors for faculty reluctance to participate in educational research?" Clearly the involvement percentages were not high in the present study. Is there a systemic problem that has previously been overlooked? Bergee (2003) was successful in having performance faculty engage in research with him, but perhaps there were extenuating circumstances that facilitated this endeavor. There are, by comparison, very few other studies that indicate performance faculty involvement. It is important for music education researchers to begin working collaboratively with performance faculty and their students in order to provide better understanding of attitudes about grading. Working toward this broader goal could then perhaps facilitate accountability to university administrators.

There is a widely held belief that because of the inherent subjectivity of music performance, college applied studio teachers need not be as accountable in their methods of assessment compared to other faculty from wider university programs. Applied studio fees are among the most expensive in higher education, and performance faculty should be held to the same levels of accountability as faculty in other departments and disciplines. Accountability is a primary concern in higher education in general, particularly in the areas of assessment and grading. The importance of consistent grading processes for performance faculty should not be underestimated, as neither should the importance of understanding the impact assessment has on undergraduate students. Outcomes for students could be improved in several areas. Levels of performance anxiety might reduce if faculty were consistent and transparent about how they are grading the performances of their students. Students may be better prepared for the exams and in turn may learn to perform with greater results. Performance faculty may increase their students' learning potential by simply explaining the mystery that surrounds the applied studio issue of grading and assessment.

The findings of this study did not reveal answers to the proposed research questions, but suggest that further research investigate both faculty and student attitudes toward grading in the applied studio are recommended. This should be undertaken in the qualitative field to uncover issues and themes that are currently counterproductive to quantitative research into this area, namely faculty hesitation to be involved. The first step toward understanding performance faculty beliefs may be through qualitative interviews and focus groups.

References

Abeles, H. F. 1973. Development and validation of a clarinet performance adjudication scale. *Journal of Research in Music Education, 21*(3):246–255.

Bergee, M. J. 1993. A comparison of faculty, peer, and self-evaluation of applied brass jury performances. *Journal of Research in Music Education, 41*(1):19–27.

Bergee, M. J. 1997. Relationships among faculty, peer, and self-evaluations of applied performances. *Journal of Research in Music Education, 45*(4):601–612.

Bergee, M. J. 2003. Faculty interjudge reliability of music performance evaluation. *Journal of Research in Music Education, 51*(2):137–150.

Boyle, D. J. and R. E. Radocy. 1987. *Measurement and evaluation of musical experiences.* New York: Macmillan.

Brand, M. 1992. Voodoo and the applied music studio. *The Quarterly Journal of Music Teaching and Learning, 3*(2):3–4.

Colwell, R. 2002. Assessment's potential in music education. In R. Colwell and C. Richardson, eds., *The new handbook of research on music teaching and learning,* 1128–1157. New York: Oxford University Press.

Duke, R. 2005. *Intelligent music teaching—Essays on the core principles of effective instruction.* Austin: Learning and Behavior Resources.

Labuta, J. A., and D. A. Smith. 1997. *Music education: Historical contexts and perspectives.* New Jersey: Simon and Schuster.

Madsen, C. K. 1963. Experimental research in applied music. *Music Educators Journal, 51*(6):63–66.

Parkes, K. A. April, 2006. *Music performance faculty perceptions about grading.* Poster session presented at the annual meeting of MENC National Convention, Salt Lake City, UT.

Saunders, T. C. and J. M. Holahan. 1997. Criteria-specific rating scales in the evaluation of high school instrumental performance. *Journal of Research in Music Education, 45*(2):259–272.

Schleuter, S. L. 1997. *A sound approach to teaching instrumentalists: An application of content and learning sequences.* Belmont: Schirmer.

Schmidt, C. P. 1992a. Systematic research in applied music instruction: A review of the literature. *The Quarterly Journal of Music Teaching and Learning, 3*(2):32–45.

Watkins, J. G., and S. E. Farnum. 1954. *The Watkins-Farnum performance scale: Form A.* Winona, MN: Hal Leonard.

Watkins, J. G., and S. E. Farnum. 1962. *The Watkins-Farnum performance scale: Form B.* Winona, MN: Hal Leonard.

Appendix A
Student and Faculty Survey Items

Student survey questions:

1. I like being graded at the end of semester in a jury exam.
2. I enjoy the grading process.
3. I am satisfied that the grade I get reflects my level of performance.
4. I usually know what grade I am going to get before I have my jury.
5. I think my teacher has already decided what grade to give me before my jury.
6. I know what I am going to be asked in my jury exam.
7. It is made clear to me during the semester how I will be graded in my jury.
8. I wonder how they assign a grade during my jury.
9. I usually feel I am prepared for my jury.
10. I am surprised by the grade I get in my juries.
11. I think my teacher knows what he/she is doing when they grade me.
12. I don't think my teacher gives me enough information about what to expect in the jury.
13. My teacher doesn't seem to know how he/she will grade me in the jury.
14. My teacher gives me plenty of information about what to expect in the jury.
15. My teacher grades me according to how well I do during the semester, not in the jury.
16. I usually get enough feedback from my teacher during the semester to know how well I am doing.
17. I would like to have more chances to be graded during the semester.
18. I don't need any more grading opportunities from my teacher.
19. I could use more feedback about how I can do better during the semester.
20. I would feel more satisfied in the grading process if I were told more often how I was doing.

Faculty survey questions:

1. I like grading at the end of semester in jury exams.
2. I enjoy the grading process.
3. I am satisfied that the grade I give reflects the level of performance I hear.
4. I usually know what grade I am going to give before I hear my students' juries.
5. I have already decided what grade to give before juries.
6. My students know what I am going to ask in their jury exam.
7. I make it clear to my students during the semester how they will be graded in their jury.
8. I don't really have a process by which I grade in a jury.
9. I usually feel I have prepared my students for their jury.
10. My students are surprised by the grades they get in juries.
11. I think I know what I am doing when I grade students.
12. I don't give enough information to my students about what to expect in the jury.
13. My students think I know what I am doing when I give grades in a jury.
14. I give my students plenty of information about what to expect in the jury.
15. I grade my students according to how well they do during the semester, not in the jury.

16. I usually give enough feedback to my students during the semester so they know how well they are doing.
17. I would like to have more chances to grade during the semester.
18. I don't need to have more grading opportunities for students.
19. I could give more feedback about how my students can do better during the semester.
20. I would feel more satisfied in the grading process if I told my students more often how they were doing.

Creative Alternative: Survey of Pre-Service Music Teachers' Perceptions of a Music Composition Project as the Final Assessment Tool in Wind and Percussion Techniques Classes

Patricia Riley
University of Vermont

Abstract

The purpose of this research was to explore perceptions of pre-service music teachers regarding the performance of a music composition project as the final assessment tool in their wind and percussion techniques classes. A survey was used to obtain the perceptions of thirty-two students enrolled in two sections of a beginning techniques course designed to prepare music education majors with major instruments of piano, guitar, or voice with the practical skills, knowledge, and understanding to teach wind and percussion instruments at the elementary level. Students were assessed in the areas of tone quality, intonation, pitch accuracy, rhythmic accuracy, appropriate tempo, articulation, technique, posture, playing position, dynamics, and phrasing. Results included twenty-two students stating that they felt that this music composition project was useful in the development of skills as a beginning wind instrumentalist; twenty-one stating that playing their music composition as the final playing examination was a fair way of demonstrating their proficiency on their techniques instrument; and twenty-three stating that they would like to be evaluated in this way again in a future techniques class.

Music is experienced in many ways, including performing, evaluating, analyzing, creating, and listening (Hickey, 1997). According to Brophy (2001), musical creativity is an "important and valued means of expression" which can be demonstrated through composing and improvising (34). Educating students musically in performance classes entails not only performance, but also a "methodology centered around creativity" (Brown, 1968, 15). Elliott (1995) states that the development of musical creativity "overlaps and extends" the development of musicianship (215). When students in performance classes engage in creating music, they "can be stimulated to think in more musical ways and ultimately achieve deeper levels of musical understanding" (Hickey, 1997, 17). Kaschub (1997) writes "creative endeavors such as composition offer a rich environment for students to develop musical thinking skills and such opportunities should be a standard component in music education experiences" (27). According to Reese (2001), "composing and improvising are processes by which we can put into practice today's emphasis on student-centered learning, creative and critical thinking, problem solving, working cooperatively with others, and new forms of student assessment (53).

Torrance (1967) asserts "the development of the creative thinking abilities [of students] is at the very heart of the achievement of even the most fundamental educational objectives" (174). He surveyed 135 students at the University of Minnesota, and lists events that participants identified as those in which creative instruction had caused changes. These changes included "lack of self-confidence and self-expression to adequate self-confidence and creative expression," "apathy and dislike of school to enthusiasm about learning," and "mediocrity of achievement among gifted pupils to outstanding performance" (Torrance, 1967, 179).

Kratus (1989) studied the music composition processes of seven-, nine-, and eleven-year-old children, and found that children use divergent and convergent thought as they progress through four stages. First, children prepare to explore problems and solutions; second, possible solutions are considered, and ideas developed; third, children arrive at tentative solutions; fourth, the final composition is evaluated and refined. He observed that children use different strategies for composing music depending on their age. Seven-year-old children compose primarily through exploration. As children become older, they compose through development and repetition. He also noted that the nine-year-old and eleven-year-old children change processes as they compose. They start with exploration, progress to development, and end with repetition. Ashby (1995), Levi (1991), Perconti (1996), Swanwick and Tillman (1986), van Ernst (1993), and Wiggins (1993) also explored music composition processes of children. Similar to Kratus, Ashby describes a three-step process, and reported that children generally moved from exploring to developing to repeating musical ideas. Perconti and van Ernst describe four-step processes. According to Perconti, children create, notate, practice and edit, and perform their music; van Ernst states that students are stimulated to compose, organize sounds, rehearse their compositions, and perform their compositions. Levi writes of a five-phase process that consists of exploring, focusing, rehearsing, composing, and editing. Swanwick and Tillman outline eight sequential stages, and refer to them as "sensory, manipulative, personal expression, vernacular, speculative, idiomatic, symbolic, and systematic" (331). åDiffering from Ashby, Kratus, Levi, and van Ernst, Wiggins reported that as children composed music, little time was spent engaging in "random exploration as a pre-compositional stage…children in this study seemed to play some version of their eventual motifs from the very first moments" (268–269). According to Wiggins, the children "represented their musical ideas through a combination of verbal and non-verbal modes, including singing, rhythmic speech, vocal imitation of musical sounds, gesture, graphic representation, and instrumental performance" (270–272).

Priest (1997), Riley (2001, 2006), and Whitener (1983) studied students in instrumental music classes to determine the effects of music composition activities on various combinations of student performance, achievement, and attitude. Priest (1997) examined the effects of an instructional approach to teaching beginning instrumental music that used music composition, listening, and performance activities. The control group experienced instruction based mainly on performance techniques, while the experimental group experienced instruction in which the children analyzed and described music, composed and improvised, performed by ear, and performed by reading traditional notation. Priest found that children in the experimental group demonstrated growth in understanding of music structure through description and analysis of music listened to, and through music composition and improvisation. Children in the experimental group demonstrated more growth than children in the control groups on some music performance skills, but less growth on others. There were few differences regarding attitude toward music and instrumental music instruction.

Riley (2001, 2006) investigated the effects of two instructional approaches on the individual music achievement, performance, and attitude of students in middle school band classes. The control group instruction consisted of music performance and listening; and the experimental group instruction consisted of music composition, performance, and listening. Statistically significant gains from pre-test to post-test were achieved by both the experimental and control groups in the areas of music achievement and performance; however, the differences between the gains of the groups were not statistically significant. The experimental group responded more favorably than the control group from pre-test to post-test to attitude survey statements. Riley concluded that students who engage in music composition activities, and students who do not engage in music composition activities, both experience gains in music achievement and music performance, and that achievement and performance are affected favorably both by an approach to teaching middle school band classes that includes music performance and listening, and by an approach that includes music composition, performance, and listening.

Whitener (1983) researched music achievement and performance skills. The experimental group was instructed using a comprehensive musicianship approach that included performing, analyzing, and composing. The control group was instructed with a performance approach. Statistically significant differences were reported between the experimental and control groups in favor of the experimental group on music achievement tests which measured interval and auditory-visual discrimination. Whitener concluded that music analysis and composition can be taught to beginning instrumentalists in conjunction with music performance skills without a loss of performance ability, and with some increases in music sensitivity.

In 1992, researchers from the Educational Testing Service and Harvard Project Zero and teachers and supervisors from the Pittsburgh Pubic Schools collaborated to examine school music instruction and assessment (Winner, Davidson, and Scripp). *Arts PROPEL: A Handbook for Music* summarizes the collaboration and guides implementation of the Arts PROPEL assessment-based curriculum. According to Winner, et al., Arts PROPEL is a tool for curriculum construction, and for the identification, generation, support, and documentation of quality instructional practices in performance and general music settings, and for the assessment of student learning. The acronym PROPEL identifies Perceiving, Producing, and Reflecting as three "ways of knowing" music (Winner, et al., 1992, 6).

According to Winner, et al., teachers and researchers involved in Arts PROPEL music believe that the fullest, most convincing learning in music occurs when students generate music (whether in performing, composing, or mapping what they hear), listen discerningly (to their own singing or playing or their own compositions or to someone else's music), and think critically about what they're producing and/or hearing (thinking on the spot and reflecting over time, whether in speech, in writing, or nonverbally). As the project developed, there was a growing consensus that learning could be described in terms of Production, Perception, and Reflection, and that the most effective learning in music occurs when these processes are integrated. (1992, 6)

The purpose of this research was to explore the perceptions of pre-service music teachers regarding the performance of a music composition project as the final assessment tool in their wind and percussion techniques classes.

Method

A survey was used to obtain the perceptions of pre-service music teachers regarding the performance of a music composition project as the final assessment tool in their wind and percussion techniques classes. Participants ($N = 32$) were students in two pre-existing sections of a beginning techniques course entitled Wind and Percussion Techniques. This course was a two-semester sequence of study designed to prepare music education majors with major instruments of piano, guitar, or voice with the practical skills, knowledge, and understanding to teach wind and percussion instruments at the elementary school level. Each student played two brass instruments one semester, and two woodwind instruments in the other semester, with special sessions one semester on percussion and the other semester on marching. Each section of this course met for fifty minutes, two times each week for fifteen weeks. At approximately the halfway point of each semester, students were assessed on their first wind instrument, and at the end of the semester, they were assessed on their second wind instrument. Students were assessed on the playing of each wind instrument in the areas of tone quality, intonation, pitch accuracy, rhythmic accuracy, appropriate tempo, articulation, technique, posture, playing position, dynamics, and phrasing. The final playing examination (during which the students performed an original music composition as the examination performance piece) counted for 15% of students' final course grades. The other 85% consisted of 50% class participation, 15% mid-term playing examination (assessment on the first wind instrument, during which the students performed a pre-existing performance piece selected by the professor), 10% on a teaching presentation, and 10% on a written examination. This research occurred at the end of the Spring 2006 semester at a university that specializes in music education.

The assignment was as follows:

Compose a duet for you and a classmate to play. It should be a piece for you and someone who plays an instrument from another instrument family (for example flute and trumpet; or clarinet and trombone). It should include at least eight measures that feature each of the techniques instruments, and also include each person's major instrument (piano, guitar, or voice), either as additional featured instruments or as accompaniment. During each featured techniques instrument section, there should be some slurred and some tongued notes, contrasting dynamics, a range of at least an octave, and should consist of a variety of note values, including eighth notes. These pieces will be performed in a recital, and (in addition to playing scales in class), will count as the final playing exam. Be creative and have fun!

The students were encouraged by the professor (researcher) to compose using their techniques instrument rather then using pianos or computers, and some class time was devoted to starting the project. Students worked in pairs, and were instructed to hand in a printed copy of their composition at the time of performance. The recital occurred during class time, and the audience was comprised only of class members and the professor. Immediately following the recitals the surveys were administered. Survey questions were:

1. Please describe the process you used in creating your final music composition.
2. Do you feel that this music composition project was useful in the development of skills as a _____ (fill in the name of your current techniques instrument) player? Why or why not?
3. Did you develop or refine performance skills to accommodate your creative musical ideas? If so, please describe.
4. Which performance skills (tone, fingerings, pitch accuracy, rhythmic accuracy, articulation, dynamics, etc.) do you feel were developed the most as a result of this project?
5. Do you feel that this music composition project was useful in the development of your overall musicianship? Why or why not?
6. Do you feel that playing your music composition as the final playing examination was a fair way of demonstrating your proficiency on this techniques instrument? Why or why not?
7. What did you like the most/least about participating in this creative project?
8. Would you like to be evaluated in this way again in a future techniques class?

Results

For each question, responses and/or response summaries will be presented, followed by a statement of how many, if any, other participants responded similarly. In order to maintain confidentiality, the phrase "my classmate" was substituted when proper names were used in responses.

Question 1: Please describe the process you used in creating your final music composition.

The processes described varied greatly. Four groups indicated experimenting and/or improvising as an early stage in their compositional process. Four indicated starting with melody and moving to harmony; one indicated melody, harmony, then the transitions between sections; and one indicated melody, then transitions. One group responded that they started by choosing a chord progression and key, and then moved to melody, followed by harmony; and one group choose the key, followed by chord progression, melody, harmony, dynamics, articulation, and text. One started with melody, followed by form, and then instrumentation; and another started with the notes they could play, followed by form, melody, and then harmony. One started with notes they know, and then moved to form, melody, and then harmony; one started with the key, followed by form; one with style, then melody and form; one with form, key, and then meter; and one with harmony, then melody and transposition.

Question 2: *Do you feel that this music composition project was useful in the development of skills as a ___ (fill in the name of your current techniques instrument) player? Why or why not?*

Twenty-two participants answered "yes"; six responded "no"; one did not respond positively or negatively, but offered a "why or why not" response; one answered "kind of"; one answered "indifferent"; and one answered "yes and no." The "why or why not" responses with each answer are shown in Figure 1.

Figure 1. Responses to Question 2: Do you feel that this music composition project was useful in the development of skills as a ___ (fill in the name of your current techniques instrument) player? Why or why not?

Response: *Yes.*

1. In composing a melody for myself, I had to consider my strengths and weaknesses as a beginning instrumentalist, and incorporate that awareness into the composition. (There were two similar responses.)
2. Instead of just playing something someone else wrote, I had to decide what I was able to play. Also, because I had more motivation to learn it and play it well. (There were two similar responses.)
3. It was more beneficial than a technical drill—at least with composing, you spend time exploring the instrument, seeing what works, and what is harder to maneuver. (There were two similar responses.)
4. I developed a more thorough understanding of the versatility of the instrument, and practiced more than usual. If I didn't practice, the piece wouldn't have sounded how we wanted. (There was one similar response.)
5. It allowed me more practice on my techniques instrument. It also put my playing in the context of a real piece with another instrumentalist, so I had to be more aware of intonation and other aspects. (There was one similar response.)
6. I really like incorporating composing into the techniques curriculum. It is important, and why not bridge theory/composition to new instruments.
7. Because I had to do phrasing and dynamics, as well as transpose for voice, my instrument, and my duet partner's instrument.
8. It forced me to expand my range, and even work on quick embouchure switches between high and low.
9. Although the composition didn't use difficult rhythms, it included most of the notes I learned.
10. I had to focus on what I remembered from class, and create something using that. I feel it solidified my skills.
11. It allowed me to create a more melodic line than the trombone is used to seeing, and helped me to play it with musicality. I had to make each slide position accurate because it wasn't a familiar song, and I wanted the audience to hear and grasp each note.
12. To meet the requirements, we had to write music that was challenging at our beginning level.

13. This assignment helped me understand the difficulty of transposing particular notes.
14. We had to do dynamic contrast and work with good tone.

Response: *No.*
1. I could have learned the same concepts learning out of a book.
2. Because I had some prior playing experience on this instrument.
3. I was so worried about the composition and voice part, that the techniques instrument was put on the back burner. There were too many requirements in this composition, that the techniques instrument was not a big part of it.
4. I really didn't learn many skills from writing for my instrument.
5. The composition assignment was far too simple to help improve myself as a vocalist.
6. I could have played a piece to fulfill that, however writing my own piece did make it easier to play.

Other responses.
1. (No "yes" or "no.") I have had trouble with the double-tonguing in the higher register on the tuba; and while still there, it is better under control.
2. ("Kind of.") It got me to be creative with what I know, but it didn't really help me understand more.
3. ("Indifferent.") It was a fun project that did take skill and time. However, I think if you want to assess every student on the same scale, we should all be playing the same piece.
4. ("Yes and no.") It seemed to be a hassle in some aspects, and others probably made the playing final harder than it could have been.

Question 3: Did you develop or refine performance skills to accommodate your creative musical ideas? If so, please describe.

Twenty participants answered "yes"; eleven responded "no"; and one did not respond in a positive or negative way. Of the "yes" responses, technique was identified five times: range, four times; articulation, three times; fingering, embouchure, breath support, and transitions between playing major and techniques instruments, two times each; and tone, style, phrasing, dynamics, and concentration and relaxation, one time each. Additional responses were: "I had to synchronize with the other player, and had to be sensitive to other sounds, not just my own"; and "Refine—do what is in the capacity of the performer."

Question 4: Which performance skills (tone, fingerings, pitch accuracy, rhythmic accuracy, articulation, dynamics, etc.) do you feel were developed the most as a result of this project?

Tone was identified fourteen times; articulation, thirteen times; pitch accuracy, eleven times; fingerings, ten times; rhythmic accuracy, five times; dynamics, three times; and switching registers was identified once.

Question 5: *Do you feel that this music composition project was useful in the development of your overall musicianship? Why or why not?*

Twenty-eight participants answered "yes"; three responded "no"; and one did not respond in a positive or negative way. The "why or why not" responses are shown in Figure 2.

Question 6: *Do you feel that playing your music composition as the final playing examination was a fair way of demonstrating your proficiency on this techniques instrument? Why or why not?*

Twenty-one participants answered "yes"; seven responded "no"; one answered "sort of"; two answered "depends…"; and one answered "for me, yes…for some, no." The "why or why not" responses are presented in Figure 3.

Question 7: *What did you like the most/least about participating in this creative project?"*

Responses to this question can be found in Figure 4.

Question 8: *Would you like to be evaluated in this way again in a future techniques class?"*

Twenty-three participants answered "yes"; seven responded "no"; one responded "maybe"; and one answered "no preference."

Figure 2. Responses to Question 5: Do you feel that this music composition project was useful in the development of your overall musicianship? Why or why not?

Response: *Yes.*
1. It forced me to use musicianship skills I had acquired in other classes and apply them to my new instrument. (There were two similar responses.)
2. I always feel composition furthers the growth of a musician. It is a different way of expressing. (There was one similar response.)
3. I had to work with other instruments I don't have any experience working with. It got me a little more familiar with them, in case, as a teacher, I have to compose something for beginning instruments. (There was one similar response.)
4. As a singer, it is useful to know information about all things dealing with music, not just voice. I enjoyed learning about these instruments. (There was one similar response.)
5. It provided the impetus to learn well enough to give a performance, not just an evaluation.
6. It was fun, and used other skills we are using/developing at the same time in other classes.

7. I don't usually get to work with transposition for different instruments. This composition allowed me to play with this aspect of my musicianship.
8. It forced me to work on my embouchure so that I could create a more musical tone and phrasing.
9. Any composition builds musical creativity, improves your ear, and helps your performance/musical skills.
10. The best way to learn is to be creative.
11. Timbre is an important musical element, and instrumentation is a subcategory of timbre. Therefore, I increased my knowledge in that area of music.
12. This project really got me to open up creatively; I didn't just plug through notes to get a grade, I played with my instrument, testing what I could do, and my voice too.
13. It got me back to the basics of composition. I write a lot of more technically difficult compositions that focus on harmonic tension, so it was fun doing something simpler that focused on line.
14. This definitely gets you doing something you normally wouldn't—learning about what other instrumentalists deal with.
15. When a piece is your own, you have a real connection to it, and know how you want it expressed. Any experience of true connection is going to benefit your other work in some way.
16. It made me more comfortable writing music.
17. It forced me to do something that I'm not very good at: composition.
18. It is nice to work on composing with another person—to use both of our ideas to form a unified composition.
19. Writing the beginning duet forced me to think what is feasible, and what is not, for me and my instrument.
20. I have never really had to play a sensitive melodic line on a low brass instrument before this class, and I feel that I now understand the techniques to do so.
21. I had to work hard at it and perfect other aspects of being a good musician (such as my tone) in order to try to make the areas I had difficulty in more accurate.
22. It involved more thinking because we actually had to write the piece and not just learn it. We also had to work together as a duo composing—being together on notes and rhythms, etc.
23. I explored aspects of the trombone that I wouldn't have otherwise.

Response: *No.*
1. I don't think it aided my musicianship, but it added to my arsenal of activities to use as a music teacher.
2. It felt like another theory assignment, but it did develop my score-writing musicianship/transposing ability.
3. I don't think that it was taken seriously enough by the performers and audience.

Other responses.
1. I'm the person who would much rather work alone on a project, and because of the nature of the assignment, I think I would have benefited more alone.

Figure 3. Responses to Question 6: Do you feel that playing your music composition as the final playing examination was a fair way of demonstrating your proficiency on this techniques instrument? Why or why not?

Response: *Yes.*
1. It allowed us to write for our own instrument and prove we were proficient on the instrument and show all of the concepts we have learned. We showcased our best skills because we decided what to play. (There were six similar responses.)
2. The performer/composer is in control of the material played. You have to compose it within the level of your own playing ability. (There were two similar responses.)
3. Because we wrote the piece, we could concentrate more on the act of performance. Because of that, we were able to set our own limits of what we could and could not do on our particular instrument. (There was one similar response.)
4. Very fair. We got to pick what we were comfortable with. (There was one similar response.)
5. It is more flexible and independent than our usual solo-playing exam.
6. But, it would probably be easier just performing in front of you in a more relaxed situation.
7. However more could have been achieved through a specific example in the book.
8. Due to the requirements outlined in the assignment, we covered all the topics taught in class. All these topics show a good level of skill for our time on the instrument.
9. However being given a piece would be good as well. Also, solo performances.
10. We could choose the level the piece would be at, and it showed our creative and artistic sides as well.
11. Because you are going to have to know how to play when teaching.

Response: *No.*
1. Students had more liberty with how difficult their piece is, hence creating uneven grading. (There was one similar response.)
2. People get nervous when playing in front of other people, so may not play as well as normal. (There was one similar response.)
3. Because we made it ourselves, in some aspects, I think it made it harder.
4. Even though I played notes I had learned, I felt the composition in whole didn't let me demonstrate the range of pitches I learned.
5. Playing something out of the book would have been a better demonstration of the proficiency because of the nerves involved with performing your own work.

Other repsonses.
1. ("Sort of.") The composition does show some degree of proficiency. I feel that one could test with the teacher privately. But, overall, the composition accomplished its goals.
2. (Depends...") On the honesty of your students. Some would just make it really easy to get a good grade.
3. On whom you're talking to. Several of the compositions were written to accommodate the performer's lack of skill.

4. ("For me, yes...") For me yes, because I played many pitches. For some no, because they played few pitches.

Figure 4. Responses to Question 7: What did you like the most/least about participating in this creative project?

What students liked most.
1. Being able to be creative and write our own music. (There were three similar responses.)
2. I enjoyed the requirement that we incorporated our major instrument in our compositions. It gave us the chance to be more creative. Also, it was nice to have clearly planned requirements laid out for us. (There were two similar responses.)
3. Performing the composition was my favorite. (There was one similar response.)
4. It was a lot of fun.
5. It was fun composing music for different instruments.
6. Creating the piece. It was a lot of fun coming up with good ideas.
7. I took pride in this composition—writing and performing. It was an overall fun assignment.
8. I love creating a piece for instruments that I might have not written for before.
9. It was fun to be creative with combining the instruments and voice. It was a little challenging to add dynamics and articulation, and to execute them well.
10. Working in groups to brainstorm.
11. Making the music and performing with my classmate.
12. We got to work on our own and have more freedom.
13. I liked that I was able to choose to show my strengths. No dislikes—good project!
14. Practicing the composition with my classmate after we were done writing it was pretty fun.
15. I liked getting to know a classmate better.
16. It gave us a chance to show some personality. We could write something that was interesting for us to play.
17. I liked that it was up to us to compose our own final.
18. It was fun writing my own song, and writing a part that I felt I was capable of playing.
19. Creating the piece. It was a lot of fun coming up with good ideas.

What students liked the least.
1. The performance. (There were four similar responses.)
2. I didn't like having to use our major instruments. It took away from the point at hand. I think we should just play our techniques instrument. (There were three similar responses.)
3. Trying to find time outside of class to meet and work on it. (There was one similar response.)
4. I'm bad at writing with a partner—our musical ideas clashed. (There was one similar response.)
5. I wasn't sure if the composition we wrote was good enough, or showed off all the concepts we had learned.
6. It fell at a very hectic time in the semester.

7. The duet made it difficult to focus on my own performance.
8. I didn't dislike anything, except that our creativity did not get evaluated.
9. I liked the act of doing it, but I didn't like being forced to work with a partner and compromising.
10. Being evaluated just on the performance, and not my improvement as a trumpet player.

Discussion

Of the thirty-two participants, twenty-two responded "yes," that they felt the music composition project was useful in their development of skills as beginning wind instrumentalists; twenty indicated that they developed or refined performance skills to accommodate their creative musical ideas; and twenty-eight responded that they felt the project was useful in the development of their overall musicianship. These results are similar to Priest (1997), Riley (2001, 2006), Torrance (1967), and Whitener (1983), who found creative instruction and/or music composition activities in some way to be beneficial to students' music performance skills, achievement, understanding, sensitivity, and/or attitude.

In describing the processes used to compose music, four groups indicated experimenting and/or improvising as an early stage in their compositional process. These results are similar to Ashby (1995), Kratus (1989), and Levi (1991), who also found that children begin their music composition processes with exploration. Similar to Wiggins (1993), who reported that little time was spent engaged in exploring early in the compositional process, thirteen groups or individuals in the current research did not indicate exploration in describing their processes.

Conclusions and Implications for Music Education

Perceptions of pre-service music teachers regarding the performance of a music composition project as the final assessment tool in their wind and percussion techniques classes varied. Of the thirty-two participants in this study, twenty-two responded that they felt that this music composition project was useful in the development of skills as a beginning wind instrumentalist; twenty indicated that they developed or refined performance skills to accommodate their creative musical ideas; twenty-eight responded that they felt this music composition project was useful in the development of their overall musicianship; twenty-one indicated that playing their music composition as the final playing examination was a fair way of demonstrating their proficiency on their techniques instrument; and twenty-three responded that they would like to be evaluated in this way again in a future techniques class. Based on the results of this research, it can be concluded that perceptions of pre-service music teachers regarding the performance of a music composition project as the final assessment tool in their wind and percussion techniques class are positive. Implications for music education appear to be that music educators should consider including the performance of music composition projects as an assessment tool in performance classes.

References

Ashby, C. L. 1995. An analysis of compositional processes used by children. *Masters Abstracts International, 34* (01):0040. (UMI No. 1375862).

Brophy, T. S. 2001. Developing improvisation in general music classes. *Music Educators Journal, 88*(1):34–41.

Brown, E. H. 1968. A study of the application of creativity in the teaching of secondary school music. *Dissertation Abstracts, 29*(05):1553A. (UMI No. 6815219).

Elliott, D. J. 1995. *Music matters: A new philosophy of music education.* New York: Oxford University Press.

Hickey, M. 1997. Teaching ensembles to compose and improvise. *Music Educators Journal, 83*(6):17–21.

Kaschub, M. 1997. A comparison of two composer-guided large group composition projects. *Research Studies in Music Education, 8,* 15–27.

Kratus, J. 1989. A time analysis of the compositional processes used by children ages 7–11. *Journal of Research in Music Education, 37*(1):5–20.

Levi, R. 1991. A field investigation of the composition processes used by second-grade children creating original language and music pieces. *Dissertation Abstracts International, 52*(08):2853A. (UMI No. 9202227).

Perconti, E. S. 1996. Learning to compose and learning through composing: A study of the composing process in elementary general music. *Dissertation Abstracts International, 57*(10):4301A. (UMI No. 9710259).

Priest, T. L. 1997. Fostering creative and critical thinking in a beginning instrumental music class. *Dissertation Abstracts International, 58*(10):3870A. (UMI No.9812743).

Reese, S. 2001. Tools for thinking in sound. *Music Educators Journal, 88*(1):42–46, 53.

Riley, P. E. 2001. A comparison of the effects of two instructional approaches to teaching middle school instrumental music: An approach using music performance and listening, and an approach using music performance, listening, and composition. *Dissertation Abstracts International, 63*(06):2172A. (UMI No. 13056497).

Riley, P. E. 2006. Including composition in middle school band: Effects on achievement, performance, and attitude. *Update: Applications of Research in Music Education, 25*(1):28–38.

Swanwick, K., and Tillman, J. 1986. The sequence of musical development: A study of children's composition. *British Journal of Music Education, 3,* 305–339.

Torrance, E. P. 1967. Creative teaching makes a difference. In J. C. Gowan, G. D. Demos, and E. P Torrance, eds., *Creativity: Its educational implications* (173–188). New York: Wiley.

van Ernst, B. 1993. A study of the learning and teaching processes of non-naïve music students engaged in composition. *Research studies in Music Education, 1,* 22–39.

Whitener, W. T. 1983. Comparison of two approaches to teaching beginning band. *Journal of Research in Music Education, 31*(1):5–13.

Wiggins, J. H. 1993. The nature of children's musical learning in the context of a music classroom. *Dissertation Abstracts International, 53*(11):3838A. (UMI No. 9305731).

Winner, E., Davidson, L, and Scripp, L. (Eds.). 1992. *ARTS PROPEL: A Handbook for Music.* Boston: Harvard Project Zero.

A Cluster Evaluation Approach to the Assessment of E-Portfolios in Music Teacher Education

Kristen Albert
West Chester University

Abstract

E-portfolios are a tool for learning, evaluation, assessment, and employment in music teacher education. Given an increasingly politicized, data-driven, accountability-focused educational environment, e-portfolios provide an electronic repository for evidence of a preservice teacher's acquisition of the "desirable attributes," "music competencies," and "teaching competencies" developed by the National Association of Schools of Music (NASM).

How effective are e-portfolios in answering questions related to candidate preparation? To what degree do candidates demonstrate evidence of satisfactory attainment of standards? How effective are e-portfolios in facilitating learning within an electronic environment? Because of the rapid development of e-portfolio technologies and their multi-faceted use, music teacher educators face the challenge of assessing the efficacy of e-portfolios to meet intended purposes.

This paper presents a research-based cluster evaluation approach to evaluating and assessing e-portfolios as part of a music education program within the jurisdiction of a university-based teacher education program. This model provides a standards-based evaluation process by which e-portfolio models may be evaluated for the ability to provide data-driven accountability in high-stakes educational environments.

Electronic portfolios have received a great deal of attention in teacher education, and improvements in technology have contributed to and facilitated rapid changes in electronic portfolio development. Changing technologies in e-portfolio development have provided a plethora of options for creating electronic portfolios throughout a candidate's undergraduate experience in music education.

With the challenges of rapidly changing technologies come challenges of assessing the efficacy of e-portfolios. This challenge needs to be addressed so that e-portfolios do not simply become the next "fad," discarded because of lack of research-based assessment. This paper proposes a cluster evaluation approach to evaluate and ultimately assess the effectiveness of e-portfolios designed for multiple uses: evaluation, assessment, reflective practice and learning, and employment. The evaluation schema presented in this paper evaluates e-portfolios from within two differing perspectives—those designed to meet the needs of a body that oversees teacher education within a university system, and those designed to meet the needs of music education at the specialized program level. The intent is to provide assessment data that will contribute to the improvement of the e-portfolio model and the programs for which the e-portfolio was developed.

Helen Barrett, a pioneer in the field of electronic portfolio development in education, explains that an electronic portfolio is a "portfolio that contains work that a learner has collected, reflected, selected, and presented to show growth and change over time" (Barrett, 2005, 2). E-portfolio artifacts can be collected, organized, reflected upon, and presented to serve the following purposes:

1. To provide a repository of work on which to base subsequent evaluation of candidates' knowledge, skills, and dispositions relative to their academic program.
2. To offer a forum for candidates to engage in and document evidence of reflective practice and learning.
3. To display an electronic portfolio product that can be used to help candidates to obtain an interview or to secure a teaching position.
4. To provide a selection of specific artifacts from which evaluation or assessment of specific outcomes may take place.

The e-portfolio model assessed in this research addressed the following expectations:

1. Expectations of teacher education programs.
   a. The e-portfolio was designed to demonstrate attainment of NCATE standards.
   b. To document candidates' attainment of knowledge, skills and dispositions in keeping with a conceptual framework.
2. Expectations of music education programs.
   a. Candidates meet NASM standards for Music Education (i.e., desirable attributes, and essential music and teaching competencies).
   b. E-portfolios provide collaborative and reflective opportunities for candidate learning.
3. Expectations common to both the music education and teacher education programs.
   a. Provide evidence for program evaluation.
   b. Provide a framework where summative e-portfolios are available to contribute to decisions regarding licensure.

Approaching a Multi-Faceted Evaluation

To design a plan for evaluation with such a variety of questions and multitude of stakeholders is a complex undertaking. When this is the case, Weiss (1998) suggests that a decision be made as to whether to approach a program evaluation as one large study, or as several smaller studies. When one large study is conducted, different stakeholders with differing perspectives may find reason to doubt the study; thus, Weiss presents Cronbach and Associates' (1980) conclusion that, in these cases it is best to plan for "a fleet of studies" (Cronbach, 1980). This approach also allows for the comparison of results from these various studies, providing opportunities for independent, yet potentially complementary findings to add credibility to the program and the evaluation (Weiss, 1998).

Weiss (1998) also points out that to adopt a purview of conducting multiple evaluations provides for:

1. The opportunity for various studies to use different methods.
2. Studies to begin at different times, rather than all at the same time.
3. Flexibility to be able to address new questions, or "newly visible questions as they arise" (Weiss, 1998, 90).

Because of the complexity of the e-portfolio framework, the multiplicity of purposes within e-portfolio models, and the interconnectedness among constituents, the evaluation developed in this paper will be approached through a number of separate evaluations that contribute to the evaluation of the whole. Components of the e-portfolio framework will be evaluated and approached separately. As such, each component will be subject to proposed changes and adaptations that will in turn affect the conglomerate e-portfolio model designed for evaluation, assessment, learning, and employment. Figure 1 shows a conceptualization of the process for approaching the evaluation of the e-portfolio model with multiple purposes in mind, as suggested by Cronbach (1980).

The fact that there are many evaluators provides a risk for the entire e-portfolio project as a whole. To draw conclusions from the total collective experience as shown in Figure 1 would not only be difficult, it would also risk disconnected or pre-mature conclusions. Thus, the provision for a synthesis of the findings of multiple evaluations by way of a meta-evaluation is the next logical step in the process.

To understand the effectiveness of the e-portfolio model as a whole, Sanders (1998) suggests "cluster evaluation" to provide a more global understanding of the "collective experience." What is learned at the point at which all studies come together contributes to the model of cluster evaluation. When conducting a cluster evaluation, the evaluator seeks to understand "whether any progress has been made in the general problem area" (Sanders, 1998, 7) and if so, to be able to specifically identify that progress. Sanders' identifies four questions to be answered by cluster evaluation. It is the task of the assessment advisory committee to collect data from each of the multiple evaluations and synthesize them to answer the following questions as they are applied to the e-portfolio evaluation at large:

1. Overall, have changes occurred in the directions of learning, evaluation, assessment, and employment as outcomes of the use of the e-portfolio model? If so, what is the nature of these changes?
2. In what contexts have different types of changes occurred and why? To what can the changes be attributed?
3. What insights can be drawn from failures and successes? How can these insights inform future initiatives?
4. What resources are needed to sustain changes that are worth continuing? (Sanders, 1998)

The answers to these questions provide a meta-evaluation bringing together each independent evaluation within the e-portfolio framework. This process is shown in Figure 2.

Evaluation Teams

As part of this evaluation model, each teacher education program seeks to evaluate its e-portfolio model(s) developed for programmatic purposes. The music education program in this e-portfolio framework reports back to the Teacher Education Unit with information that supports the needs for NCATE accreditation.

With several sets of evaluative questions to be answered by separate groups of stakeholders, it is important to identify evaluation groups and the questions that guide the evaluation processes. Figure 1 shows evaluation schema for the multiple evaluation teams identified for the purpose of this e-portfolio evaluation. This scheme shows the questions that guide the evaluations of each interest group.

Figure 1. Evaluation Schema for Multiple E-portfolio Evaluation Teams

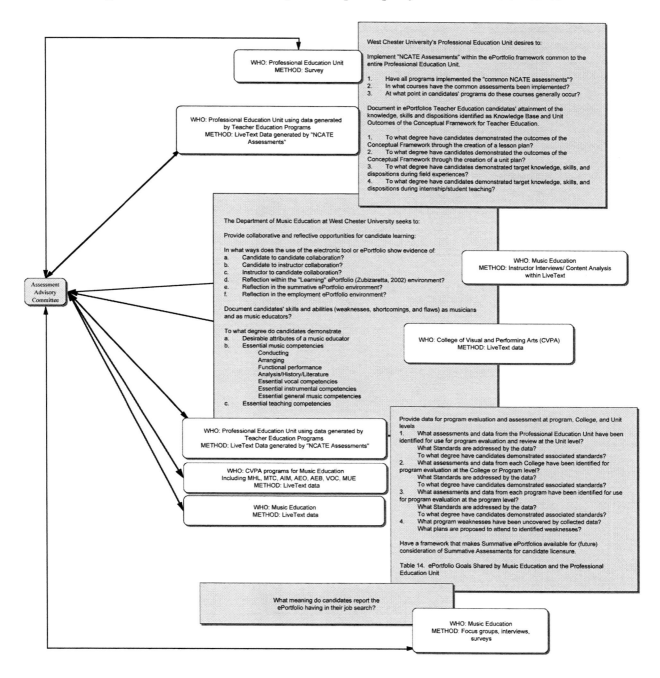

Assessment Advisory Committee

Keeping in mind the intention to conduct "cluster evaluations" (Sanders, 1998), there is a need to establish a governing body that will work to synthesize the findings of each of the evaluations. Weiss suggests that an advisory committee be established to address methodological and political issues (Weiss, 1998). An advisory committee can provide advice with regard to design, measurement, and analysis. From a political point of view, the committee established for this purpose should have representation from all colleges whose stakeholders may be affected by multiple evaluations. By way of membership on such a committee, members will have input into evaluation design, interpretation, and recommendations that stem from the work of the committee. An Assessment Advisory Committee appears at the left of the framework illustrated in Figure 1.

The charge to an Assessment Advisory Committee is to receive reports of all evaluation studies conducted in Figure 1 and synthesize the findings to evaluate the effectiveness of the entire e-portfolio model. This process, a meta-evaluation conducted by the Assessment Advisory Committee, is shown in Figure 2.

Figure 2. Meta-Evaluation Process for the E-Portfolio Model.

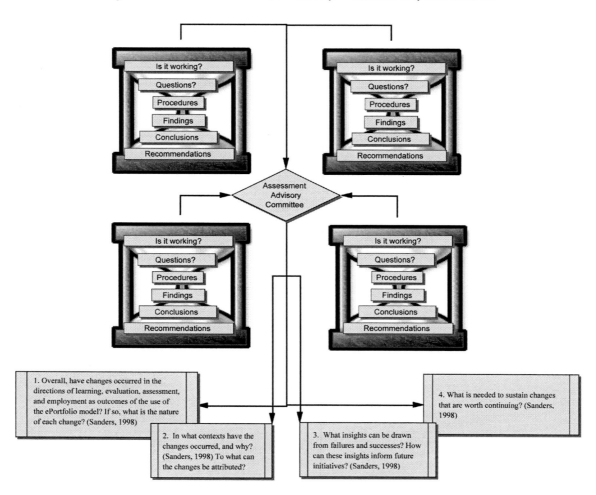

Program Evaluation Standards

When planning and implementing evaluations, it is critical that accepted standards be observed and maintained. To design a well-founded evaluation plan, Program Evaluation Standards created by Sanders and approved by the American National Standards Institute in 1994 are used to guide this evaluation design. The standards are broken down into the areas of "utility," "feasibility," "propriety," and "accuracy." These are defined by Sanders (1994) as follows:

1. *Utility Standards*. The utility standards are intended to ensure that an evaluation will serve the information needs of the intended users.
2. *Feasibility Standards*. The feasibility standards are intended to ensure that an evaluation will be realistic, prudent, diplomatic, and frugal.
3. *Propriety Standards*. The propriety standards are intended to ensure that an evaluation will be conducted legally, ethically, and with due regard for the welfare of those involved in the evaluation, as well as those affected by its results.
4. *Accuracy Standards*. The accuracy standards are intended to ensure that an evaluation will reveal and convey technically adequate information about the features that determine worth or merit of the program being evaluated (Sanders, 1994).

Utility Standards

Utility standards apply to issues relating to stakeholders, selection of evaluators, content and process of the evaluation, and the adherence to a timely schedule for evaluation. In the case of the e-portfolio framework presented here, a variety of stakeholders have interest in the e-portfolio evaluation on multiple levels. Stakeholders include:

1. Professional Education Unit Head
2. Deans, including Associate and Assistant Deans of Colleges
3. Department Chairpersons
4. Unit e-portfolio developers/leaders
5. Committee members
   a. NCATE steering committee
   b. Assessment Committee members
6. Faculty members within the Professional Education Unit as they relate to "NCATE assessments"
7. Departmental e-portfolio developers
8. Faculty members from specific teacher education programs
9. Candidates
10. Employers

Individuals from this list of stakeholders take part in the evaluative process and serve on evaluation teams. Citing his own work "Why Transformation Efforts Fail," Kotter stresses the importance of creating a coalition of leaders within a system to serve a variety of purposes to help to facilitate acceptance and success of programs (Kotter, 1996). This "coalition of leaders" is provided for by choosing stakeholders who have vested interest in the process and outcomes of various e-portfolio projects. According to Sanders' Program Evaluation Standards, "the persons conducting the evaluation should be both trustworthy and competent to perform the evaluation" (Sanders, 1994, 1).

Members of the evaluation teams should look to collect information that provides a broad representation of the work in e-portfolios within Teacher Education. In planning their evaluation strategies, evaluation teams should clearly describe the "perspectives, procedures, and rationale used to interpret the findings...so that the bases for value judgments are clear" (Sanders, 1994, 1).

Evaluation teams must provide clear descriptions of the programs being evaluated, including purpose of the use of e-portfolios within the context of the program. It is also critical that the evaluation be guided by questions that provide information pertinent to the purpose of the evaluation. In the case of the evaluations of the e-portfolio model presented for this paper, Figure 1 elaborates upon the guiding questions within a Professional Education Unit, a department of Music Education, and the common questions that these two constituencies share.

The Assessment Advisory Committee is responsible for setting expectations for respective evaluation committees, including setting dates and deadlines for evaluations to be planned, conducted, and reported. The Program Evaluation Standards stress the importance of reporting in ways that "encourage follow-through by stakeholders" whereby increasing the likelihood that evaluation results will be used.

Feasibility Standards

Feasibility Standards relate to "practical procedures," "political viability," and "cost effectiveness" of a program evaluation (Sanders, 1994). The configuration of this evaluation plan uses in-house evaluation teams, overseen by an established Assessment Advisory Committee at the level of the Professional Education Unit. The intent is to minimize disruption by the evaluation process.

Propriety Standards

The intent of the Propriety Standards is to "ensure that an evaluation will be conducted legally, ethically, and with due regard for the welfare of those involved in the evaluation, as well as those affected by its results" (Sanders, 1994, 4). The evaluation of the e-portfolio model is intended to be conducted legally and ethically.

Accuracy Standards

All evaluations, whether individual evaluations conducted by teams, or cluster evaluations synthesized by the Assessment Advisory Committee are subject to follow Accuracy Standards detailed in the Program Evaluation Standards (Sanders, 1994). These standards ensure the technical accuracy of evaluations such that they will accurately represent determinations of "worth or merit of the program being evaluated" (Sanders, 1994, 4).

Methods of Data Collection

As can be seen in Figure 1, a variety of methods have been recommended to serve various purposes in the evaluation of the e-portfolio model. These include data collection through LiveText[1], surveys, interviews, and focus groups. Questions that drive the evaluation also determine the need for various evaluative strategies.

Surveys are used in this evaluation to gain information about the delivery of "NCATE assessments." The information gathered is critical; the evaluator must know how much of the picture is represented by the data that has been collected. Surveys may also be used along with individual interviews and focus groups to help evaluators to understand what e-portfolio development has meant for those who have used e-portfolios in their search for employment.

In the e-portfolio framework that provided the basis for this paper, the use of e-portfolios as learning tools in music education is a primary focus of the e-portfolio design. Instructor interviews and content analysis help program evaluators to identify evidence of collaboration and reflection within the e-portfolio model. At this point in the evaluation, only the presence of reflection and candidate to candidate and candidate to instructor collaboration is being monitored, although the quality of reflection and collaboration is a topic for further study.

The most common method for evaluating the e-portfolio model is based within LiveText, the tool that provides the electronic infrastructure for data collection. With its back-end data-driven design, the e-portfolio model was developed to allow for a variety of evaluations and assessments to be designed and implemented within the e-portfolio framework. The data generated by formative and summative evaluation and assessment tools will provide the answers to the key questions for the evaluation of the e-portfolio model.

Conclusions

In evaluation, there are no ultimate answers. This evaluation plan mainly deals with issues of utility, and less with feasibility, propriety, and accuracy. Weiss suggests that the best case scenario is to collect objective information on the implementation and outcomes of the e-portfolio model, and from that information, to make wise decisions with regard to further program planning (Weiss, 1998). From a variety of evaluators comes the potential for a variety of information, conclusions, and further questions. The provision of a cluster evaluation, serving the function of a meta-evaluation, brings objective information to the fore for the purpose of affecting needed adaptations or changes to the e-portfolio model as a whole. Some questions that remain to be answered are:

1. How much progress toward desired outcomes marks success?
2. How do these results guide further action, or set direction for changes in programs or policy?

---

1 LiveText is "a web-based, data-driven web-site that enables registered users to create and share documents, perform document reviews and assessments, and have others assess and review the documents that you've created" (LiveText, 2005). LiveText was the tool used in e-portfolio development in this case. LiveText provides for back-end data collection within the context of the electronic tool.

3. In what ways to the results of the evaluations reinforce or affirm prior beliefs?

With answers to these questions, evaluators can come together with the intent to make wise decisions with regard to the e-portfolio model and the impact of its use in learning, evaluation, and assessment within teacher education programs.

Questions for Further Investigation

The e-portfolio model for which this evaluation was designed was intended to provide opportunities for learning, evaluation, assessment, and employment within one e-portfolio framework and working e-portfolio model. The uses for e-portfolios within this framework were very specific; thus, questions of quality of e-portfolios and their content, impact on candidate learning, and the reasons for candidate success in relation to e-portfolios have not been addressed. Considerations regarding cost or risks to candidates who provide information within the context of e-portfolios have not been explored. Neither have the effects of e-portfolios on employment, longitudinal effectiveness of e-portfolios, nor the reliability of faculty evaluation and assessment of e-portfolios been explored. These questions require further study following the implementation of the e-portfolio model. These questions include:

1. What impact does the use of the electronic tool and/or e-portfolio process have on candidates' learning? How much of the learning can be attributed to the electronic tool?
2. What impact does the use of the e-portfolio have on a candidates' success in obtaining employment?
3. What characteristics are associated with success? Disaggregate the data to determine:
   a. Characteristics of recipients who experienced success.
   b. Types of services associated with success.
   c. Surrounding conditions associated with success (C. Weiss, 1998, 273).
4. What are the costs associated with the electronic system for e-portfolio development? Where are the funds coming from over time to develop, maintain, and support e-portfolio development and implementation?
5. Are there any questions about privacy, self-incrimination, placing students at risk who are involved in implementing the e-portfolio system?
6. How accurate are the judgments rendered by faculty who use the e-portfolios for evaluation and assessment? Are they reliable?
7. What degree of quality is demonstrated with regard to candidate reflections as evidenced within an e-portfolio for learning? To what can be attributed the quality (or lack of quality) of reflections?

A cluster evaluation, or meta-evaluation of an e-portfolio model leaves room to question the effectiveness of e-portfolios, especially in the areas of feasibility, propriety, and accuracy. Once implemented, the field of music education will be ripe to examine more specifically the efficacy e-portfolios, especially in the area of learning. Leaving with more questions than with which you began is not undesirable. As more questions are uncovered, there will be more opportunities to scrutinize the use of e-portfolios for learning, evaluation, assessment, and employment, and ultimately improve e-portfolios practices.

References

Barrett, H. 2005. White paper: researching electronic portfolios and learner engagement. Retrieved February 3, 2005, from http://www.electronicportfolios.com/reflect/whitepaper.pdf

Cronbach, L., and Associates. 1980. Toward reform of program evaluation. San Francisco: Jossey-Bass.

Kotter, J. 1996. Leading change. Boston: Harvard Business School Press.

LiveText. 2005. Retrieved June 5, 2005 from http://college.livetext.com/college/index.html

Sanders, J. 1994. The program evaluation standards. Retrieved February 26, 2006 from http://www.behav.com/program_evaluation_standards.html

Sanders, J. 1998. Cluster evaluation. [Electronic Version]. The evaluation exchange: Emerging strategies in evaluating child and family services, IV(2):7–8. Retrieved February 26, 2006 from http://gseweb.harvard.edu/~hfrp/content/eval/issue11/eval11.pdf

Weiss, C. 1998. Evaluation, 2nd ed. Upper Saddle River, NJ: Prentice Hall.

The Teacher Work Sample Methodology: A Tool to Develop Pre-Service Music Teachers' Understanding of Assessment

William I. Bauer
Case Western Reserve University

Abstract

The Teacher Work Sample Methodology (TWSM) is a model for instructional design and delivery that involves participants in planning, teaching, and assessment of disciplinary content. Used with both pre-service and in-service teachers, it is a process that facilitates the understanding of how the collection and analysis of data can inform instructional decision-making, thereby increasing student achievement. This article describes an application of the TWSM in pre-service music teacher education. A sample music-student-teacher work-sample is included and suggestions for successful implementation are provided.

Assessment in music education has often been thought of strictly in terms of the evaluation of students in order to assign a grade. To utilize assessment as an integral component of the teaching and learning process requires teachers to have a more comprehensive understanding of the practices and procedures involved. Originally developed by faculty and researchers at Western Oregon University, the Teacher Work Sample Methodology (TWSM) is "an approach in which teacher candidates are explicitly taught and practice a model that links pre-instructional planning, conduct of the instructional process, and subsequent reflection with a strong emphasis on assembling and analyzing data about their students' learning and growth" (Imig and Smith, 2002, ix-x). The purpose of this paper is to (a) describe the Teacher Work Sample Methodology, (b) discuss the implementation of the TWSM in teacher education, (c) present an example of a music student teacher work sample, and (d) provide suggestions for implementation of the TWSM with music student teachers.

The Teacher Work Sample Methodology

The Teacher Work Sample Methodology involves creating and teaching a complete instructional unit. The unit's development, implementation, and evaluation are driven by assessment data collected by the teacher. The TWSM utilizes a prompt to guide teachers to consider "seven teaching processes identified by research and best practice as fundamental to improving student learning" (Renaissance Partnership, 2002, 3). These seven processes include:

1. Contextual factors
2. Learning goals
3. Assessment plan
4. Design for instruction
5. Instructional decision-making
6. Analysis of student learning
7. Reflection and self-evaluation

Student teachers are directed to follow a series of steps that provide a framework to address these processes. The steps are:

1. *Identification of the context and setting where teaching/learning will take place.* Student teachers first create a profile of the community, school district, school building, and classroom that may include information related to:
   a. Demographics
   b. Socio-economics
   c. Cultural values that are evident
   d. Number of students, their grade level, racial/ethnic makeup, gender, and perceived knowledge and ability in the subject
   e. Students with exceptionalities in the class
   f. Classroom management practices and the environment produced by those practices
   g. The physical set-up of the classroom
   h. The resources available for instruction, including technology
2. *Identification of a unit topic.* Next, the student teachers write the unit topic in a single sentence, taking into consideration the curriculum for the class as well as the materials and resources that are available.
3. *Selection of standards and development of learning goals.* Student teachers then select state and/or national content standards that are aligned with the unit topic and long-term learning goals.
4. *Creation of an initial outline of the unit.* The unit's sequence of lessons is outlined, with specific learning outcomes, teaching materials, teacher methods, student activities, and means of assessment indicated for each lesson.
5. *Development of an assessment plan.* The means and processes to be used to assess K–12 student learning are fully described. Specific assessment instruments are developed.
6. *Pre-assessment of students.* Each K–12 student is pre-assessed on the learning outcomes using the pre-assessment instrument. The student teacher analyzes students' current level of understanding of the topic.
7. *Design of lessons that are aligned with the unit goals.* Based on the results of the pre-assessment, the first lesson plan is developed. Subsequent lesson plans are written following formative assessment of K–12 students during each lesson taught.
8. *Teaching and learning.* The student teacher teaches the unit. Following each lesson, the student teacher reflects in writing on the lesson's strengths and weaknesses, as well as the K–12 students' progress toward meeting the lesson outcomes and long-term learning goals of the unit. Each subsequent lesson is designed following this period of reflection.

9. *Post-assessment of students.* After the final lesson of the unit has been taught, the student teacher conducts a post-assessment. Most often the post-assessment processes and instrument are the same as those used in the pre-assessment. In addition, a narrative discussion that interprets the observed learning gains (or possible absence of learning gains) is written.

10. *Reflection by the teacher.* The student teacher completes a written reflection on the entire process of developing and teaching the unit. In the reflection, student teachers consider what they learned, what worked well, what they would change if they taught the unit again, etc.

Steps 5 (assessment plan), 6 (pre-assessment of students), and 9 (post-assessment of students) explicitly involve the role of assessment in teaching and learning. In developing an assessment plan, the pre-service teacher is asked to provide an overview of the assessment strategies to be utilized. For each learning goal a (a) pre-assessment, (b) formative assessment, and (c) post-assessment—along with the format, type, or mode of the assessment—is identified. In addition, in a narrative statement, the assessment process (logistics of the assessment) is discussed. The pre-service teacher also develops pre- and post-assessment instruments appropriate for measuring progress towards the learning goals. These may take many different forms, including paper-and-pencil tests, checklists, rating scales, and rubrics. The student teacher writes a narrative statement that describes how s/he will evaluate and score the assessments, also discussing the formative assessments to be utilized and how they will be implemented in order to assess students' progress toward the goals.

When conducting the pre-assessment, the student teacher is asked to determine what each student knows about each objective prior to completing the final design of the individual lessons in the unit. After administration of the pre-assessment, an analysis of the data collected is conducted to determine students' pre-instructional understanding of the unit objectives. This is described in a written narrative. In addition, each K–12 student's name and score are listed in an Excel spreadsheet.

At the completion of the unit, the post-assessment is administered and the resulting data analyzed. The post-assessment data is entered in the Excel spreadsheet and learning gains are calculated. Pre-service teachers are encouraged to use a table, chart, or graph to visually display the assessment data. A narrative discussion is written that interprets the observed learning gains seen (or, possibly not seen), including an explanation of why they did or did not occur.

The Teacher Work Sample Methodology in Teacher Education

The Teacher Work Sample Methodology has received a great deal of attention as a tool for teacher education (Girod, 2002; Tucker and Stronge, 2005; Renaissance Partnership, 2006a). The Renaissance Partnership Project (2006b) involves a consortium of eleven teacher preparation institutions whose goal "is to become accountable for the impact of teacher graduates on student achievement by developing systems to measure and improve teacher candidates' ability to facilitate student learning." The partnership's web site contains extensive information about the Teacher Work Sample Methodology. Among the resources available are downloadable PowerPoint presentations, training materials, model teacher work samples, rubrics for assessing work samples, papers and publications, and links to each of the participating institutions.

Fredman (2004) stated that the Teacher Work Sample Methodology is one means by which colleges of education can document the quality of both their teacher education programs and candidates for national and state organizations, including accrediting bodies such as NCATE. In particular, the TWSM is a way to provide evidence of the impact of a teacher candidate's teaching on student learning. Tucker and Stronge (2005) reported on studies that found the TWSM to have face, content, and construct validity. The authors also stated that it is possible to achieve good inter-rater reliability in scoring teacher work samples, discussing one study where inter-rater agreement between college and school supervisors ranged from 81–98%.

Two researchers have studied the TWSM process and made recommendations based on their findings. Mallein (2003) investigated "the benefits and challenges of completing the teacher work sample during the student teaching field experience from the perspective of K–12 student teachers and their cooperating teachers" (10) by surveying 134 student teachers. The study participants indicated that additional training, support, and resources to support their implementation of the TWSM would be beneficial. The researcher also suggested that the TWSM should be appropriately adapted for various grade levels and disciplines. In addition, it was recommended that the TWSM be streamlined in order to alleviate its demands on the student teacher's time, potentially avoiding a detrimental impact on the student teacher's other instructional responsibilities.

Pratt (2000) conducted a content analysis of fifty math education work samples completed by student teachers at Western Oregon University. The researcher reached the following conclusions:

1. Teacher Work Sample Methodology (TWSM) as employed with student teachers at Western Oregon University has not yet made significant contributions to ensuring standards-based instruction in mathematics, if the standards under consideration are the NCTM standards.
2. TWSM as developed at Western Oregon University has the capacity to identify a student teacher's instructional strengths and weaknesses (such as aligning instructional objectives with assessment methods, understanding of assessment and test construction, understanding and ability to reflect on instructional process, and improvement on the weaknesses).
3. Teacher Work Sample Methodology has the capacity to demonstrate a pre-service teacher's (student teacher's, teacher intern's) ability to facilitate learning/academic growth.
4. Teacher Work Sample Methodology has the capacity to identify strengths and weaknesses in teacher preparation programs (v-vi).

An Example of the Teacher Work Sample Methodology in Music Education

The following is an example of how the Teacher Work Sample Methodology could be applied to a music education setting, in this case a fifth-grade trumpet class, and an *abbreviated* version of the work sample that might result from it.[1]

Context and Setting

The city could be considered upper-middle class with a median family income of about $65,000 per year. Caucasians comprised 75% of the population and the largest minority group was African-American. The school district was rated as "Effective" for the 2005–2006 school year by the state department of education. In addition to the public schools, the area was home to several prominent parochial schools.

The community seemed friendly towards education and the arts in general. School and community facilities for music and drama were very good. The school district had a wide array of arts offerings in their curriculum. Based on an examination of the instrumental music curriculum, it appeared the school district viewed music education as a way to enrich the overall learning abilities of students in all subjects. According to the curriculum, "The instrumental enrichment program systematically reinforces the cognitive functions that enable learners to define problems, make connections and see relationships, motivate themselves, and improve their work habits."

The elementary school, a fifth- and sixth-grade building, appeared to be an extremely child-centered environment. The corridors of the three-story building were decorated wall-to-wall with student artwork which was frequently replaced. In the stairwells there were motivational posters that praised different school subjects and encouraged social practices such as tolerance and friendship. Most of the classrooms were also decorated with brightly colored posters.

The instrumental music classroom had posters of instruments, as well as progress charts with stickers used to track the achievement for each student who had class in that room. Chairs and music stands were neatly arranged in rows. The wall at the front of the room was covered with two chalkboards, where the class agenda was listed each day. There wasn't very much technology immediately available in the classroom, but the students and their teacher alike seemed comfortable in this low-tech atmosphere. If audio-visual equipment was needed for a specific lesson, it could be reserved and brought into the classroom.

The fifth-grade trumpet students themselves were a varied and interesting group. There were seven students total, four girls and three boys. The majority of the class was Caucasian, with three students who seemed to be of African-American descent. None of the students stood out as having specific learning or developmental disabilities or exceptionalities, but there was a fairly wide range of ability levels and learning styles evident in the class. English was the primary language for all of the students.

---

1 Portions of this example have been adapted, with permission, from Teacher Work Sample Methodology projects completed by Erin Grady and Trista Emmons, students of the author.

Unit Topic

This unit will focus on the development of fifth-grade trumpet students' playing fundamentals, including embouchure formation, left and right hand positions, posture, and playing position.

Standards and Learning Goals

National Standard:	Performing on instruments, alone and with others, a varied repertoire of music (MENC, 2006).
Achievement Standard:	Students perform on at least one instrument accurately and independently, alone and in small and large ensembles, with good posture, good playing position, and good breath, bow, or stick control (MENC, 2006).
Learning Goals:	Fifth-grade trumpet students will play with a correct embouchure, left and right hand position, posture, and playing position.

Unit Outline

Class 1: Administer the pre-assessment.

Class 2: Review the fundamentals of embouchure, right and left hand position, posture, and playing position by re-teaching each of these elements to the students. Throughout the lesson, the teacher will correct improper fundamentals as necessary, as well as provide reinforcement to students when fundamentals are being properly executed. Formative assessment will occur through teacher observation.

Class 3: The teacher will model correct and incorrect instances of the playing fundamentals. Students will be asked to identify these instances. Throughout the lesson, the teacher will correct improper fundamentals as necessary, as well as provide reinforcement to students when fundamentals are being properly executed. Formative assessment will occur through teacher observation and an analysis of students' ability to identify correct/incorrect fundamentals.

Class 4: The teacher will ask selected students to model correct and incorrect instances of the playing fundamentals. The rest of the class will be asked to identify these instances. Throughout the lesson, the teacher will correct improper fundamentals as necessary, as well as provide reinforcement to students when fundamentals are being properly executed. Formative assessment will occur through teacher observation and an analysis of students' ability to identify correct/incorrect fundamentals.

Class 5: Students will conduct peer assessments of each other using the pre-/post-assessment instrument (see Appendix). Half the class will perform an exercise from the method book while the other half conducts the assessment. Then, the students will switch roles. The teacher will collect the completed assessment instruments. Throughout the lesson, the teacher will correct improper fundamentals as necessary, as well as provide reinforcement to students when fundamentals are being properly executed. Formative assessment will occur through teacher observation and an analysis of students' ability to indicate correct/incorrect fundamentals on the assessment instrument.

Class 6: Administer the post-assessment.

Assessment Plan

At the beginning and conclusion of the unit, the teacher assessed each trumpet student using the *Trumpet Checklist* (see Appendix). During each lesson, formative assessment occurred. This formative assessment took the form of teacher observation, student verbal response to models, and student peer assessment. Figure 1 shows the Assessment Plan for this unit.

Figure 1. Unit Assessment Plan

Learning Outcome	Assessment Type	Means of Assessment
The student will play utilizing a proper embouchure.	Pre-assessment	Trumpet fundamentals checklist
	Formative assessment	Teacher observation, student verbal response to models, student peer assessment
	Post-assessment	Trumpet fundamentals checklist
The student will play utilizing proper left hand position.	Pre-assessment	Trumpet fundamentals checklist
	Formative assessment	Teacher observation, student verbal response to models, student peer assessment
	Post-assessment	Trumpet fundamentals checklist
The student will play utilizing proper right hand position.	Pre-assessment	Trumpet fundamentals checklist
	Formative assessment	Teacher observation, student verbal response to models, student peer assessment
	Post-assessment	Trumpet fundamentals checklist
The student will play utilizing proper posture.	Pre-assessment	Trumpet fundamentals checklist
	Formative assessment	Teacher observation, student verbal response to models, student peer assessment
	Post-assessment	Trumpet fundamentals checklist
The student will play utilizing proper playing position.	Pre-assessment	Trumpet fundamentals checklist
	Formative assessment	Teacher observation, student verbal response to models, student peer assessment
	Post-assessment	Trumpet fundamentals checklist

Pre-assessment

While students were playing exercises from their method books, the teacher observed each individual and completed the *Trumpet Checklist* (see Appendix). Pre-assessment scores are shown in Table 1.

Table 1. Pre-assessment scores for the trumpet unit.

Student	Embouchure	Left-Hand Position	Right-Hand Position	Posture	Playing Position	Total Score
1	4	3	4	3	2	16
2	3	3	4	3	1	14
3	3	5	4	3	1	16
4	4	4	4	2	1	15
5	5	4	5	3	2	19
6	2	3	3	2	1	11
7	3	4	3	3	1	14
Total Students	24	26	31	13	9	

The students' execution of playing fundamentals was quite varied. Common problems observed included embouchures with puffed cheeks, bent wrists on the left hand, and elbows which were too close to the body. Overall, basic posture was quite good. The mean overall score was 15 out of a possible 20 points. The mean scores for each fundamental (with possible scores in parentheses) were:

Embouchure 3.43 (5)
Left-hand position............3.71 (5)
Right hand position..........3.86 (5)
Posture.............................2.71 (3)
Playing position................1.29 (2)

Lessons/Teaching and Learning

Detailed lesson plans including objectives, materials, procedures, assessment procedures, and reflections by the teacher for each class would appear in this section of the work sample. Each successive lesson builds from the formative assessment conducted, and the teacher's reflection on that assessment, in the previous lesson.

Post-assessment

The post-assessment scores are shown in Table 2. The overall mean score for the post-assessment was 17.43. A comparison of the pre- and post-assessment means by individual student is shown in Figure 2. Means for each of the individual fundamentals that were assessed were:

Embouchure 4.43
Left-hand position............4.29
Right-hand position 4.14
Posture.............................2.71
Playing position................1.86

The overall mean student scores improved by 2.43 points from the pre- to post-assessment, increasing from 15 to 17.43—a 14% gain. A comparison of the pre-and post-assessment scores for each fundamental is shown in Figure 3. Scores on nearly all of the individual fundamentals, with the exception of posture, also increased from the pre-to post assessment. The mean increase for each fundamental, with percentage of increase in parentheses, was:

Embouchure ....1.0 .... (23%)
Left-hand position............0.58 .... (14%)
Right hand position..........0.28 .... (7%)
Posture.............................0.0 .... (0%)
Playing position................0.57 .... (31%)

While there was some variation among individual students, and some student's scores actually dropped slightly in a specific area from pre- to post-assessment, overall, students improved their ability to perform with proper fundamentals. That there was no measurable increase in posture was not surprising, given that students' posture was good from the beginning of the unit.

Table 2. Post-assessment scores for the trumpet unit.

Student	Embouchure	Left-Hand Position	Right-Hand Position	Posture	Playing Position	Total
1	4	3	5	3	2	17
2	4	4	3	3	2	16
3	4	5	4	2	2	17
4	5	4	5	2	1	17
5	5	5	5	3	2	20
6	4	4	4	3	2	17
7	5	5	3	3	2	18
Total	31	30	29	19	13	

Figure 2. Comparison of Pre-and post-assessment scores for the trumpet unit.

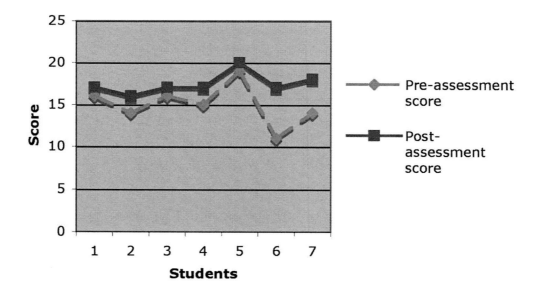

Figure 3. Comparison of pre- and post assessment scores by fundamental.

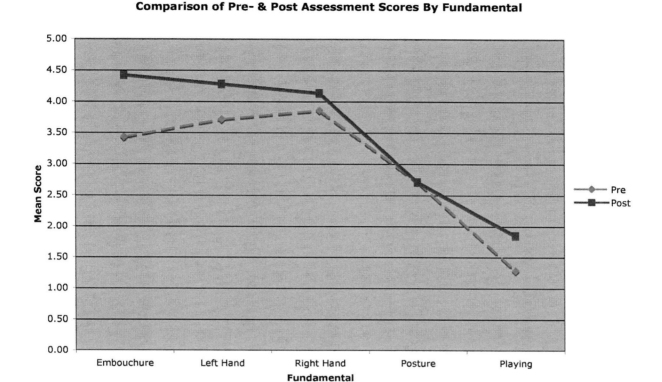

Reflection

The TWS project is a formalized way of approaching what a teacher should be doing every day. Teachers should design lessons built around standards that address the specific needs of their students. Teachers should develop assessment plans prior to teaching a specified unit and then implement meaningful assessments that students can understand and from which they can learn. Teachers should develop assessments that actually provide useful information and document student learning.

This topic obviously addressed a basic component of instrumental performance. From my private teaching experience, I knew that this concept was crucial to student success. Developing learning goals was not difficult, and creating the initial outline for the unit was fairly simple. The challenge was to come up with multiple ways to approach this topic so that the ideas could be reinforced without the students getting bored.

Developing the assessment instrument (*Trumpet Checklist*) caused me to clearly define the details of each of the fundamentals. Using a checklist approach worked well in this setting. During the course of a lesson, a checklist could easily be completed for each student while the class was playing exercises out of the method book. Implementation of the lessons went well, and teaching the classes was fun. The post-assessment data show that the students improved their ability to play with good fundamentals.

While the Teacher Work Sample Methodology may be valuable in helping student teachers design and teach units of instruction grounded in the collection and analysis of assessment data, certain aspects of the process need to be considered if the overall experience is to be successful. All parties involved—student teachers, cooperating teachers, and university supervisors—must fully comprehend the purpose and processes of the TWSM. The project must also be structured so that it doesn't become an additional huge requirement added to the frequently stressful experience of student teaching. Based on the perceptions of student teachers, cooperating teachers, and university supervisors with whom the author has worked in implementing TWSM projects, the following recommendations are provided for successfully implementing the TWSM with music student teachers.

The TWSM project can be complicated and confusing if students are not fully prepared for it, or if they aren't provided with adequate support. It requires a significant investment of time, which, if not properly structured and incorporated into the overall student teaching experience, can become overwhelming. Students need to have practiced planning for instruction and developing assessment instruments prior to student teaching. Assignments related to this should be part of methods classes. Along with this, if students can be introduced to the TWSM model before their teaching internship, it may help them to feel more comfortable in completing their work sample during student teaching. One way to do this is to have students complete a TWSM project as a class during a pre-student teaching field experience or practicum.

While most student teachers will have developed lesson plans and taught individual lessons prior to student teaching, relatively few will have tackled an entire unit of instruction. Scaffolding the Teacher Work Sample Methodology project by requiring specific components to be completed by certain dates can assist students in managing this large assignment. For instance, the *Context and Setting* section could be finished by the end of the first week of student teaching. This part of the project can be partially addressed prior to beginning student teaching by examining web sites of the school, community, and the state department of education reports on individual schools and school districts. During the first week of student teaching, which often consists primarily of observation, information to finish the rest of this section can be gathered and the narrative can be written.

Likewise, the *Unit Topic, Standards and Learning Goals,* and *Assessment Plans* could be written prior to the end of the first month of student teaching. By this time students should be well acquainted with the school, their cooperating teacher, and students. They should have been able to determine what topics will be taught over the next several weeks and have had a chance to discuss potential units of instruction with their cooperating teacher and university supervisor. At this point, there will still be time for student teachers to adjust their TWSM plan based on formative feedback from their cooperating teacher and university supervisor. There will also be sufficient time left in their student teaching experience to teach and assess the unit. Continuing with specific due dates for the remaining portions of the TWSM may help students to better stay on task with the project. These suggestions for scaffolding the project are similar to those provided by the Renaissance Partnership (2004).

Providing adequate support for student teachers while they are completing the TWSM project is also important. The project should be a topic that is addressed regularly during student teaching seminars, allowing student teachers to ask questions of the seminar leader and to discuss successes and challenges they are facing with each other. The student teachers' cooperating teachers also need to fully understand the rationale and processes involved with the TWSM. A student teacher should not be placed with a cooperating teacher who is not receptive to and supportive of this project. By providing cooperating teachers with an in-service session on the Teacher Work Sample Methodology, not only will they be better prepared to assist their student teacher in its completion, but they may also develop professionally in their own understanding of unit teaching and assessment practices. The university supervisor can continue to provide support to both the cooperating teacher and student teacher during visits to the school setting, via phone, or by email.

Summary

While finding the process challenging, student teachers have generally stated that they believed the Teacher Work Sample Methodology project had educational merit and was a good model to help them consider all the aspects involved in planning and teaching units of instruction. They report that completing the work sample positively impacted their way of thinking about music curriculum, instruction, and assessment. Most student teachers came to appreciate the value of developing an assessment instrument, utilizing it with actual students, and analyzing the data to determine whether student learning occurred. One student teacher said, "It helped me to focus on what it means to be a professional educator."

The Teacher Work Sample Methodology is growing in popularity among faculty of colleges and schools of education. It appears to be applicable to music teaching and learning, and may be an important way to help pre-service teachers not only think like a teacher, but also to integrate the knowledge and skills they have developed through their collegiate study. It provides a structure that can enable student teachers to develop assessment instruments, utilize various assessment practices, analyze assessment data to inform the delivery of instruction, and reflect on assessment processes and procedures. It may be a means through which pre-service teachers' understanding of assessment can be developed in a way that will ultimately make them more effective educators.

References

Fredman, T. 2004. Teacher work sample methodology: Implementation and practical application in teacher preparation. *Action in Teacher Education, 26*(1):3–11.

Girod, G., ed. 2002. *Connecting teaching and learning: A handbook for teacher educators on teacher work sample methodology.* NY: AACTE Publications.

Imig, D. and C. Smith. 2002. Forward. In Gerald R. Girod, ed., *Connecting teaching and learning: A handbook for teacher educators on teacher work sample methodology.* Washington, D. C.: AACTE Publications.

Mallein, D. J. 2003. Assessing the benefits and challenges of completing a teacher work sample during student teaching from the perspective of K–12 student teachers and cooperating teachers. *Dissertation Abstracts International, 64*(08):2848A. (UMI No. AAT 3100567).

Music Educators National Conference. 2006. *Performance standards for music: Grades 5–8.* Retrieved December 10, 2006 from http://www.menc.org/publication/books/performance_standards/5–8.html

Pratt, E. O. 2000. Teacher Work Sample Methodology: A content analysis of the mathematics work samples produced by student teachers at Western Oregon University between 1991–1999. *Dissertation Abstracts International, 61*(06):2171A. (UMI No. AAT 9973491).

Renaissance Partnership for Improving Teacher Quality. 2002. *Teacher work sample: Performance prompt, teaching process standards, scoring rubrics.* Retrieved December 12, 2006, from http://fp.uni.edu/itq/PDF_files/June2002promptandrubric.pdf

Renaissance Partnership for Improving Teacher Quality. 2004. *Manual for teacher candidates: Tips for preparing the teacher work sample.* Retrieved December 12, 2006 from http://fp.uni.edu/itq/PDF_files/student_tws_manual_june_2004.pdf

Renaissance Partnership for Improving Teacher Quality. 2006a. Retrieved December 12, 2006 from http://fp.uni.edu/itq/

Renaissance Partnership for Improving Teacher Quality. 2006b. *Project overview.* Retrieved December 12, 2006 from http://fp.uni.edu/itq/ProjectOverview/Index.htm

Tucker, P.D. and J. H. Stronge. 2005. *Linking teacher evaluation and student learning.* Alexandria, VA: Association for Supervision and Curriculum Development.

Fundamentals Checklist

Trumpet

Student _____

I. Embouchure Formation (5 points)

Embouchure (1 point each)

_____ Mouthpiece is place in the center of the lips horizontally.

_____ One-half of the mouthpiece is on the upper lip and one-half is on the lower lip.

_____ The chin is firm and flat.

_____ The corners of the mouth are firm.

_____ The cheeks stay flat (not puffed).

II. Hand Position (10 points)

Left-Hand Position (1 point each)

_____ The thumb is placed along (around) the first valve casing. (If the instrument has a thumb trigger, the thumb is placed on the trigger.)

_____ The first and second fingers are wrapped around the third valve casing.

_____ The third finger is inserted into the trigger ring. (If the instrument does not have a third valve trigger ring, the third finger is wrapped around the valve casing.)

_____ The fourth finger is placed on the third valve slide.

_____ The wrist is straight

Right Hand (1 point each)

_____ The thumb is placed under the mouthpipe between the first and second valve casings.

_____ The fleshy pads of the first, second, and third fingers are placed on the valve pearls.

_____ The fingers are curved.

_____ The fourth finger is placed on top of the finger loop.

_____ The wrist is straight.

III. Posture and Instrument Playing Position (5 points)

Posture (1 point each)

_____ The back is straight and away from the back of the chair.

_____ The shoulders are relaxed.

_____ The feet are comfortably apart and flat on the floor.

Playing Position (1 point each)

_____ The instrument is positioned to the center of the body with a slight angle to the floor.

_____ The elbows are slightly away from the body.

Total Points _____/20

Contributors

Kristen Albert......................................West Chester University

Janet R. Barrett..................................Northwestern University

William I. Bauer..................................Case Western Reserve University

Mary Birkner ....University of Florida

Timothy S. Brophy ....University of Florida

Rebekah Burcham ....University of Florida

Ming-Jen Chuang...............................National Taichung University, Taichung City, Taiwan

Richard Colwell..................................Professor Emeritus, University of Illinois, New England
Conservatory of Music

Colleen Conway ....University of Michigan

David Edmund....................................University of Florida

Helen Farrell......................................Department of Education, Melbourne, Victoria, Australia

Dee Hansen ....The Hartt School of Music, University of Hartford

Aurelia W. Hartenberger ....University of Missouri—St. Louis

Sarah Hearn.......................................Dorothy Pullen Elementary School, Rowlett, Texas

Christopher Heffner...........................Lebanon Valley College

Maud Hickey ....Northwestern University

Al D. Holcomb...................................University of Central Florida

Charles R. Hoffer...............................University of Florida

Paul R. Lehman..................................Professor Emeritus, University of Michigan

Jay McPherson...................................Board of Studies, New South Wales, Australia

James D. Merrill ....Milton Terrace Primary School, Ballston Spa Central
School District, New York

Glenn E. Nierman ....University of Nebraska—Lincoln

Denese Odegaard...............................Fargo Public Schools, Fargo, North Dakota

Douglas C. Orzolek............................University of St. Thomas

Mary Palmer ....University of Central Florida

Kelly A. Parkes ....Virginia Polytechnic Institute and State University

Tara Pearsall......................................University of South Carolina

Patricia Riley......................................University of Vermont

Philip Shepherd ....Kentucky Department of Education

Scott C. Shuler...................................Connecticut Department of Education

Bret P. Smith ....Central Washington University

Robyn Swanson..................................Western Kentucky University

Sandra K. (Tena) Whiston.................Beattie Elementary School, Lincoln Public Schools,
Lincoln, Nebraska

Melanie Wood....................................Kentucky Music Educators Association

Ching Ching Yap................................University of South Carolina

About the Editor

Timothy S. Brophy is Associate Professor of Music Education at the University of Florida. A highly-awarded classroom teacher, he received an Ashland Teacher Achievement Award (1996), a Memphis Rotary Club Rotary Award for Teacher Excellence (1999), and was the first elementary music teacher to be honored at the Disney American Teacher Awards in Los Angeles in 1998.

An active music education writer and clinician, Dr. Brophy has published over 40 articles, which have appeared in numerous journals, such as the *Journal of Research in Music Education*, *Music Education Research*, the *Music Educators Journal*, and the *Journal of Music Teacher Education*. He is sole author of three books and co-author of over 30 books and modules as part of the music textbook series *Music Expressions* (Warner Bros./Alfred Publications, 2003–6). Dr. Brophy has conducted music education workshops and conference presentations throughout the United States and in Canada, England, Spain, China, Australia, New Zealand, Holland, Sweden, Norway, Malaysia, Indonesia, and Taiwan.

His research has focused on the development of children's melodic improvisations and music assessment. He has been a member of the editorial boards of *The Music Educators Journal,* the *Orff Echo,* and currently is a member of the Editorial Committee for *Teaching Music Magazine*. He is the past editor of *Research Perspectives in Music Education* and co-editor of *The International Journal of Music Education: Practice*. He is a past Research Chair for the Florida Music Educators Association (FMEA) and chair of the Florida Music Assessment Task Force.